AF251610

THE ARCHITECTURE OF
MARIO BOTTA

THE ARCHITECTURE OF MARIO BOTTA

INTRODUCTION BY CHRISTIAN NORBERG-SCHULZ
TEXT BY MIRKO ZARDINI
EDITED AND PHOTOGRAPHED BY YUKIO FUTAGAWA

RIZZOLI
NEW YORK

MARIO BOTTA

1943	Born in Mendrisio (Switzerland) on April 1, 1943.
	Primary school at Genestrerio (Canton Ticino).
	Secondary School at Mendrisio.
1958-61	Apprentice building draftsman in the architectural studio of Carloni and Camenish at Lugano.
1961-64	Art college in Milan.
1964-69	Attended the Istituto Universitario di Architettura in Venice.
1965	Practical work in the studio of Le Corbusier (new hospital project) in Venice, with Jullian de la Fuente and José Oubrerie.
	Worked in the studio at rue de Sèvres, 35, in Paris.
1969	Met Louis Kahn in Venice and helped install the exposition of the project for the new Congress Building.
	Graduated from the IUA, in Venice.
	Examiners: Carlo Scarpa and Giuseppe Mazzariol.
1969	Began work as a professional architect with a studio in Lugano.
1976	Visiting professor at the Ecole Polytechnique Fédérale in Lausanne.
1978	Member of the F.A.S. (Federation of Swiss Architects).
From 1979	Lectured in North America and in Europe.
1982	Member of the Commissione Federale Svizzera delle Belle Arti.
1983	Honorary fellow of the BDA (Bund Deutscher Architekten).
	Titular professor at the Ecole Polytechnique Fédérale in Lausanne.
1984	Honorary fellow of the AIA (American Institute of Architects).
	Lectured in Europe, North America, and Latin America.

First published in the United States of America in 1985 by
RIZZOLI INTERNATIONAL PUBLICATIONS, INC.
597 Fifth Avenue, New York, NY 10017

Copyright © 1984 A.D.A. EDITA, Tokyo Co., Ltd.
3-12-14 Sendagaya, Shibuya-Ku, Tokyo 151, Japan

Design Gan Hosoya
Text translation into English from the Italian original : Norberto Massi

Library of Congress Cataloging in Publication Data

Zardini, Mirko.
    The architecture of Mario Botta.

    Originally published as : Mario Botta.
    Bibliography : p.
    1. Botta, Mario, 1943-   2. Architecture,
Modern-20th century-Switzerland. I . Botta, Mario,
1943-   . II. Futagawa, Yukio, 1932-
III. Title.
NA1353. B67Z37 1985   720'.92'4   85-2328
ISBN 0-8478-0619-7
ISBN 0-8478-0620-0 (pbk.)

Printed and bound in Japan

Contents

Introduction

Christian Norberg-Schulz

Mario Botta's buildings are distinguished by a singular image quality. Like powerful "things" they stand forth in our confused present-day environment and create order and meaning. They are easily comprehended and remembered, and satisfy man's need for orientation and identification. Botta's success as an architect is undoubtedly due to this image quality. Thus his works prove that we are no longer satisfied with an architecture which is merely "functional," but want that the buildings should tell us *where we are*, and hence "explain" the world to us.

Botta's houses and large-scale buildings in fact appear as such explanations. With self-assurance they stand on the ground, and rise up in space to form a distinct "figure." At the same time they communicate with the environment to which they belong; a dialectical relationship is created which reveals the landscape as what it is. Botta himself over and again emphasizes this aim. Thus he defines architecture as the "taking possession of a particular place."[1] "Taking possession," however, to Botta does not mean dominance. Rather it implies a rediscovery of the site and the memories connected with it. Vernacular buildings always served this purpose, but in our time we tend to get alienated from our environment and as a consequence lose our own identity.

What Botta proposes is a return to *architecture*. "In the 'sixties architects fled towards other disciplines: sociology, for example, or urbanism — or in the 'seventies semiology," he says, and continues. "I think that above all man must look for his roots and his condition of being within his cultural and historic domain, in his own country."[2] The words "in his own country" are important, because what Botta wants is a concrete "establishment of a rapport between man and the elements of nature, of the countryside, of the different seasons, the values of the cosmos, the values of the sky."[3] His works demonstrate that this rapport does not imply passive adaptation. Rather it means a promotion and reinterpretation of the environmental values.[4]

Botta's approach to the environmental problem is most significant. In a time when we tend to oscillate between senseless exploitation on the one hand and nostalgic protection on the other, he wants to use architecture to reveal what a place *is*. Thus he helps us to recover our identity, or, in his own words: "Through the expression of the profession, one could also help society."[5] This approach is valid regardless of the site in question, be it rural or urban, and with his houses and civic buildings Botta in fact proves that it works. Before we take a closer look at his achievement, however, we have to say a few general words about architecture as the taking possession of place.

The current interest in *place* is of relatively recent date. During the last decade several books have been published where place is proposed as a key to architectural theory and practise.[6] During the history of the modern movement, on the contrary, the term was hardly used. Interest was rather concentrated on the problem of "space," in connection with functional fit and technological production. Space was intended as a measurable continuum, abstracted from the concrete phenomena of daily life. As a result, environmental qualities tended to disappear, and a general "loss of place" came about. The reaction against this "development" has taken many forms, but what they have in common is the wish for *meaningful* architecture, that is, buildings which communicate something more than mere utilitarian purpose. In general "meaning" is today understood in terms of the qualities of a particular location and the "memories" which are connected with a certain way of life. In the past both contents became manifest as a "building tradition" or *Bauweise.*[7] Architecture therefore acted as an *imago mundi*, making life in a locality "visible" as a built form, and thus it helped man to gain an existential foothold. A tradition of this kind does not consist in a mere repetition of given types and motifs, but rather in a continuous reinterpretation which relates the locally given to the temporal changes. In this way the place is taken into possession, or rather, the *site* is transformed into a *place* where life may "take place."

The task of the architect therefore has to be understood as the *visualization of a world*. Through his buildings the architect keeps and presents the transient phenomena, and explains their meaning. The term "world" here comprises a given physical environment as well as a set of social and cultural traditions. The translation of such a world into architecture may seem an obscure problem. In general it consists in revealing the structural properties of the site and in adding what the site "lacks" to become a true place. At the same time the spatial implications of the way of life have to be embodied in the built form. It is not possible to give a further explanation of the process here, but an analysis of the works of Botta will serve as an illustration.[8] Botta in fact subscribes to the idea of architecture as an *imago mundi*. Thus he says explicitly that the work of the architect consists in: 1) "An interpretation of the environment as a given physical entity," and 2) "An interpretation of the environment as a testimony of history and memory."[9] Our first problem, thus, is to define the world of Mario Botta, not in terms of his personal idiosyncracies, but as something to which he belongs.

Botta's world
Botta himself repeatedly has referred to *Ticino* as his immediately given world, and his architecture cannot be understood without grasping the properties of this geographical and cultural region. The location of Ticino on the southern slopes of the Alps determines its particular quality as a *meeting place* on the European continent. The worlds of the "North" and the "South" here come together, with the latter as a dominant element. (Ticino in fact *faces* the South and turns its back to the North!) Anybody who has travelled across the Alps will have experienced the profound change in environmental character which becomes manifest as one leaves the narrow mountain passes and proceeds towards the sunny and fertile Lombardian plain.[10] A high, blue sky determines the general atmosphere, the vegetation becomes lush and almost tropical in character, and the dramatic mountains calm down to form comprehensible masses which define spaces where man may settle and belong. These spaces are moreover distinguished by lakes which contribute signifi-

cantly to the quality of the region. In general, the landscape is simultaneously powerful and idyllic, colourful and distinct. It possesses the definition and identity of the "classical" world of the Mediterranean, at the same time as it reverberates with an echo of the "romantic" world of the Alpine countries. No wonder, hence, that this rich world traditionally was considered a *paradise*. Here the austere and demanding world of the mountains is left behind and the promise of an easier life is offered.[11]

This does not mean that Ticino was a prosperous country during the course of time. The cultivable land is scarce and a difficult history created severe living conditions. As many other meeting places, however, Ticino has been blessed with a rich cultural life, notably in the field of building. Already in the Middle Ages Ticinese architecture blossomed, and during the Baroque epoch Ticinese architects gained a leading position on the European scene. Numerous craftsmen and builders thus left their homes to construct churches and palaces all over Europe. Well known are the cases of the Fontana-brothers, Maderno and Borromini, all of whom were born on the shores of the Lake of Lugano.[12] Borromini particularly well represents the synthetic character of his native land, combining in his works the Classical architecture of the South with "nordic" traits.

In the vernacular architecture of Ticino we encounter a similar architectural symbiosis. The folk architecture of the South-Alpine valleys is characterized by the meeting of basic formal characters and technological systems. Hans Soeder thus tells how above the shore of the Lake of Como he found a house which on the valley side consisted of a massive "Roman" block with gently sloping roof, to which a "Germanic," steeply gabled volume in wooden construction was added on the mountain side.[13] Significantly the structure was located near a village called Germasino, a name which indicates the presence of immigrants from the North. In the same region we also find the same kind of units placed side by side.[14] More common, and typical of several regions on the southern slopes of the Alps, are houses where a gabled wooden structure is built over a massive ground floor in stone. Often the two volumes interpenetrate due to vertical slits in the main façade.[15] A relationship to earth and sky which combines southern solidity and repose with nordic transparency and ascension is thus achieved. Vernacular buildings of this kind do not only illustrate the meeting of cultural traditions, but also visualize the character of the landscape to which they belong, which unites Mediterranean definition and Alpine drama. In general the vernacular houses of the region are simple, erect bodies which tend towards a symmetrical disposition. Due to the sloping land they do not, however, appear as enclosed, self-sufficient volumes like the typical Italian *casale*. In the lower parts of Ticino and the neighboring regions a stronger North-Italian influence becomes apparent.[16] Thus the houses tend to extend horizontally, and repetitive arcades and *loggie* are used as distinguishing elements. In this way the local architecture expresses the transition of the territory towards the plain of Lombardy, with its different topographical and solar conditions.

The characteristics of the Ticinese vernacular reappear in the works of

Mario Botta. We shall later take a closer look at how he reinterprets the local typologies. So far we only want to point out that his one-family houses recall the traditional values without making use of superficial, nostalgic imitation. Evidently Botta has arrived at his solutions through a more profound "reading" of the physical properties of the territory as well as the traditional building types and motifs.

But Botta's world does not only comprise regional elements. In characterizing Ticino as a meeting place, we have already suggested that the memories which constitute its cultural inheritance have a wider scope. First of all they recall the meanings of the classical South, that is, a general sense of regular order and individual bodily form.[17] In nearby Milan the classical tradition was kept alive through the Middle Ages, and came again into full blossom during the second half of the *quattrocento,* notably in the works of Bramante. Already at the beginning of the following century full-grown Renaissance forms appear in churches in Lugano and Locarno. In general, classical architecture aims at expressing inter-human values rather than a particular situation. A classical building therefore opposes nature instead of blending with it, creating a dialectic relationship with its environment. This does not mean, however, that it is self-sufficient and place-less. Classical works also have to be rooted to become truly meaningful, and the history of Western architecture in fact shows how the classical language was varied to allow for adaptation to different situations. In this way the particular task is related to a general understanding of the world, and its true meaning is revealed. Mario Botta adheres to the classical tradition, a fact which spontaneously was proved when a couple of years ago he visited Scandinavia and was confronted with eminently Nordic works of Aalto-like character. Their anti-classical blending with nature was entirely foreign to him and produced a rather negative reaction.

When we emphasize Botta's affinity to the vernacular and the classical traditions, it might seem that he is mainly concerned with the past. The contrary is true. We have already pointed out that Botta is concerned about reinterpretation rather than nostalgic protection, and in fact he above all considers himself a *modern* architect. His modernism is however different from the abstract utilitarianism of late-modern architecture. The basic aim is evidently to revive what is essential and timeless, that is, to reveal creatively what Louis Kahn has called the *beginnings.* Mario Botta worked for Kahn in 1969, and he has never forgotten Kahn's lesson. From Kahn he learned to ask: "What does the building want to be?," and he also apprehended the answer: "It is not what you want, it is what you sense in the order of things which tells you what to design."[18] Botta's interest in the past is therefore guided towards the order of things rather than the sentimental motif, and as a consequence he refuses those "post-modern" currents which return to superficial historicism.

From what has been said above, we may conclude that Botta's world is local as well as general, ancient as well as modern. Like few architects of the present he has managed to unite these polarities, and the singularly convincing significance of his works resides in their wide range of content. Thus they possess immediate, local presence, at the same time as they recall the basic structures of our being in the world. Our second task is to investigate the means Botta employs to set his world into work.

Botta's architecture

The image quality of Botta's buildings expresses a unity of content and means. In his works we do not feel that a functional pattern has been "translated" into a form by means of some kind of system of "signs"; Botta's buildings *are* their meaning, just like man himself or the things of nature.[19] Thus they embody an integral *vision* of an existential situation, and explain what it means to be "here." His works therefore prove Heidegger's statement: "Only image formed keeps the vision."[20] To keep the vision of an existential situation through an *architectural* image, means to realize a built form which relates earth and sky in a particular way. Botta is quite explicit about this, saying: "It is always a question of a problem of attitude between man and his environment, man vis-à-vis the earth, man vis-à-vis the sky, man vis-à-vis the sun – and that, in my opinion, is the true nature of architecture."[21]

If we consider the more recent houses of Botta, they all seem to embody the same basic vision. We could also say that they appear as *variations on a theme*. This theme comprises several motifs: a block-like main form (which often, but not necessarily, rises up in space like a tower), a symmetrical main façade which is related to earth and sky by means of a vertical slit in the middle which also unifies the stories of the house, a crowning skylight over the slit which lets the sun penetrate into the interior, and an embracing masonry shell which contains recessed areas of glazing. The theme was introduced in the house at Pregassona in 1979, whereas Botta's earlier houses appear as "freer" compositions. To understand what the theme means, it is useful first to take a look at the earlier works.

Botta's first one-family house built in Stabio 1965–66, is evidently inspired by the post-war architecture of Le Corbusier.[22] It possesses a characteristic modern "open form," and shows a will to communicate with the landscape by means of guiding walls and varied openings. It does not, however, make any wish for image quality manifest. The houses in Cadenazzo from 1970–71 and Riva San Vitale from 1972–73 represent important steps on the way towards the architectural image. Both are block-like structures rather than open forms, and have a pronounced *Gestalt* quality. The house in Cadenazzo stands on a wide and gentle slope articulated by old vine terraces. On this slope the house introduces an axis which is directed towards the plain below and the more distant mountains in front. The direction is emphasized by two large, circular openings in the end wall which relate to the landscape. The upper half of the circle thus mirrors the vaulted sky, whereas the lower embraces the plain. A horizontal division across the ground-floor opening acts like a "horizon," giving definition and stability to the spatial rapport. On the top floor the unbroken circle appears as the image of a "total" world. A similar opening is also found on the back side of the house towards the hill. Here the upper part is reduced to a slit visualizing the vertical rise of the land. The motif is furthermore varied on one of the relatively closed lateral façades. Here the circle is subdivided by a vertical pillar, as to indicate the stepping down of the site. The circular opening as such is derived from Kahn, but it is used by Botta to articulate the relationship between the house and its environment. An ingenious solution to the problem of making a building reveal the spatial properties of a situation! The surrounding houses with their arbitrary directions and roof shapes are on the contrary unrelated to the site, and Botta's structure acts like an axis which gathers the other buildings around itself.

The house at Riva San Vitale has a certain basic affinity to the one in Cadenazzo, but is also quite different. Here the site is much steeper and the space in front more narrow, embracing the reflecting surface of the Lake of Lugano under the dramatic masses of Monte Generoso. To stand up to this magnificent landscape, a concentrated powerful form was needed, and Botta as a consequence designed a "tower," which like a vertical *axis mundi* embodies the desired quality of place. Standing slits in the elevations emphasize the verticality, whereas more limited horizontal openings echo the expanse of the lake. Within the unified volume the different rooms interact vertically, evidencing the up-and-down movement. The house is reached on the top floor by a bridge from the rising slope behind. A direct experience of the spatial composition is hence achieved. In general, the house at Riva San Vitale shows how the qualities of strong *Gestalt* and environmental rapport may be combined.

A third house from Botta's earlier period carries on similar intentions. In 1975—76 he built a dwelling in Ligornetto which again demonstrates how a unified block-like volume may interact meaningfully with its surroundings. The site is here located at the outskirts of an agricultural village, and the land is quite flat. In the past, such villages had a pronounced figural quality, being densely clustered and clearly delimited. Today this quality tends to get lost, due to the scattering of the new buildings. Botta counteracts this unfortunate development intending his structure as an "urban wall" which marks the limit of the settlement. The house is therefore designed as a simple prismatic volume extending horizontally. Towards the countryside it is cut through by a centrally placed vertical slit which is repeated on the inside in connection with a larger opening. Thus the volume interacts meaningfully with the space to which it belongs, at the same time as the rooms inside are integrated around the opening. A general simplification and quasi-symmetric equilibrium is achieved, which points towards the basic theme of Botta's more recent houses. The simplicity of the layout is however complemented by a new wish for sophisticated detailing. The walls are composed of horizontal stripes of grey and red masonry, and the volume terminates in an articulate cornice. A new sense of scale and rhythm becomes manifest, which is echoed in a number of small, sensitively placed holes in the facades. Whereas the former houses first of all reflected the influence of Le Corbusier and Kahn, the lesson of Botta's teacher Carlo Scarpa here becomes evident.

In general, the three houses in Cadenazzo, Riva San Vitale and Ligornetto revive the archetypal themes of directed axis, tower and delimiting wall, at the same time as they demonstrate the eternal validity of the simple, prismatic volume. In doing this, they echo basic typologies of the South-Alpine vernacular, and make the landscape come to life again. They do not, however, possess the general image quality which distinguishes Botta's later houses. A project for a house in Manno from 1975 represents a decisive step in the quest for the image. Here a quasi-symmetrical, triangular volume is cut through by a narrow vertical space in the middle which terminates in a skylight. The main front is dominated by a large arched opening which acts as a powerful integrating motif. We see, thus, how the "open" forms of modern architecture are becoming subject to a more general kind of order. One could also say that the circumstantial solutions of modernism are augmented to comprise a wider range of meanings.

With the house in Pregassona from 1979 the conquest of the image as a fully developed theme is accomplished. The united volume is still there, and the four elevations relate in different ways to the surroundings. The main front, however, has now gained a figural quality which embodies more general values. The symmetrical vertical slit unifies earth and sky at the same time as it makes the "between" of human life visible as a set of interacting spaces. On the ground, the extended surface of the earth interpenetrates with the enclosing volume of the house, and up towards the sky light is received and crystallized as a visible form by the triangular skylight. Thus the slit opens and contracts as it rises up. The relationship to the immediate surroundings is hence interpreted as a case of our general being in the world, and the solution gains a profound human value.

In 1979 Mario Botta also built a house in Massagno where the theme is varied in accordance with a different situation. Here the site is a steep slope which is approached from below. The house therefore primarily has to act as a frontal plane in the hillside, rather than a free-standing volume. To relate this façade to the "total" world it faces, Botta placed a large, circular opening in its middle. This opening is subdivided by a floor which echoes the horizon and relates the circle to the orthogonal directions of lived space. Thus he recalls the motif introduced at Cadenazzo, but now as a dominant image. Through the circular opening we recognize a vertical space which runs up through the house, terminating in a triangular skylight. Again, thus, the house is meaningfully related to the sky and the sun. Just as convincing is the relation to the earth, which is expressed by a cut-away corner containing the entrance. A cave-like feeling is achieved which is emphasized by a narrow view of the land below through the lower part of the main circular opening. The detailing is again very sophisticated, and the frontal plane is defined by grey and red stripes like in Ligornetto.

The meaningful articulation in Massagno was carried another step forward in the house in Viganello from 1980. Here motifs from the former two houses are brought together and reinterpreted. Thus we find again the frontal elevation on the steep slope, the cave-like entrance, and the integrating, central opening. Now the latter has become a wide interval between the two massive halves of the embracing volume. It is covered by a generous semicircular skylight which indeed visualizes the presence of the sun. The surface articulation is more elaborate than in the earlier houses, and is now partaking actively in the intended relationship of earth and sky. By placing cement blocks obliquely in the wall certain areas are characterized as being more "open" than the wall around, in correspondence with the living spaces inside. The cornice is also differentiated from the wall below, as to suggest the influence of light and sky on the volume. Lastly, the front steps out at either end as it rises, creating a liberating counter-movement to the enclosing façade around the cave-like entrance. In the house at Viganello the built form thus reflects in its plastic articulation the spatial being of the structure, giving the solution a new sense of presence. We could also say that the general existential theme is embodied as a "here," and the creation of a true place is accomplished.

A similarly meaningful relationship between space and built form distinguishes the Medici house in Stabio from 1980. Due to its round form, it has become Botta's perhaps best-known work.[23] In Stabio the land is flat and the house ought to function as a gathering centre to the scattered buildings around. A tower-like shape was therefore chosen, but without the orthogonal orientation determined by the slope in Riva San Vitale. The round form is hence a function of the site, but as the house also has to take the directions of north, south, east and west into consideration, the volume is articulated by means of Botta's characteristic motifs. Towards the south, a vertical slit unites earth and sky, at the same time as it widens out to reveal the interior living room. A small triangular skylight terminates the vertical space running up through the volume. On the opposite side the wall is opened up in a way which recalls the solution in Pregassona. At Stabio, however, the stepped outline is counterpoised by the round shaft of the staircase which like a large column rises up and fans out at the top to form a kind of capital. The cornice recalls the one at Viganello, but gains added importance due to the roundness of the main volume. In general, the house at Stabio shows how Botta's theme is capable of adaptation to varied situations, and that in all cases it may secure a meaningful relationship between the particular and the generic. The fertility of his "method" is also proved by the house in Origlio from 1981, where motifs already encountered at Pregassona, Viganello and Stabio are combined in a fascinating way. A house under construction in Morbio Superiore (1982-83) again varies the basic theme, this time on a sloping site. Again the frontal relation to the landscape is expressed by horizontal stripes, and is moreover emphasized by the concave curvature of the façade. Curved walls inside add to the Late-Baroque flavor of the project.

Beyond their successful adaptation of domestic functions to various sites, the importance of the houses of Mario Botta resides in their having revived archetypal forms of the human dwelling. Thus they represent reinterpretations of the original cave-like enclosure, the interior "hall," as well as the extrovert "veranda."[24] A spontaneous feeling of coming close to the essence of house is thus created. At the same time they are truly modern in their spatial interaction with the environment, their technological honesty and their refusal of sentimental imitation of the past. Last but not least, their powerful imagery opens up a new phase in the development of the contemporary house.

Botta himself recognizes the importance of his domestic architecture, saying: "The single-family house can be interpreted as an archetype in the organization of the relation between man and nature, in as much as it is the constant of man's inhabiting, throughout history and in different places, and in as much as it is a space, a microcosm, which defends and characterizes man in relation to his environment. The single-family house is a constant to be found throughout the course of the history of human settlements, from the primitive dwellings to the recent history of modern architecture."[25]

How, then, do Botta's large-scale projects implement the general aims and means so far illustrated by his houses? Evidently the aim of relating to a given environment by revealing its meaning, pertains to any work of architecture.[26] But the means may differ. The image of the house is not the same as the image of the school, the church, the factory or the office-building. And still, there are forms of imagery of a more general kind which reveal that any building stands forth between earth and sky. We could also say that the "between" where human life takes place is always concretized "as something." Botta's works illustrate this fact.

The first large-scale projects by our architect from the beginning of the 'seventies, are conceived in "structuralist" terms.[27] Open, repetitive systems of spatial organization are used in the competition entries for the Lausanne Polytechnic (1970) and the Housing Estate at Mendrisio (1974). The executed secondary school at Morbio Inferiore (1972–77) shows how Botta imagined such projects to be carried out. The structuralist derivation is also here evident, but in contrast to the abstract, technological character of most works of this kind, Botta's school possesses a strong plastic and spatial identity which meaningfully complements the given situation. Already here, in fact, Botta emphasized that it is not the task of the architect to "construct on a site, but to construct *that site*, so that the building becomes part of a new geographical configuration in direct connection with the qualities of history and of memories peculiar to that place."[28] The school satisfies this aim in its relation to the surrounding landscape and through its powerful presence which makes it gather the surroundings into a totality. The formal articulation and the interior spaces with their suggestive play of light and shadow reflect the influence of Kahn, at the same time as they prove the extraordinary figurative talent of Mario Botta. In spite of its presence and gathering function, however, the building does not possess the image quality characteristic of Botta's later work.

With the project for the enlargement of the railway station in Zürich (1978), a new attitude becomes apparent. Again the existing situation is taken as the point of departure, but now the solution consists in one great gesture. More concretely, it is conceived as a bridge-structure which links the two parts of the city separated by the railway. This bridge is designed as one great form spanning between towers of access. Due to the utilitarian character of the task, monumentality, in the usual sense of the word, is avoided, but the solution all the same acts as a unifying and powerful element in the cityscape. Several details give testimony to a new quest for image quality. In general, the project possesses a genuine urban value and shows how Botta's environmental approach may be used within an existing city.

A similar understanding of an urban situation distinguishes the State Bank at Fribourg (1977–82). The building is located at a corner facing the square in front of the railway station. Thus it had to adapt to the existing structures along the flanking streets, as well as the urban space at their intersection. Botta solved the problem through a differentiation into three kinds of subordinate volumes: two wings which continue the rhythm and scale of the street walls, a transitory element facing the square, and a semicircular volume which turns the corner at the same time as it suggests an interpenetration of building and urban space. Different formal means are used to characterize the three volumes. The wings are articulated by a repetition of separate windows like the adjacent buildings, the transitory volume has *fenêtres en longueur* to express the large, open spaces it contains and the main entrance on the ground floor, and the semicircular "bow window," a transparent curtainwall. The volumes are unified by means of a sophisticated use of materials, detailing and proportions.[29] Of particular interest is the main bank hall with its arched entrance, symmetrical disposition and vaulted skylight. It shows how Botta's theme may be transferred to an interior. A grand space, indeed, which teaches us how a utilitarian function may gain expressive value! The restaurant in the basement is a *tour de force* of interior design, proving how Botta is able to obtain festive and fascinating effects by simple and controlled means.

The project for an office-building in Lugano (1981, under construction) significantly varies the solution in Fribourg. Again the site is located on a corner in front of a public square. Also here Botta picks up the scale and rhythm of the adjacent buildings, and again he opens up the corner to obtain an interaction with the urban space in front. The orthogonal layout of the city blocks, however, demands a simpler volumetric composition. Thus the building is conceived as a unitary body which steps back at both sides of the corner in a way which resembles the slit introduced in the house at Pregassona. A meaningful visualization of the horizontal extension of the ground as well as the rising up of the building towards the sky is thus achieved. A powerful tower-like element marks the corner and keeps the whole volume together, unifying itself with the crowning cornice. In general, the Lugano project represents an ingenious reinterpretation of the traditional urban *palazzo*, and fully satisfies the current wish for an architecture which is simultaneously "new" and "old."

In several other works Botta has shown how his themes and motifs may be varied to take care of different situations and building tasks. The library in the Capuchine monastery in Lugano (1976–79) thus makes use of the enclosed symmetrical space with a central slit and crowning skylight to obtain a certain silent solemnity. The Crafts Center at Balerna (1977–79) belongs to the same family, but the utilitarian function here determines a spreading out of the closed volumes, to transform the central slit into a hall covered by a series of triangular skylights. The symbolic importance of the theme is thereby lessened and the "industrial" nature of the building revealed.

In some other recent large-scale projects Botta's quest for image quality becomes forcefully manifest. The design for a second Crafts Center in Balerna (1979) thus consists of two elementary juxtaposed volumes: a "thick" entrance wall pierced by a large archway, and a rotunda behind, which is subdivided by one of the architect's characteristic vertical slits on the main axis. A powerful solution, indeed, which gives testimony to the capacity of Botta's approach. The design for a Centre of Culture in Chambéry, France (1st prize in competition 1982) finally shows how our architect intends a public insitution of monumental character.[30] The lesson of Kahn is still evident in the simple juxtaposition of elementary volumes and in the structural articulation. The symmetrical stage façade, however, possesses that image quality which is characteristic of Botta's later work and suggests how his universe of forms may serve to give distincition and meaning to a civic place.

Botta's lesson
Mario Botta's works show what the return to architecture means. Sociological and semiological considerations are left behind, and even functional analysis is reduced to an aid of secondary importance. Instead Botta takes the basic forms of human existence in a certain place as his point of departure, and as a result architecture comes back to life. What, then, are these "basic forms," in terms of building? First of all they are the archetypal relations of earth and sky, and of man's being "between" the elements of nature. In architecture this rapport becomes manifest as front, tower and wall, gateway, cave and hall, arch, gable and embodied light.[31] These are the primary "images" which serve to interpret and explain our situation. But the primary images have to be set into work "as something," that is, as house, as school, as *palazzo*. And every something has its own archetypes, which consist in a certain choice between the primary ones. Thus we may talk about the basic forms of dwelling and institution. Louis Kahn understood that when he said: "Everything that an architect does is first of all answerable to an institution of man before it becomes a building."[32] But Botta also considers a third level of meaning. Thus he points out that the primary forms have to be interpreted *locally* to become real. Man does not only live on the earth and under the sky, but in a particular *here*. When living "here," for instance in Ticino, is adequately understood, the memories of life will belong to a tradition which is visualized as a *Bauweise*. Botta's interest in the vernacular therefore aims at helping man to find roots in our modern world of abstrac-

tions. A tradition also represents a choice between the primary images, and consists in a set of locally meaningful types.

The lesson of vernacular architecture tells us that forms do not have to be invented over and over again from "zero." They are handed down to us as a *language*, which it is our duty to know and use. Botta's return to architecture implies a rediscovery of this language. In his pursuit of the language of architecture, Botta has been aided by a keen interest in history. His "reading" of the vernacular has been of decisive importance, but also his ability to understand its archetypal basis. The classical sources of inspiration are less obvious, but a certain affinity to Palladio may be pointed out. Palladio also aimed at combining general typologies with the characteristics of the individual site, as is expressed in his own explanation of the Villa Rotonda: ". . . as it enjoys from every part most beautiful views, some of which are limited, some more extended, and others that terminate with the horizon, there are loggia's made in all the four fronts . . ."[33] Palladio's "typical" villas are echoed by Botta's one-family houses which are distinguished by an analogous unity of the general and the particular.

Botta's houses moreover represent a continuation of a most important tradition in modern architecture. The modern movement in fact considered the dwelling the primary building task, expressing thereby a deep concern for the human condition in the new "open" world. This concern was concretized as the *plan libre,* which is not only a practical aid to accommodate various "functions," but a symbol of the simultaneity of places characteristic of the modern world.[34] Botta adopts the free plan, and as a fourth level of meaning he thus subscribes to the conviction that an authentic work of architecture has to belong to its own time. In relating the modern house to archetypal and local memories, however, he gives it a new profound significance.

What, then, is Botta's professional position at the present moment? We have already pointed out that the common denominator of the actual currents is the wish for a meaningful architecture, and that Botta has given a most important contribution to it fulfillment. In general, the problem is approached in two different ways. Robert Venturi and his followers propose an architecture of "complexity and contradiction" to express the multifarious contents of the modern world. The result are collage-like compositions where various memories or "conventional forms" are brought together. Venturi's concept of the "decorated shed" well expresses the approach.[35] Its artistic validity is obvious, but the danger of a return to superficial historicism cannot be negated. Botta's refusal of "Post-modernism" must be understood in this context. Aldo Rossi and the Italian *Tendenza* on the contrary advocate an architecture based on elementary "types," to secure easy comprehension and popular appeal.[36] The danger inherent in this approach is a certain schematism and loss of the immediately given. Botta is evidently related to the *Tendenza*, but his sense of concrete local values as well as his respect for the modern tradition give his works a nearness to life which lacks in those of his Italian colleagues. In this respect he comes closer to some of the leading

American architects, notably the Moore, Lyndon, Turnbull, Whitaker group, whose condominium at the Sea Ranch north of San Francisco (1963) represents a fundamental contribution to the development of a meaningful architecture. If we consider the local values involved there, the solution may be compared with Botta's *Ticinese* works.[37] In a more general sense Botta is also related to the Dane Jörn Utzon, who already in 1957 proposed an architecture derived from the archetypal relationships of earth and sky.[38] As Utzon has grown up under the Nordic sky, it is not surprising that he conceives of the "between" as an open and fundamentally "romantic" continuum, in contrast to Botta's distinct, "classical" buildings.

A last, and particularly interesting, relationship may finally be pointed out. The fundamental importance of image quality in Botta's works brings him close to Michael Graves, who in a series of projects has aimed at the development of a "figurative architecture."[39] In contrast to many colleagues who use the forms of the past as separate "motifs," Graves looks for essential archetypes, and in his designs he chooses those which "fit" the situation.[40] Being an American, he does not have local roots in the sense of Botta, but his attempt at unifying the general and the particular is similar. And even more: his quest for the "figure" or "image" is essentially the same. The architecture of the modern movement was "non-figurative," Graves says, and therefore brought about a "dismemberment of our formal language of architecture."[41]

We have seen how Mario Botta revives the language of architecture, and his singular success proves that this revival is needed. Botta in fact is one of the few architects of the moment who is accepted by "everybody." The reason is undoubtedly that he brings us back to the "beginnings" without losing contact with the present. In doing this he carries on the search initiated by his master, Louis Kahn. "What will be has always been," Kahn says, and adds: "I am trying to find new expressions of old institutions."[42] The words of Kahn tell us that the works of Botta should not be imitated. As a reinterpretation, an authentic architecture may always be realized in several ways, and Botta's buildings represent *one* possible solution. His lesson, however, ought to be understood. It teaches us that architecture to be valid has to comprise all the four levels of meaning mentioned above. Thus it has to be founded on the archetypes of our being in the world at the same time as it incorporates the characteristics of institution (in Kahn's sense of the word), locality and historical moment. The total *world* which is constituted by these four levels is visualized by means of the language of architecture. Only when we are able to do that, architecture becomes a taking possesion of place, and a help to human society.

Notes:
1 *GA Document* 6, p.7
2 *GA Document* 6, p.9
3 op.cit.
4 *Mario Botta 1978–1982*, Milano 1982. p.115
5 *GA Document* 6, p.8
6 In particular we may recall Moore, Allen, Lyndon: *The Place of Houses*, New York 1974 and Norberg-Schulz: *Genius Loci*, London/New York 1980.
7 The German term covers both the formal and technical aspects.
8 See Norberg-Schulz: *Genius Loci*.
9 *Mario Botta 1978–1982*, p.116.
10 The present writer crossed the Alps on bicycle in 1946.
11 See Stieler, Paulus, Kaden: *Italia, viaggio pittoresco*, Milano 1876.
12 See U.Donati: *Artisti ticinesi a Roma*, Lugano 1942.
13 H. Soeder: *Urformen der abendländischen Baukunst*, Köln 1964, p.150
14 Soeder: op.cit. Abb. 49
15 Numerous examples are given in W. Blaser: *The Rock is my Home*, Zürich 1976.
16 See G. Bianconi: *Costruzioni cantadine ticinesi*, Locarno 1982.
17 In general see V. Scully: *The Earth, the Temple and the Gods*, New Haven 1962.
18 See C. Norberg-Schulz: Kahn, Heidegger and the Language of Architecture. *Oppositions* 18, 1979.
19 Thus they prove the failure of semiology to explain the meaning of works of architecture.
20 Heidegger: The Thinker as Poet, *Poetry, Language, Thought*. New York 1971.
21 *GA Document* 6, p.7. Botta here explicity refers to Kahn as his source of inspiration.
22 See *GA Houses* 3, Tokyo 1977.
23 See *Mario Botta, la Casa Rotonda*. Milano 1982.
24 See L. Veltheim-Lottum: *Kleine Weltgeschichte des städtischen Wohnhauses*. Heidelberg 1952.
25 *GA Houses* 3, p.73.
26 Heidegger thus uses a Greek temple as an example to explain how a building makes a landscape appear as what it is. See The Origin of the Work of Art, in *Poetry, language, Thought*.
27 For the architecture of structuralism, see A. Lüchinger: *Strukturalismus in Architektur und Städtebau*. Stuttgart 1981.
28 *Mario Botta 1978–1982*, p.82.
29 See *GA Document* 6, Tokyo 1983. Also *Werk, Bauen+Wohnen* Nr. 1/2, 1983.
30 See *GA Document* 6, pp. 28ff.
31 The terms have an indicative function, and do not pretend to be complete.
32 See Norberg-Schulz: Kahn . . . p.31.
33 Palladio: *The Four Books on Architecture*, II, ii.
34 See C. Norberg-Schulz: *Roots of Modern Architecture* (ed. Y. Futagawa), Tokyo 1985.
35 See R. Venturi: Une définition de l'architecture comme abri décoré, *L'Architecture d'Aujourd'hui*, Nr. 197, Juin 1978.
36 See A. Rossi: *L'architettura della città*, Padova 1966.
37 See Moore, Allen, Lyndon: op.cit.
38 See J. Utzon: Platforms and Plateaus, *Zodiac* 10, Milano 1957.
39 See M. Graves: A Case for Figurative Architecture, in *Michael Graves Buildings and Projects 1966–1981* (ed. K.V. Wheeler, P. Arnell, T. Bickford), New York 1982.
40 A particularly important example is offered by the project for the Humana Corporation Building in Louisville. See: *A Tower for Louisville* (ed. P. Arnell, T. Bickford), New York 1982.
41 Graves: op.cit. p.13.
42 Norberg-Schulz: Kahn . . . p.32.

The project for the new complex (to replace the old parish house, demolished when the road intersecting the village was widened) was given to the eighteen-year-old Mario Botta, at that time a draftsman in the studio of Tita Carloni. This was not Botta's first assignment; he had already been entrusted with the building of a small house and with some renovations.

The new building is located on the site of the old one, next to the church, facing the valley rather than the village. Its presence reinforces on the one hand the visual impact created by the façade of the church; on the other hand it underlines and embellishes the square in front of the church. The desire to create a new public space, to not leave the church isolated, and to establish at the same time a transitional element between the old church and the new edifice resulted in the creation of a portico. The building is articulated by well-defined volumes — the portico, bedrooms, living room, and fireplace — having precise functions. These volumes based on primary forms, with only two exceptions, decline toward the valley; the inclination of the roofs follows the downward slope of the land.

In this early work Botta does not use traditional windows. Instead he substitutes a system of openings that includes the loggia, the portico, and the long horizontal opening in the external wall of the bedrooms, in which the concrete entablature is supported by metal columns that do not interrupt the continuity of the opening.

The building is made of "poor" materials typical of the local building tradition. The masonry is in plain stone, as is the lateral side of the church, the main façade of which is covered instead with plaster. The walls are a solid 50 cm. thick. The roofs are covered with curved terra-cotta tiles; doors are of wood and window shutters are painted dark green. In the interior only the dividing walls are plastered; the flooring is ceramic tile.

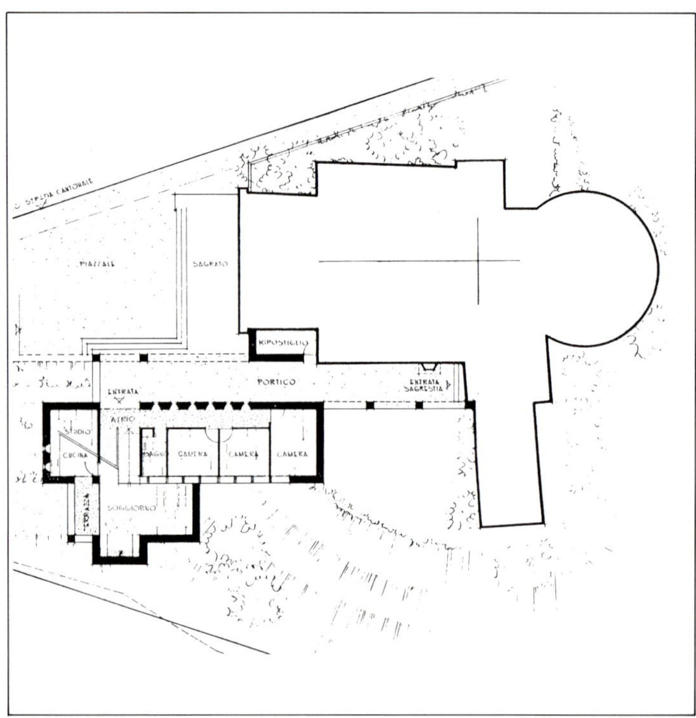

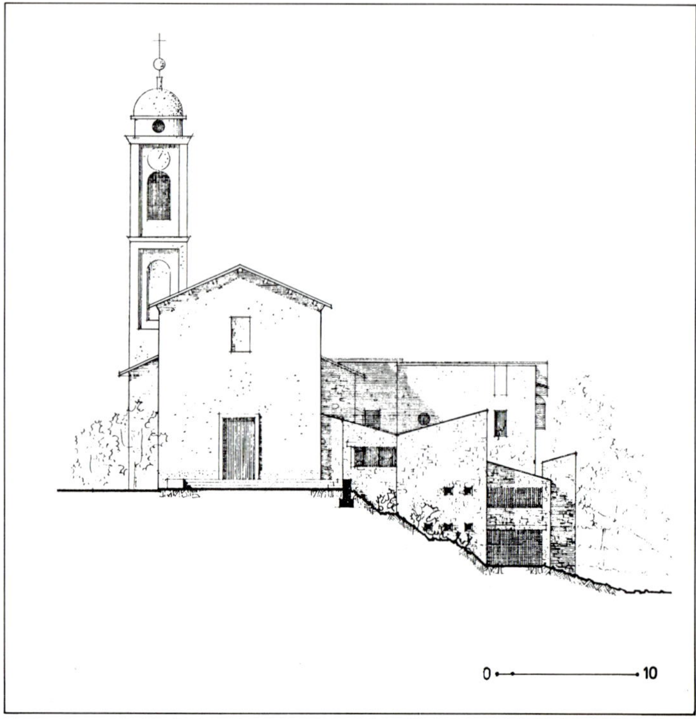

View from street

General view

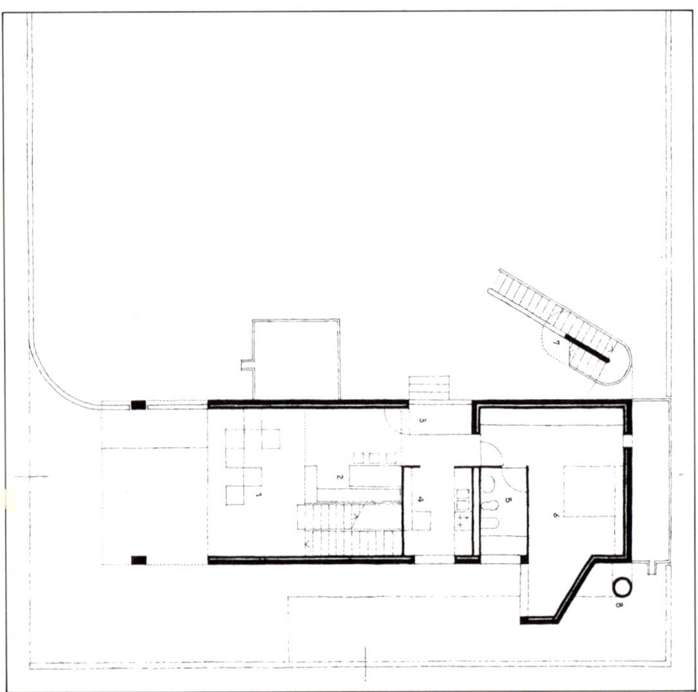

First floor

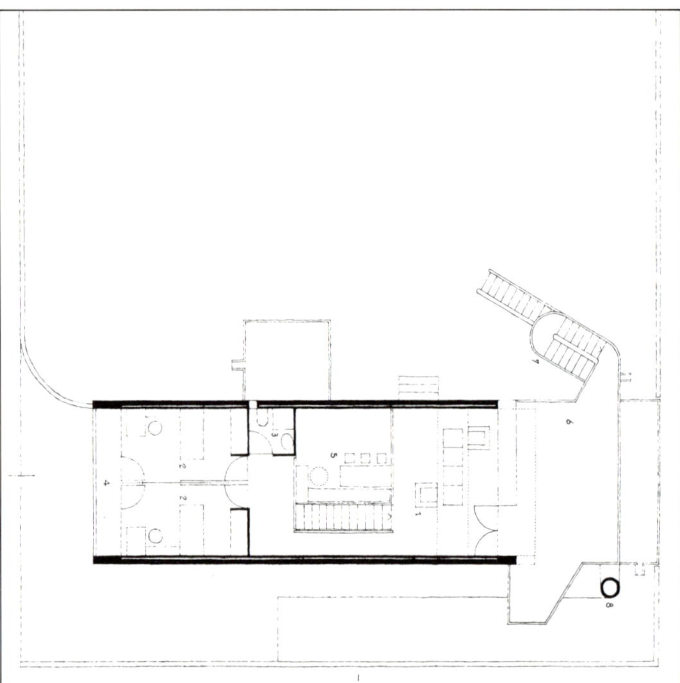

Second floor

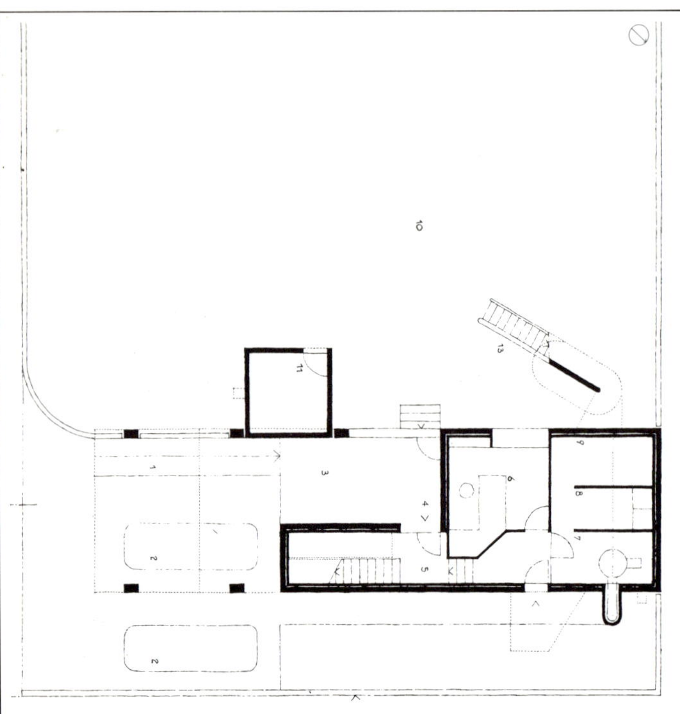

Ground floor

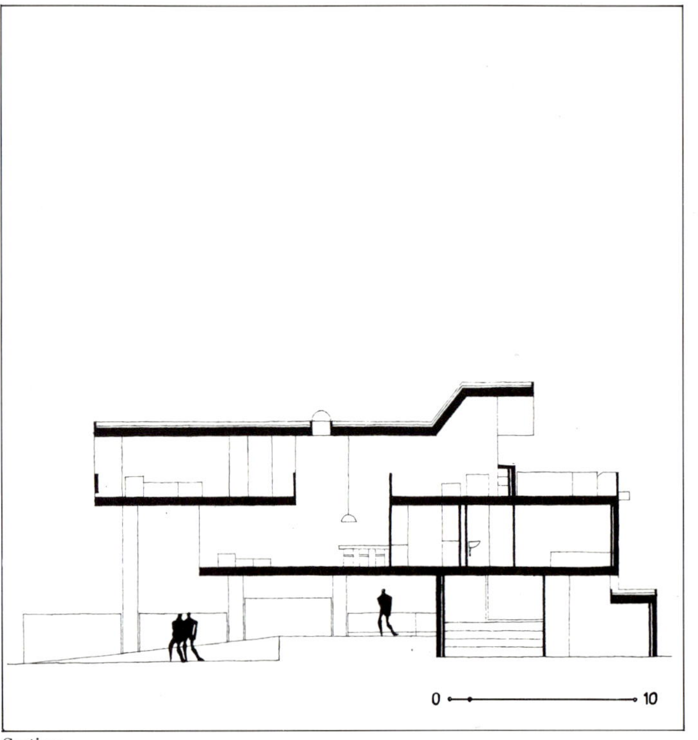

Section

Botta planned this house soon after his meeting with Le Corbusier in Venice, and as such the house represents an homage to Le Corbusier, while at the same time it is a reflection on the architectural poetry of that master.

The rectangular ground, located at the outskirts of Stabio, is enclosed within a continuous wall — actually, a fence — that separates and emphasizes the garden vis-à-vis the surrounding countryside. The new construction, planned as a "living cell" (according to the ideas of Le Corbusier), faces south on flat grounds and occupies a short side of the enclosing wall, and by its location underlines the role played by the wall of bounding and limiting the property.

Extending the relation between internal and external space within the perimeter of the large grounds, a perfect continuity exists (made possible by the stairway that directly links the second floor with the garden) between building and garden, the garden being considered, in this case, an extension of the house.

Two parallel walls, with only a small opening in the northern side and a larger one in the southern side, enclose the living area. The building is more open toward the east, where the continuity of walls is broken in two places, and where a large glass window is substituted for small openings or vertical cuts. The building has three floors — a characteristic that will often reappear in future works by Botta. On the ground floor are the entrance, the porch, services, cellars, and a playroom for children. The kitchen and the bathroom that separate the living room from the parents' bedroom are on the first floor, while on the second floor there is a studio, the children's bedroom, a large central space, twice as high as the others, and a glass window opening onto the balcony connected with the garden.

The whole building is marked by elements — the fireplace, the stair connecting the balcony of the studio with the garden, and the masonry element that on the first floor protrudes from the parents' bedroom to let in the morning light — that, according to Le Corbusier, facilitate a poetic response on the part of the viewer.

In the structure itself, which is made of exposed concrete, traditional windows are replaced by thin openings or large glass windows. All the internal walls are plastered and whitewashed. The entrance gate, the doors of the balconies (set inside black frames), and the doors inside the house, are painted yellow, blue, or red.

View from north

View from east

Living room

Dining room

Living room seen from dining room

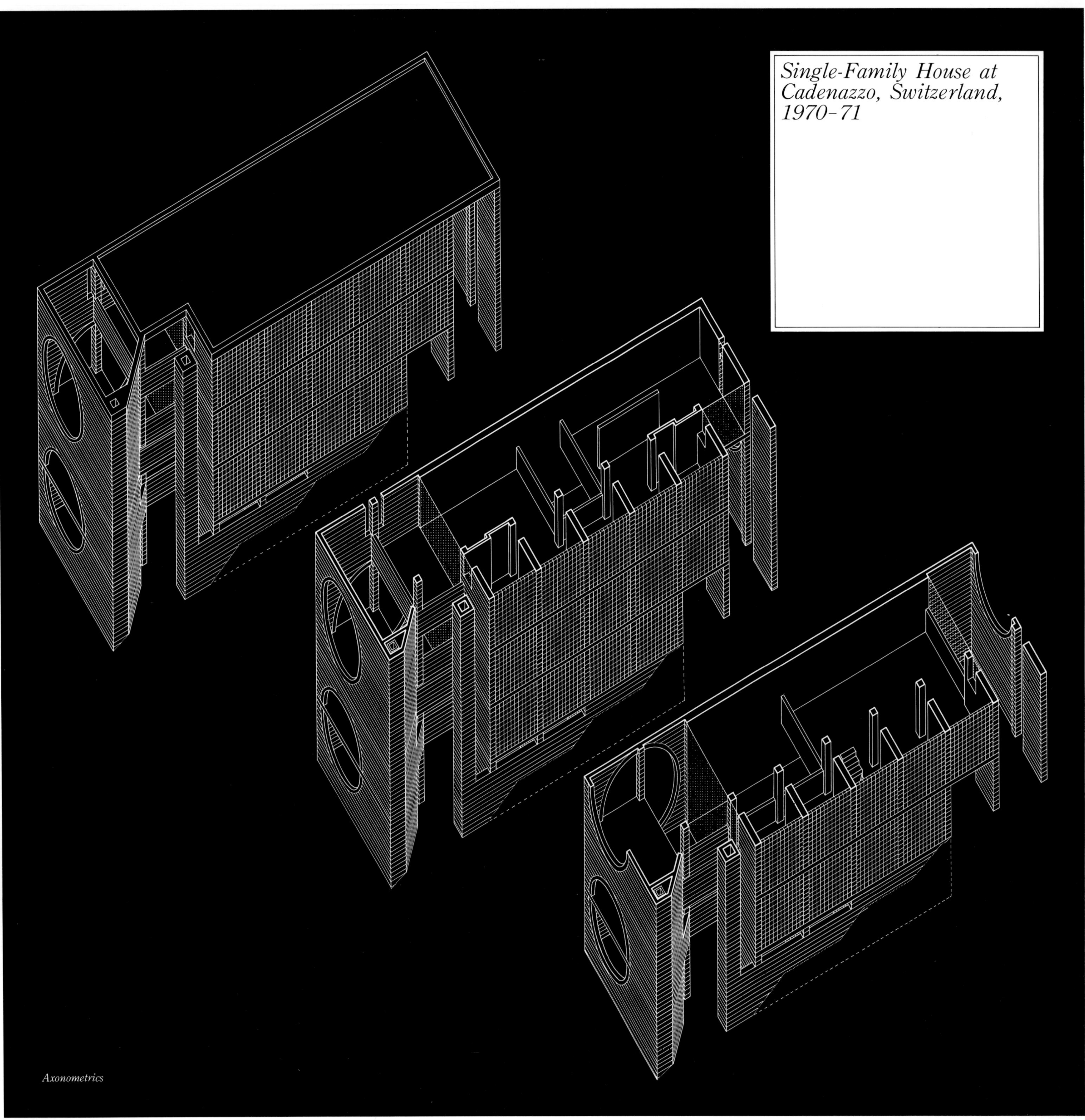
Single-Family House at
Cadenazzo, Switzerland,
1970–71
Axonometrics

1 LOCALE RISCALDAMENTO
2 LAVANDERIA
3 VANO SCALA
4 CANTINA
5 VESPAIO
6 INGRESSO
7 PORTICO - GARAGE
8 SERVIZIO
9 PRANZO
10 SOGGIORNO
11 CUCINA
12 TERRAZZA SOGGIORNO
13 CAMINO ESTERNO
14 GALLERIA
15 STUDIO
16 BIBLIOTECA
17 TERRAZZA
18 CAMERA GENITORI
19 GUARDAROBA
20 BAGNO
21 CAMERA BAMBINI
22 TERRAZZA
23 VUOTO

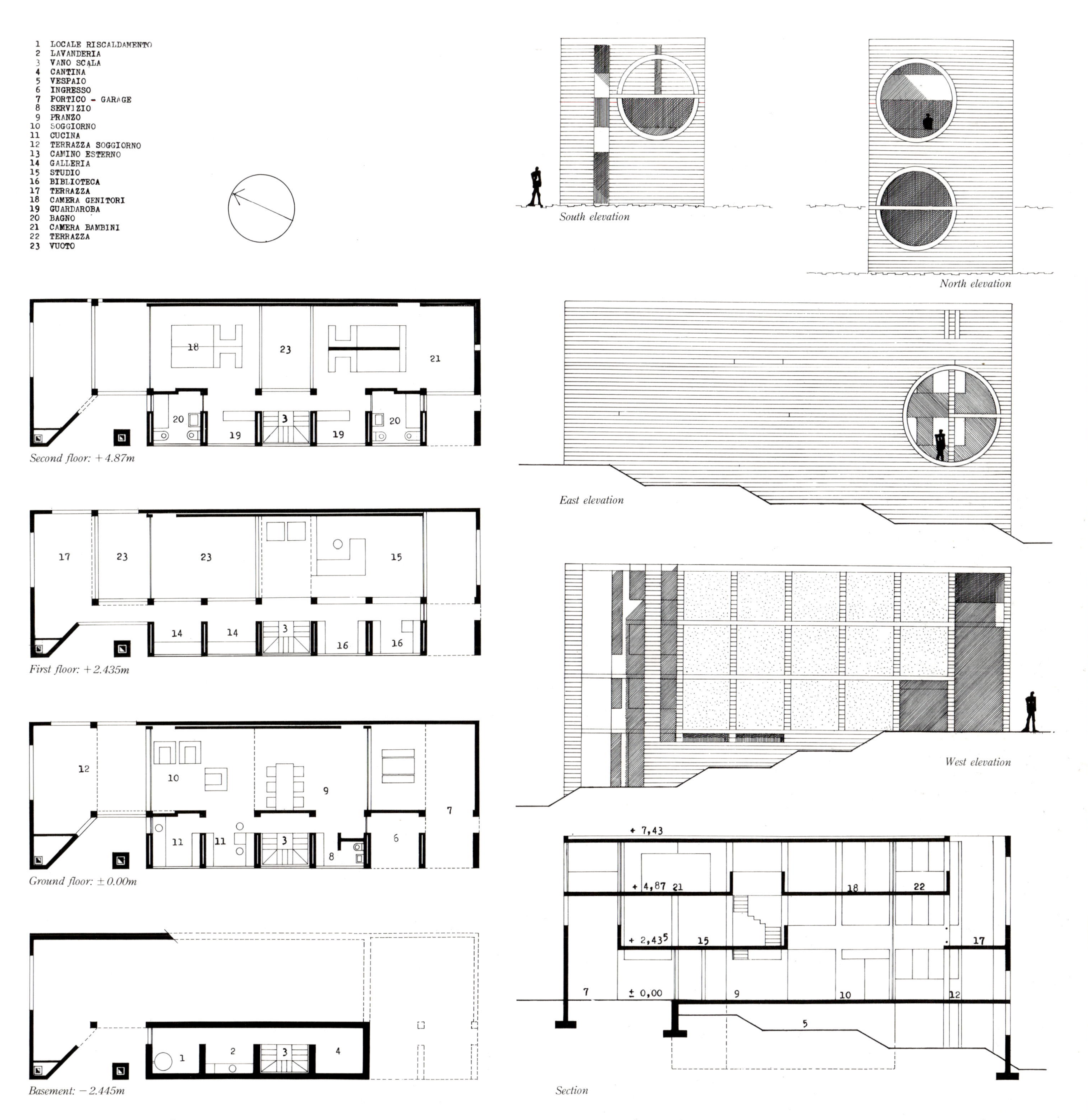

South elevation
North elevation
East elevation
West elevation
Section
Second floor: +4.87m
First floor: +2.435m
Ground floor: ±0.00m
Basement: −2.445m

△ View from southwest ▽ View of west façade
Detail of south wall ▷

View of terrace from study

As was the Stabio house, this project was also influenced by the architecture of another master. Botta met Louis Kahn a short time after his graduation. It is only on a purely theoretical side that Kahn's influence is felt, however, since the building continues and develops the plan adopted for the preceding family house, with a counterbalanced play of full volumes and deep openings that are the negation of traditional windows. In this case, as in the previous one, the choice of the plan is dictated by the particular character of the surrounding environment.

The house, built on a slope with mountains on the south and a valley to the north, is surrounded by a random proliferation of residential buildings. The house is constructed on a north-south axis and attempts to relate the internal space of the building to the positive elements of the landscape: the broad plain and the mountains. On the eastern side the house is totally closed by a continuous wall, while in the western portion a wall of glass and concrete gathers the afternoon light and distributes it to the small spaces allotted to services, bathrooms, and stairs. This deep portion is divided into regular bays, which can be further subdivided on different levels by partitions.

The linear organization of the plan, an evident development of that of Stabio, is highlighted by the two façades, north and south, in which the two large round openings connect the outside space with the intermediate space of the two loggias that protect the house from rain and snow. The compact volumes and the large openings that regulate the flow of light inside the building offer, unlike the surrounding construction, a different relation with the landscape.

The internal space, articulated on three levels, has the entrance and the living room on the ground floor, a studio on the first floor, and the bedrooms on the second floor; all of the western side is given over to space for secondary uses. For the first time concrete brick is used. This technique will be often found in later works. Bricks are left exposed on the outside while inside they are painted white. Floors are covered with slate; the large surfaces of glass windows are regularly broken up by black frames.

View of staircase

Block plan

Plan

Since the middle of the nineteenth century the city has expanded northward beyond its medieval perimeters. In the most recent decades this trend has resulted in a large, densely built-up area outside the old city and, within the boundaries of the historic center, the massive intrusion of banking and business activities, with the consequent disruption of the old fabric of the trade life of the city. This project intends to underline the particular characteristics belonging to both the old and the new cities. The architectural and other elements of the plan are intended to highlight at the same time the conflicting functions and structures of the old and new, to create an alternative to the existing city center, and to check the proliferation of commercial activities that are incompatible with the character of the old city. The project does not aim to build *in* a specific place but rather to *create* a place, so that the new architectural elements will become a direct part of the urban landscape as are the natural and geographic elements. The proposed site is set between the old and the more modern parts of the city, representing an extension of the city park, and as such establishes a relationship with the nearby lake. The plan is divided into four elements: the arcade, the towers, the pedestrian square, and the geometrized "forest." The pedestrian arcade, with a portico on the ground floor and various shops above, marks the boundary between the old and new cities and represents, at the same time, a physical and spatial link with the park and the lake; while the towers, with their commercial center, hotel, and administrative and recreational spaces, underline even more strongly the feeling of separation, dividing the two different civic textures already created by the arcade. The square situated at the end of the arcade will have playgrounds and recreational areas, and below it an underground parking lot on four levels. The forest and green areas are to be a continuation of the city park inside the old historic center and are to offer a shelter for activities such as open markets or games, which can become integral assets for the center. The project is to be realized in two building campaigns: the first includes the square, the underground parking lot, and the planting of part of the forest; the second, which is to follow soon after, comprises the towers, the arcade, and the rest of the forest.

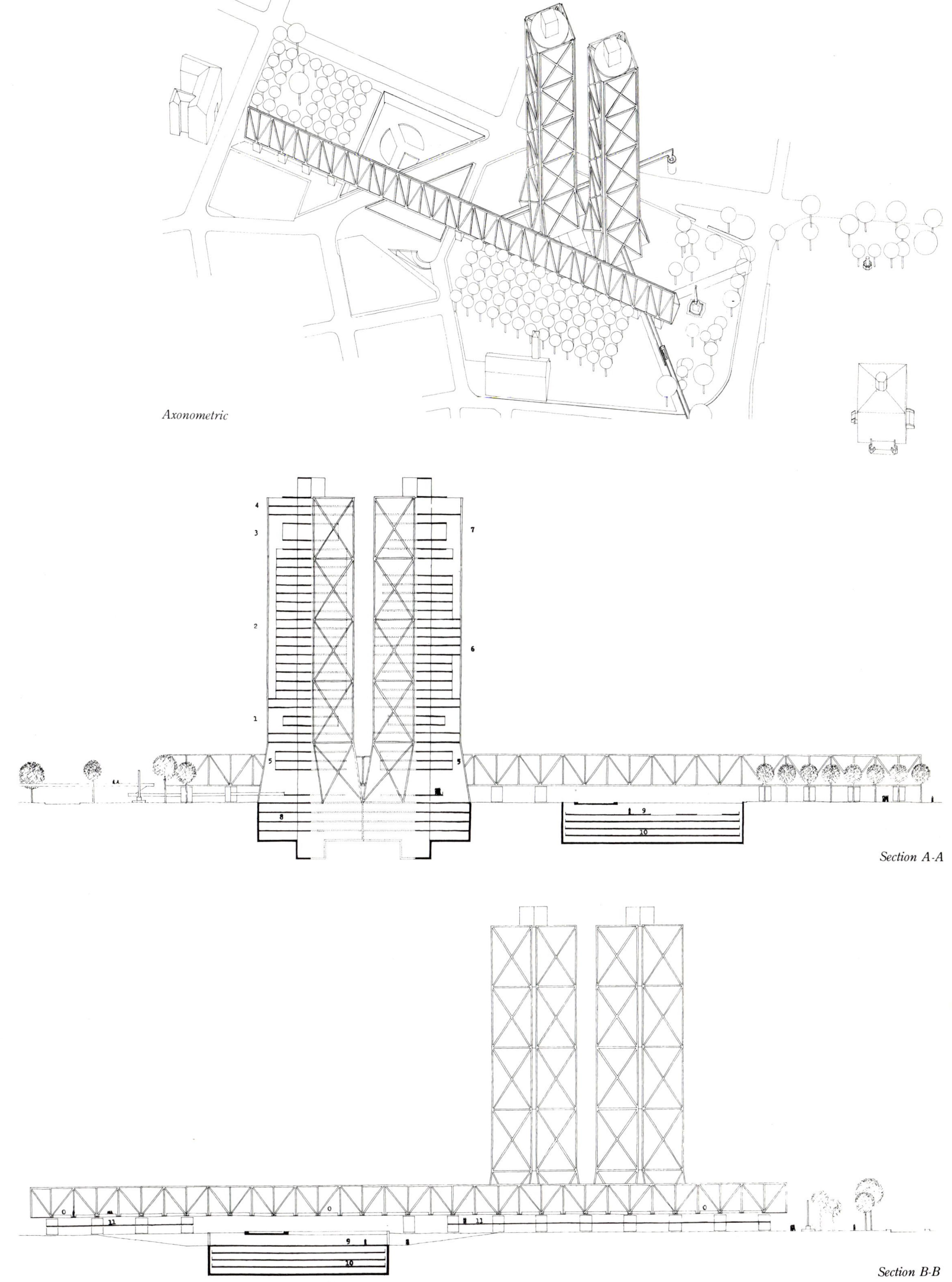

Axonometric
Section A-A
Section B-B

Competition for the Master Plan of the new Lausanne Polytechnic, Switzerland, 1970 (project)
with Tita Carloni, Aurelio Galfetti, Flora Ruchat, and Luigi Snozzi

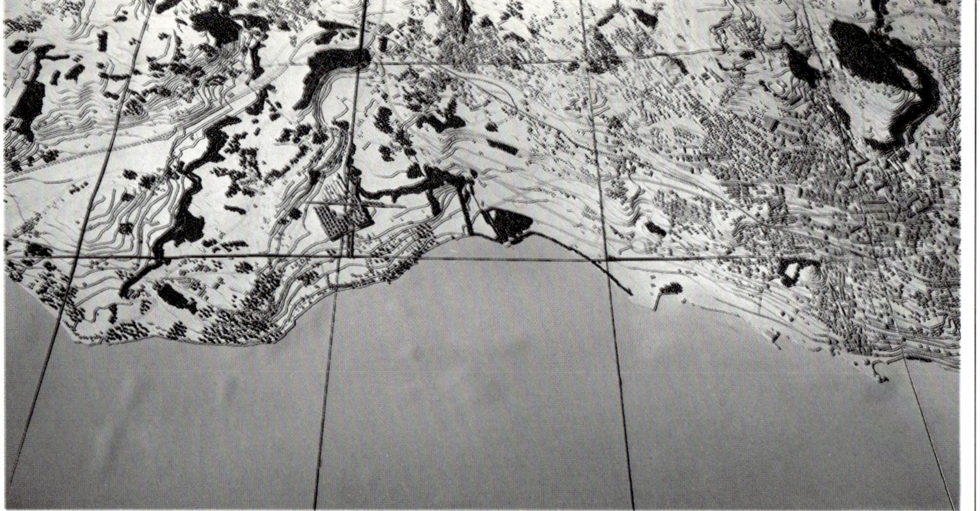

Model photo

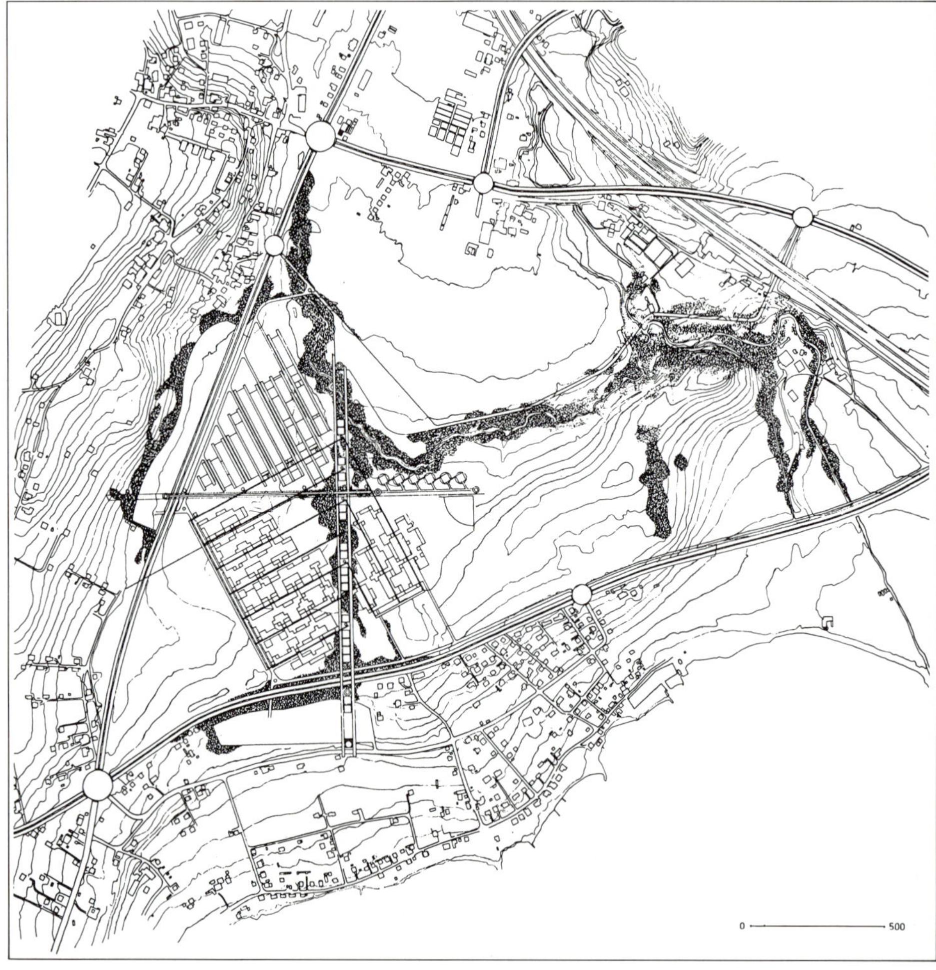

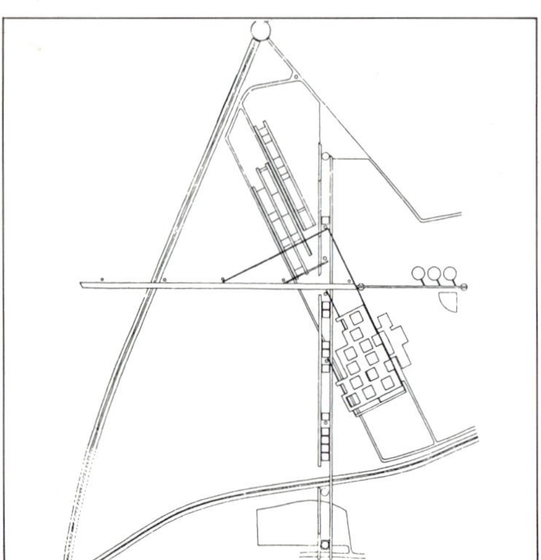

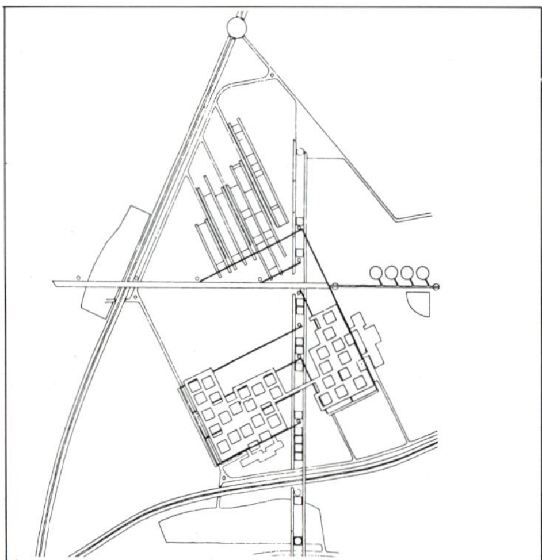

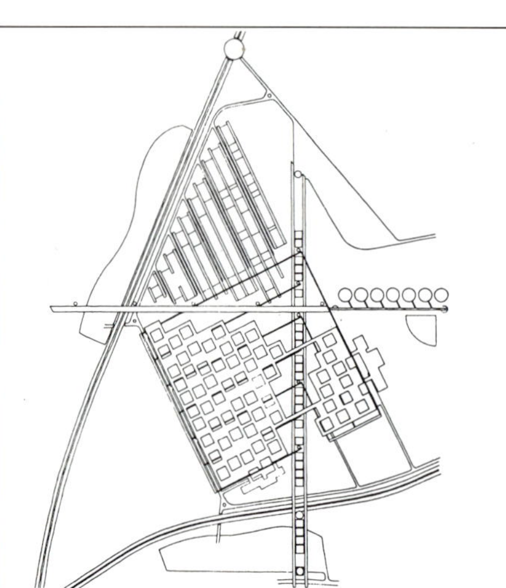

The general plan for the new polytechnic required a structure whose internal space would be highly flexible and would allow for future expansion. This is obtained by upsetting the organizational principles of the 1960s. From the outset a precise relationship of building to landscape is established through volumes that are aesthetically integrated with the surrounding space. Once the core and the enclosing perimeter are built, any modification or expansion can be made within the built structure, since the different parts that compose the project offer the logical possibility for further development.

The area where the polytechnic is to be built is located along the banks of Lake Geneva, a few kilometers from the city, near the university, which is separated from the polytechnic by a small valley cut through by a stream.

The project is articulated by three architectonic elements, each having a distinct role in the preestablished compositional system. The great cross, created by the intersection of the two axes (north-south and east-west), each about 800 meters long, is the first element that organizes and shapes the site. The living quarters for the staff and students are located within the two sides of the north-south axis; The remaining spaces are for secondary and collective activities. This long axis bridges the road leading to the south and, as well as linking the two parking lots at the extremities, is the intersection of the principal pedestrian walks. The east-west axis houses, on different levels, schoolrooms and spaces related to instructional activities, and, at the end nearest the university, cylindrical sections intended for auditoriums and an open theater.

As in a kind of industrial landscape, research facilities are grouped together in the northern area; they are built on a grid of parallel lines with large areas between them that offer possibilities for future growth. This area is intersected by roads.

A large square, whose sides are about 400 meters long and whose inner space is left empty, houses different departments. This structure has three floors: the ground floor given to research laboratories, the uppermost floor to classrooms, while the first, directly linked to the pedestrian walkways of the north-south axis, is a free space that allows the flow of people to their different activities. The elements that coordinate and link the different parts that compose the general plan of the polytechnic consist of vertical passages, empty spaces, and courtyards.

△▽ *Model photos*

The site for the school is located on the outskirts of Locarno, next to a highway that runs south, delimiting the site. The north side of the school is close to the existing urban development, and in the opposite direction it delineates and shapes the peripheral region of the developed area.

The project includes three distinct volumes: the gymnasium and swimming pool, the school itself, and the cylindrical house of the caretaker. The peculiar form of this house (a shape that will appear again in Botta's round house of Stabio in 1980) is used to underline the proportional and aesthetic relations between the other two volumes.

The swimming pool is housed on the ground floor of the gymnasium, whose central area includes showers and bathrooms, while the parking lot for bicycles is left outside. Four stairways at the corners lead to the upper floor, the gymnasium itself.

The caretaker's residence has three floors: the entry on the ground floor, the kitchen and living room on the first floor, and the bedrooms on the second floor.

The plan of the school includes a linear succession of small units, each having four classrooms serviced by two stairs. The building has three floors. On the ground floor the portico area is regularly divided by entrances and openings to the exterior; on the first floor are special classrooms, spaces for different uses, and a central corridor that links the single units, while the second floor consists of a series of isolated blocks, each containing four classrooms that lead to a central communal space. The different spatial treatment observed on the three levels permits not only an articulated merging of different systems but also allows the penetration of natural light on the different floors, the portico, and the first-floor corridor.

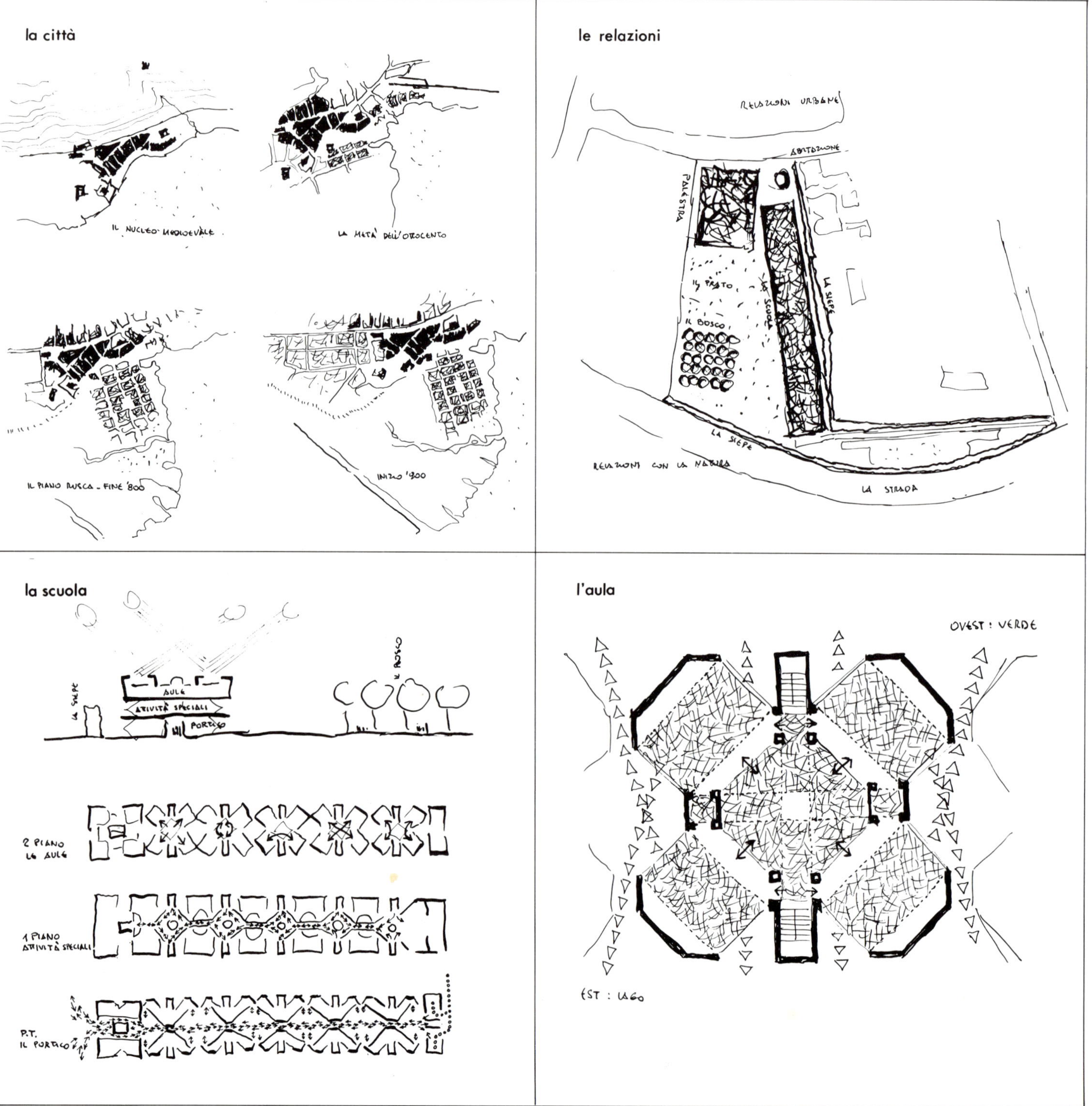

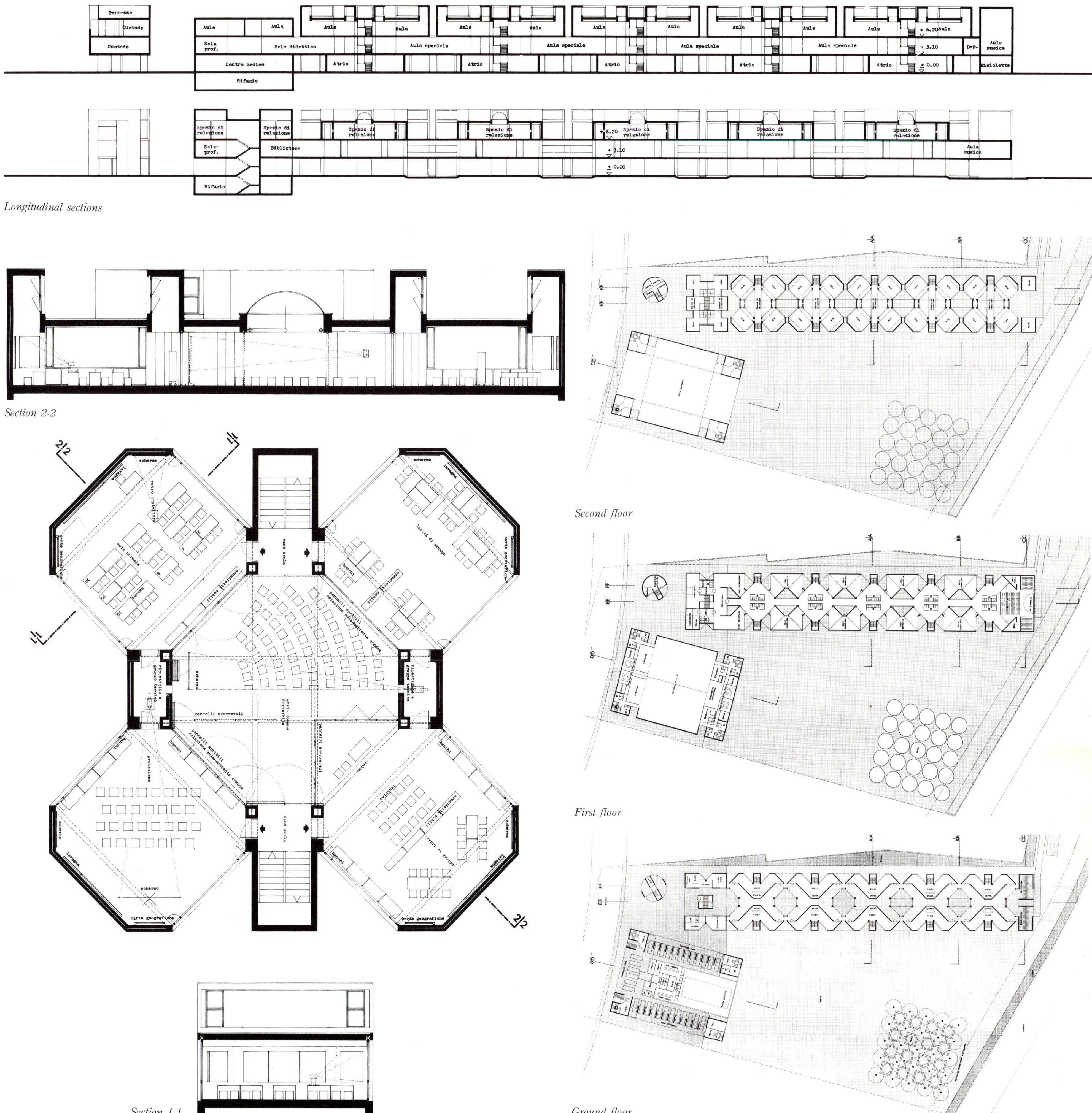

Longitudinal sections

Section 2-2

Second floor

First floor

Section 1-1

Ground floor

Competition for a New Administrative Center at Perugia, Italy, 1971 (project)
with Luigi Snozzi

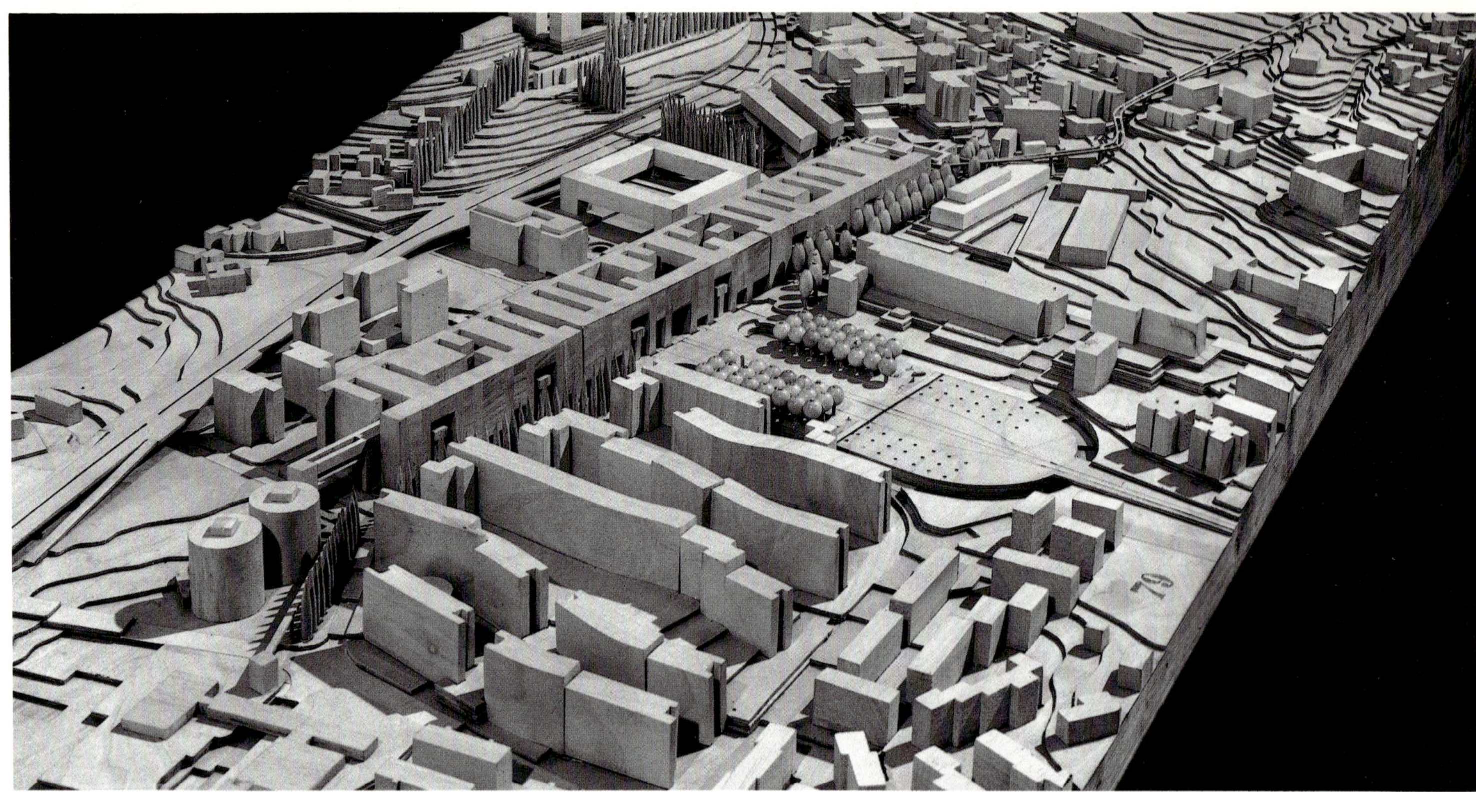

△▽ *Model photos*

Although within the limits imposed by the competition and the urban master plan, this project proposes a new primary structure that defies the ongoing relationship between empty and full spaces at the site, an area divided by the railway station, located between the north hill of the city and the nineteenth-century expansion of the city toward the south.

A compact volume, whose solidity is broken by a few squares, bridges the railway station and joins on the western end the new parking lot, and at the other end the small railway that directly links the Administrative Center with the old city. The new complex, which also includes two separate lateral wings for city offices and a quadrilateral section of houses, becomes, therefore, an intersection for different kinds of traffic.

A long pedestrian tunnel crosses the whole building: on the ground floor and below it, like negative volumes dug out of the ground, other parking lots are planned; commercial activities and offices are placed instead along the tunnel on the upper floors. Several rectangular courtyards bring light to the pedestrian spaces located on the ground floor; the external surface of the façade of this enormous "viaduct" is broken by the rhythmical alternation of stairs. The open spaces, in particular those next to the railway station, are planned as living parts of the city rather than empty spaces between existing volumes. It is from this viaductlike construction that the new park begins, extending out from it to the north.

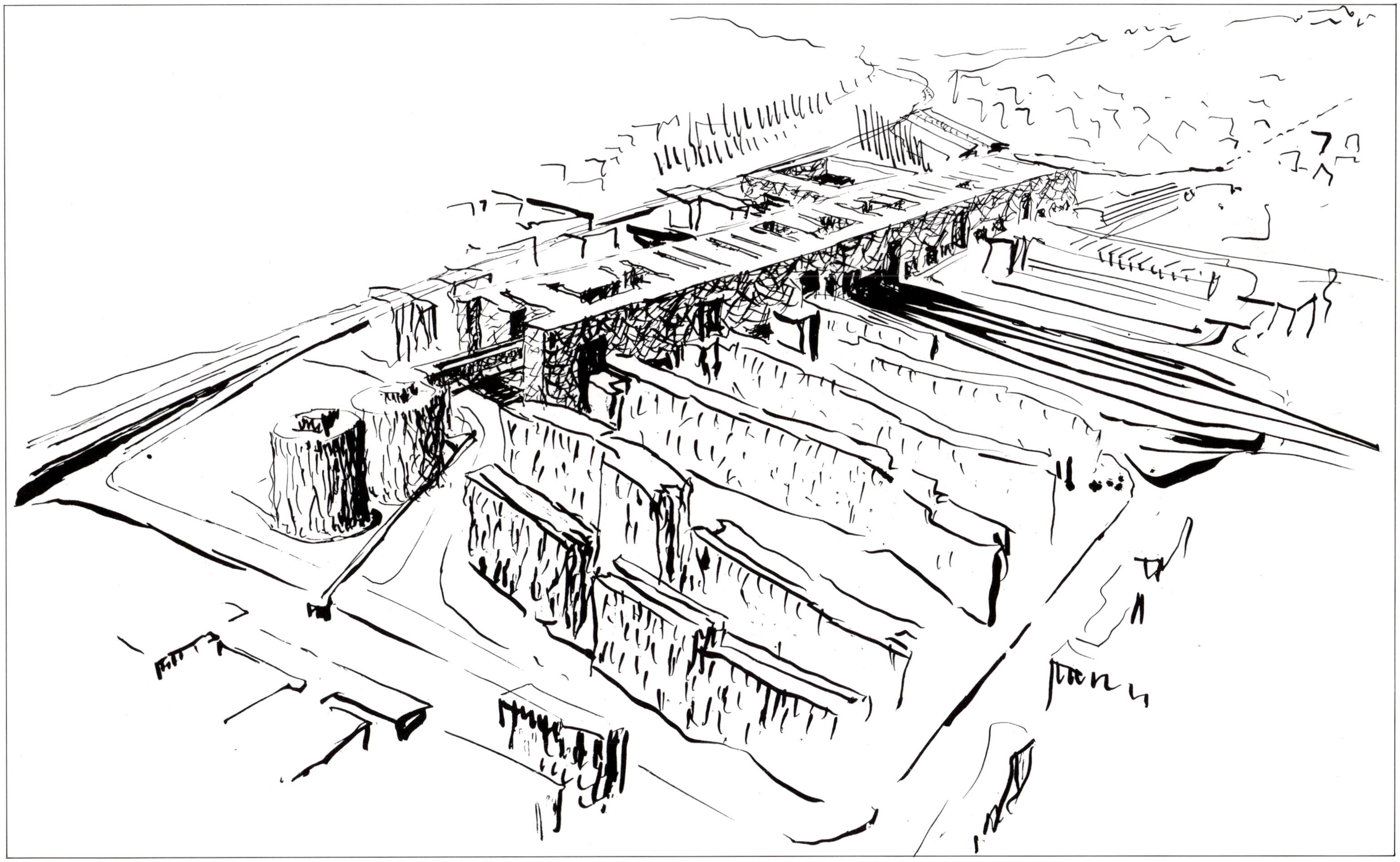

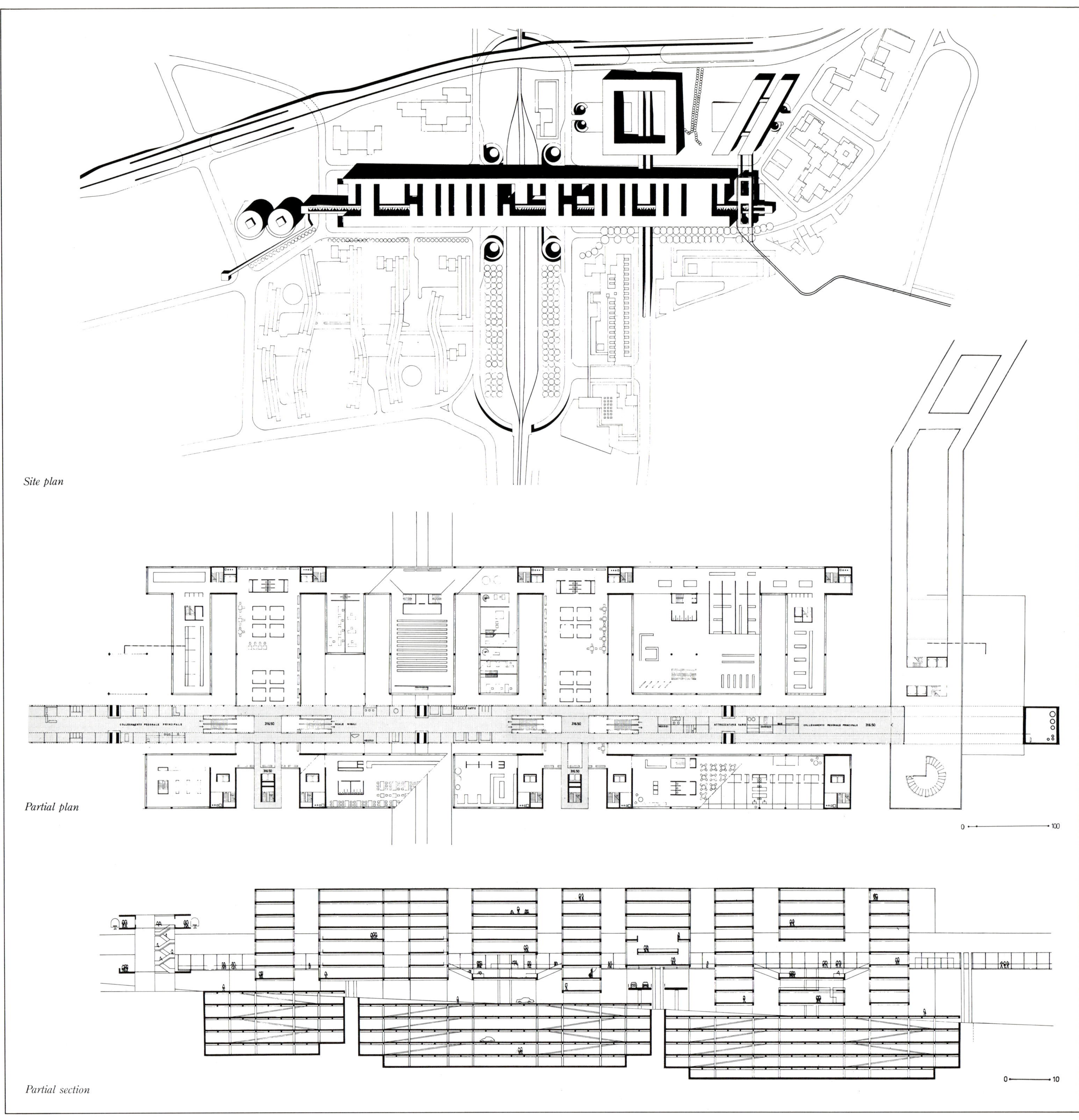

Site plan

Partial plan

Partial section

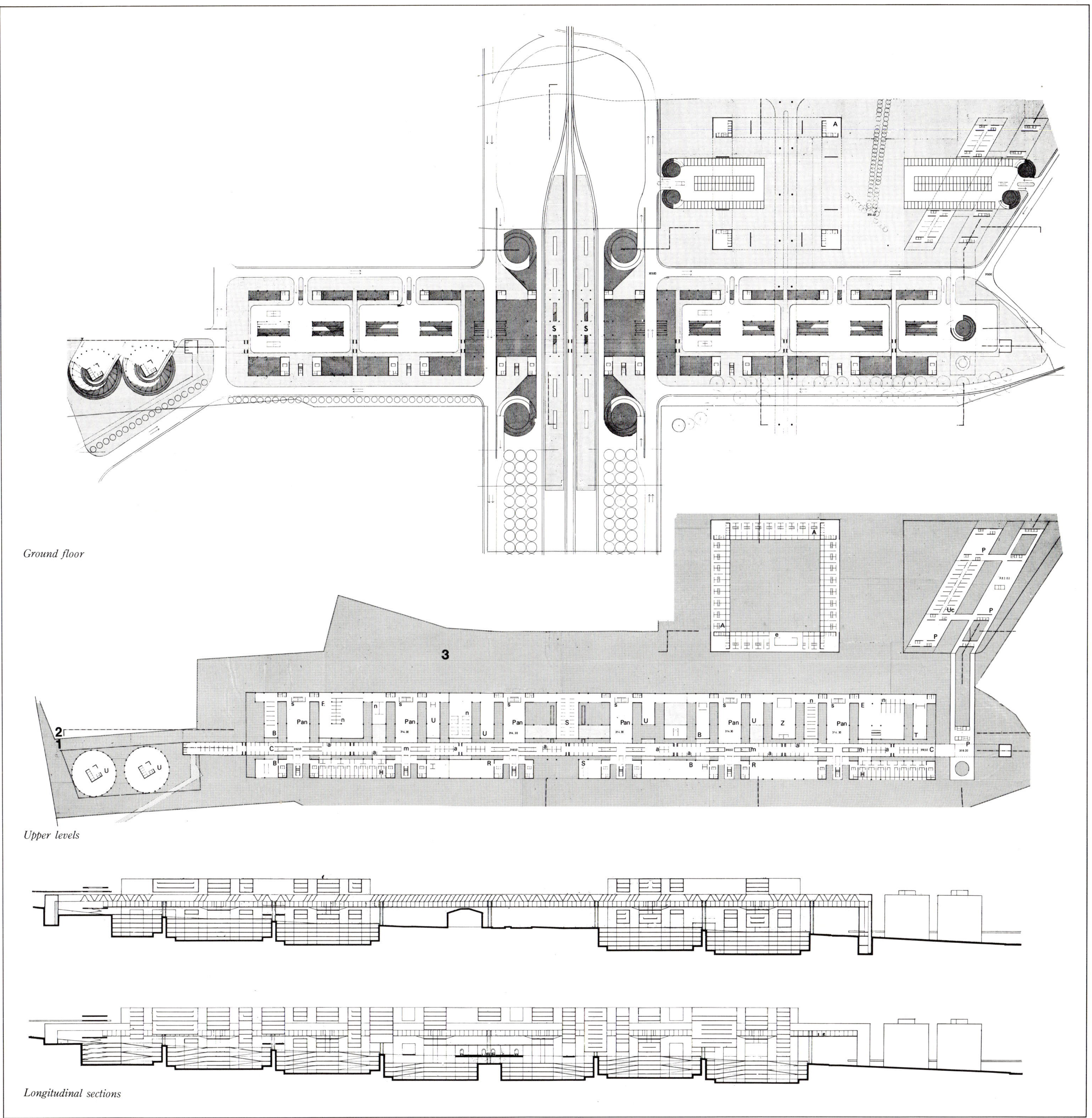

Ground floor
Upper levels
Longitudinal sections

Single-Family House at Riva San Vitale, Switzerland, 1972-73

Located on the mountainside overlooking Lake Lugano, the house emerges from the ground like a tower facing the different elements of the surrounding landscape, not totally integrated with its background and yet not foreign to it. Its primary volumetric shape and its sense of isolation make it a kind of ideal reference placed between the old village and the untouched woods that border the property.

From the old road alongside the mountain, a small metal bridge leads to the building. The bridge underlines the separation of land and building; negating the traditional sequence of road, gate, and garden, it substitutes an immediate revelation of the site and tower that becomes a kind of observation point in the surrounding landscape. The four sides of the building face different types of landscape: toward the lake, the distant landscape and the mountain; the meadows on the south; the woods to the north; and the road with the bridge at the west entrance.

This is one of Botta's key works — the first in which he demonstrates a complete formal autonomy, as well as being the preferred building in which he has gathered themes and elements that will be used and further developed in the future. The form of the tower is defined by the four corners that with their roofs make up the principal structure. The internal volumes lead to four glass walls and loggias that act as filters between the inhabited area and the landscape.

The vertical organization of the house presents the studio on the upper floor and then, in descending order, the parents' bedroom, the children's room, the kitchen and living room, the cellar (partially above ground), and a portico.

Simple and common materials reappear in the construction; walls consist of blocks of double-thick concrete and are painted white only on the interior. Floors are tile; doors are black metal; and the iron frame of the bridge is painted red.

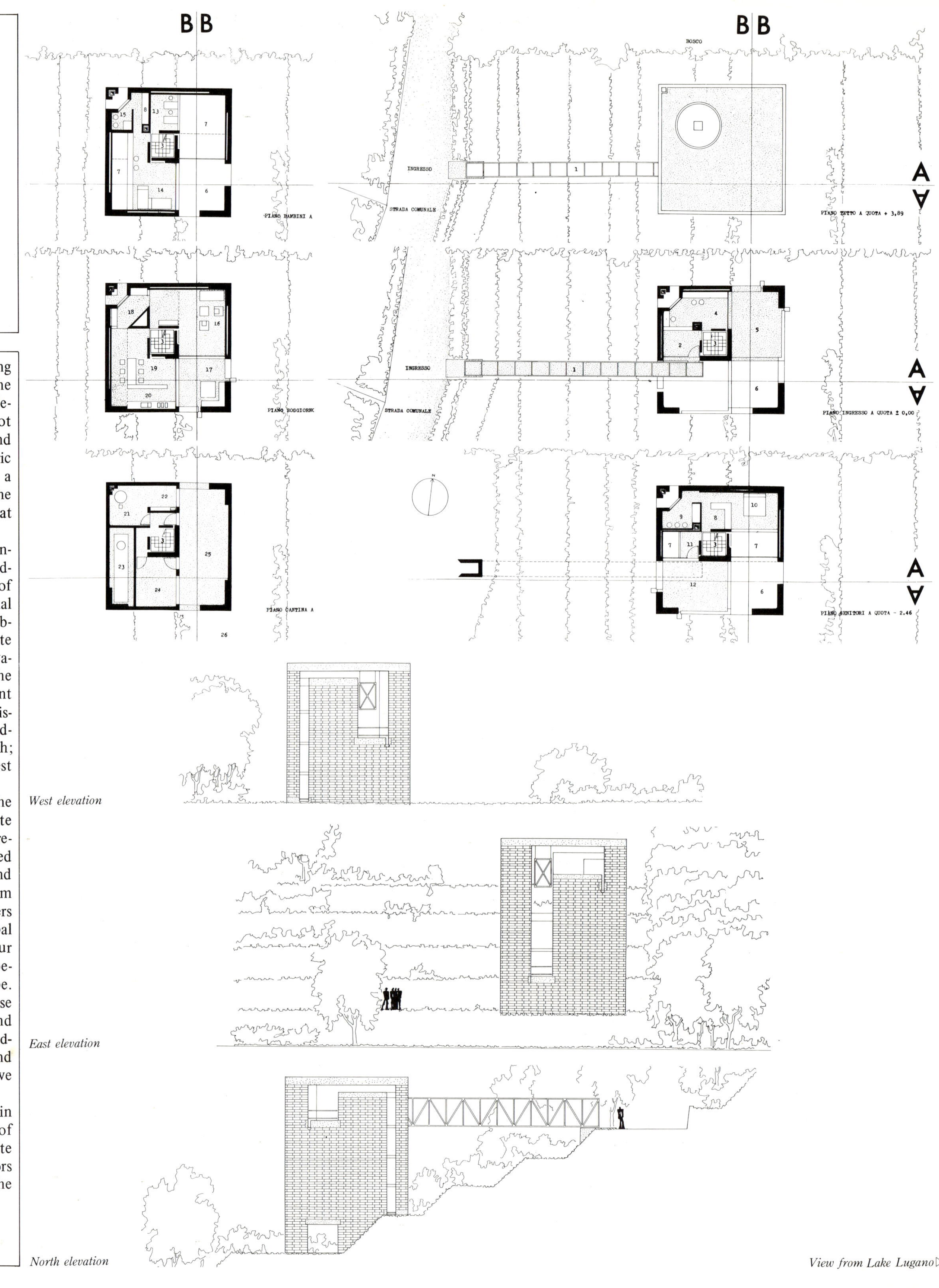

West elevation

East elevation

North elevation

View from Lake Lugano ▷

View of terrace from living room

◁ View of approach bridge

Dining room

Secondary School at Morbio Inferiore, Switzerland, 1972–77

The plan for this school, the first large project to be realized, continues and develops the ideas proposed in the competition for the school at Locarno in 1970. In this structure, also, separate buildings correspond to different functions: the school, the gymnasium, and the custodian's house. As in the school plan for Locarno, the convergence point for the different elements is integrated with the nearby buildings, while the long structure of the school delineates and shapes the open space: the view beyond the school to the east is of a forest and a small valley. In the opposite direction, on the slope of the hill, the vista includes the Romanesque church of San Giorgio and the nearby cemetery.

The school itself runs along the north-south axis and stands as the farthest limit of the developed area in this part of the village; its glass windows, therefore, open on a landscape free of constructions. The fundamental building unit, consisting of four classrooms, is repeated eight times. On the ground floor is a portico, the entrances to the different sections, and offices for the teachers. On the first floor are the classrooms, open on the sides toward the landscape; and on the top floor are the laboratories, which are illuminated by small skylights and small horizontal openings.

Large skylights illuminate the central passage, the most important spatial element, in which the regular sequence of the eight units decreasing into space visually resemble the unfolded section of a telescope. As one walks through this central passage, the different sections and the articulation of spaces and volumes create an internal urban landscape. The two large skylights, oriented from east to west, act like sundials and indicate, by the changing amount of light in the building's interior, the different times of day.

Between the farthest unit of the school, housing the library, the *aula magna,* and the block of the gymnasium, the natural shape of the ground has been transformed into a small open theater.

The caretaker's house and the gymnasium, divided into three sections, function as screens that separate the area from the parking lots and the recent constructions. The locker rooms, showers, and bathrooms of the gymnasium are located above the porch that serves as an entrance.

The whole structure is of reinforced concrete; the internal walls are covered with a colored transparent film, blue on the stairs, red for the *aula magna.* The ceilings are made of soundproof prefabricated elements; the floors are made of Klinker; doors are metal and painted black; the movable partitions of the interiors are wooden, and are painted a rich mustard-yellow.

Southwest façade of gymnasium

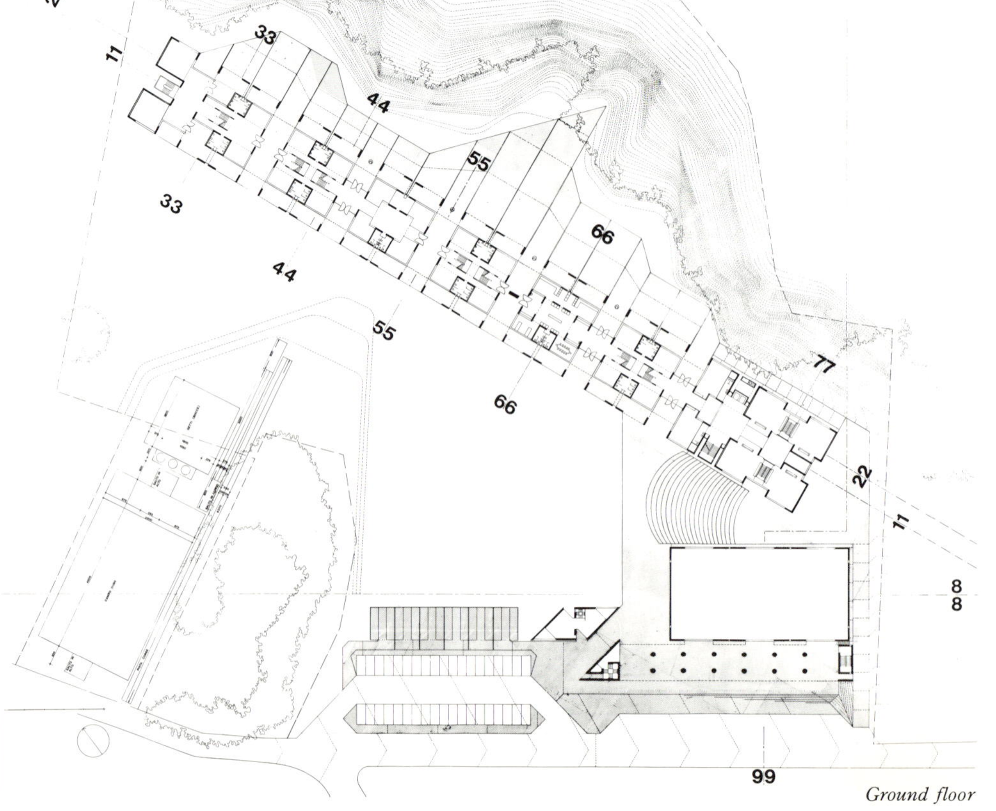

Ground floor

First floor

Second floor

△ Main approach
▽ General view from east

△ View of west façade

View toward gymnasium▷

△*Detail of east façade* ▽*View through north-south axis*   *Skylit central passage* ▷

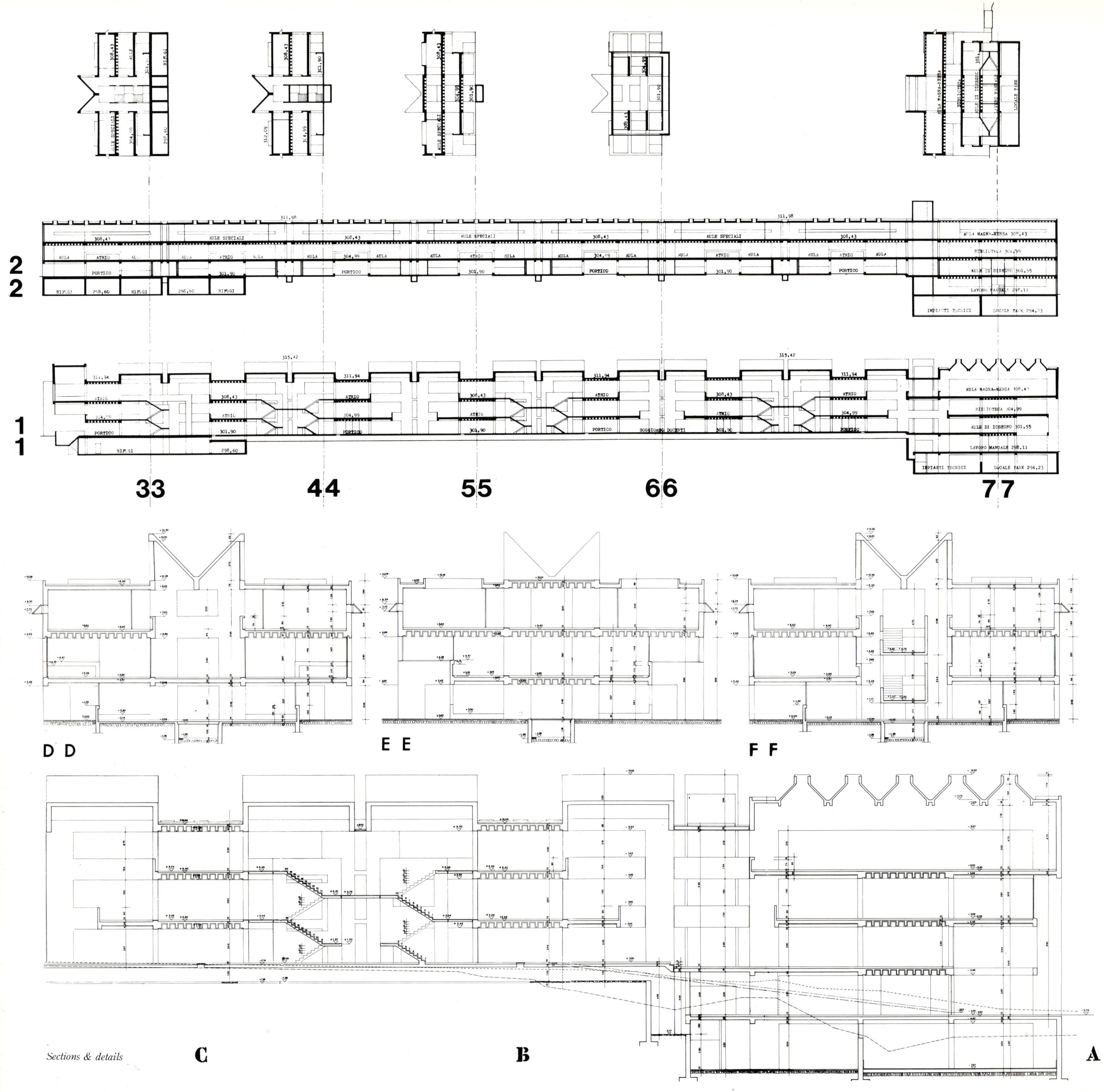

AULE SPECIALI
AULA   ATRIO
PORTICO
RIFUGI
AULA MAGNA-MENSA 308,43
BIBLIOTECA 304,99
AULE DI DISEGNO 301,55
LAVORO MANUALE 298,11
IMPIANTI TECNICI   LOCALE TANK 294,23
ATRIO
SOGGIORNO DOCENTI
Sections & details

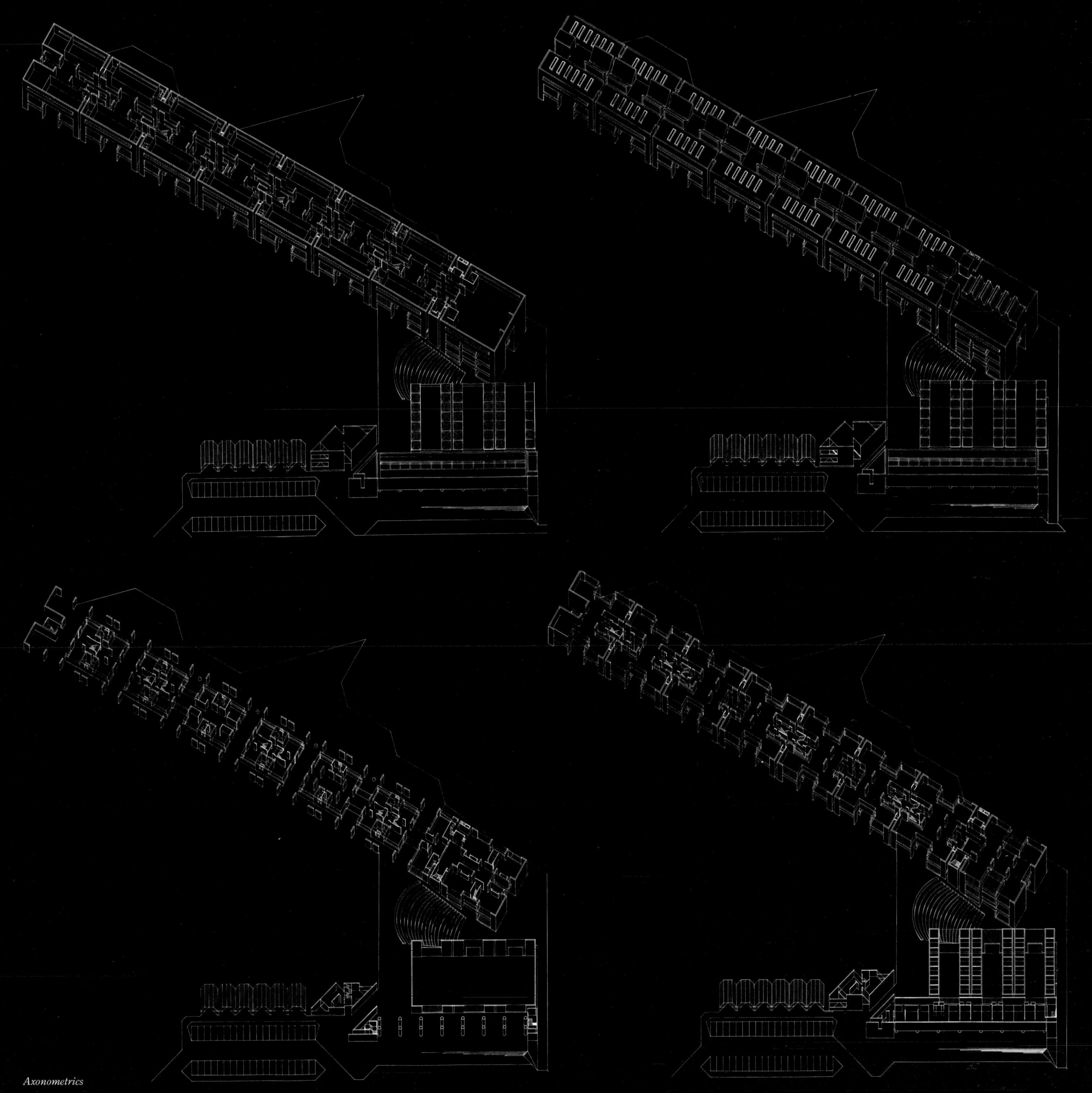

Axonometrics

Single-Family House at Manno, Switzerland, 1975 (project)

The site for the house is located near the village. A wooded mountain is on the north, and the valley, partially occupied by the extended village, is on the south. Because of this, the house is to be built on the northeast corner of the property and offers, on the side facing the valley, a closed surface with walls characterized by thin vertical cuts; it opens onto the garden, woods, and mountain on the opposite side. On this side a row of poplars marks the boundary between garden and woods, through which the road that connects the surrounding villages runs.

A thick, fortress-like wall, nearly one meter deep, is marked on the exterior by a rhythmical series of cuts, while on the interior it shelters the stairs, the fireplace, and the rooms for secondary purposes.

The front, leading to the garden, is articulated by its wall/façade, where two dividing walls correspond to the transversal cuts that cross the building and bring natural light up to the stairs. This façade is characterized by a large arch, typical of the entrance in old local buildings, an intermediate space between the construction and the garden. All rooms, either through glass windows or terraces, overlook the garden.

The building has two floors. The first, illuminated by natural light, houses the kitchen and the living room (double-height at the fireplace). Bedrooms and the large terrace are on the upper floor.

The house is to be constructed in traditional or concrete bricks.

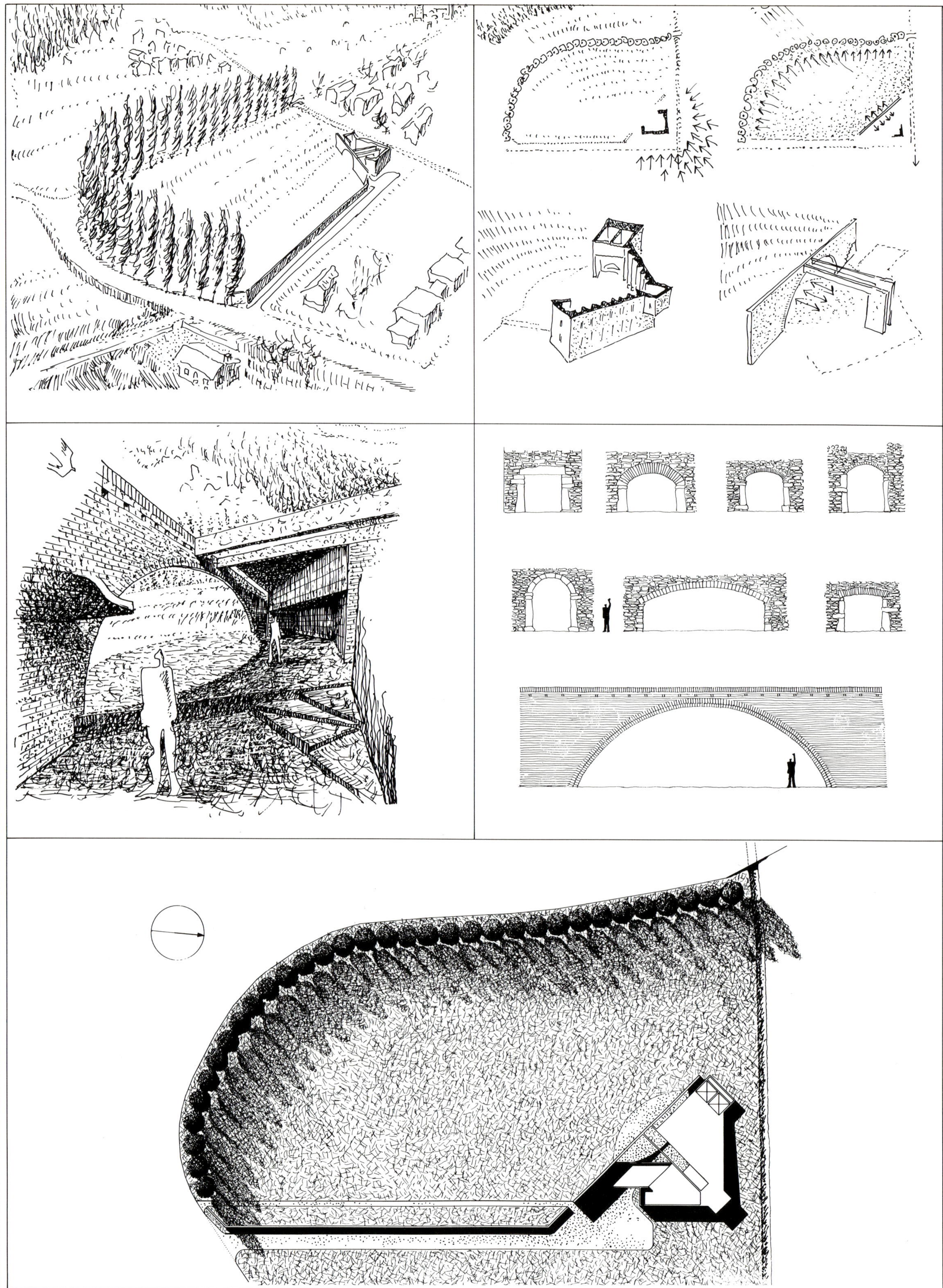

△ ▽ *Model photos*

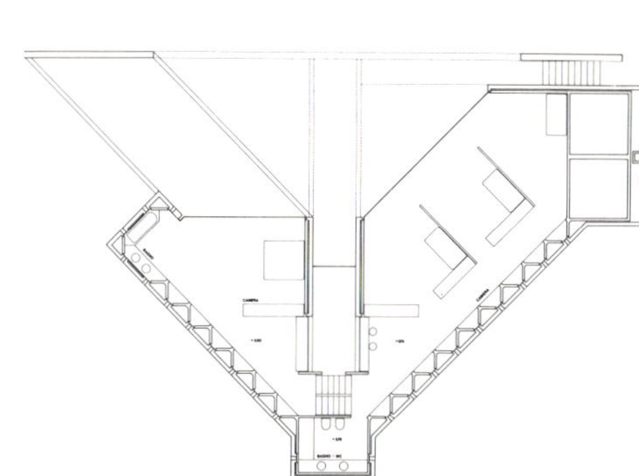

First floor

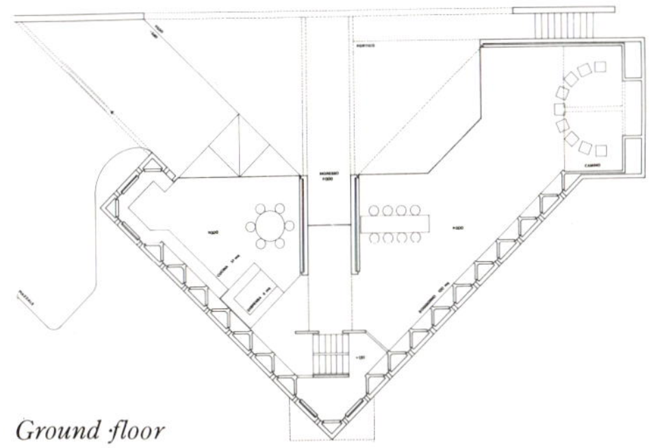

Ground floor

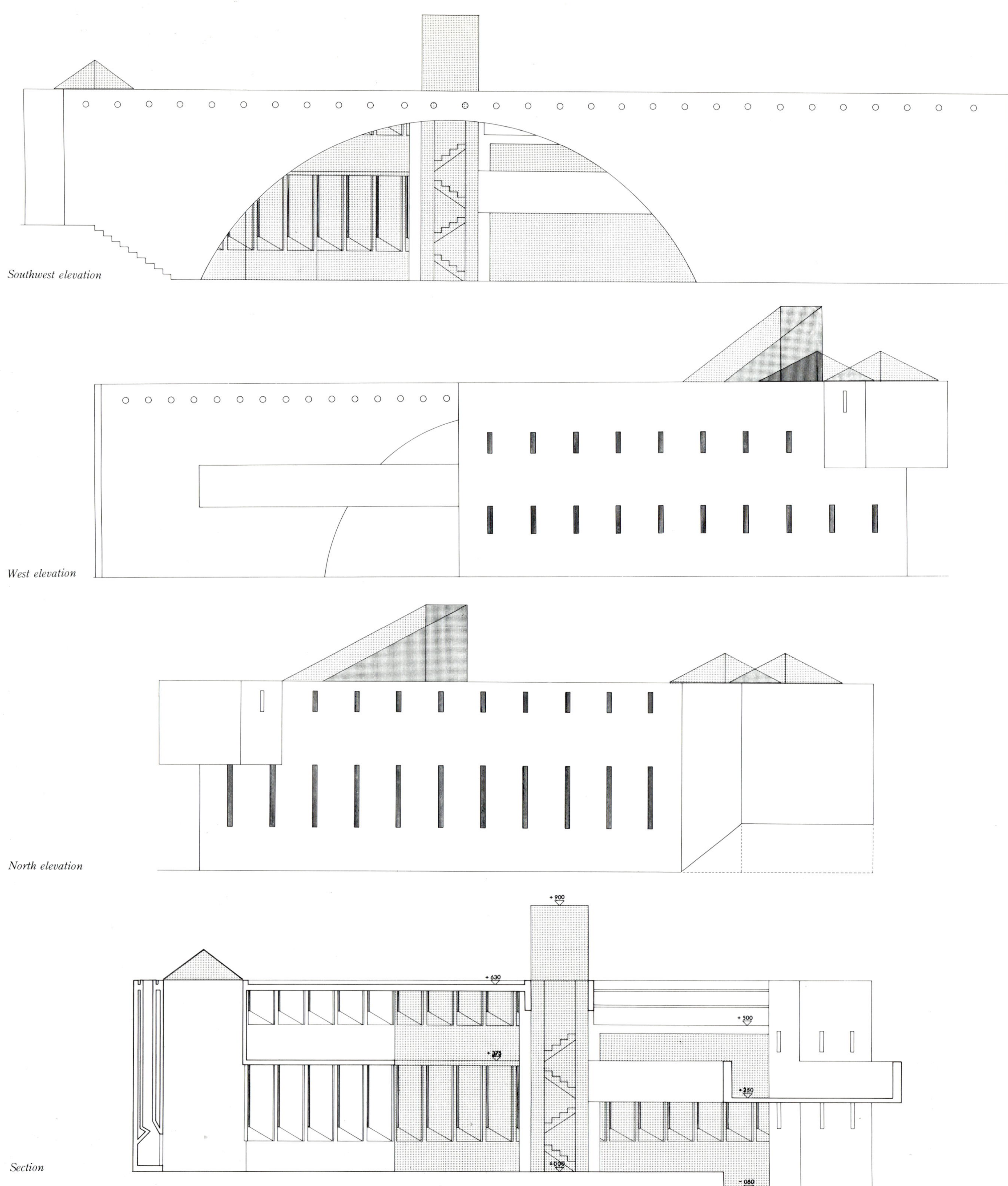

Southwest elevation
West elevation
North elevation
Section

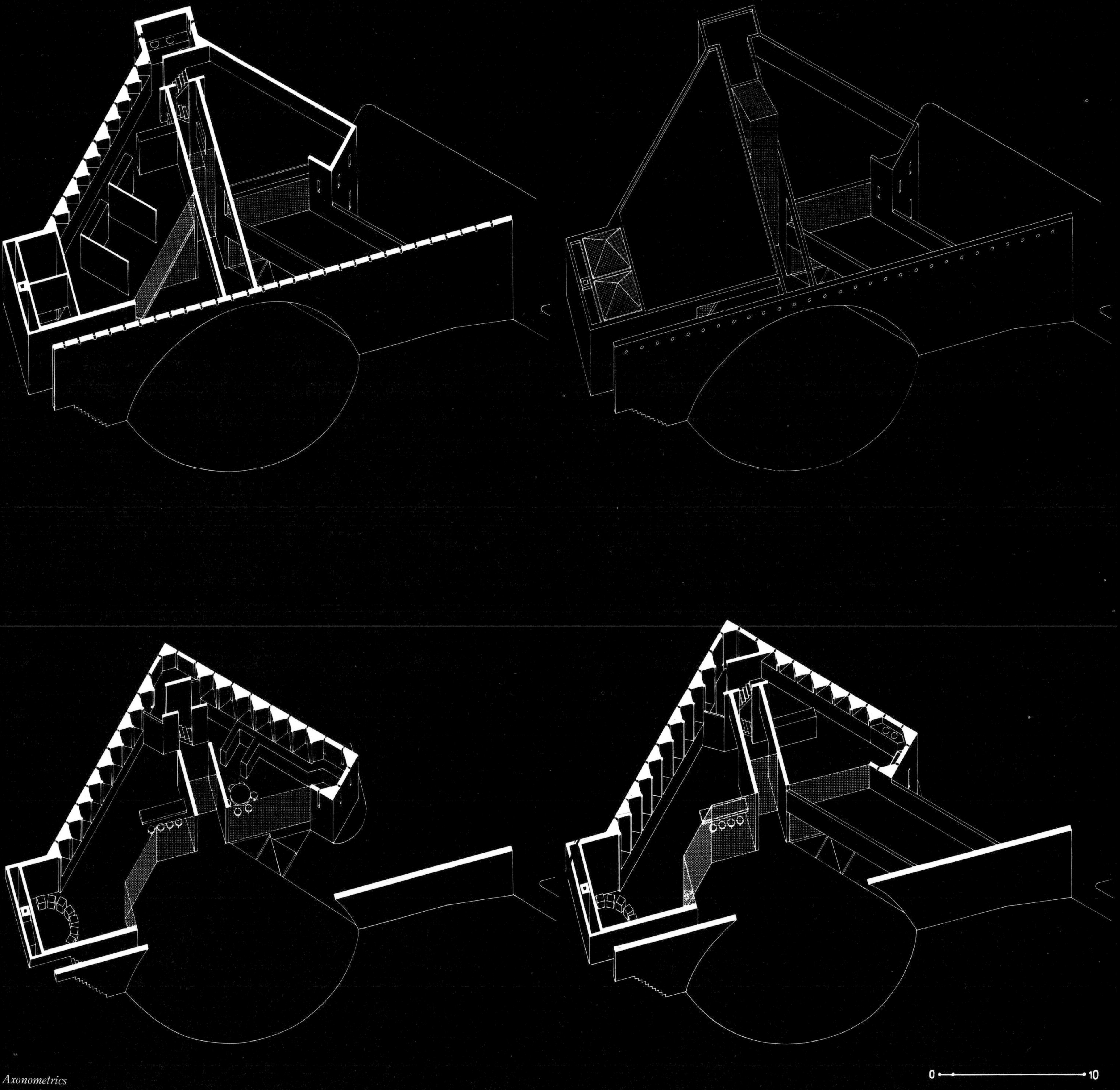

Axonometrics

Axonometrics

The house is located on the outskirts of the village. The countryside is on one end and the new residential buildings, following the old partition of the fields, run along the road that leads to Mendrisio. The family house, which occupies one end of the property, constitutes the farthest limit for buildings allowed by the general plan that regulates the growth of the village.

The house, conceived as a single, thick screen, is bound by two walls; its compact volume on the side facing the countryside is broken only by a thin vertical cut in the center, while toward the village it opens into two lateral blocks. The space between them, on different levels, is given over to glass windows and balconies. Nearly all the rooms of the house face the large opening and the garden beyond.

The house has three floors. The portico, the entrance, and the cellar are on the ground floor; the living room, the kitchen, and the children's rooms on the first; the master bedroom and the studio on the second.

The only opening toward the west is provided by the portico, while two thin vertical cuts underline the presence of the fireplace located between two walls, upon which falls the light of the roof skylight. Toward the east the wall is cut by the balcony of the two rooms for the children. These rooms, the only rooms turned toward the exterior and not toward the large central empty space, function as a filter between the house and the garden.

The building has walls made of concrete blocks of double thickness. The layer of blocks on the exterior consists of three bands made of strips of alternating color, gray and reddish. The thin space between the three bands slightly recedes, so that the bands seem to protrude. These horizontal strips derive from the local tradition, which consists of the decorative use of simple and poor materials. The possibilities offered by the skillful use of common materials and concrete bricks as decorative elements inserted into an articulated grid will appear again in the future, although with different intentions and goals. In this case the bands of bricks underline the artificiality of the construction and the resulting contrast with the surrounding nature, reinforcing at the same time its single, volumetric quality. In the interior of the house floors are tiled, the ceilings are exposed reinforced concrete, and doors and other openings are framed in black painted iron.

Ground floor

First floor

Second floor

△General view from southwest
▽North façade

△ Detail of south wall

▽ View of entryway from second floor terrace

Living room seen from study

Living room

View toward living room from kitchen

View from second floor terrace

View toward master bedroom from study

Dining room

Master bedroom

View of second floor terrace

Library in the Capuchin Monastery at Lugano, Switzerland, 1976-79

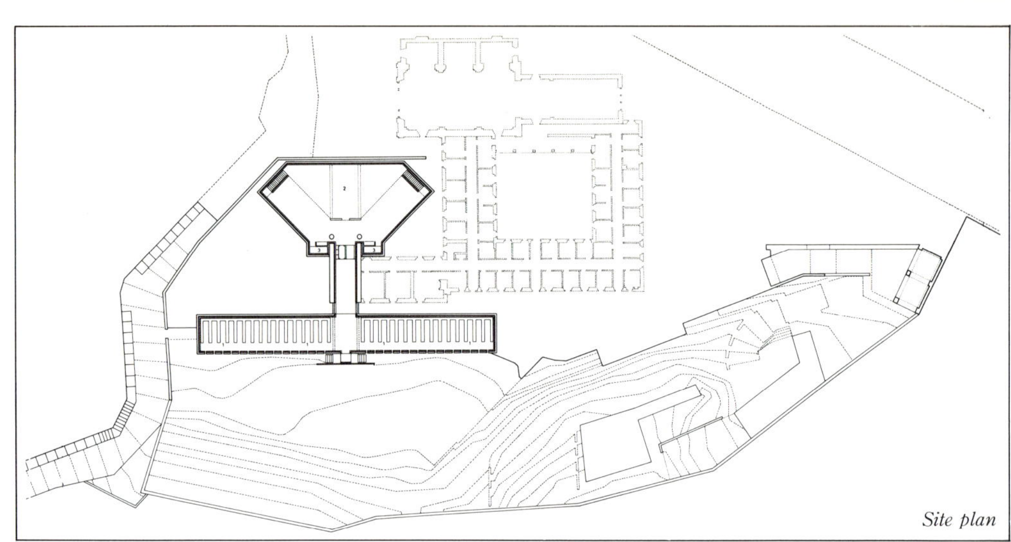

Site plan

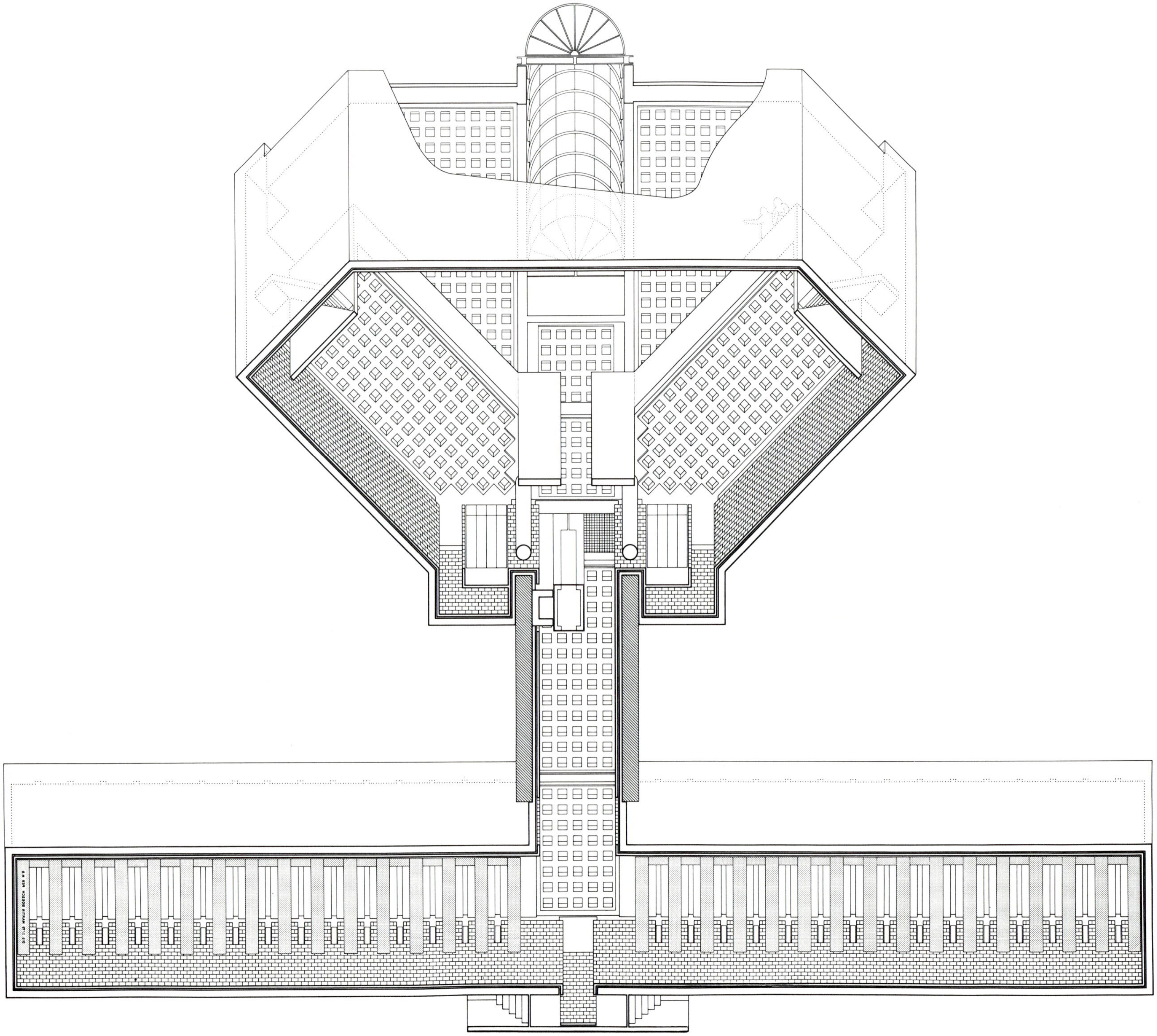

Axonometric

The monastery is on a hill, between the nine-teenth-century developments around the railway station in the upper part of the city and the lower historic center. A series of initial projects suggested placing the library in a new building next to the existing complex of the monastery. The solution decided upon, however, proposed a sunken structure that would leave the plan of the old monastery unchanged and that would underline, at the same time, the innovative quality of a new, independent structure which integrates itself with the preexisting one.

The project also contemplates the demolition of the additions to the monastery built in the twentieth century and the restoration of the eighteenth-century section of the eastern part, where the portico with its old arches will be provided with new doors. This restored section will become the entrance to the new library buried in the ground.

The reading room is located between the perimetric wall that delimits the space in front of the church and the eighteenth-century part of the monastery. The library is totally sunk in the ground, and only the central skylight emerges from it; this skylight allows for the establishment of an immediate visual relationship between the space of the library and the church above it, while at the same time it provides light for the central interior of the reading room, which is high enough for balconies (at entrance level) designed for newspaper and magazine reading.

The storeroom for the books, about 100,000 of them, also sunk in the ground, is a long structure located on the eastern side of the convent, toward the valley, and its roof provides the path leading to the new library. The storeroom, its terrace, and the external wall that emerges slightly more than a meter from the ground, merge with the existing configuration of the garden, built on different levels.

All the walls are constructed of reinforced concrete, each with a second wall of concrete blocks painted white that, like a lining, runs along the internal perimeter. In this second wall the bricks touch neither the ceiling nor the floor. The section left free by the bricks is filled in with an iron band painted black, while in the reading room, at the end of the central axis, a long vertical cut allows for visual measurement, at a glance, of the degree to which the library is buried in the ground. Ceilings are composed of soundproof, prefabricated coffers; floors have sisal matting, and furniture in the interior is black metal.

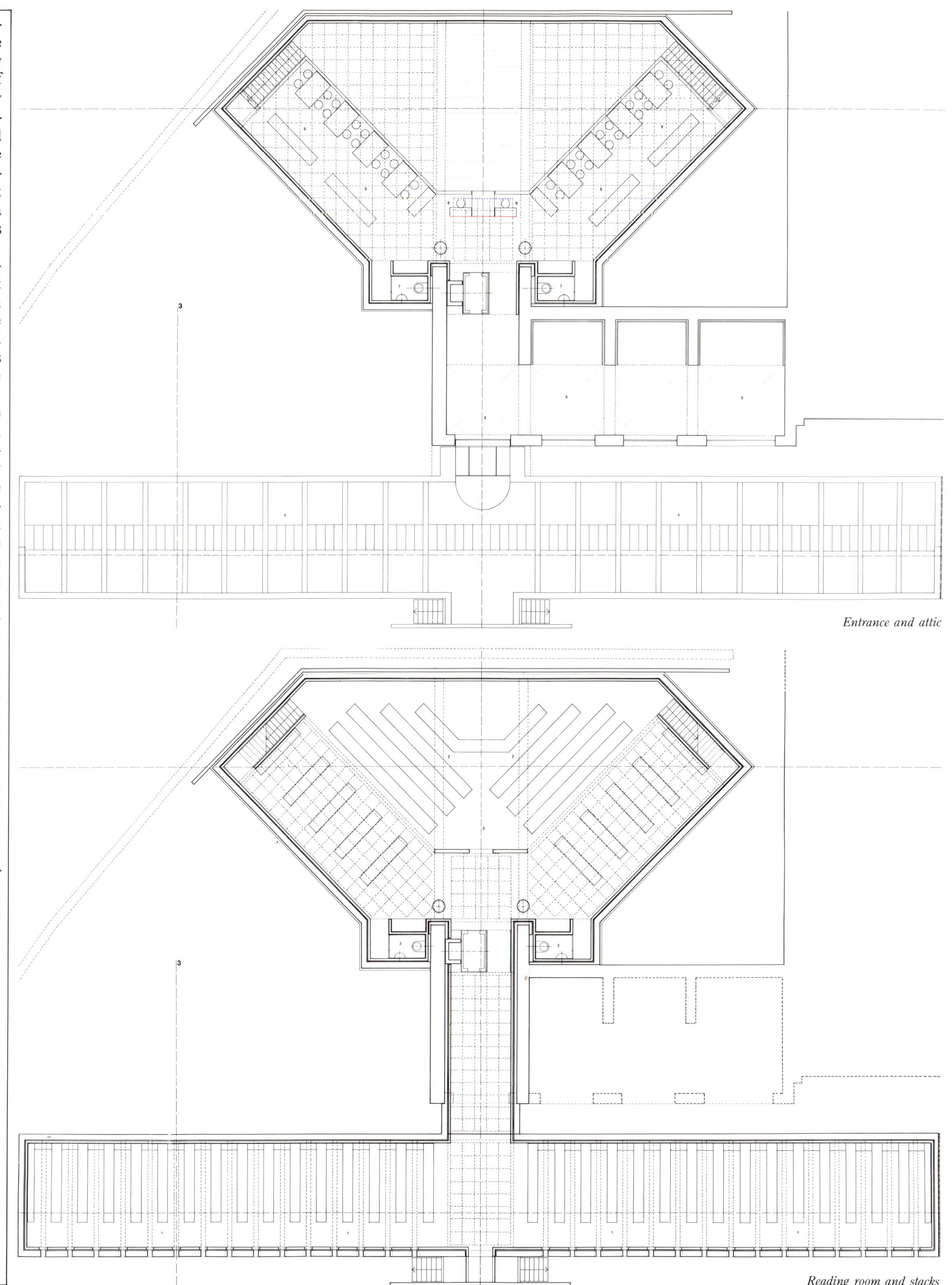

Entrance and attic

Reading room and stacks

Reading room (pp.78-81)

This structure, built after a competition held by the local city council, is surrounded by a dense inhabited area and has a school next to it. The dimensions of the lot, and the ordinances that determined the amount of land that could be built on at the site, have dictated the placement of the gymnasium and its secondary spaces within a single volume (12 x 24 m. wide) articulated by the presence of several distinctive elements.

A long skylight, placed above the entrance, traverses the length of the building and provides natural light to its interior. As in the library of the Capuchin Monastery, although here in a more evident way, the skylight provides not only light but a direction for the internal space. The role played by lateral openings is, in fact, secondary.

The skylight divides the northern part into two volumes: a receding wall on the ground floor in concrete and glass that appears to be an invitation to enter the building; and the slanted volume of the stairway leading to the lower and upper areas. All the secondary spaces of the gymnasium are, on different levels, located in this section. On the upper floor, in correspondence with the balcony above the gymnasium, there is room for therapeutic gymnastics; the storeroom for the equipment is on the ground floor, while the lockers and the showers are on the lower level. The entrance to the lower level is provided by a stairway placed in front of the building, while the access to the gymnasium from this area is supplied by another stairway whose volume protrudes from the side of the building.

The structure is made of insulating, light concrete, painted a bluish color on the interior. The ceiling is of soundproof, prefabricated coffers. Doors and window frames and sashes are of iron, painted black, while the flooring is of synthetic material, painted green.

Street façade

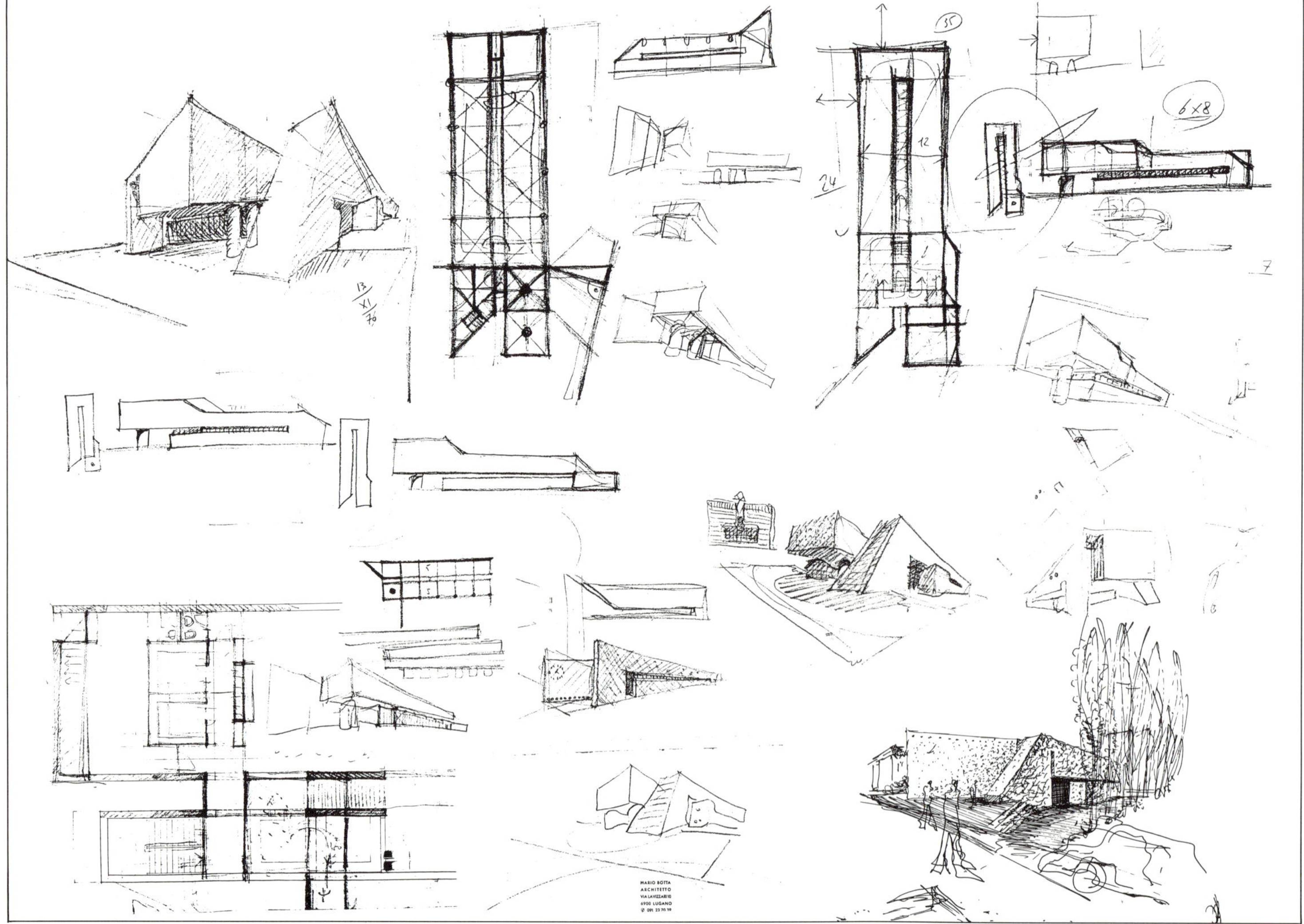

Preliminary study

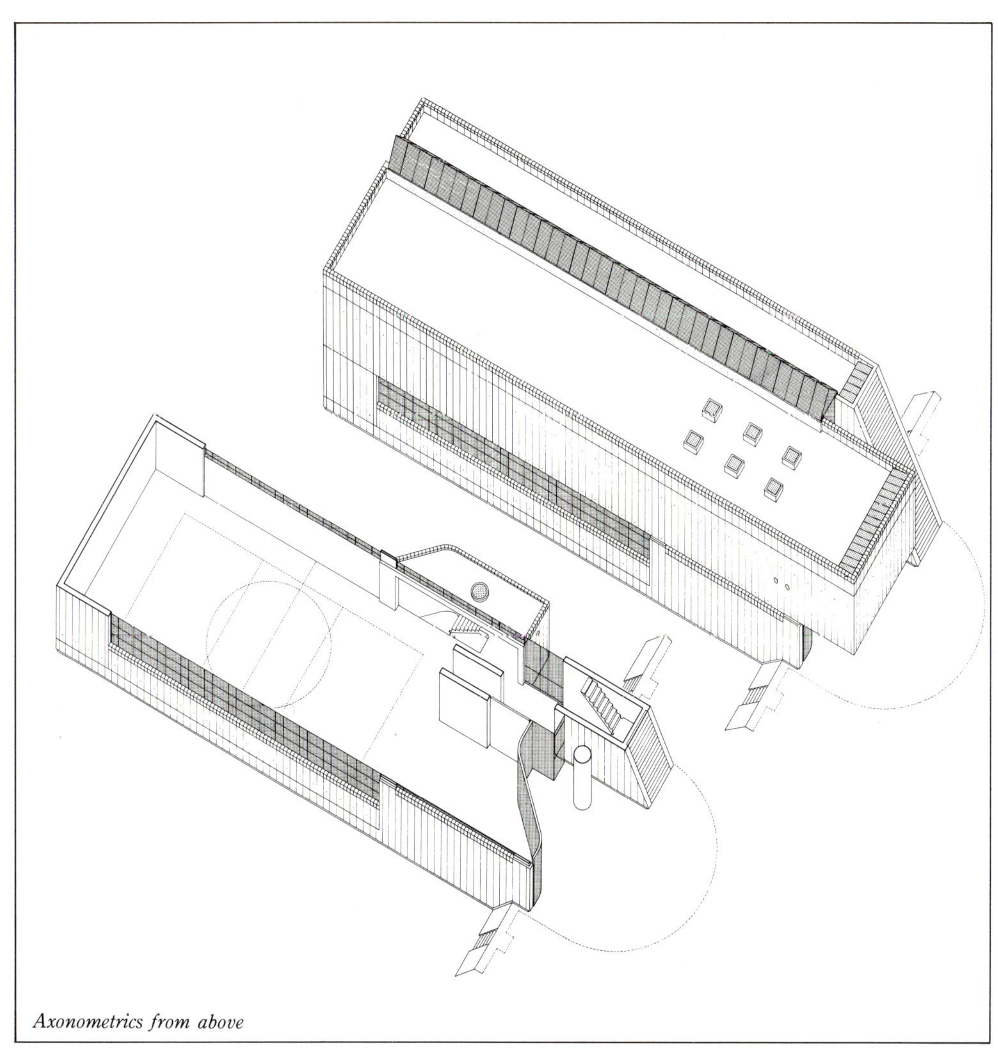

Axonometrics from above

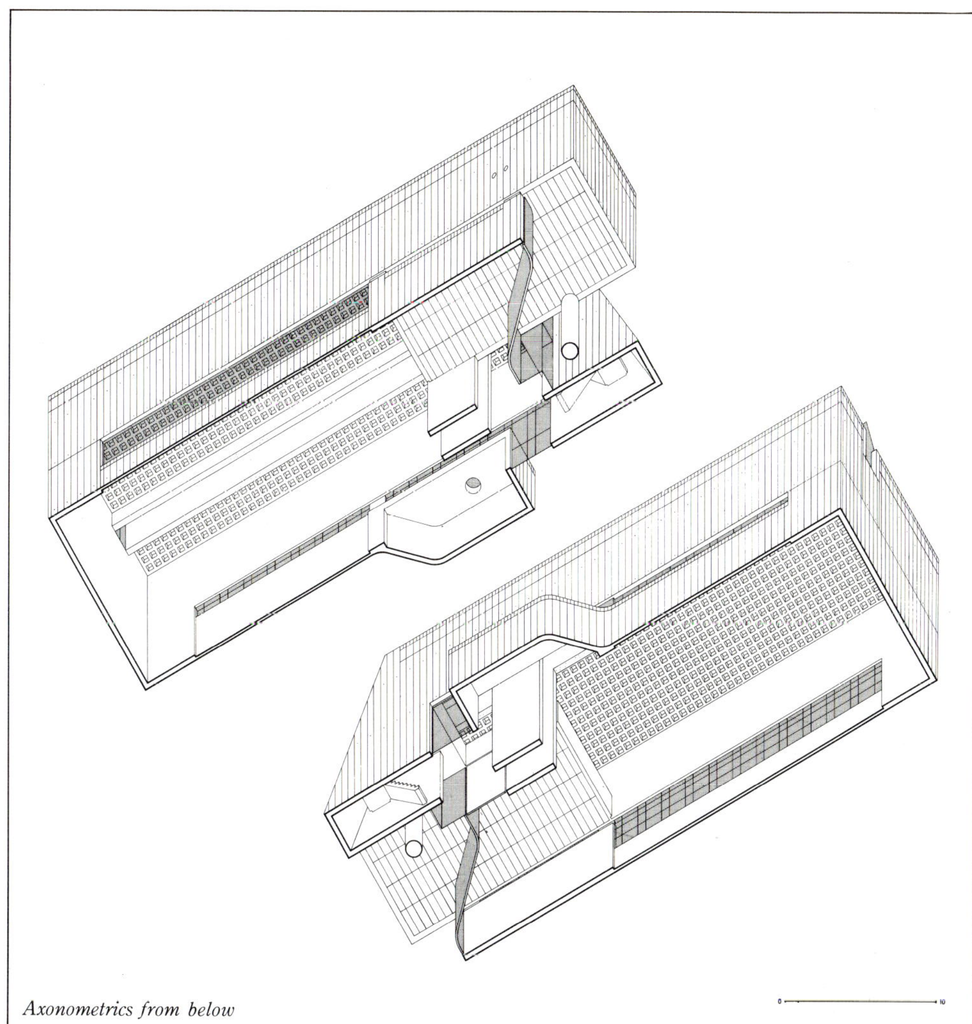

Axonometrics from below

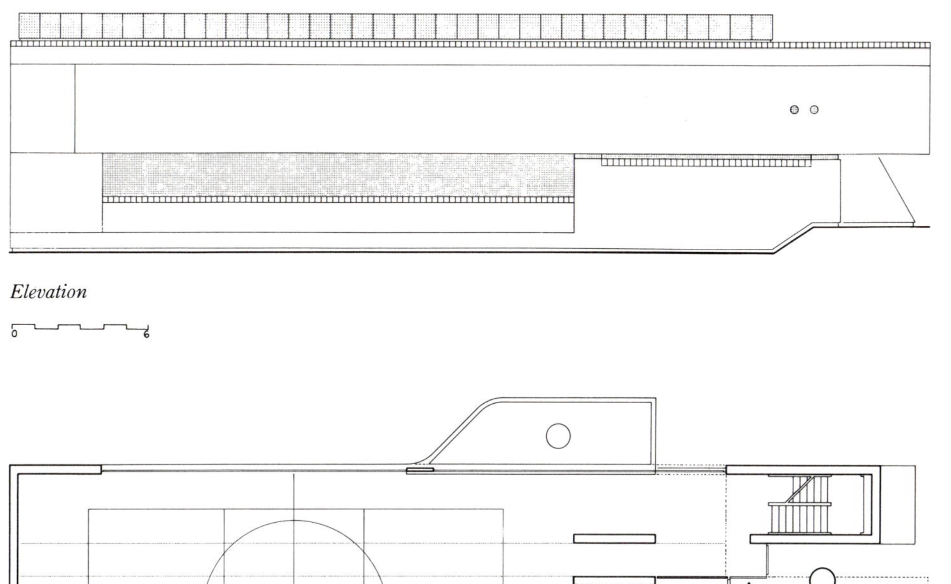

Elevation

Section

Ground floor

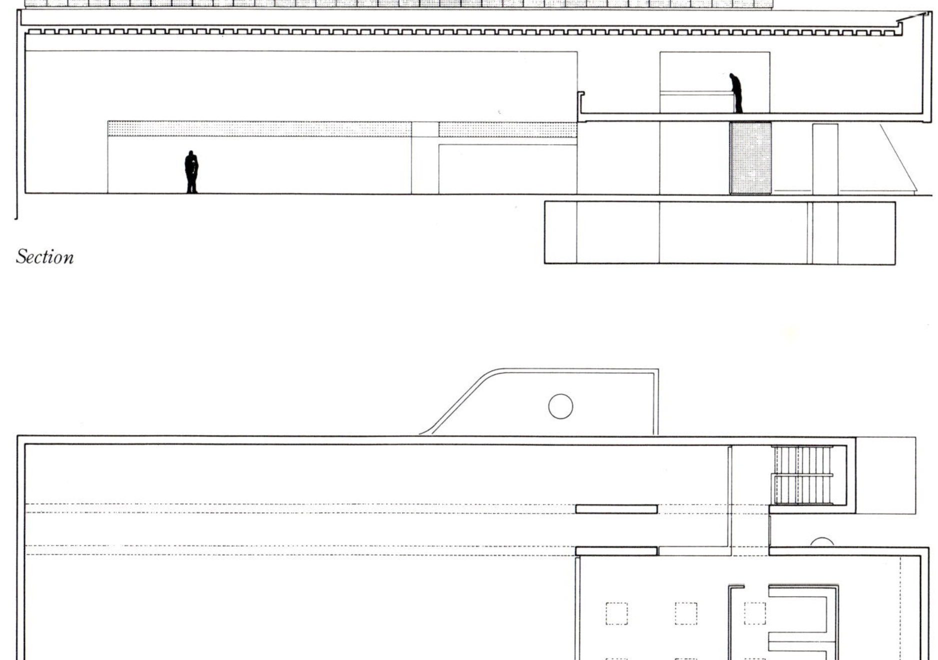

First floor

Interior of gymnasium

The farm complex to be converted, situated in a valley sloping toward Chiasso, consisted of many structures haphazardly built around the main areas. The plan of the conversion took into consideration only a part of the complex, the part facing east, which includes a house with its courtyard and a barn and cow shed built along the road next to them.

In conversion, the original courtyard space has been preserved and enlarged by adding an open shed area. In a similar way, reversing to a certain extent the notions of exterior and interior, or open and closed elements, the structure housing the barn and the cow shed was transformed into a new entrance. In this part the old roof, the constant element that defines the total volume, was kept, but beneath it half of the existing masonry was demolished and the main wall replaced by two thick columns of concrete blocks and by iron beams. The resulting portico, the new entrance, is screened on the ground level toward the courtyard by a low wall and between the two columns by a perforated partition.

The perimetric wall that encloses the courtyard on the side where the other sections of the farm are located, next to which runs the paved walk that leads to the house, presents a further variation on the use of concrete bricks. For the first time they are laid at an angle of 45 degrees. This arrangement of bricks is used again in later constructions to define the volumes more clearly.

The modifications to the main house have been limited to the façade, where the openings on the ground floor have been redefined and the form of the traditional door-window adopted. All the internal structures of the building have been reinforced, and the ceilings and attics reconstructed. The internal subdivisions have been retained; the only exception is the central section of the house, where the space is now twice as high as it used to be.

The coating of plaster on the walls of the interior is painted white; the fireplaces are covered with glossy, painted stucco. The roof of the attics has lintels of exposed iron beams; the floors are tiled with a band of polished granite that runs along the walls. Doors and window frames and sashes are made of iron, painted black. The outside walk is also granite, and the open space on the ground floor is paved with local stone.

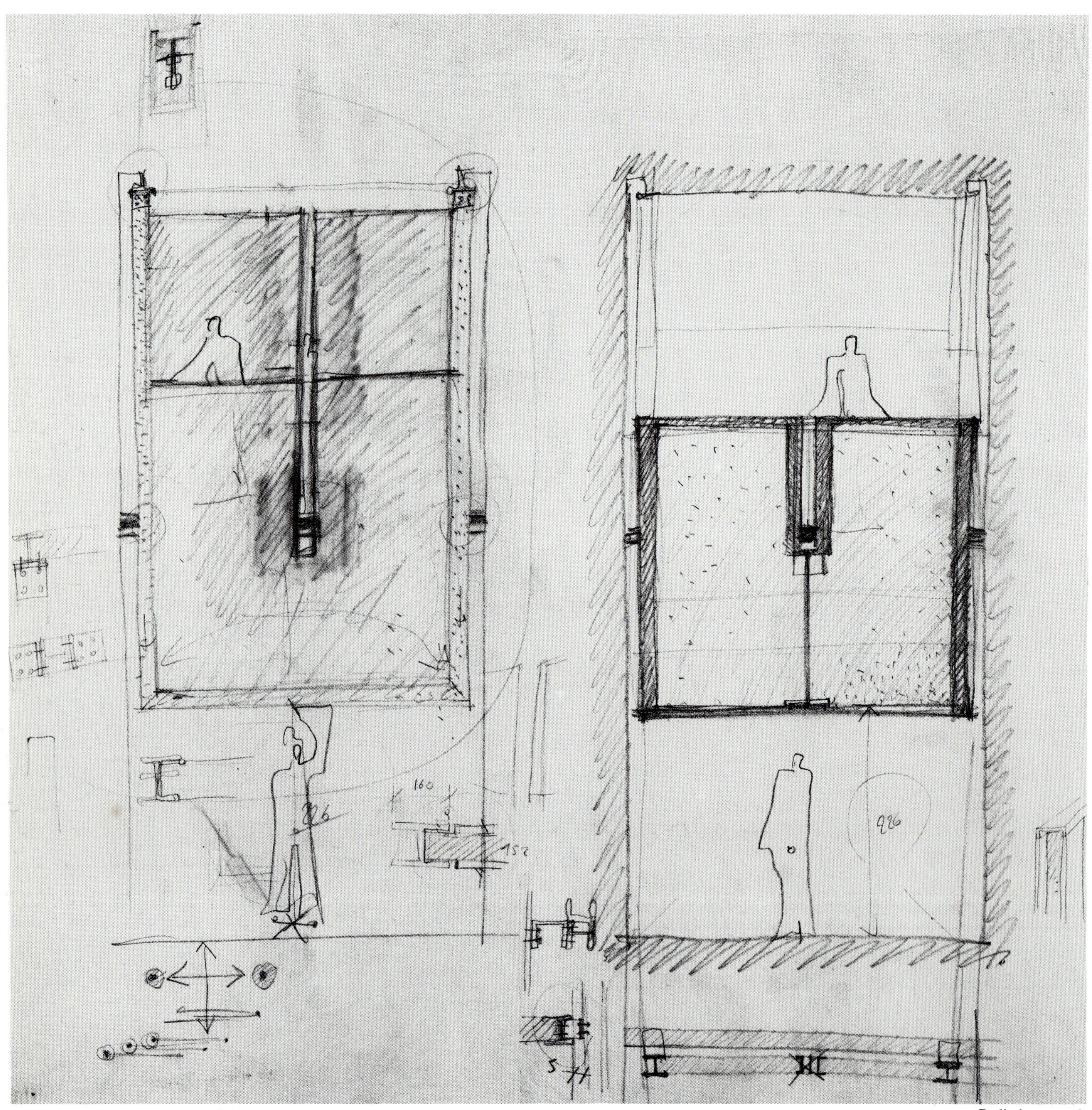

Preliminary study

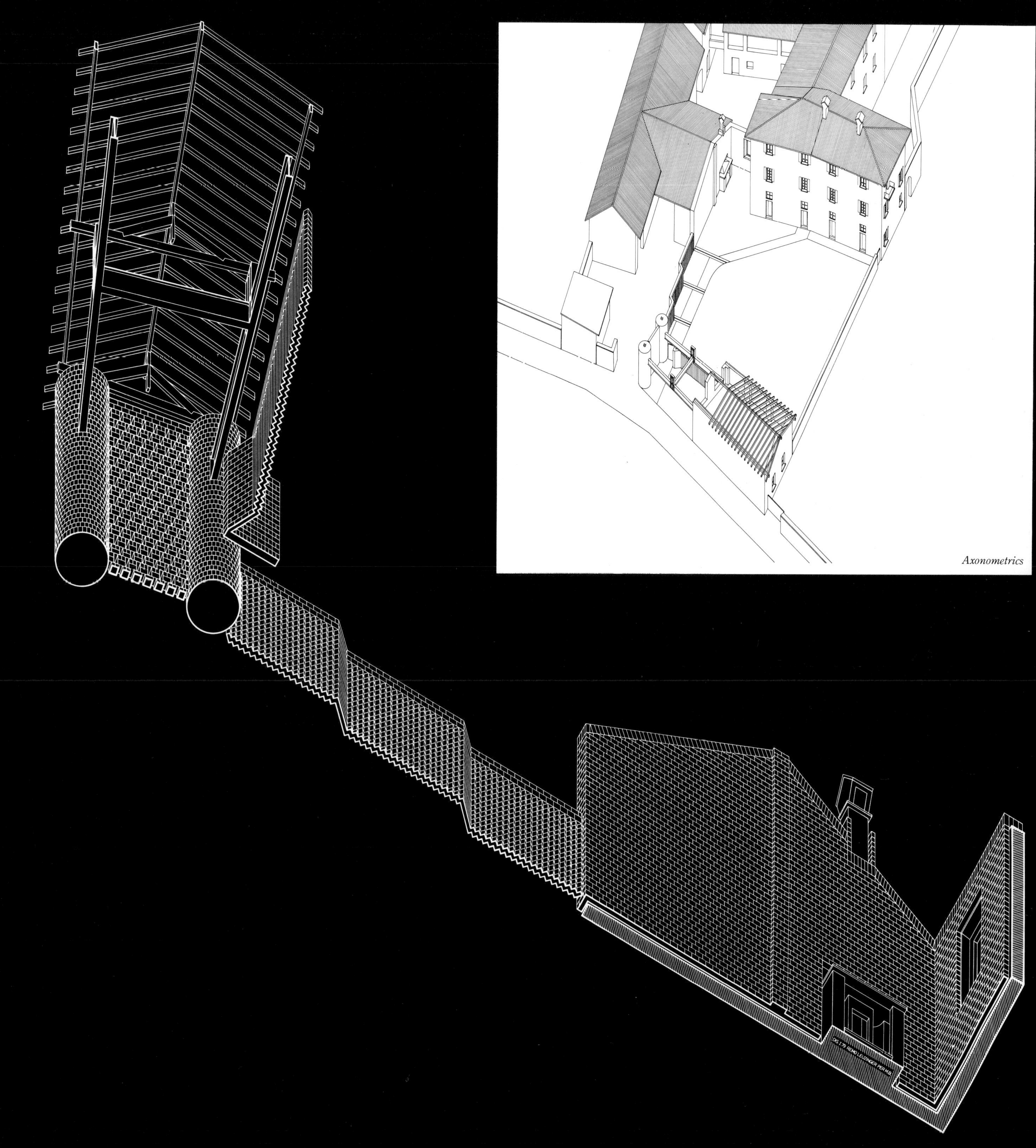

Axonometrics

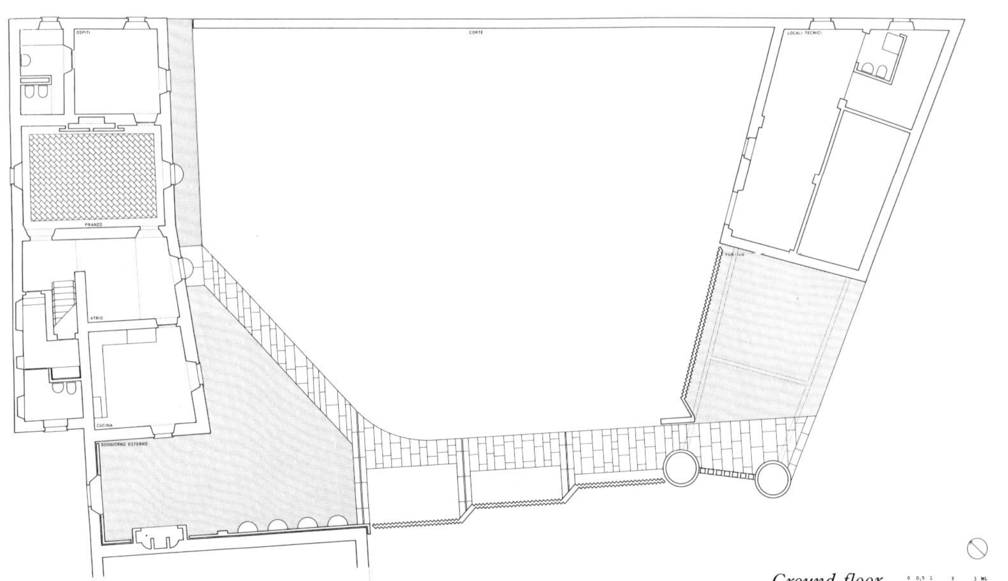

Southwest façade of barn

Ground floor

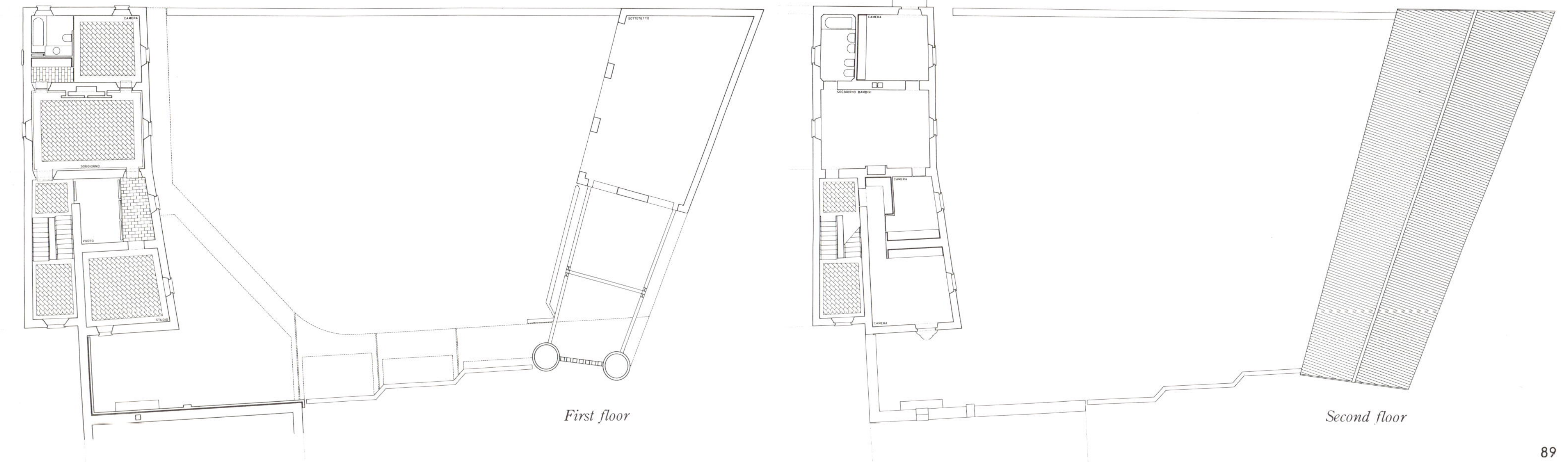

View of barn from courtyard

First floor

Second floor

Dining room fireplace

Refusing again to follow the example offered by the confused and fragmentary proliferation of nondescript architecture surrounding the site, Botta pulls the four units of the crafts center into a single, compact volume. The process adopted, involving the multiplication of single architectural units, although in this case not in a purely linear sequence, had already been employed by Botta. In the center at Balerna the four units are clustered around the central space, the area allotted for communal work. The four separate buildings become therefore the corners, the pillars of the complex, a complex that finds in the central covering of the structure its most characteristic element.

Every unit has three floors. On the ground floor, twice as high as the others, are located the laboratories and the workshops; above it are offices, and on the upper floor are apartments. Offices and apartments overlook the large loggia and the landscape beyond it on one side, and on the other, the internal courtyard where the stairs and secondary spaces are located.

The large central covering is divided into three elements: the first above the communal courtyard, the other two above the intermediate spaces and the stairs.

The structure is composed of concrete bricks, painted white in the interior; attics are of reinforced concrete, flooring is tile on the ground floor and wood on the other two. Doors and window frames and sashes are made of iron, painted black, while the metal structure of the central roof is painted white. The roof has panels of glass set in metal frames.

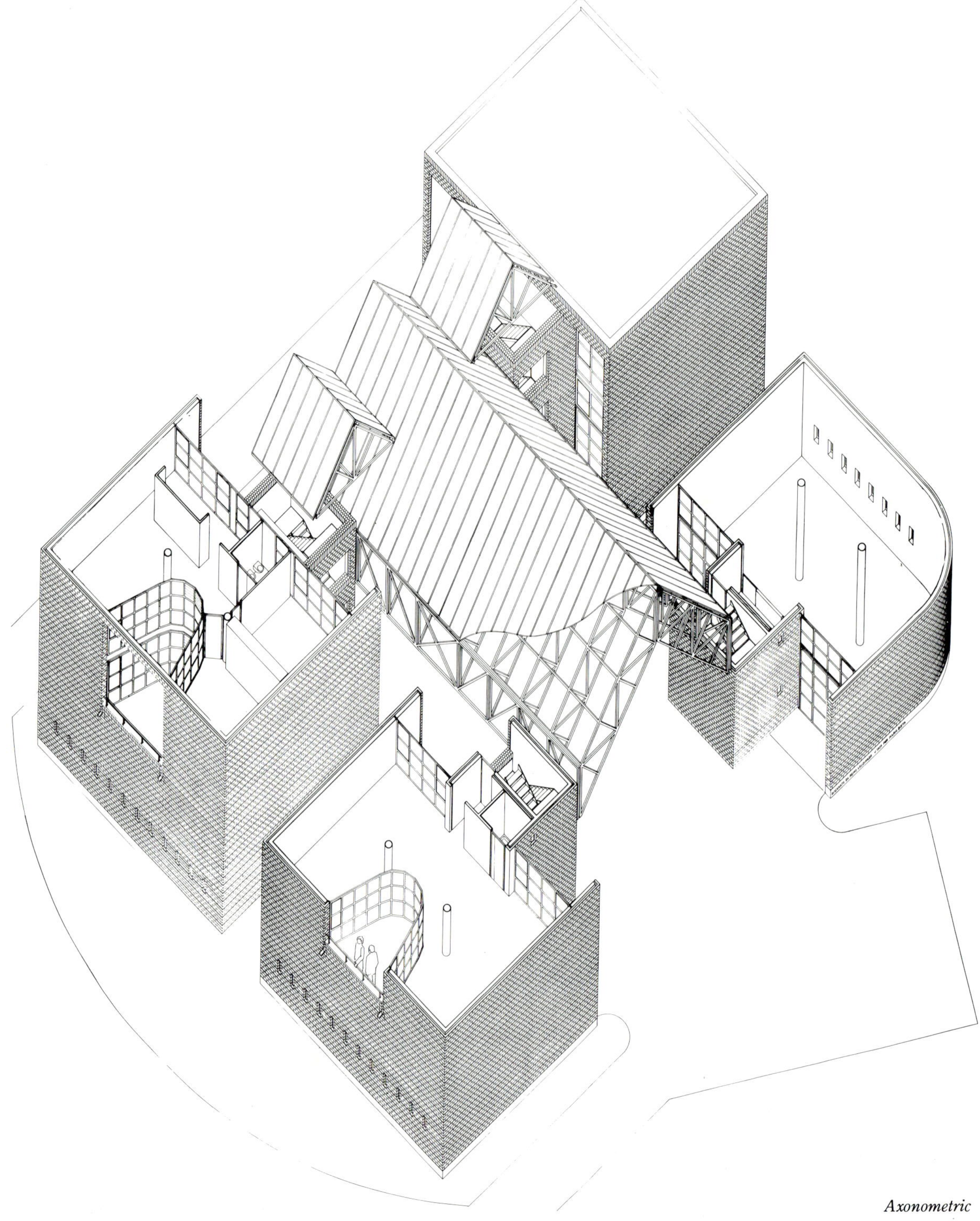

Axonometric

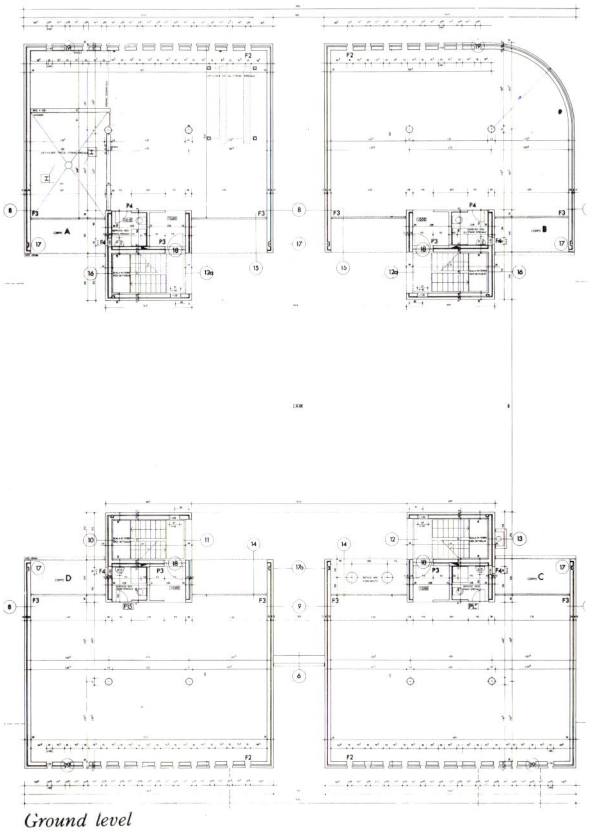

West façade

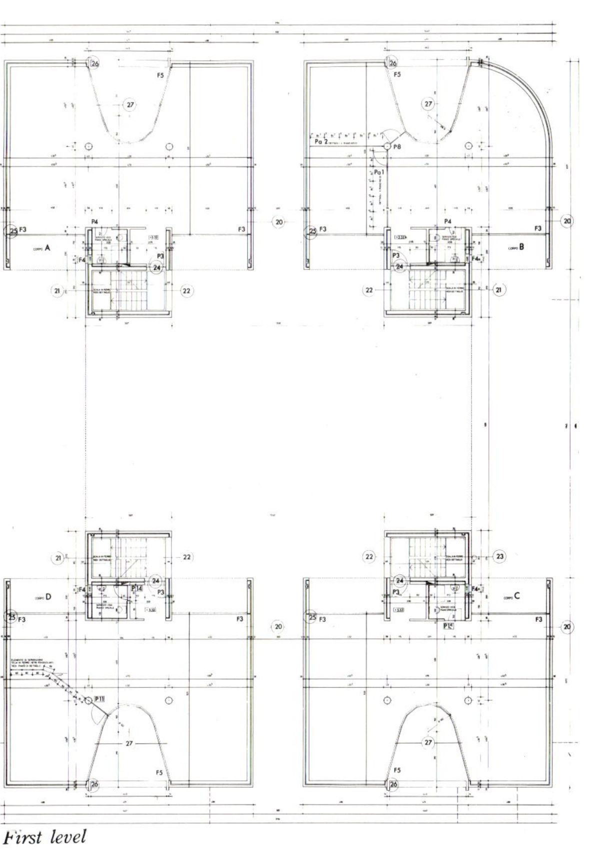

Ground level

First level

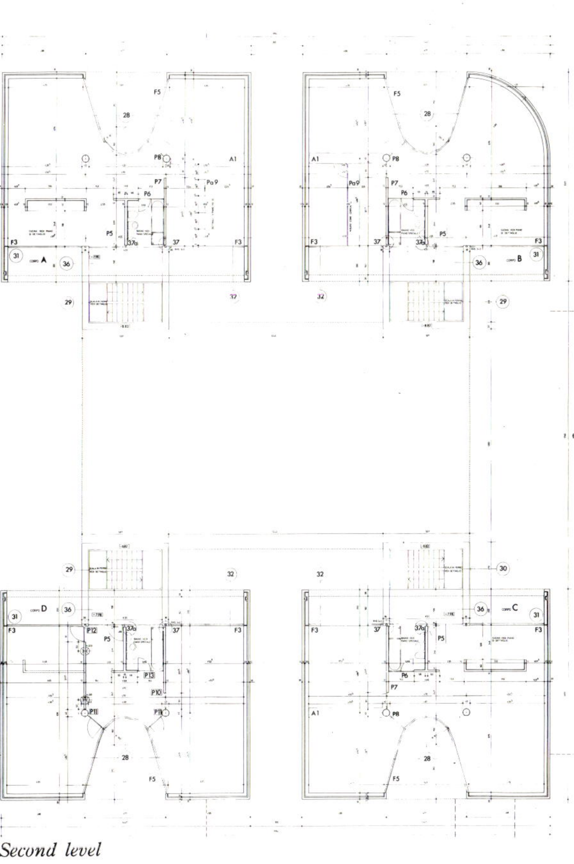

Second level

East façade

△ *Detail of glazed truss*

▽ *South façade*

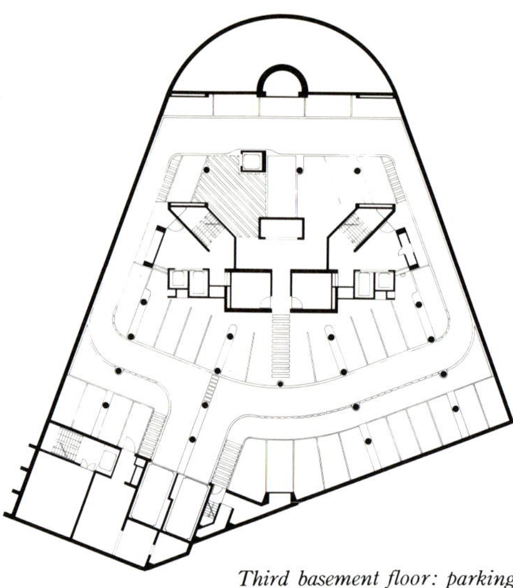

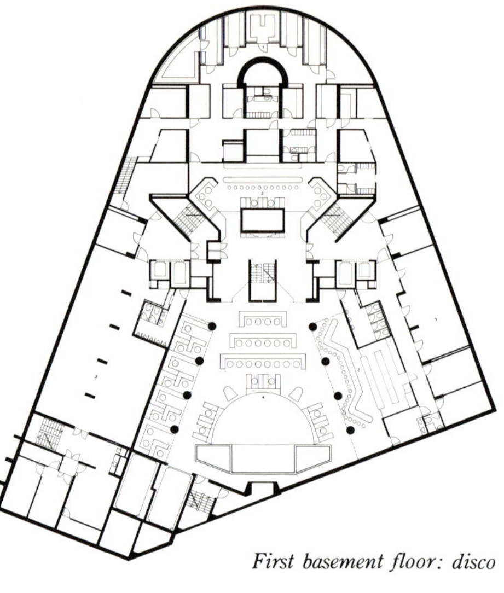

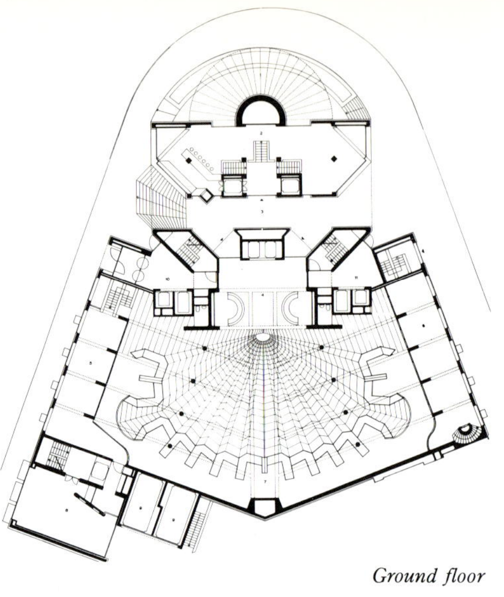

Third basement floor: parking

First basement floor: disco

Ground floor

The bank, built after a competition for the commission, occupies a triangular site, located between a boulevard, a street, and the railway station. The section of the city around the railway station has undergone considerable urban development since the beginning of the century, which has resulted in the concentration of business and banking activities in this area. This part of the city has a distinct and well-defined plan, a system of regular blocks divided by a network of streets.

The particular location of the bank underlines the characteristics of the nearby urban spaces: therefore different solutions were posed for each one of the sides facing either the boulevard, the street, or the railway station. The building has, as a result, three distinct sections: two lateral wings that continue the preexisting street front, and a central volume that constitutes the link with the square, and which at the same time, articulates the space around the railway station. The pedestrian walk that crosses the structure on the ground floor and separates the two wings from the section facing the square underlines the presence of different elements: three buildings gathered into a single complex.

A different treatment of the exterior corresponds to this precise subdivision: the buildings that face the street and the boulevard continue the theme of the "façade," forming an extension of the existing succession of building fronts and at the same time reinforcing the figurative value of these urban spaces. The block toward the square is instead an isolated, monumental, single volume. Whereas in the two wings, where a mediation with the already existing buildings was necessary, traditional windows are used, in this single volume they have been eliminated. Botta uses, instead, walls of stone and glass that tend to underline the unity of the structure through a distinct architectural and plastic organization that sets it apart from the other two sections.

All of the exteriors are covered with slabs of granite of different shades of green, a color quite common in the city. In the section

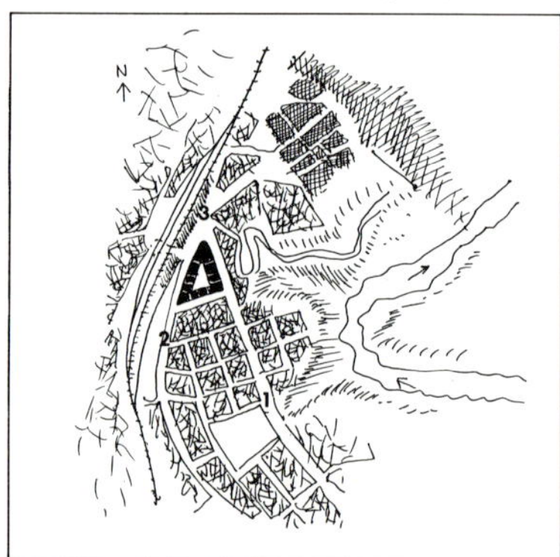

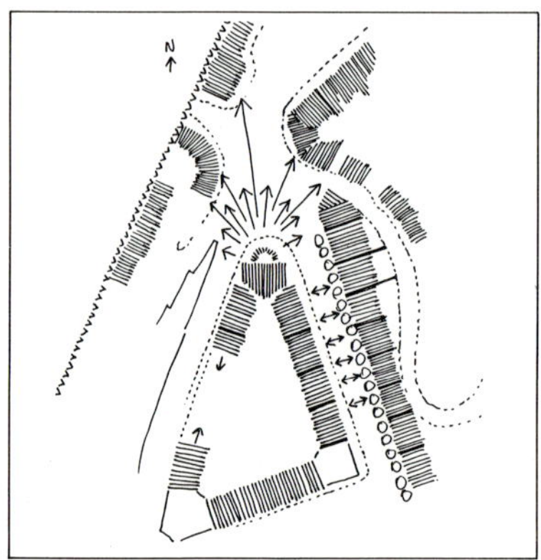

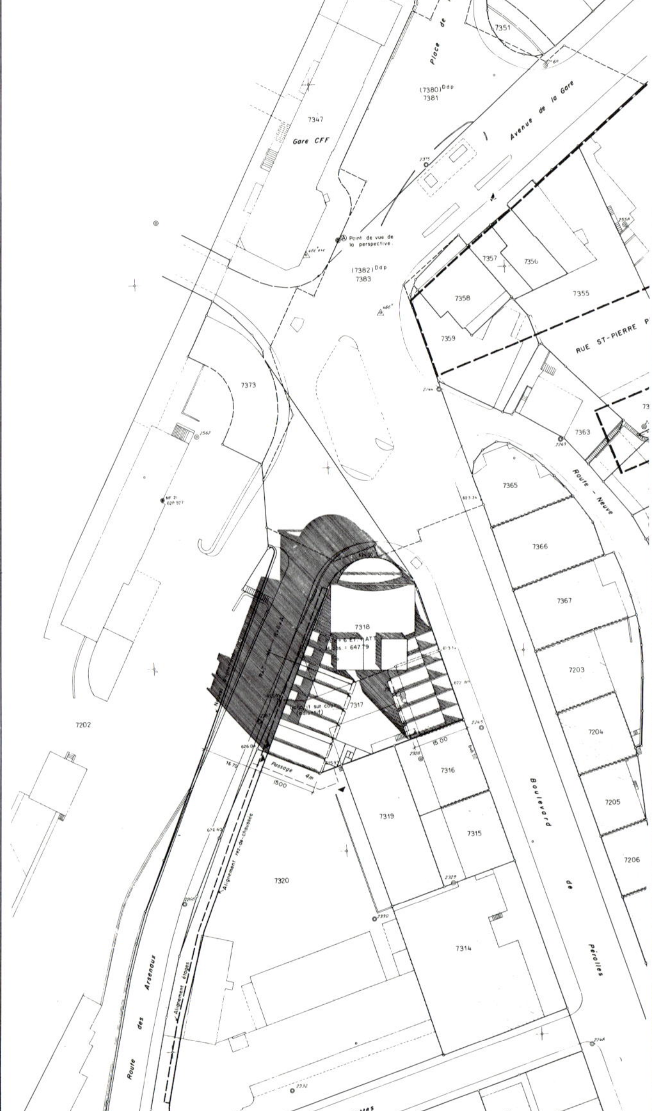

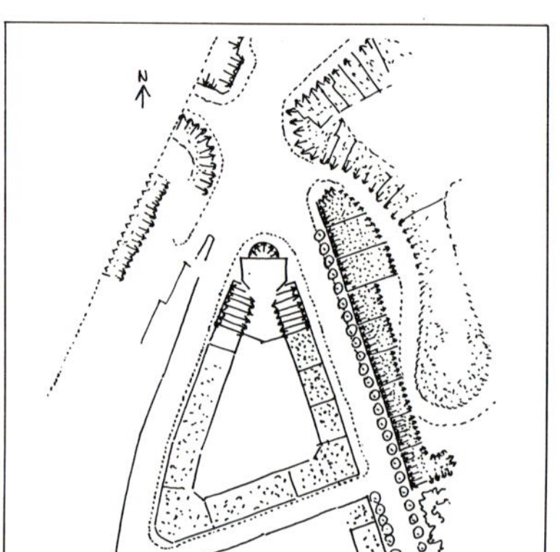

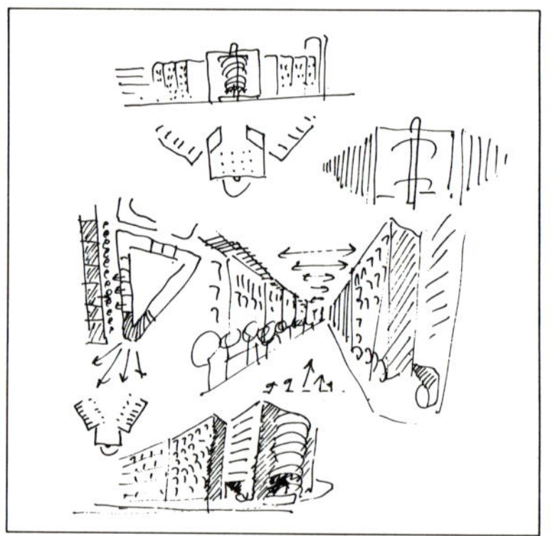

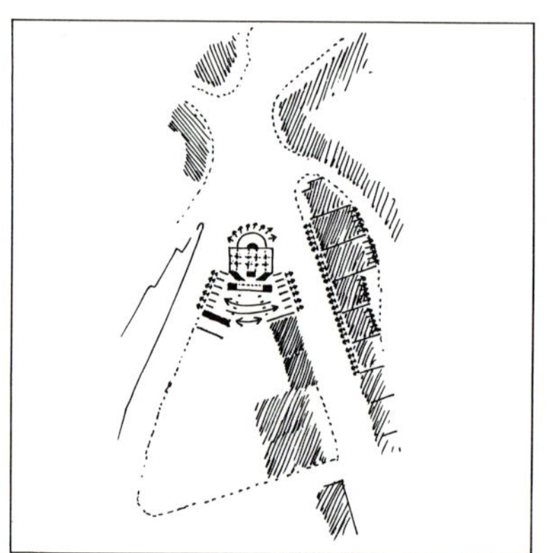

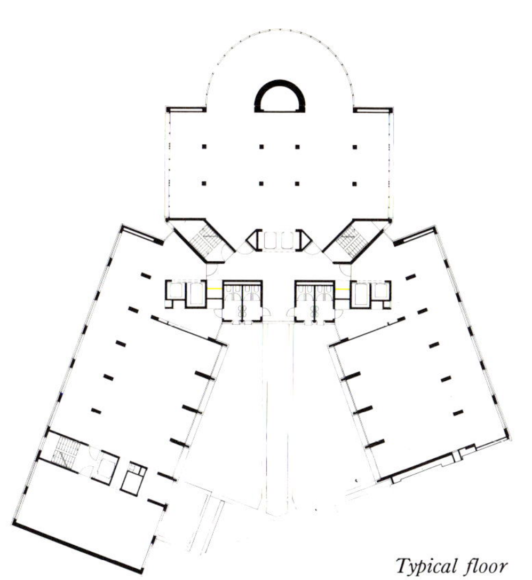

Typical floor

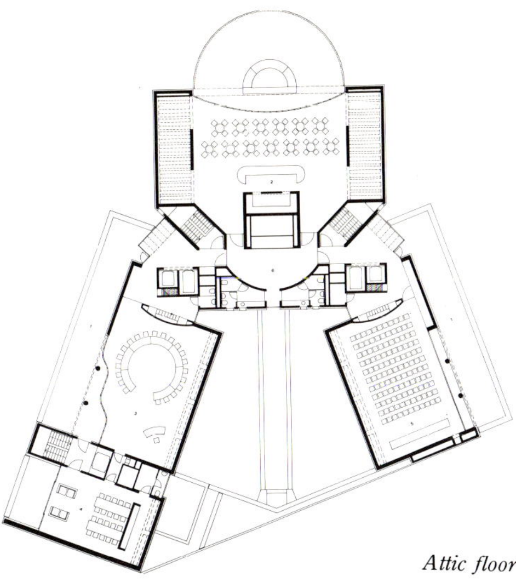

Attic floor

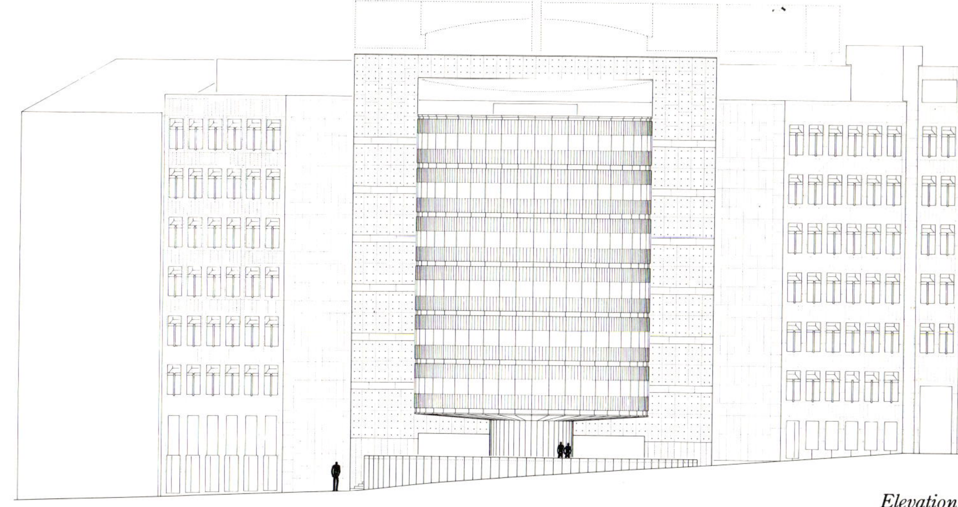

Elevation

facing the railway station the heads of the bolts used to fix the slabs to the wall are used as a means to articulate and decorate its large surface. The windows are also green, while the curtain wall overlooking the square is made of glass, either transparent or opaque.

In the basement of the building there is a discotheque, a parking lot, and bank offices; on the ground floor toward the square is a café and a restaurant, and, toward the interior, in the covered courtyard, are banking windows. In the upper floors of the three buildings the space is given over to other offices. On the top floor of the bank there is a large conference room, space for special banking services, and a large terrace (facing the railway station) with the employees' cafeteria.

In the large hall on the ground floor, where the banking windows are located, the walls are covered with gray and pink stone, and the floor with black and white stone. Spaces between the banking windows and the ceiling, whose undulating form follows the rhythm of its beams, are covered with wood.

A large central skylight, located above the arch of the entrance, illuminates the entire hall.

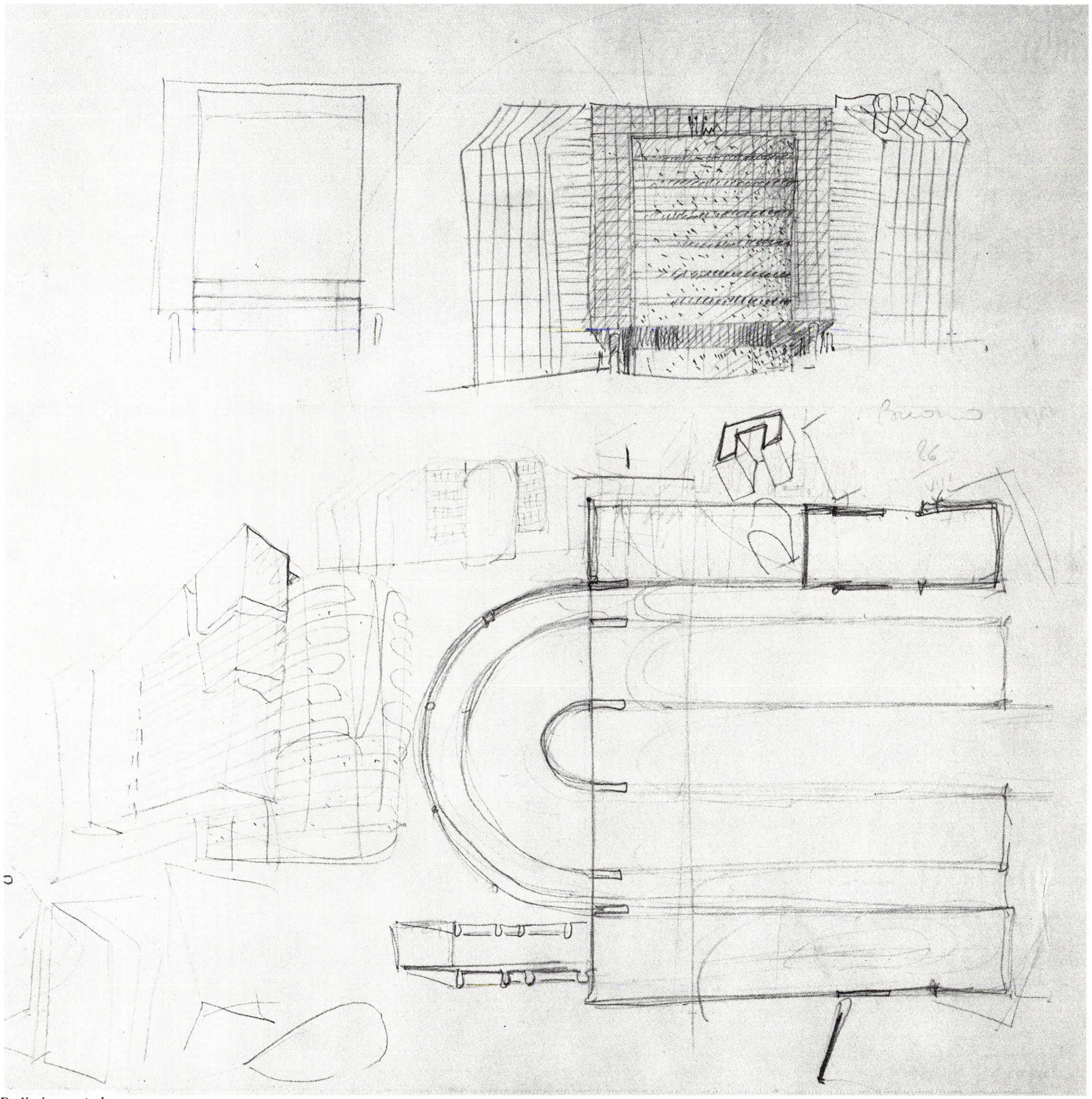

Preliminary study

BANQUE DE L'ETAT DE FRIBOURG
FREIBURGER STAATSBANK

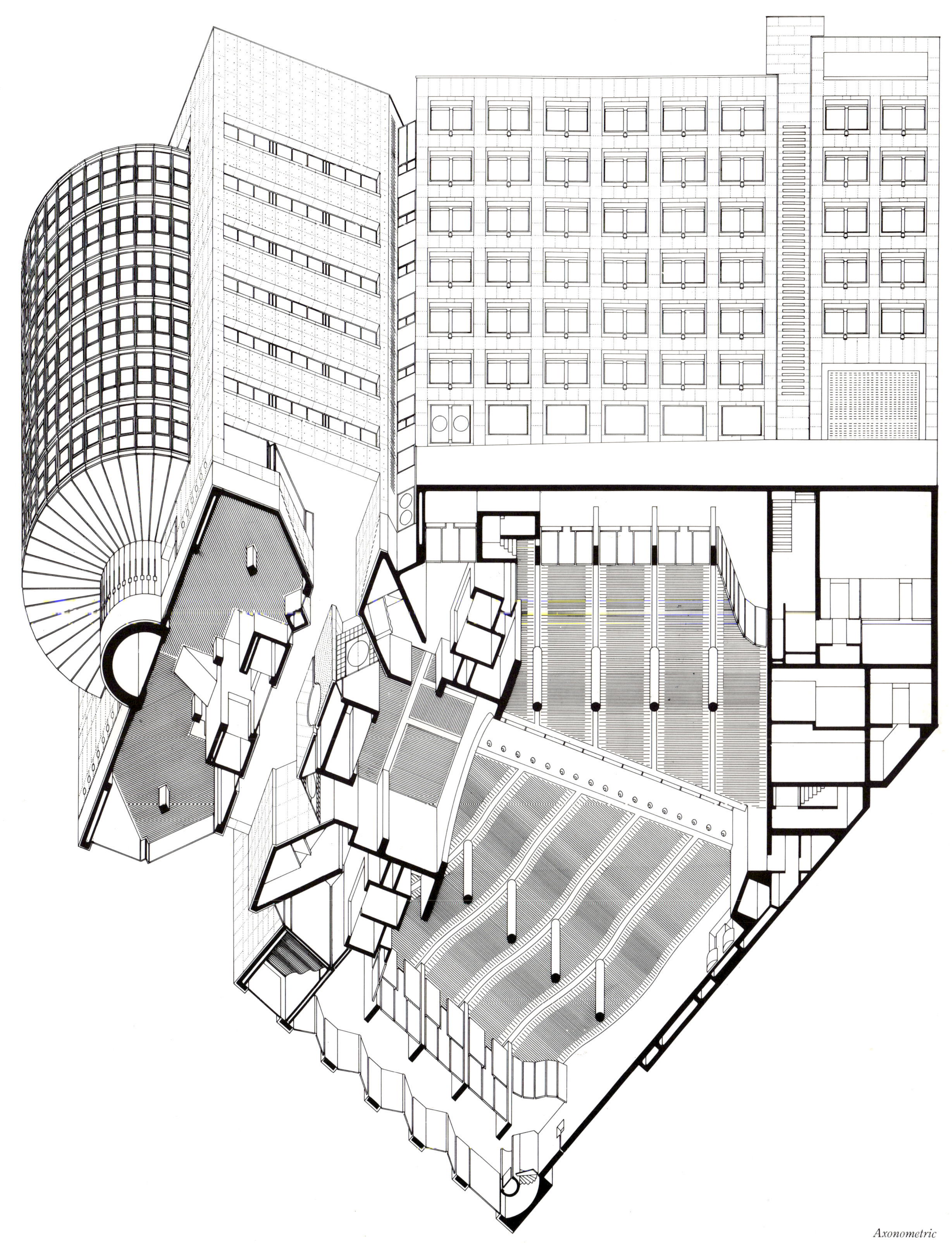

Axonometric

Detail of exterior wall

Detail of façade

Banking hall

Banking hall

Banking hall

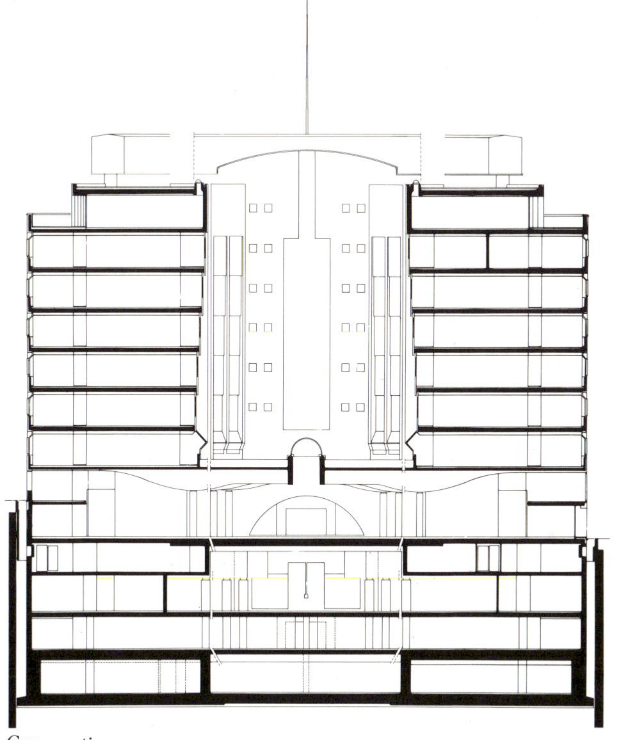

Cross section

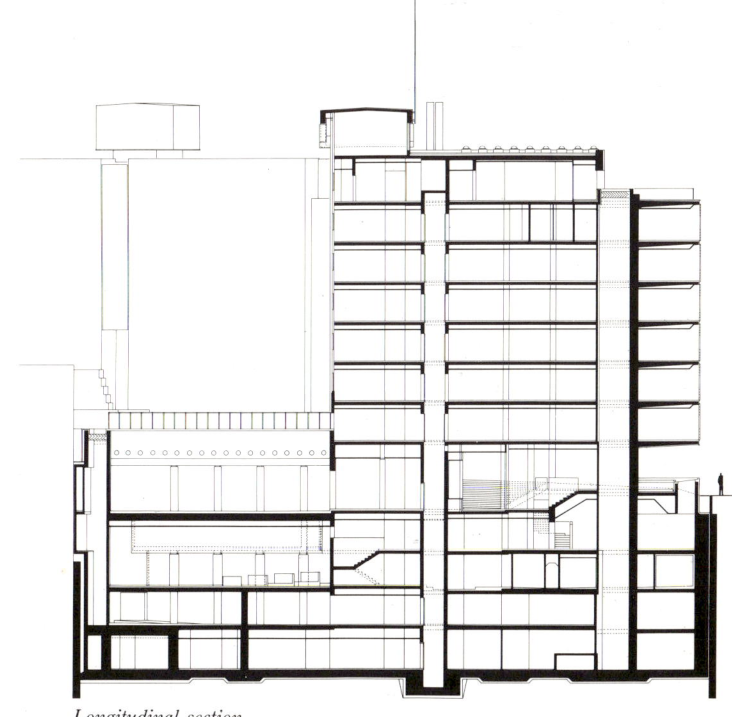

Longitudinal section

Restaurant

Banking hall

Dining hall

Disco on basement level

Meeting room

South façade

△Living room fireplace

▽Living room

Repeating the compositional method adopted in, for example, the school at Morbio, this complex is characterized by a linear succession of independent constructive and distributive elements. The house at Pregassona is the prototype from which the Riva San Vitale buildings are derived. The entrance is on the ground floor; the kitchen, the living room, and the protruding balcony on the first floor, and bedrooms are on the upper floor. The continuity between buildings is assured by the area allotted for secondary spaces inserted on the second floor between each house. A reference to the house at Pregassona is also evident in the definition of volumes, with their large central openings, the decreasing area of the wall as it rises toward the sky, and the skylight.

All buildings are planned to be in red brick on the exterior; the interiors will be painted white.

The linear development of the project parallels the slope of the hill and aspires to offer an architectural dialogue with the nearby constructions of the village of Riva San Vitale.

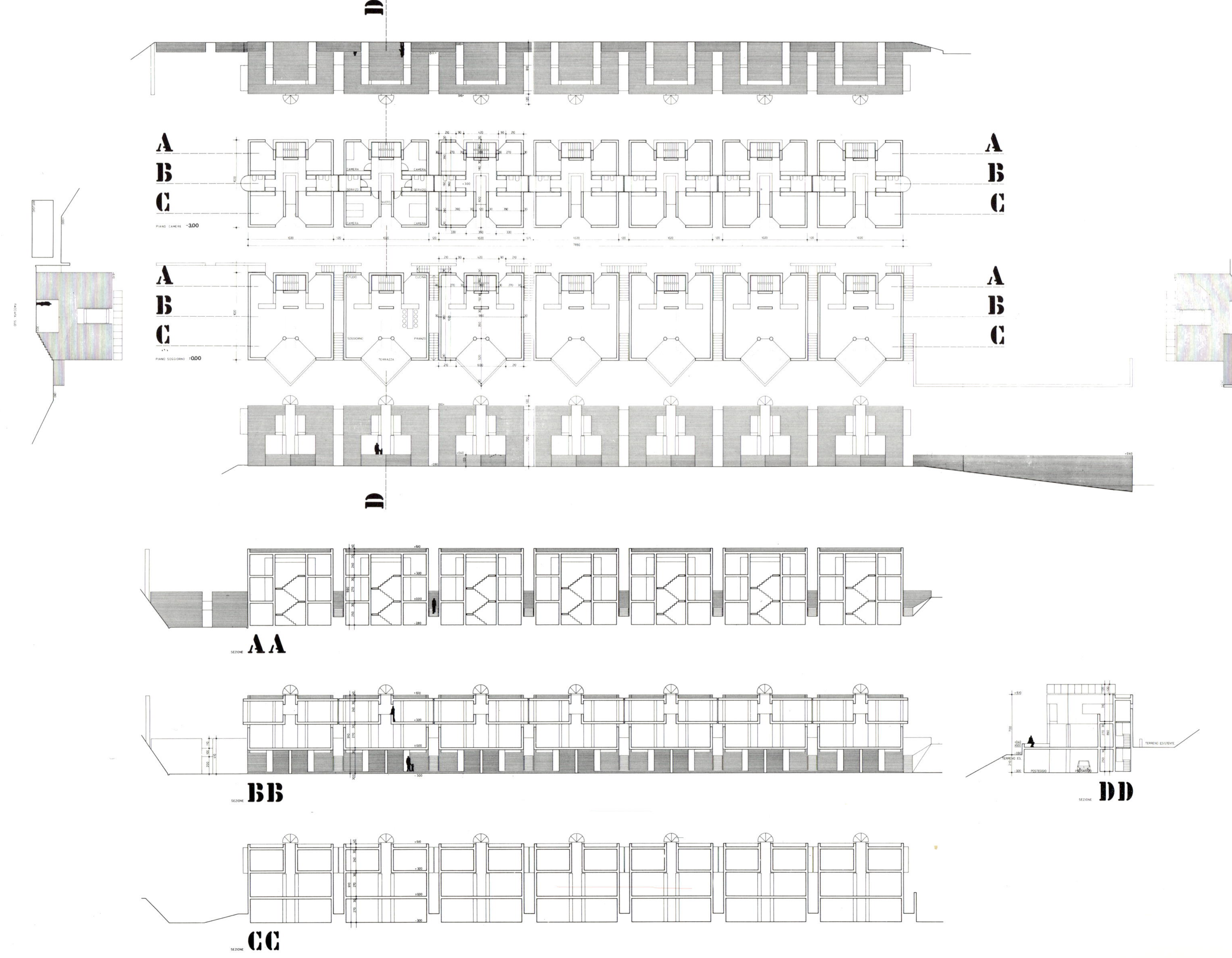

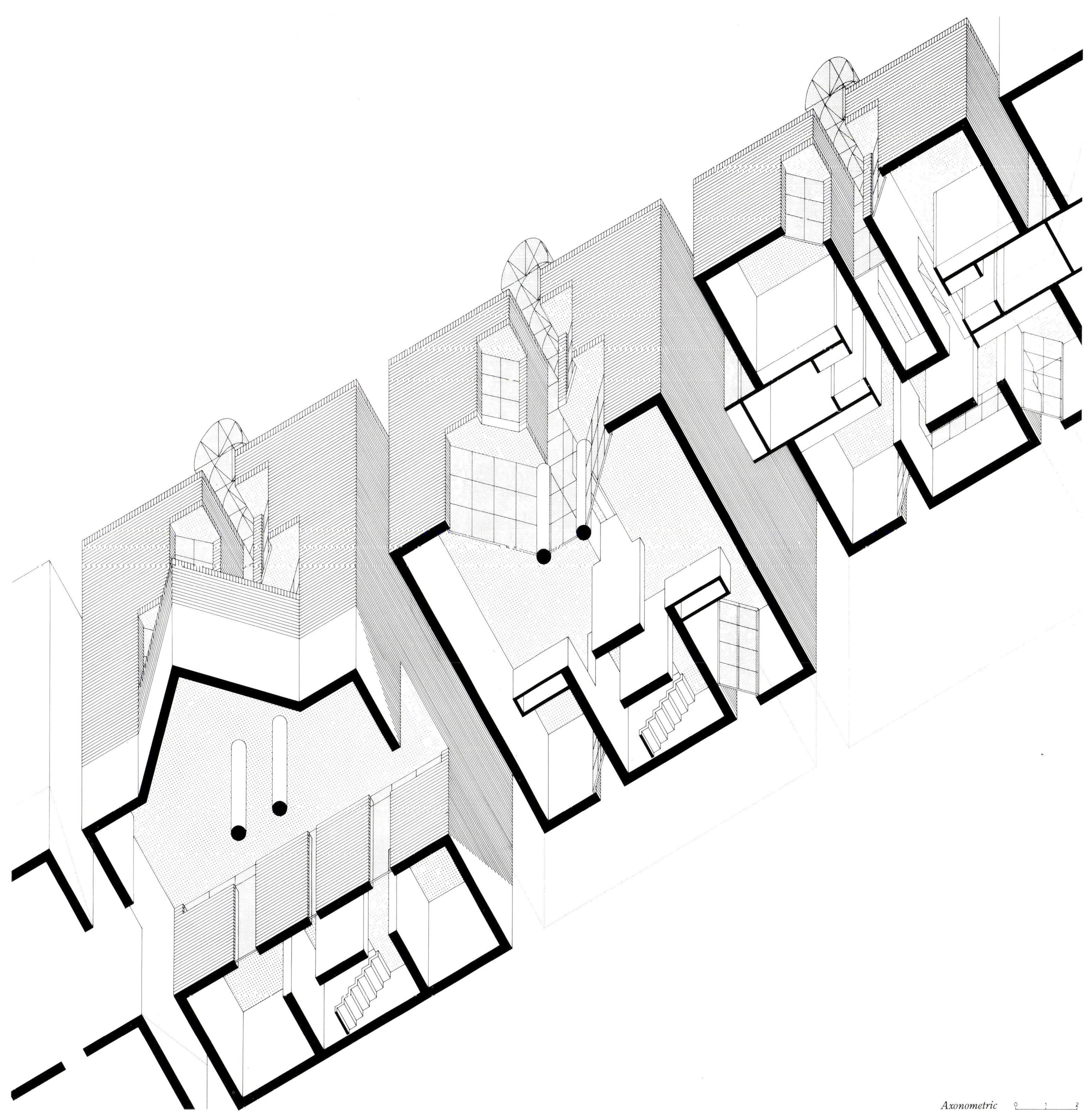

Axonometric
0   1   2

The Zurich Railway Station is located inside the city, beyond the Sihl River. The mass of tracks act as a physical barrier, separating this section of the city into north and south districts.

The competition for the enlargement of the railway station offered the opportunity to reorganize all the urban space next to it, a space that today is negatively characterized by the presence of rolling stock and rails. The new building, located toward the west, along the Sihl River, restores the old conformation of the station, once lost by the multiplication of railway lines. At the same time the structure, which will be as tall as the adjacent building of the Sihlpost, will form a bridge over the rails and create a connection between the two districts. The enlargement integrates itself with the already existing underground space, and offers, with its shops and restaurants gathered along the longitudinal walk, a new element that even further unites the two sections of the city. The roof of the new building will be partially occupied by an avenue whose trees, although on a different level, are a repetition of those along the river.

Next to the building/bridge, on the western side, there will be a bus station and above it a parking lot for taxis. These two levels are directly linked to the building/bridge; the structure becomes therefore the transitional element between different kinds of traffic: that of the railway station, cars, and pedestrians.

The third part of the project concerns the section along the Zollstrasse, and redefines the space between the station and the city behind it. In this section will be housed the spaces for tertiary activities requested by the competition. This element is characterized by a wall where, on the side facing the railway station, there will be space for different services, while on the other there will be on the east-west axis a sequence of architectural units. The front of this structure, facing the station, has in the basement and on the ground floor the equipment for the restaurant cars (as dictated by the requirements of the competition). On the first floor there will be a playground for children, opening toward the street with a large arch.

△▽ *Model photos*

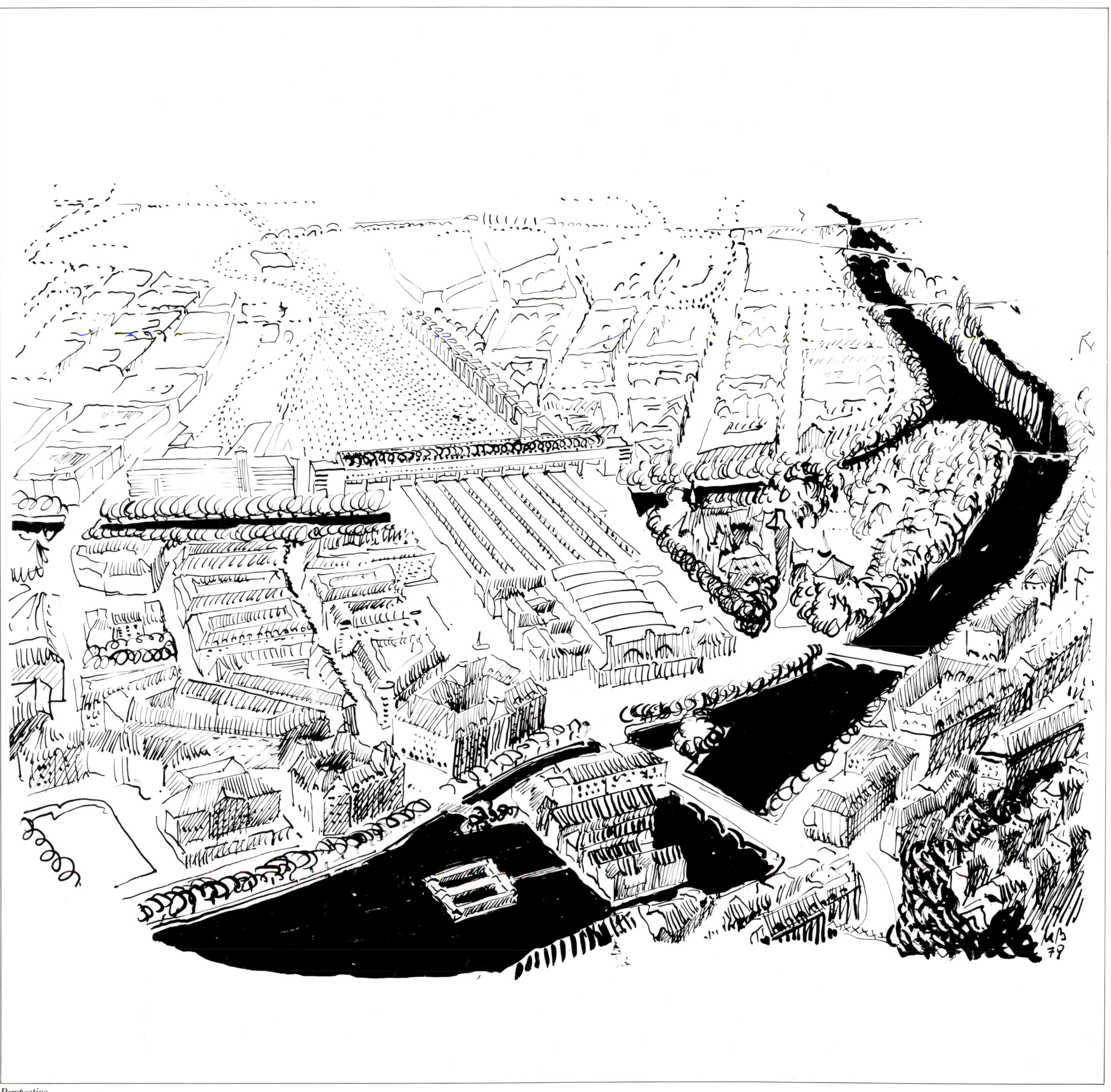

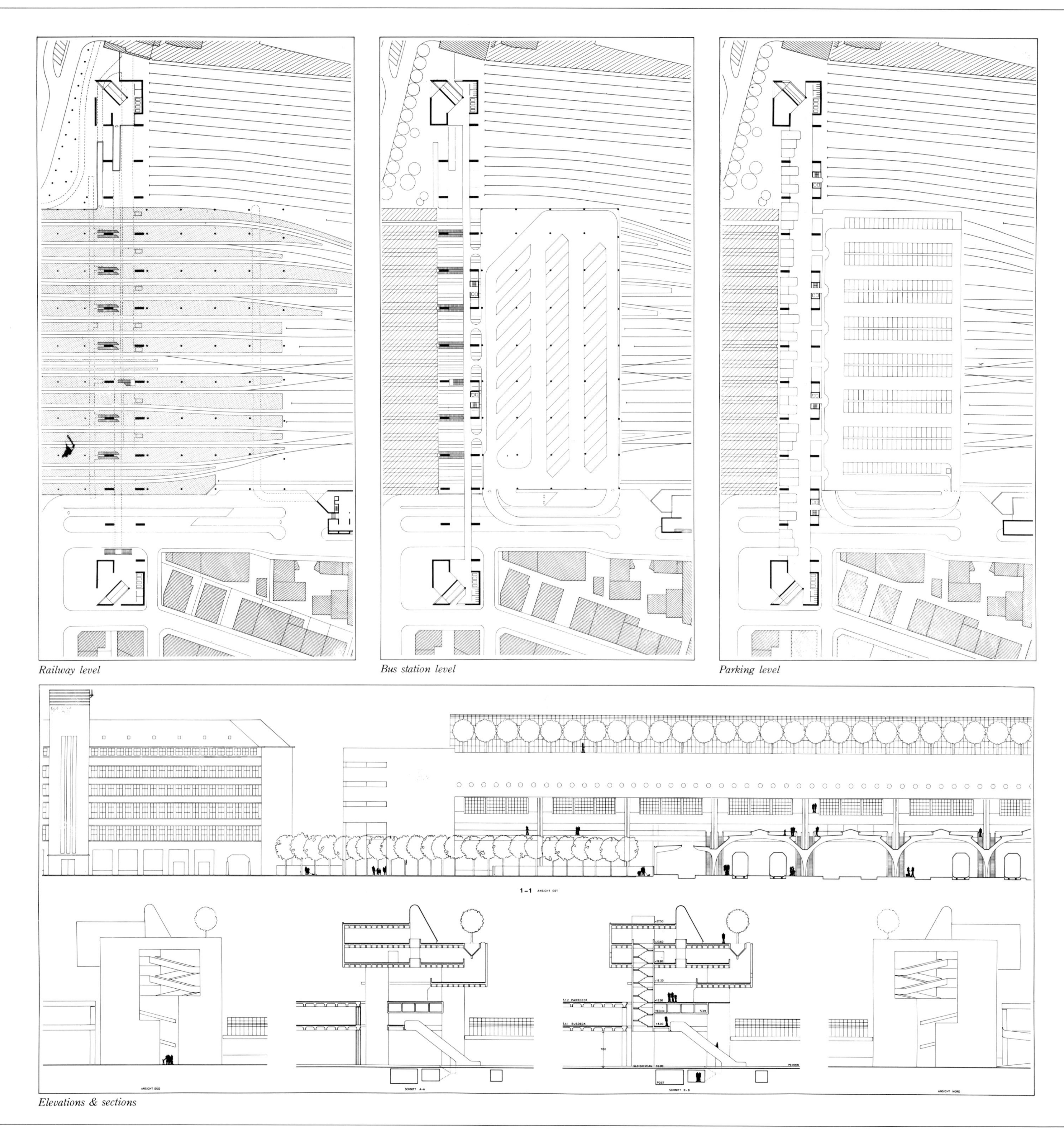

Railway level

Bus station level

Parking level

Elevations & sections

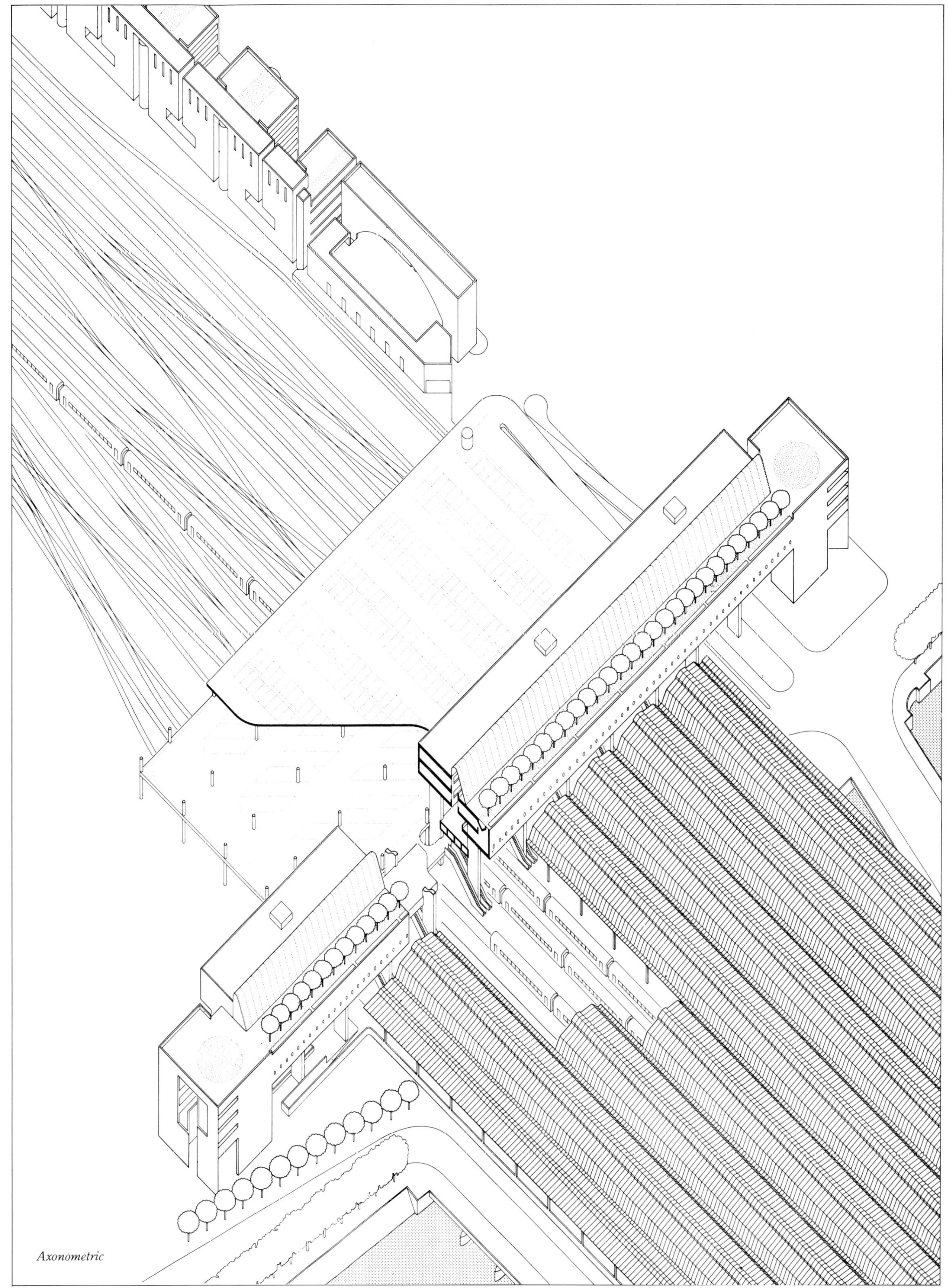

Axonometric

The tract of land on which the house is to be built is a steep slope between the road above and Lake Maggiore below. The house, planned as a vacation house, is very small and adapts itself to its particular location. The garage for cars is on the roof and can be entered directly from the road; the cubic volume of the house is partially sheltered by the slope. The large open space facing the lake is dominated by the fireplace, which when seen from the lake, takes on a symbolic value. Around the central loggia, the kitchen and living room are on the ground floor, with the bedrooms on the upper level.

The closed form surrounding the central fireplace respects the natural vegetation, keeping it intact in its original configuration.

The building thus describes the relationship of the lake with the road running above the house.

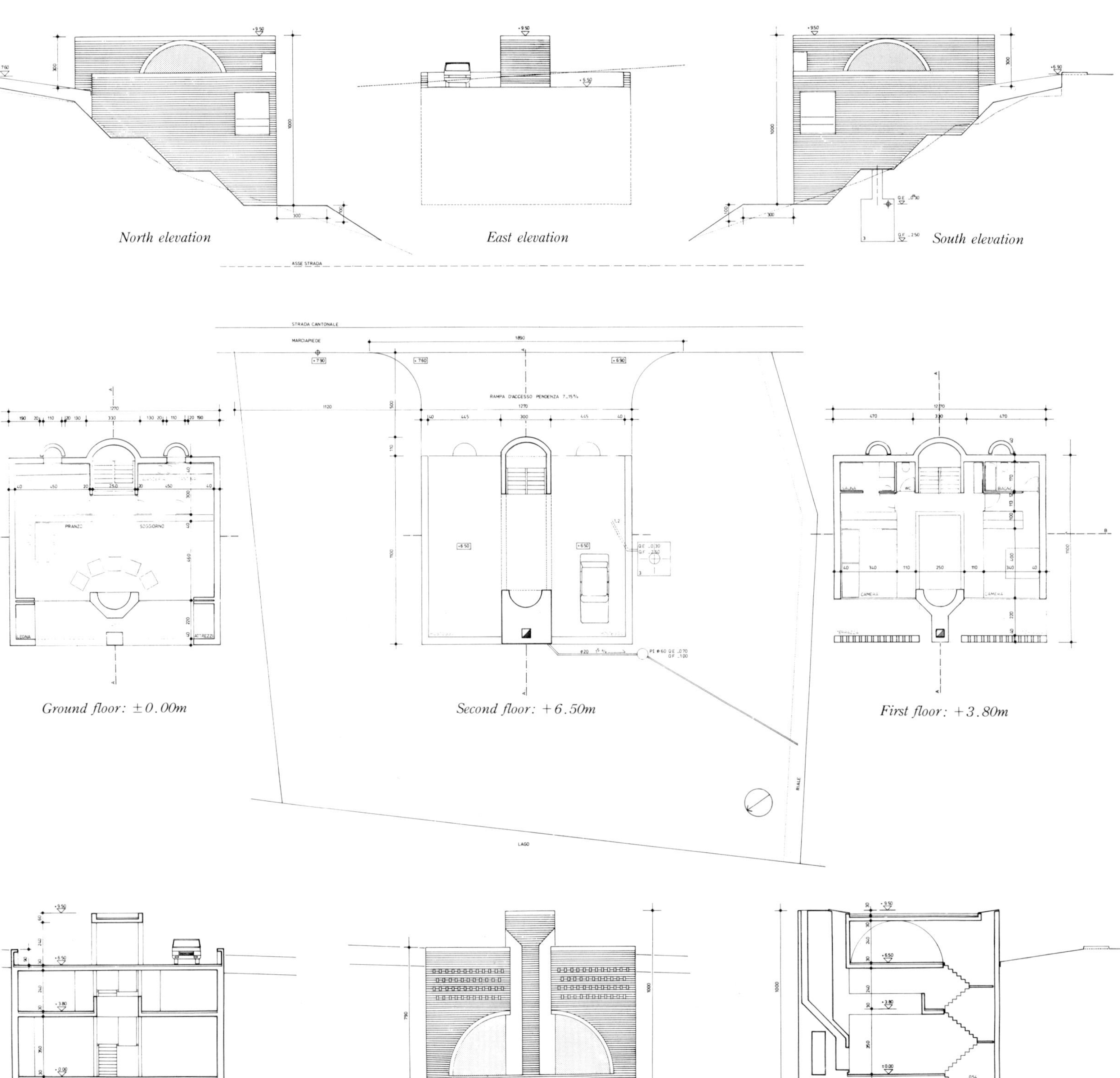

North elevation   East elevation   South elevation

Ground floor: ±0.00m   Second floor: +6.50m   First floor: +3.80m

Section B-B   West elevation   Section A-A

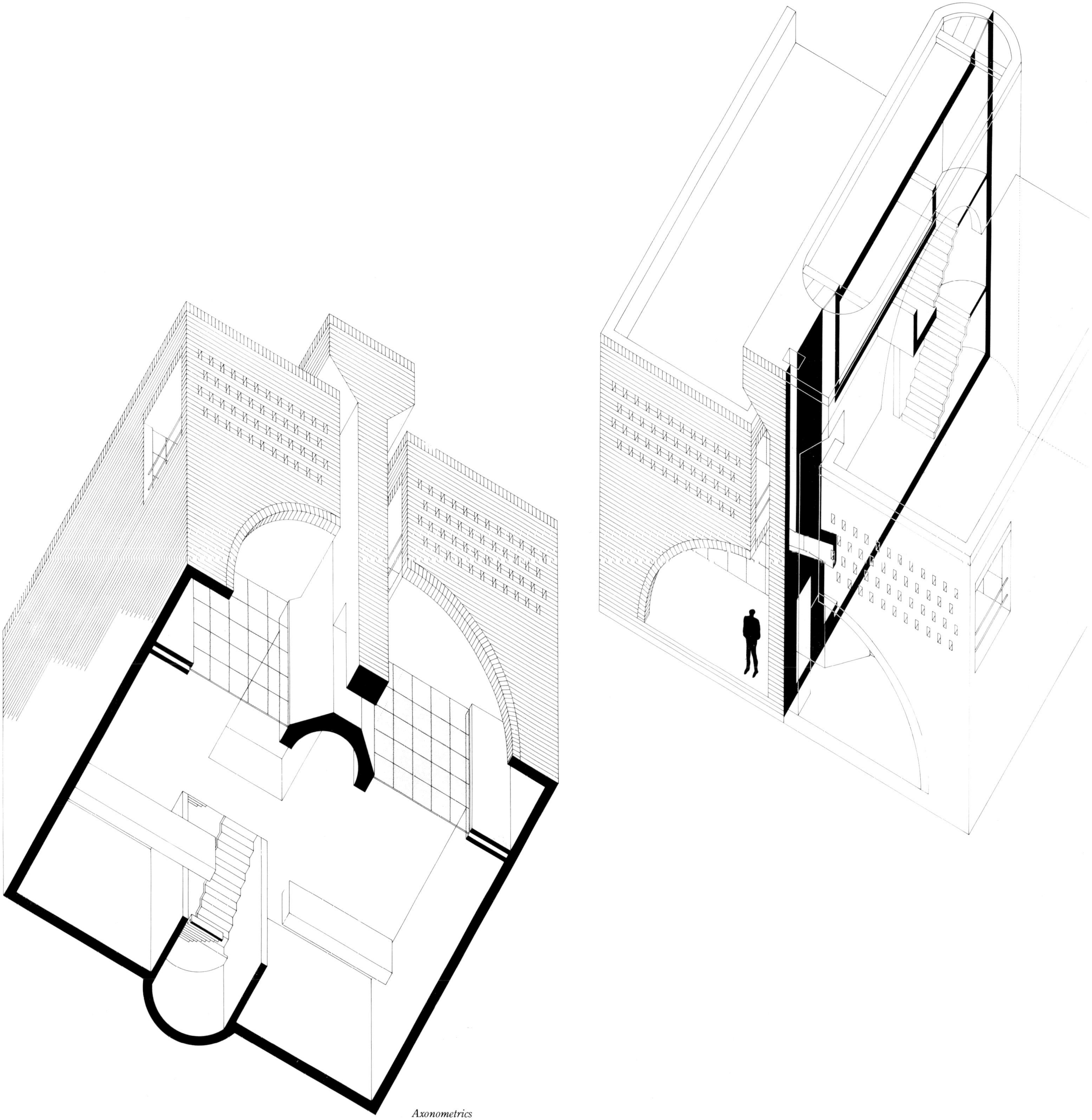

Axonometrics

The site selected for the competition is located between the outskirts of the old city and the highway along the stretch of the old walls between the historic city and the nineteenth-century additions. The parking lot, housing units, and buildings for community services (all required by the competition) are assigned to different structures. These structures and a historic building are gathered around a central public space. The project is an attempt to establish anew the boundary between the old and the modern city.

The side of the site facing south is defined by a long group of houses that echoes the topography of a medieval hamlet: each house has two superimposed duplexes with long balconies overlooking the courtyard. The central part of the area, once occupied by a garden, is used for parking. The parking lot is sunk into the ground and its roof is transformed into a paved square. Greenery, formerly provided by the garden, is supplied by trees placed in movable containers, which underline the artificiality of their surroundings.

The historic building and the new section for community services define two limits of the paved square, while the long western wall continues the perimeter of the old walls and reestablishes the boundary of the old historic city. The large central arch of the western wall represents a material separation from the rest of the city, and at the same time its scenographic quality enhances the view of the distant historic building.

Along this wall stairs are located: in the center they lead to the underground parking space; on its extremities they lead to the housing units and the community services.

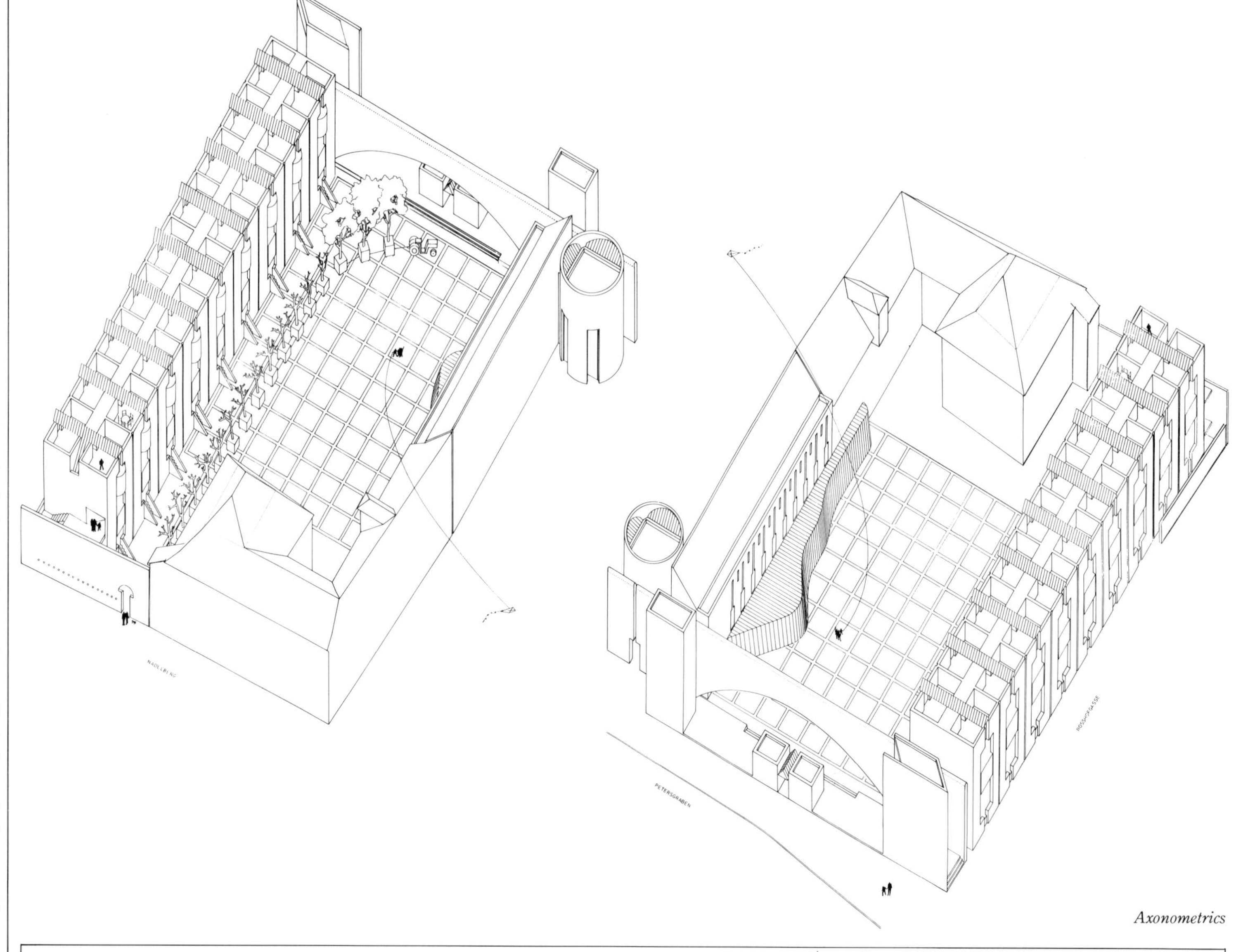

Axonometrics

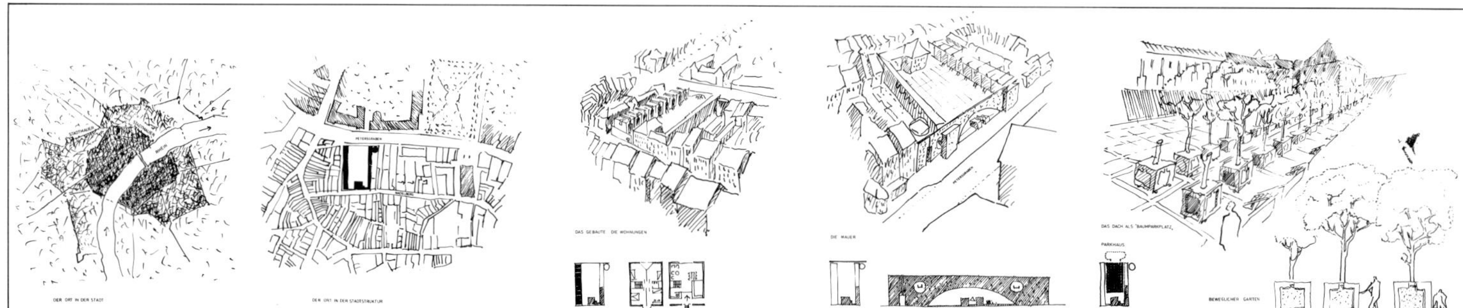

PETERSGRABEN + 270.40
BAUMPARKPLATZ
NADELBERG
+ 267.00
+ 264.20
+ 261.40
+ 258.60

PETERSGRABEN
NADELBERG

0 —— 10

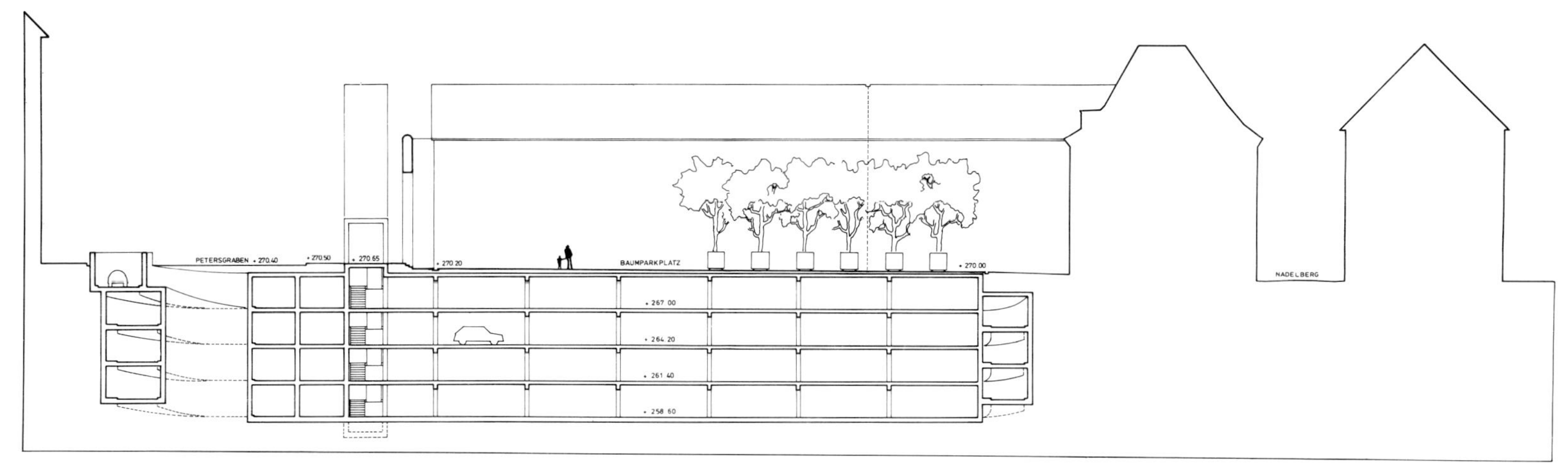

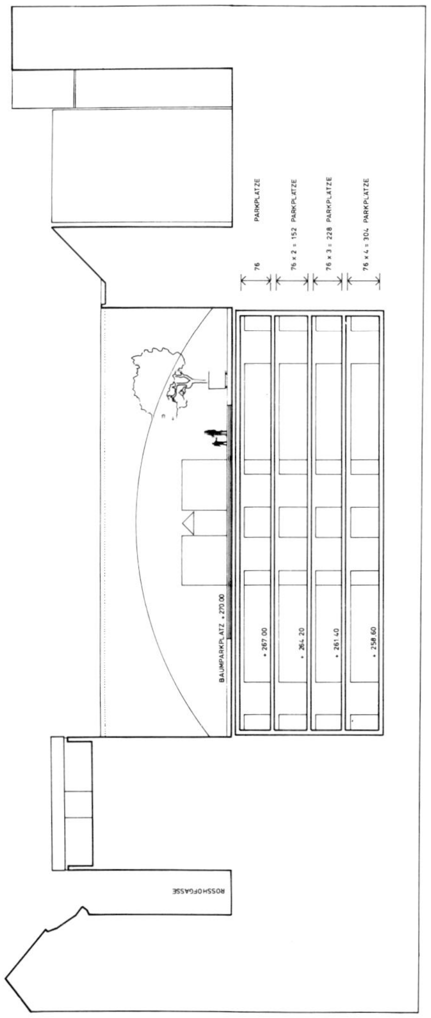

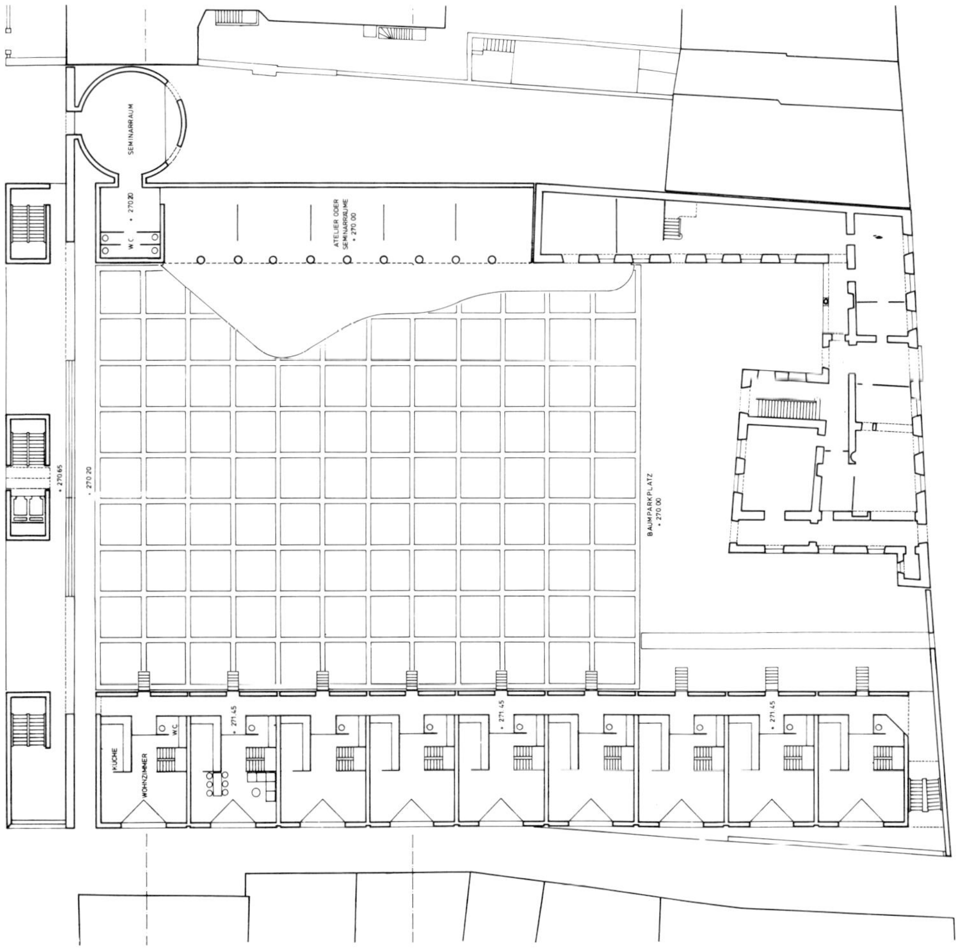

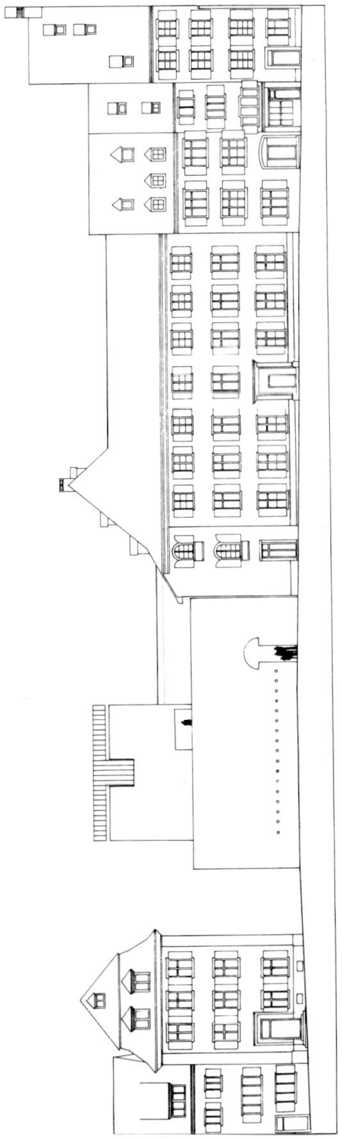

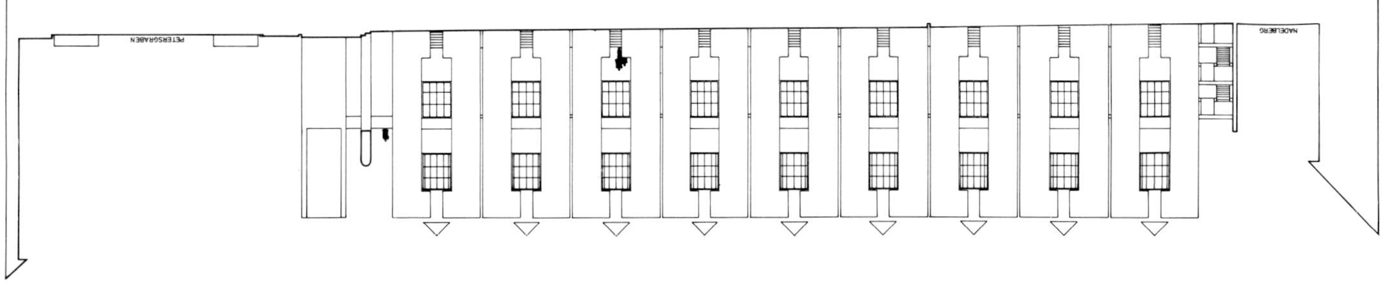

The competition allows for the reorganization of a large area that underwent considerable transformation two decades ago, at which time the streets in particular were enlarged beyond local needs. The mending of this torn urban fabric is achieved through the recomposition of city blocks and the creation of new pedestrian walkways (elevated and ground-level) around which new structures will rise.

The project totally eliminates motor traffic from the entire area. The square facing the castle is linked to the new post office (required by the competition) by a glass arcade that crosses a throughway. This arcade, a commercial and pedestrian axis, is abutted by buildings. There is a covered square and an open one; through them the articulation of the existing public space is accomplished.

The planned buildings give a new façade to the streets in which they are located and reconstruct the grid of city blocks destroyed twenty years ago by the expanding amount of space given over to parking for cars. The new office building, located at one end of the arcade, is a duplication of the one already existing, while the post office, divided into three buildings, repeats the plan proposed for the State Bank at Fribourg.

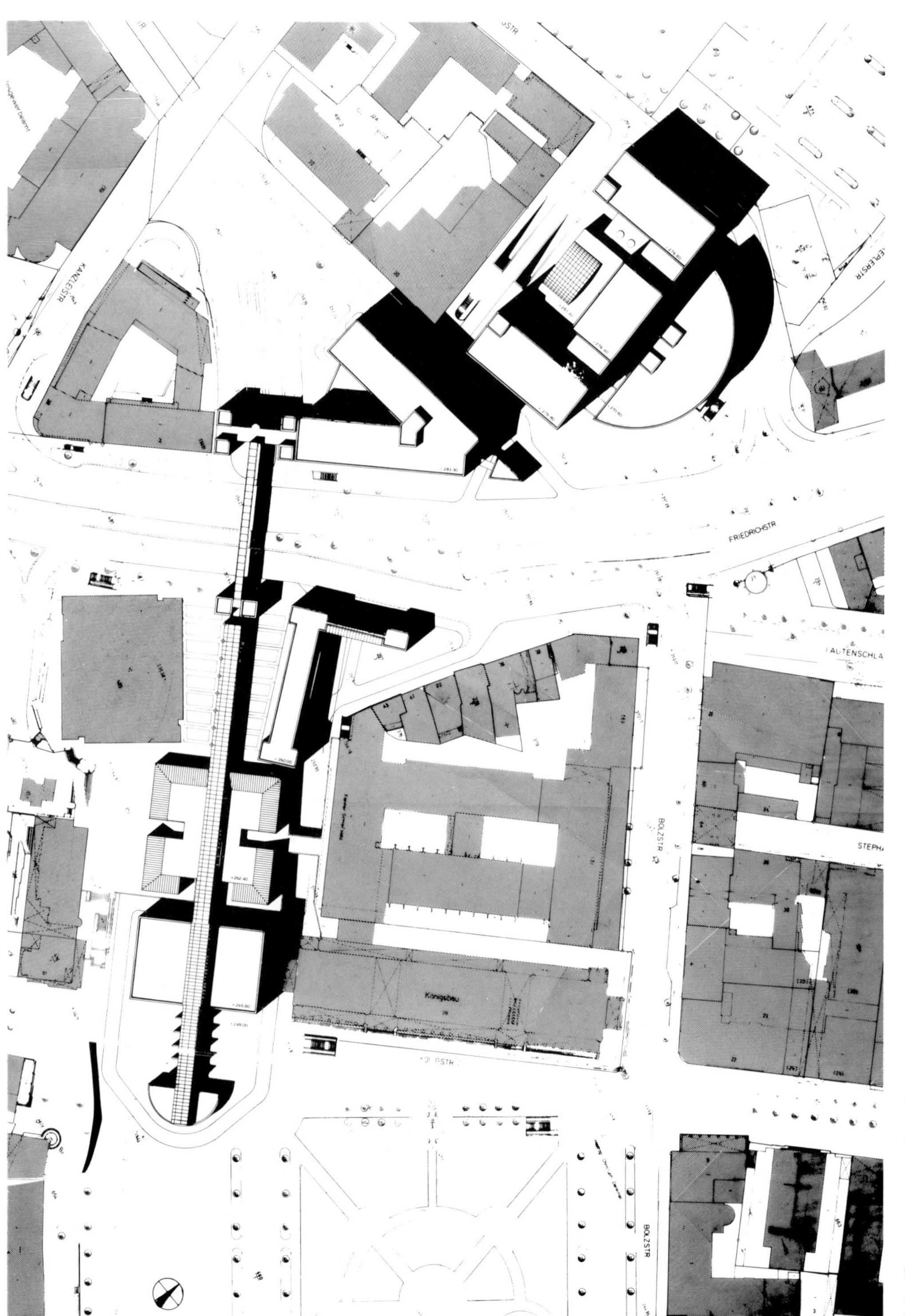

Site plan

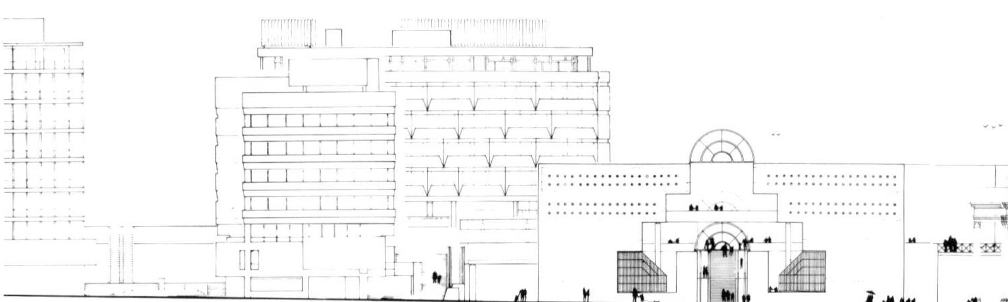

Königstrasse elevation

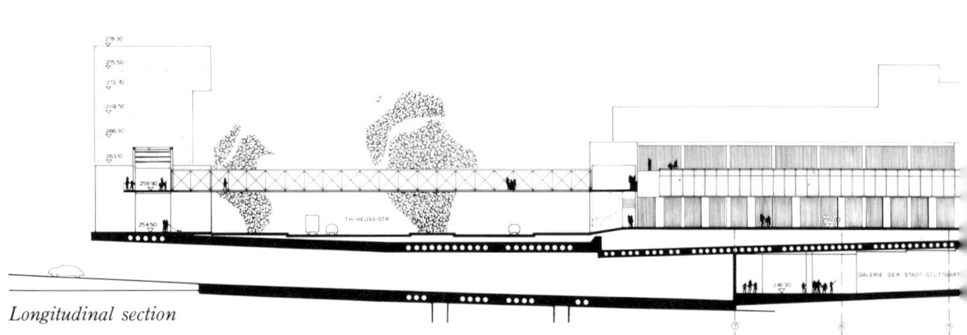

Longitudinal section

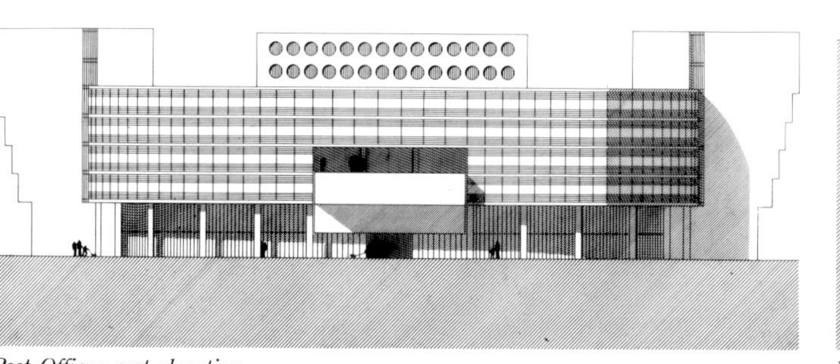

Post Office: east elevation

Post Office: section

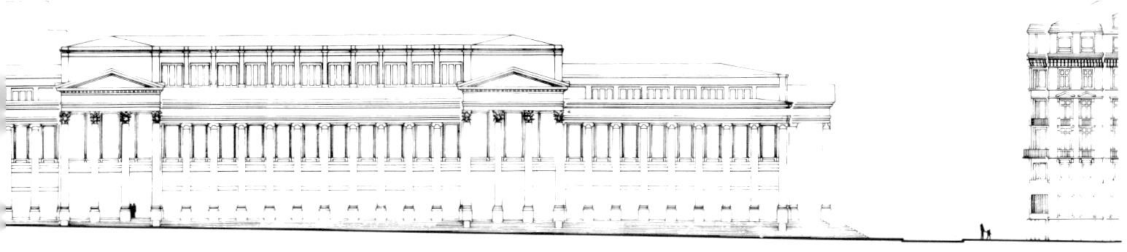

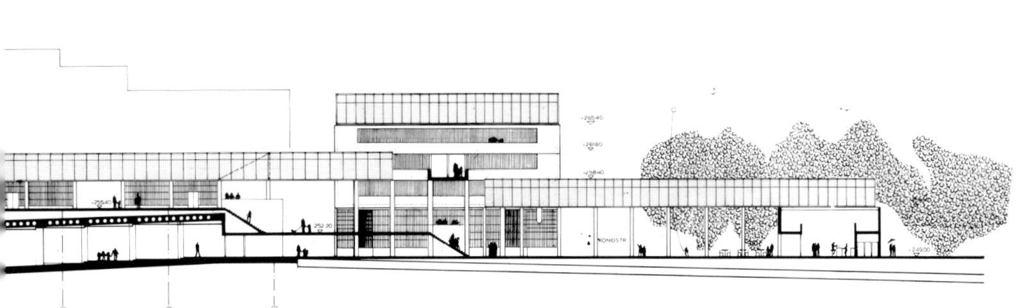

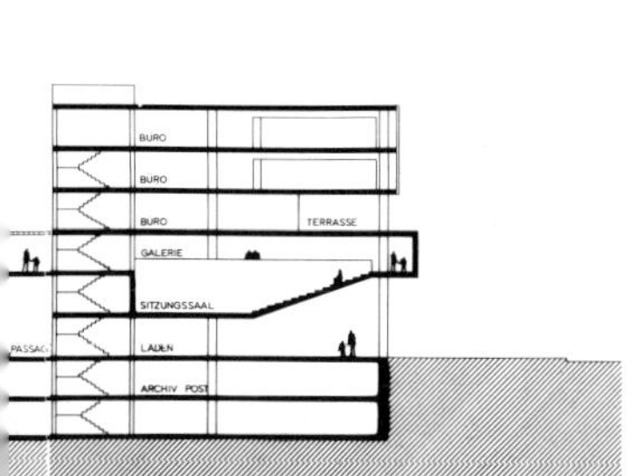

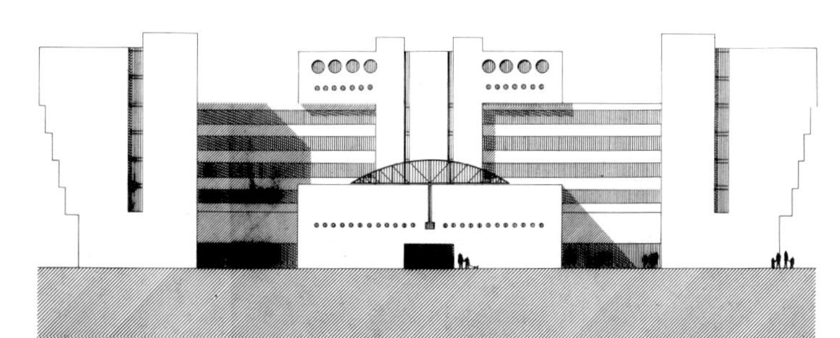

Post Office: west elevation

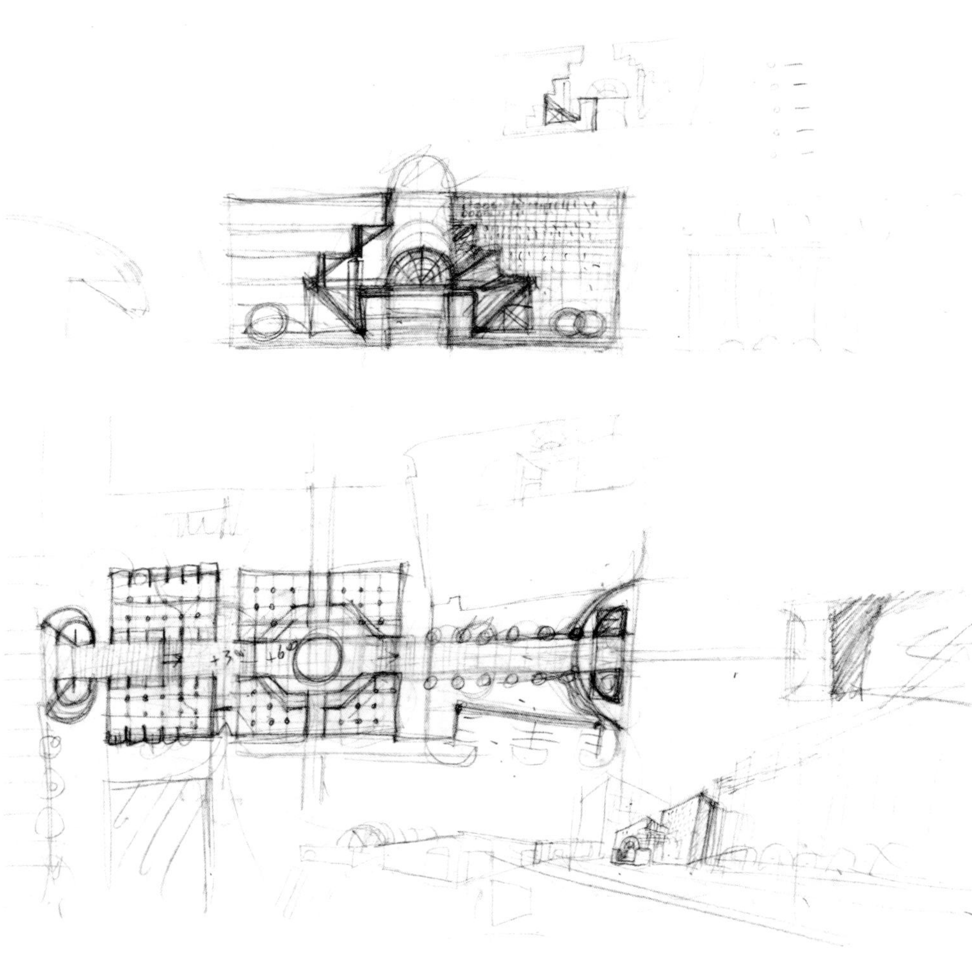

Preliminary study

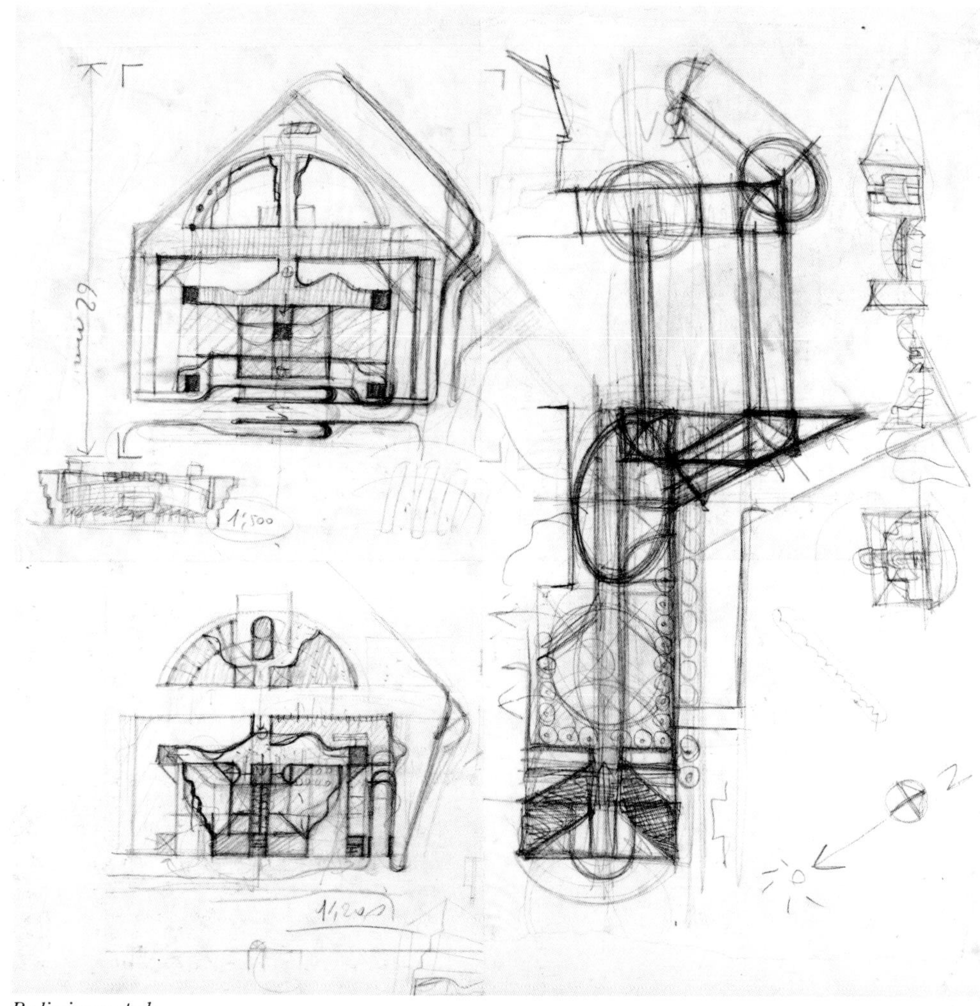

Preliminary study

Perspective

△▽ Model photos

Competition for an Administrative Building at Brühl, West Germany, 1980 (project)

The firm DOM (key manufacturers) needed a new building, next to the existing one, which would serve as an advertising "billboard" for the company. By reorganizing the parking lot area along the tree-lined street, the new building becomes the entrance to an entire industrial complex. The long pedestrian walk, whose covering is supported by the cylindrical volumes of the security check and of secondary spaces, crosses the new building along the path marked by the large central opening.

The structure is formed by a central body, with stairways placed at its extremities, and by two lateral wings with façades executed in glass and concrete; the façade of the central building is covered with slabs of stone. The contrast resulting from the different materials employed in the façades is emphasized by variations in the treatment of the corners and of the central opening. The top floor, intended for exhibitions, has a single wide space illuminated by a central skylight.

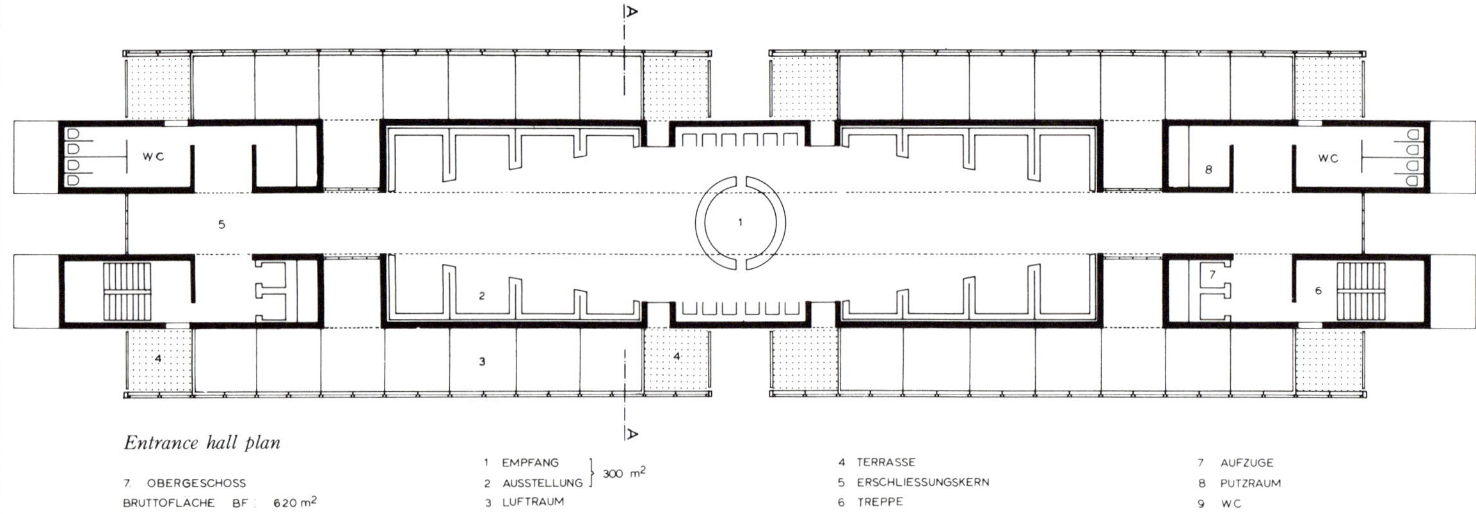

Entrance hall plan

7. OBERGESCHOSS
BRUTTOFLACHE BF : 620 m²

1 EMPFANG
2 AUSSTELLUNG } 300 m²
3 LUFTRAUM

4 TERRASSE
5 ERSCHLIESSUNGSKERN
6 TREPPE

7 AUFZUGE
8 PUTZRAUM
9 WC

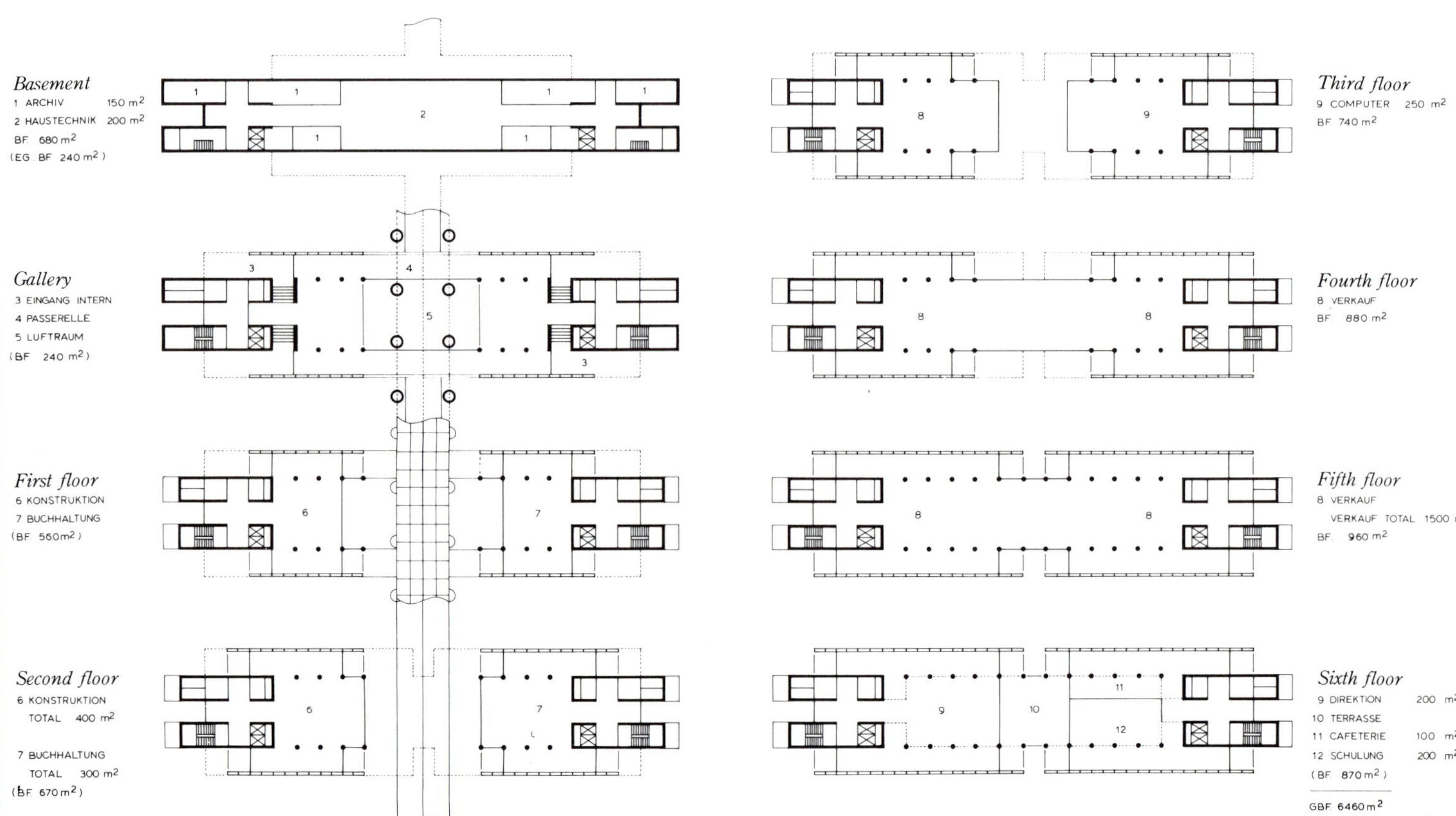

Basement
1 ARCHIV   150 m²
2 HAUSTECHNIK 200 m²
BF. 680 m²
(EG. BF 240 m²)

Gallery
3 EINGANG INTERN
4 PASSERELLE
5 LUFTRAUM
(BF 240 m²)

First floor
6 KONSTRUKTION
7 BUCHHALTUNG
(BF. 560 m²)

Second floor
6 KONSTRUKTION
   TOTAL 400 m²

7 BUCHHALTUNG
   TOTAL 300 m²
(BF. 670 m²)

Third floor
9 COMPUTER 250 m²
BF. 740 m²

Fourth floor
8 VERKAUF
BF. 880 m²

Fifth floor
8 VERKAUF
   VERKAUF TOTAL 1500 m²
BF. 960 m²

Sixth floor
9 DIREKTION   200 m²
10 TERRASSE
11 CAFETERIE   100 m²
12 SCHULUNG   200 m²
(BF. 870 m²)

GBF. 6460 m²
(GESAMT-BRUTTO-FLACHE)

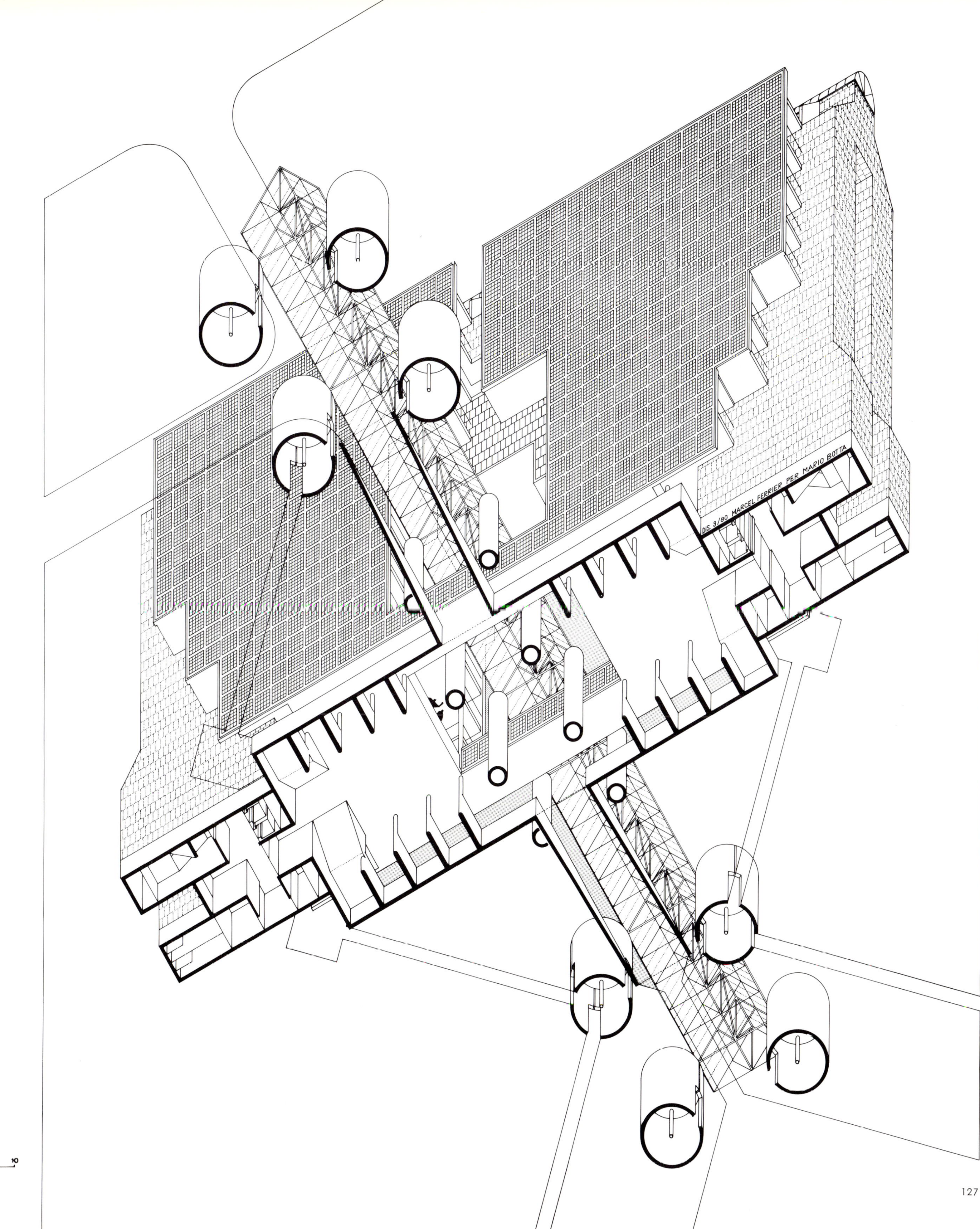

Axonometric

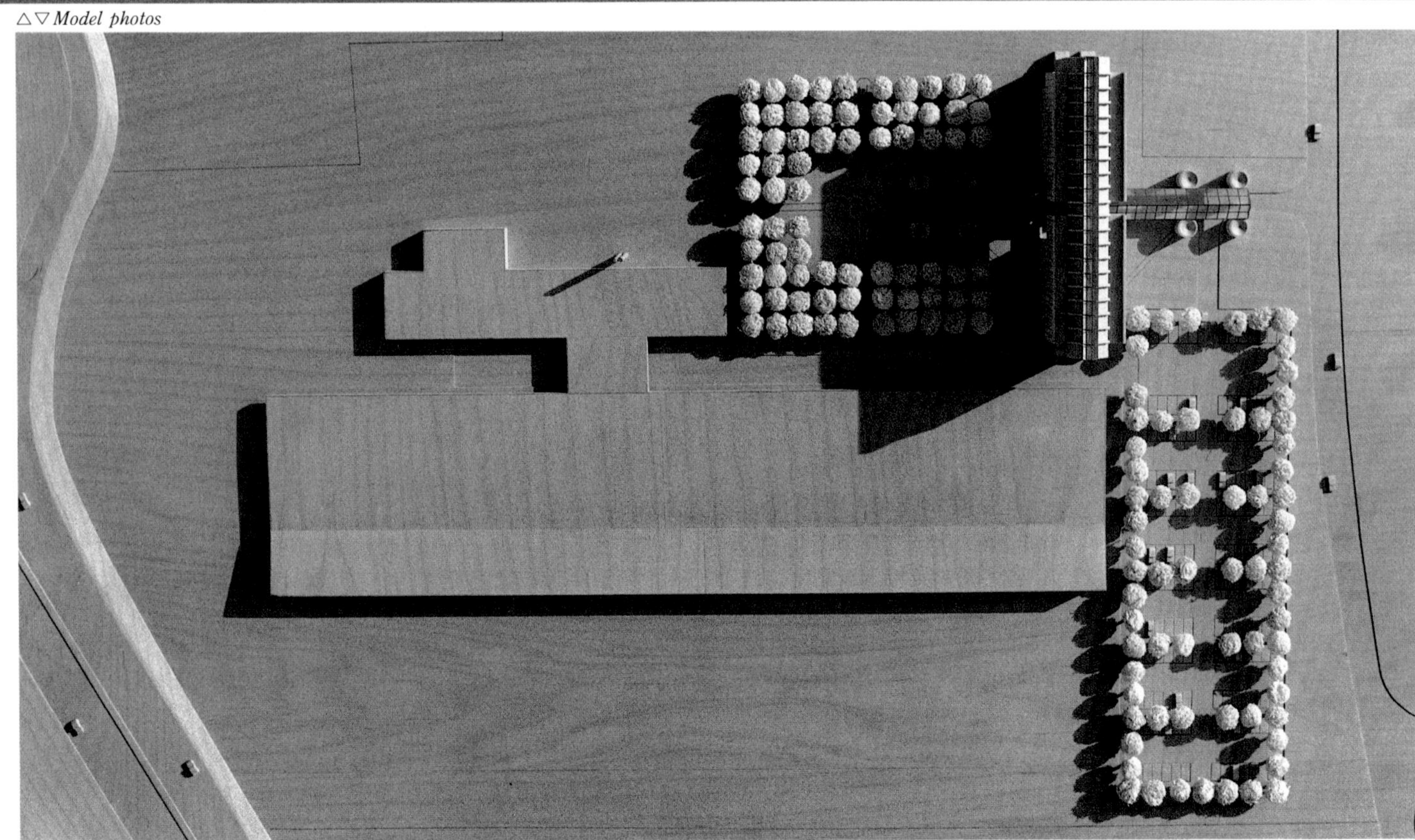

△▽ *Model photos*

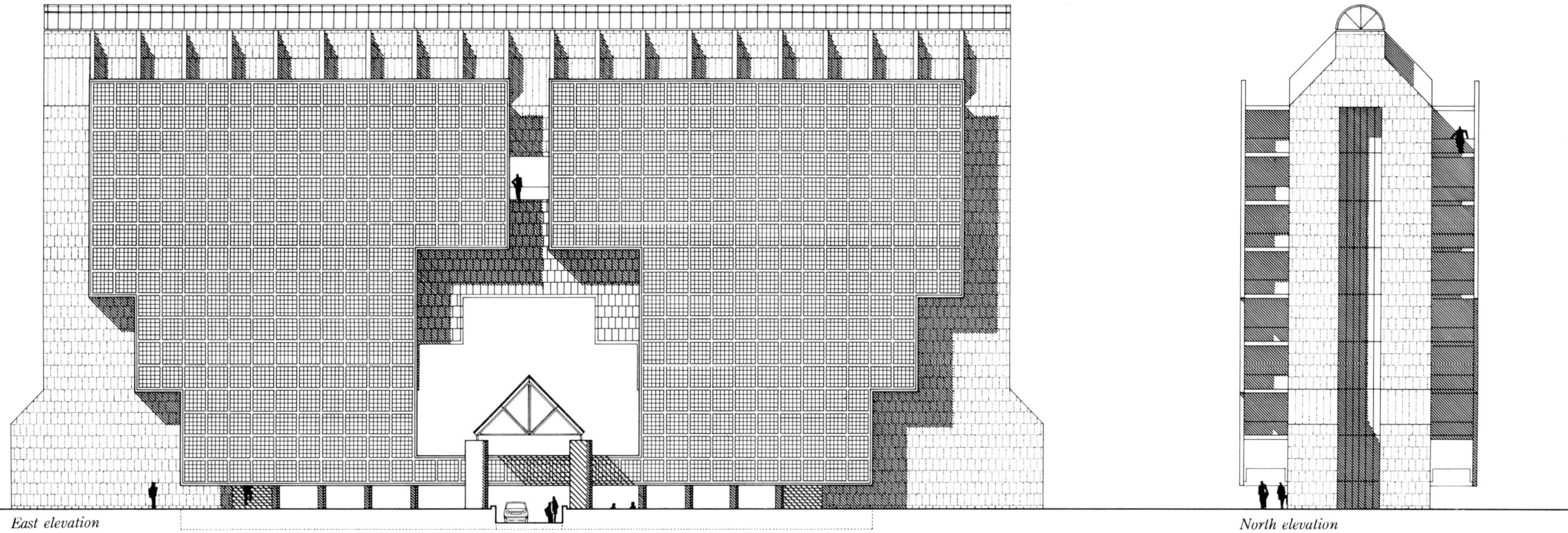

Model photo

East elevation   North elevation

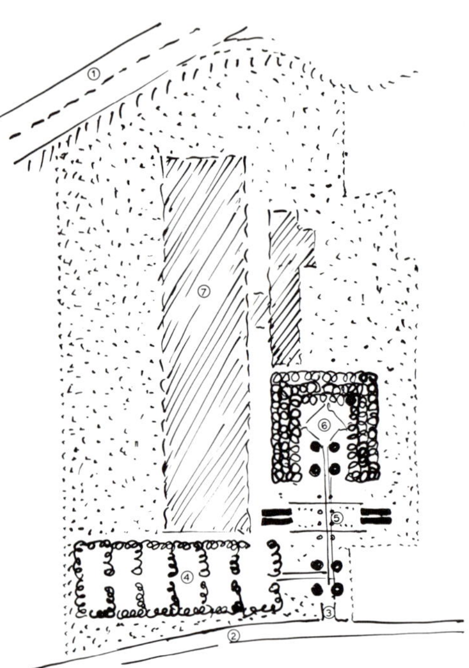

Situation

1 AUTOBAHN
2 WESSELINGER STRASSE
3 EINGANG
4 PARKPLATZ
5 VERWALTUNGSGEBAUDE
6 PLATZ
7 FABRIKATIONSGEBAUDE

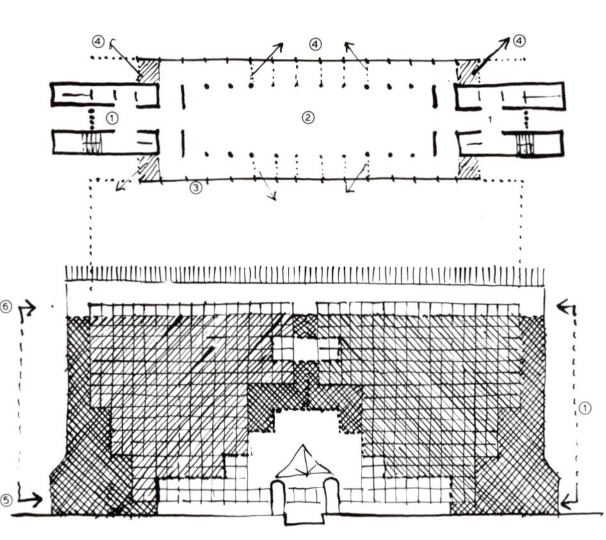

Building elevation & plan

1 VERTIKALE ERSCHLIESSUNG
2 GEBRAUCHSFLACHE
3 GLASBAUSTEINFASSADE
4 VENTILATION
5 EINGANG
6 EINGANG • EMPFANG

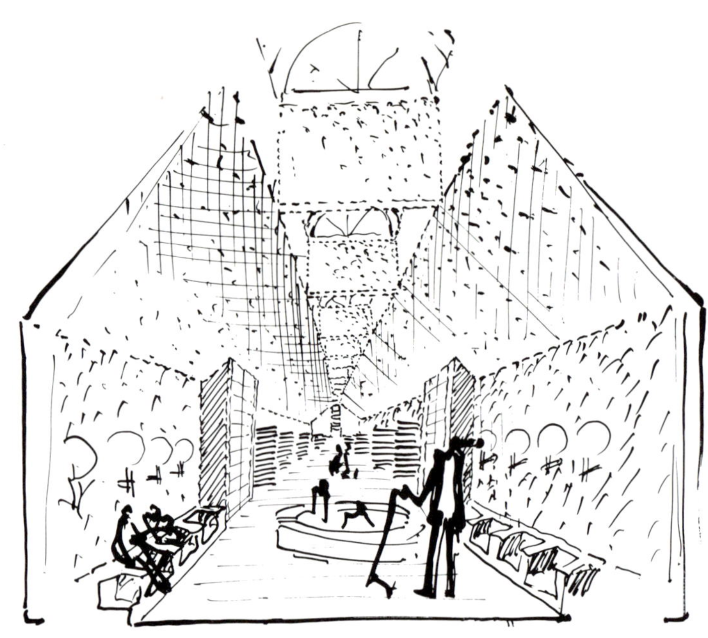

Perspective: Entrance hall

(7 GESCHOSS)

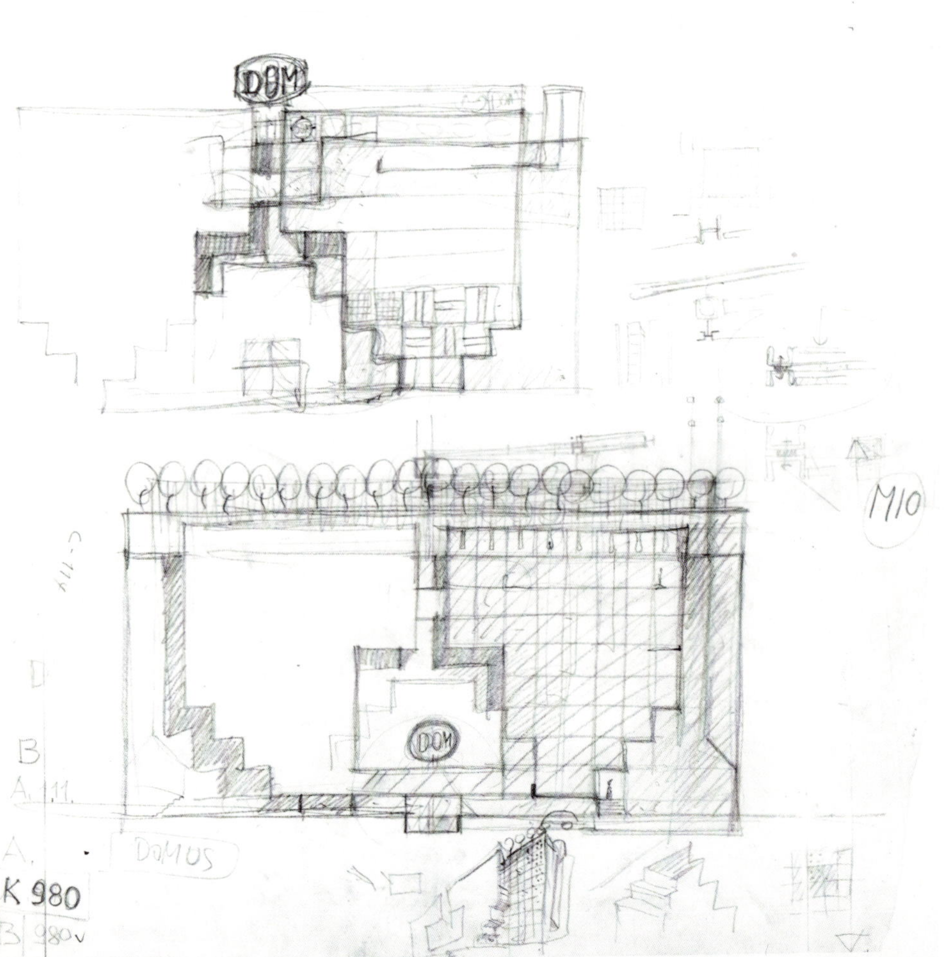

Preliminary study
130

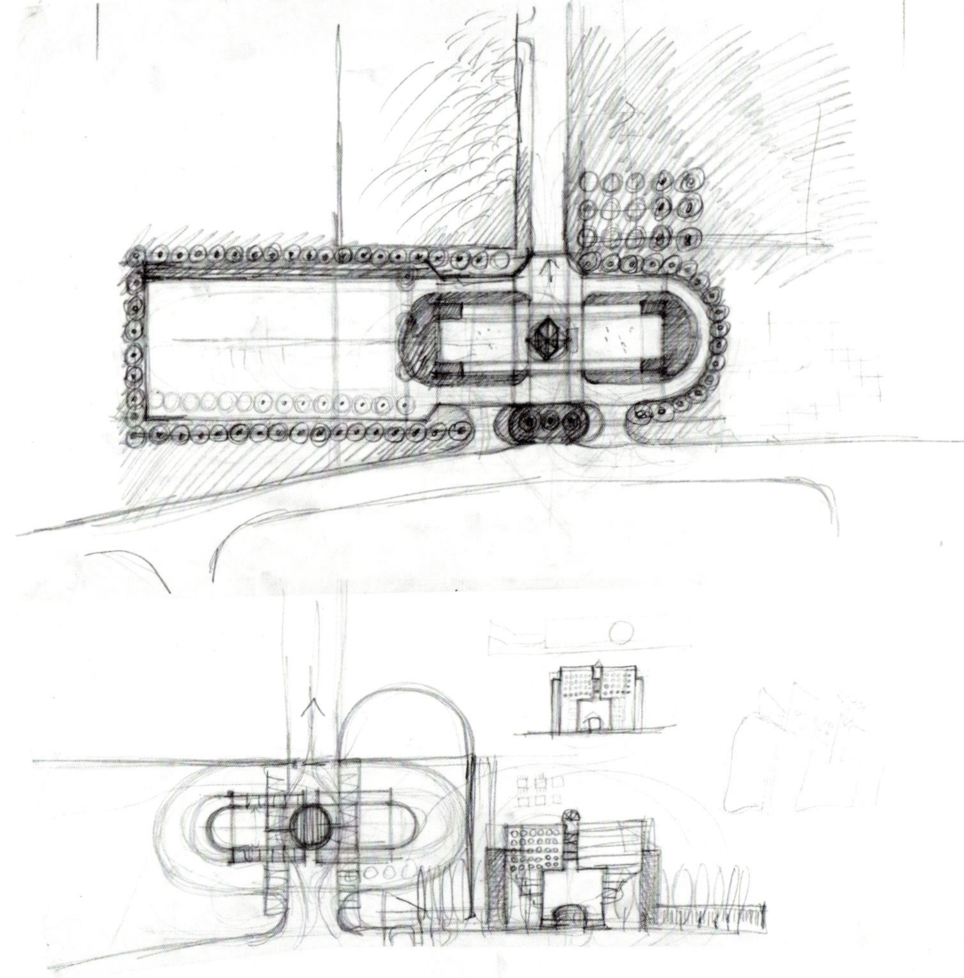

Preliminary study

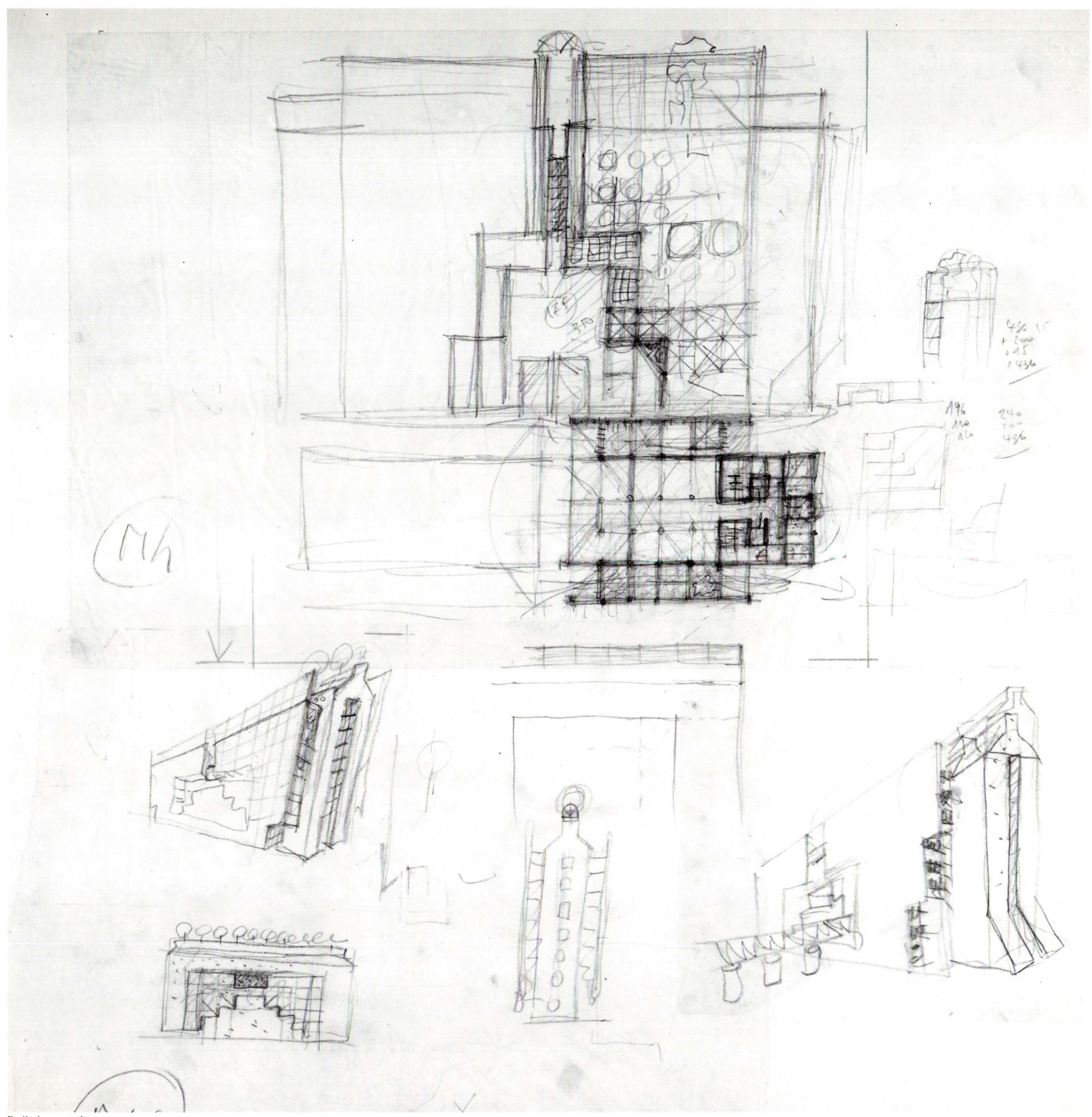

Preliminary study

The projected site is located on the left bank of a river, next to a vast public park toward the west and an undistinguished harbor toward the east. Located along the existing road, facing north and directly related to the city, whose urban façade they will define, will be all the planned structures: pavilions for sporting equipment, cabins, the solariums, a beach, a covered swimming pool, and (at the back of the new harbor) worksites for the repair and sheltering of boats.

All of the area facing the lake is kept free of buildings; its expanse is divided into smaller sections by rows of trees. Tennis courts are toward the west, in the center there will be a large field, an open swimming pool and a beach, the harbor will face east.

A floating tree, planted on a buoy at a distance from the shore represents one of the apexes of the project. A bridge, located across the river's mouth, establishes the continuity between the already existing public walk of the park that runs across the lake and the new one that from the left bank of the river winds up to the pavilions, where, flanked with trees, it continues and reaches the open zone facing the lake.

The goal of the project is to strongly characterize the open spaces in order to create through them a geometrically well-defined area between the lake and the city.

△▽ *Model photos*

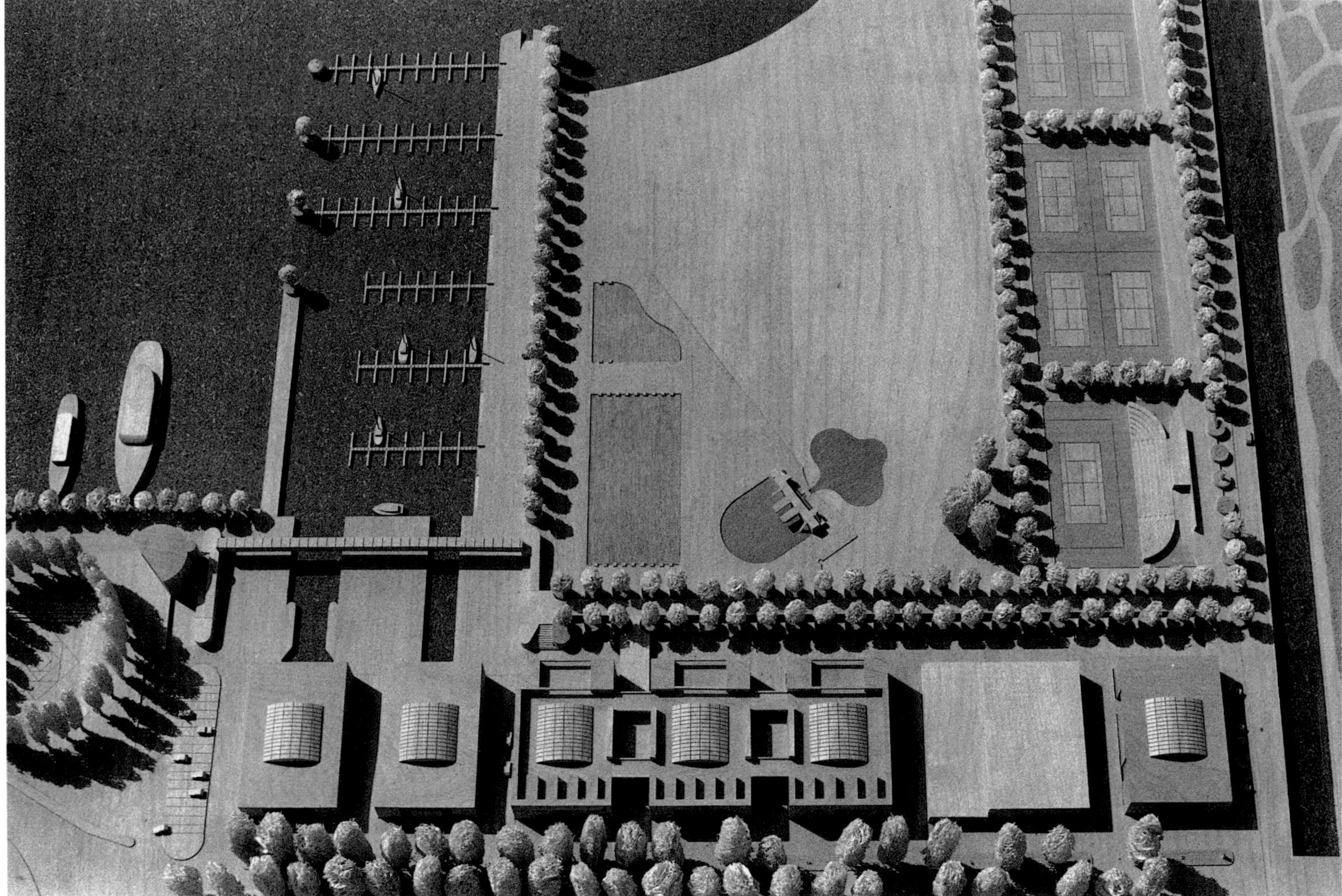

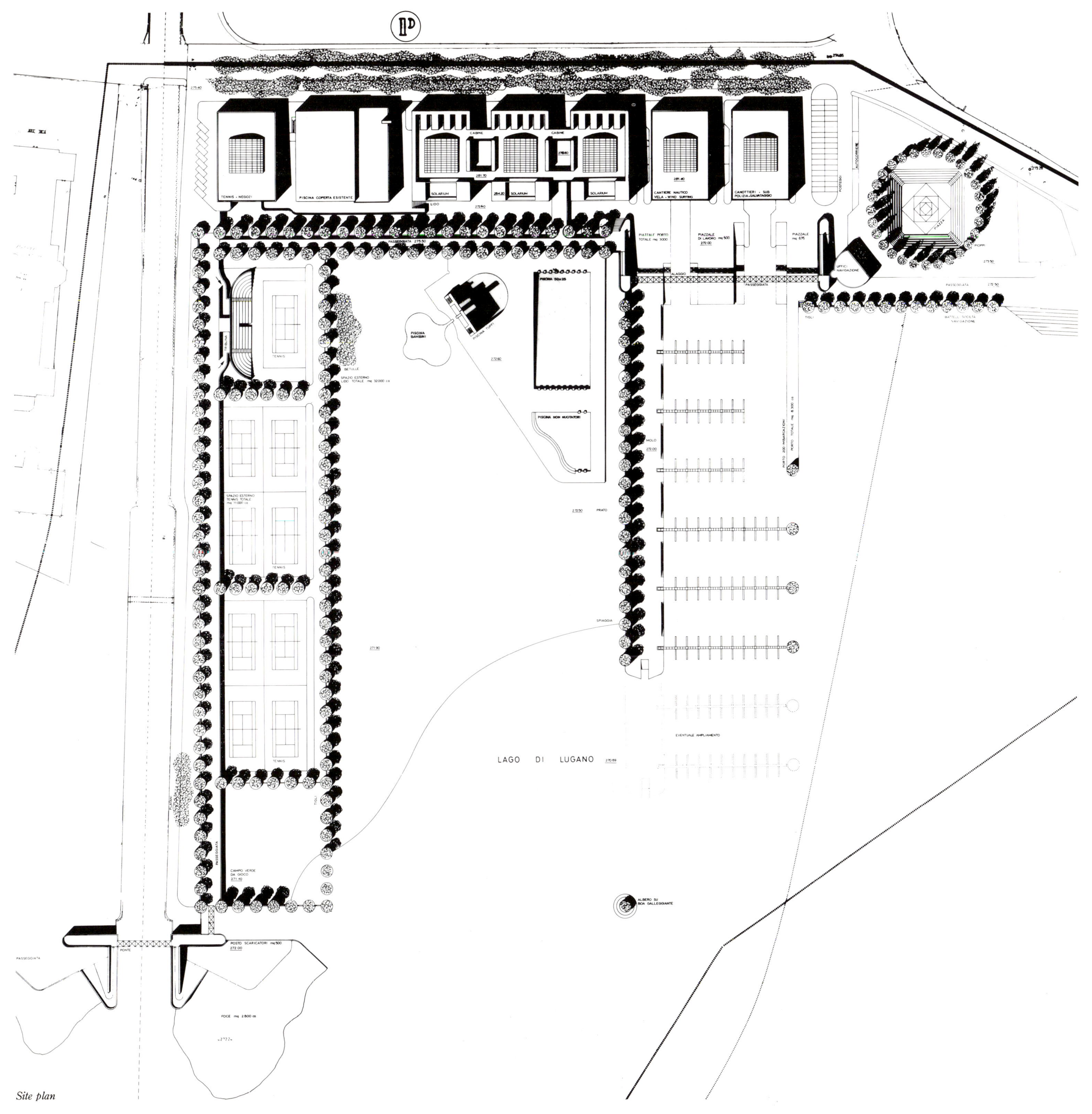

Site plan

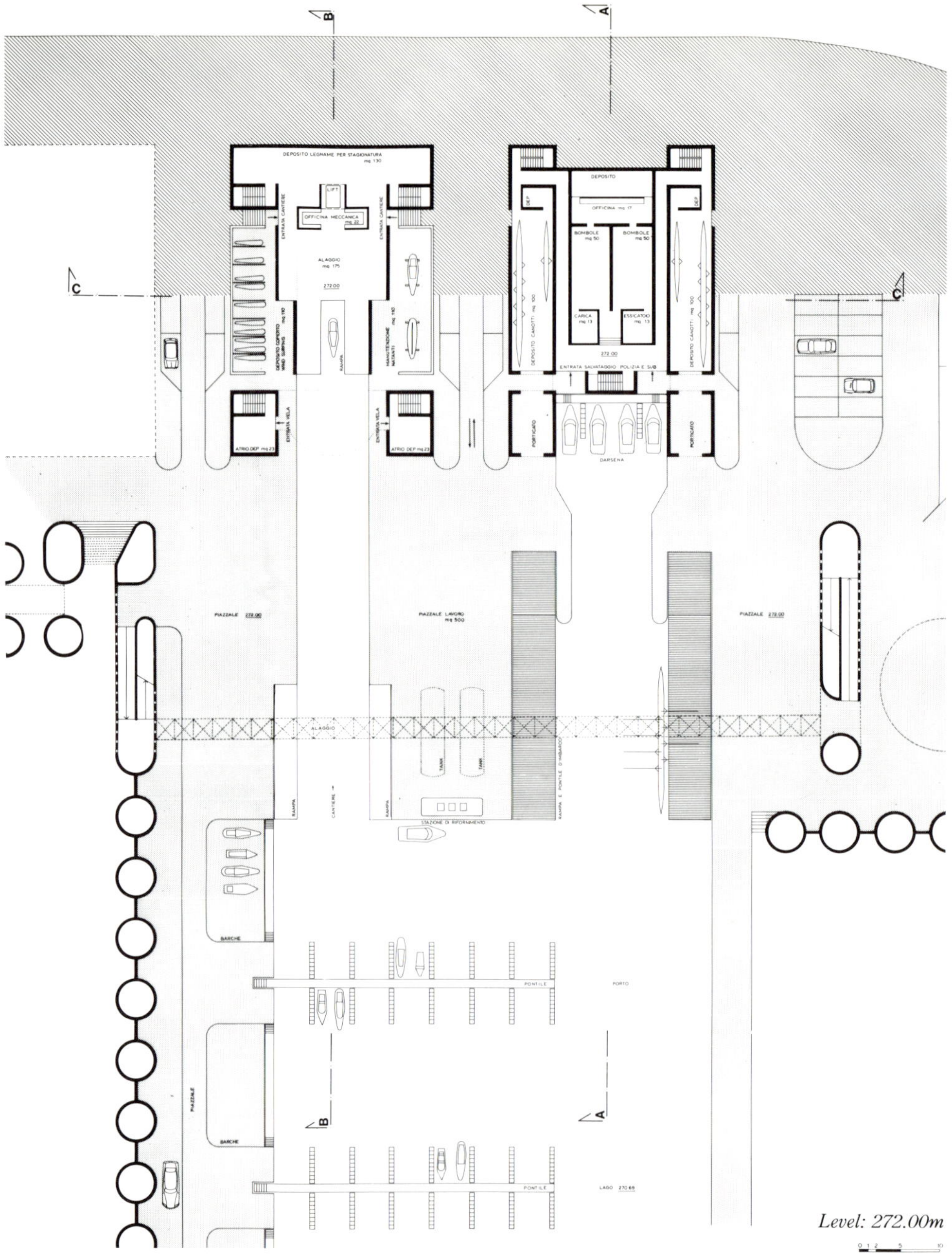

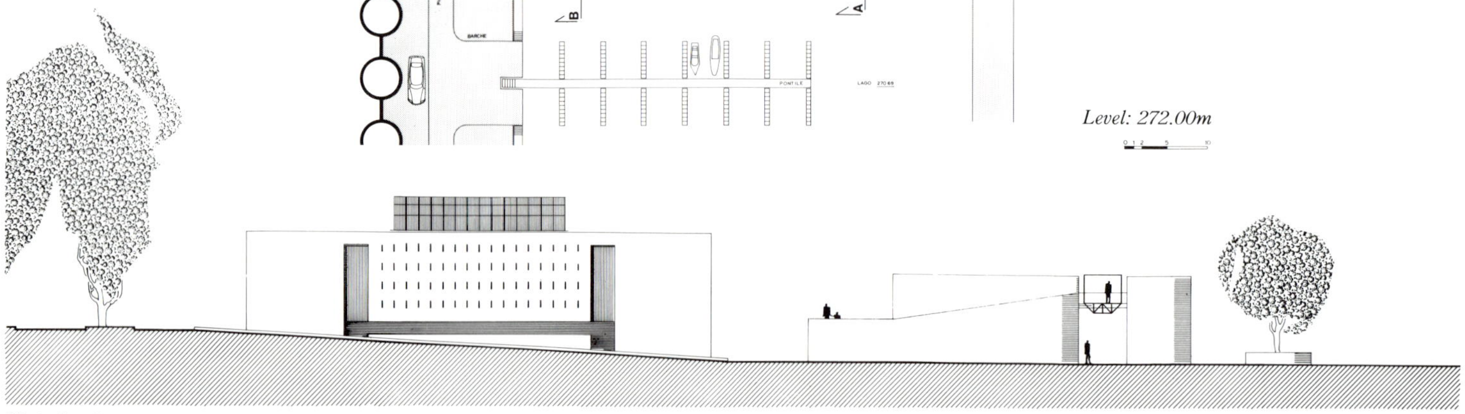

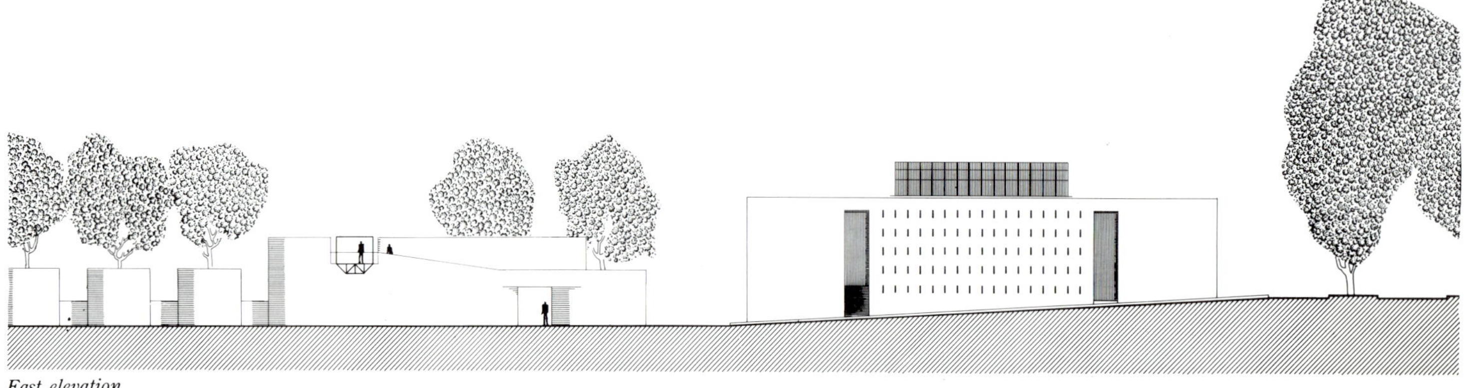

West elevation

East elevation

Level: 272.00m

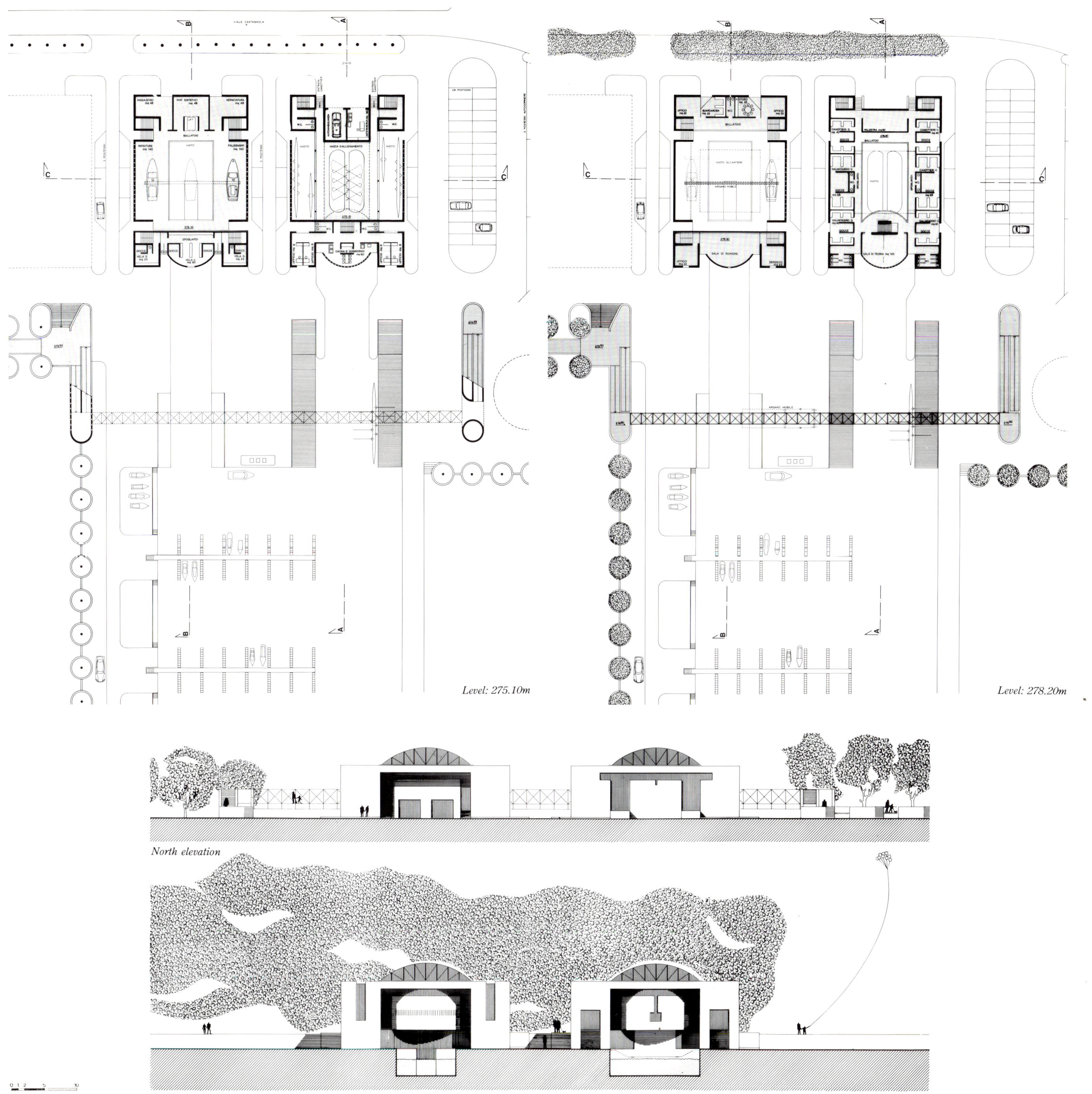

Level: 275.10m
Level: 278.20m
North elevation
South elevation

The complex is near the village, on the slope of a mountain, and appears like a compact citadel that opens itself toward the magnificent surrounding landscape. Its residential buildings, like sections of a fan, are arranged around the central core that houses different services.

The plan has six towers, placed along the perimeter of a large, covered hall, and a lower section with parking lots, housing for personnel, and space for various other uses. The entrance to the residence is provided by this building; its roof provides a square opening over the landscape.

Every tower shelters rooms on the ground floor (that function as an extension of the central hall) for special equipment or services, a restaurant, the kitchen, stores and banks, medical equipment, the entrance, and a church. A swimming pool and various equipment for different sports are located in the lower levels. From the large central hall, illuminated by natural light, one can reach a solarium, located on the mountain slope, nearly level with the towers' roofs.

All vertical connections in each tower are located toward the interior and all are linked together by a balcony that, at mezzanine level, lines the inside central hall. All of the upper floors of the towers house different kinds of living quarters. Bedrooms face the interior of the towers while living rooms overlook the valley. The particular triangular form of the loggias allows a view over the landscape to people sitting in them, creates a protected area, and at the same time lets natural light penetrate from above the interior.

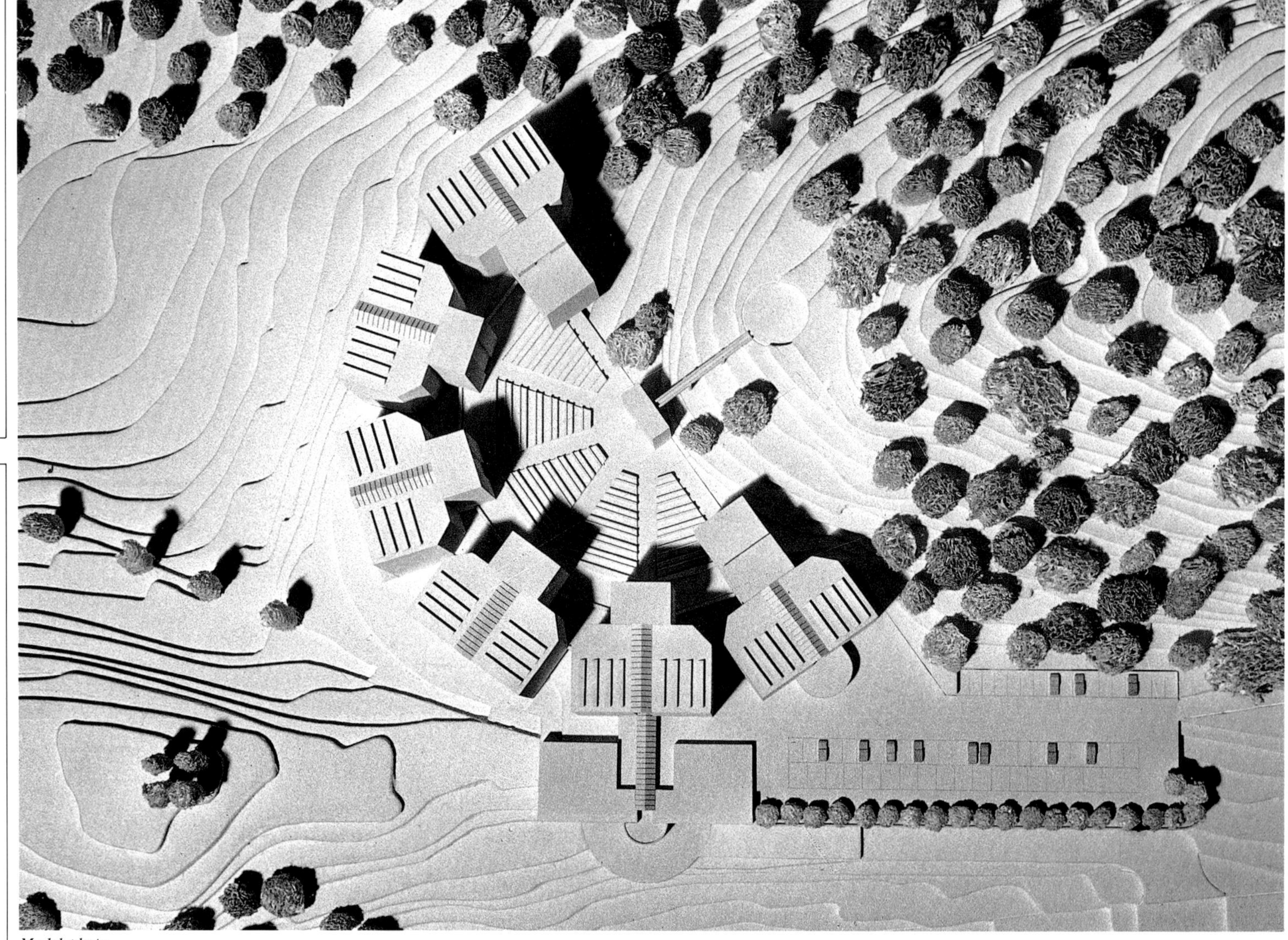

Model photo

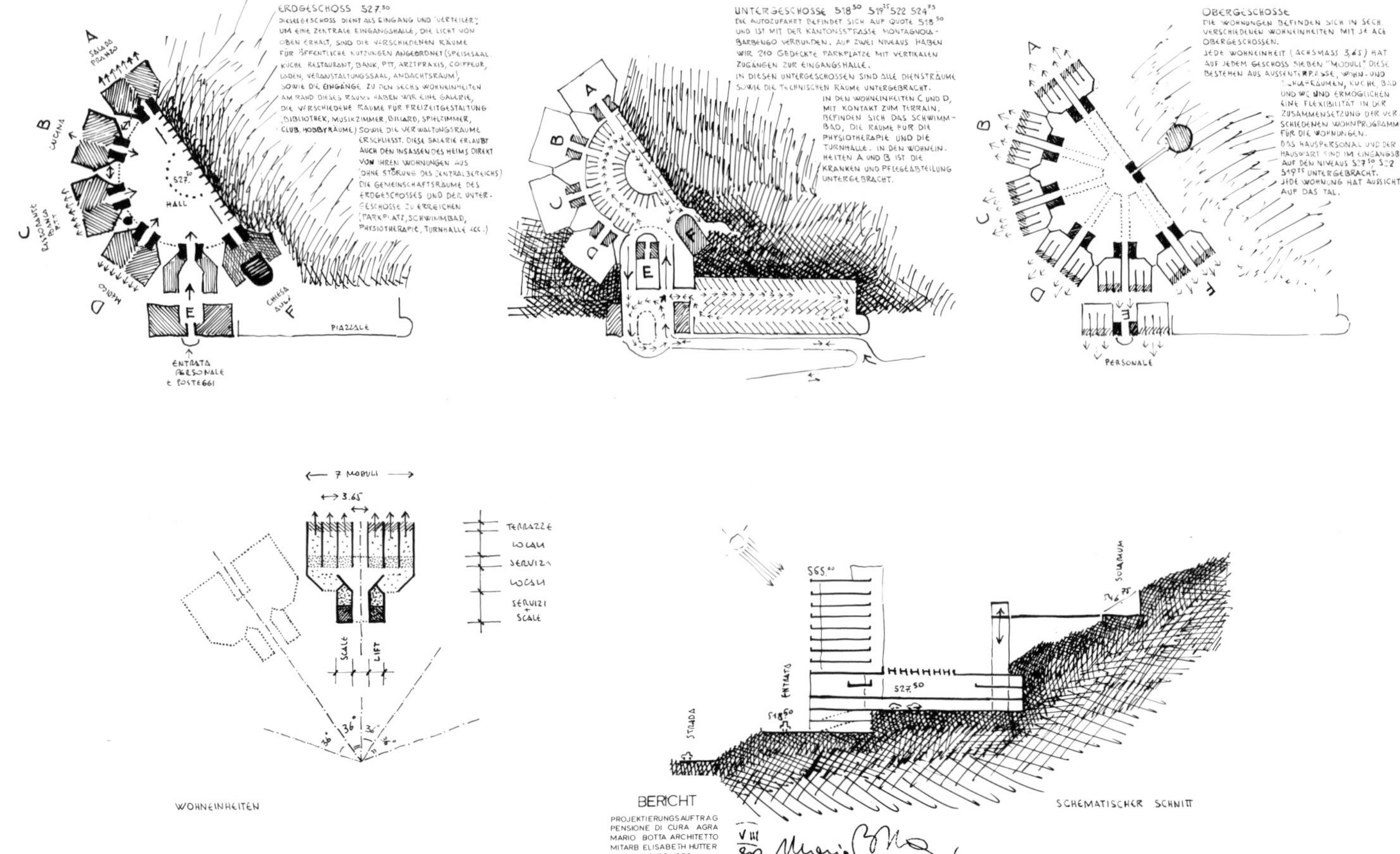

Gallery

First & second floors

Typical floor

Basement level 2

Basement level 1

Ground floor

Basement level 3

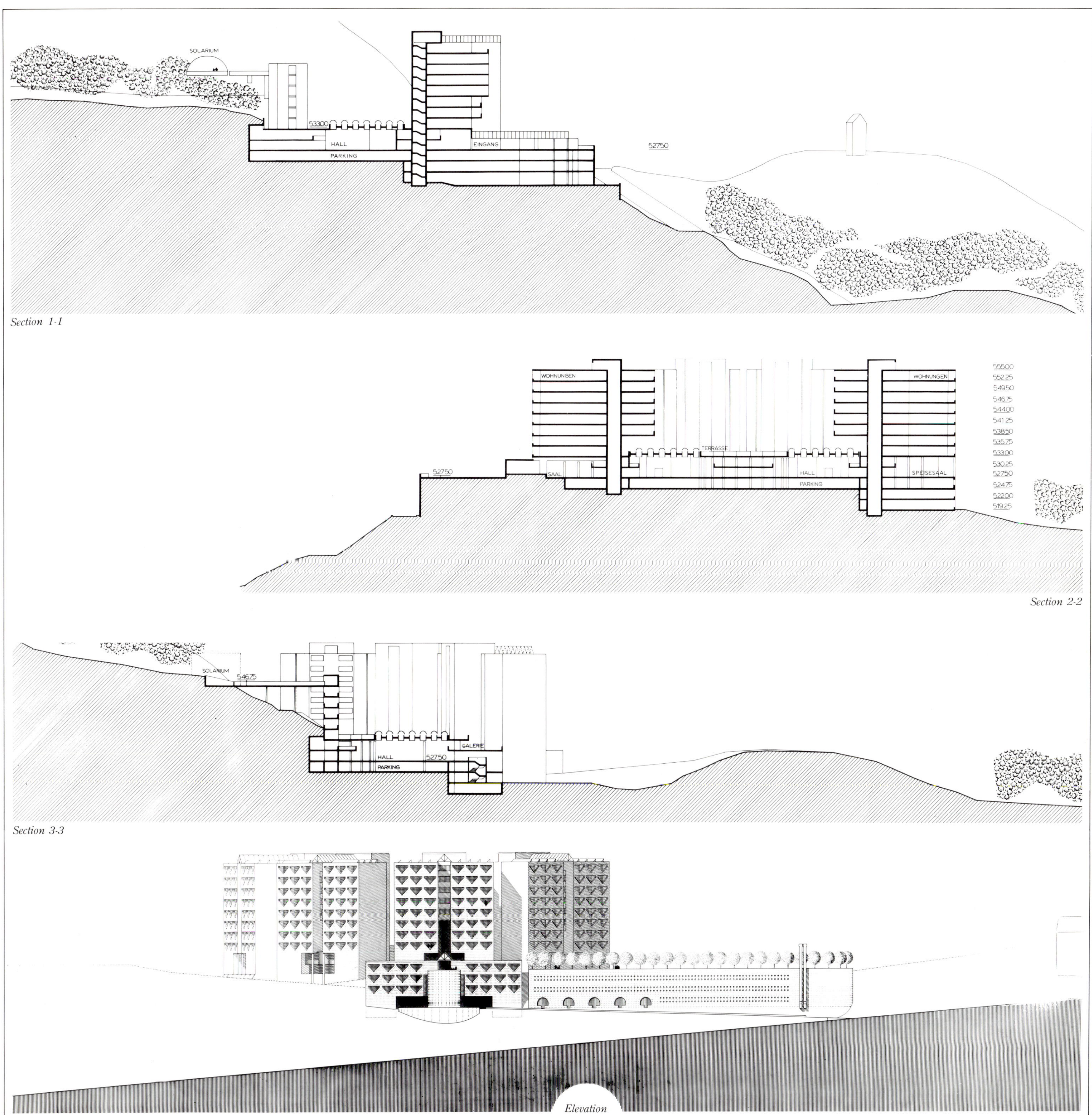

SOLARIUM
53300
HALL
PARKING
EINGANG
52750
Section 1-1
WOHNUNGEN
WOHNUNGEN
55600
56225
54950
54675
54400
54125
53850
53575
53300
53025
52750
52475
52200
51925
52750
SAAL
TERRASSE
HALL
PARKING
SPEISESAAL
Section 2-2
SOLARIUM
54675
GALERIE
HALL
52750
PARKING
Section 3-3
Elevation

Model photo

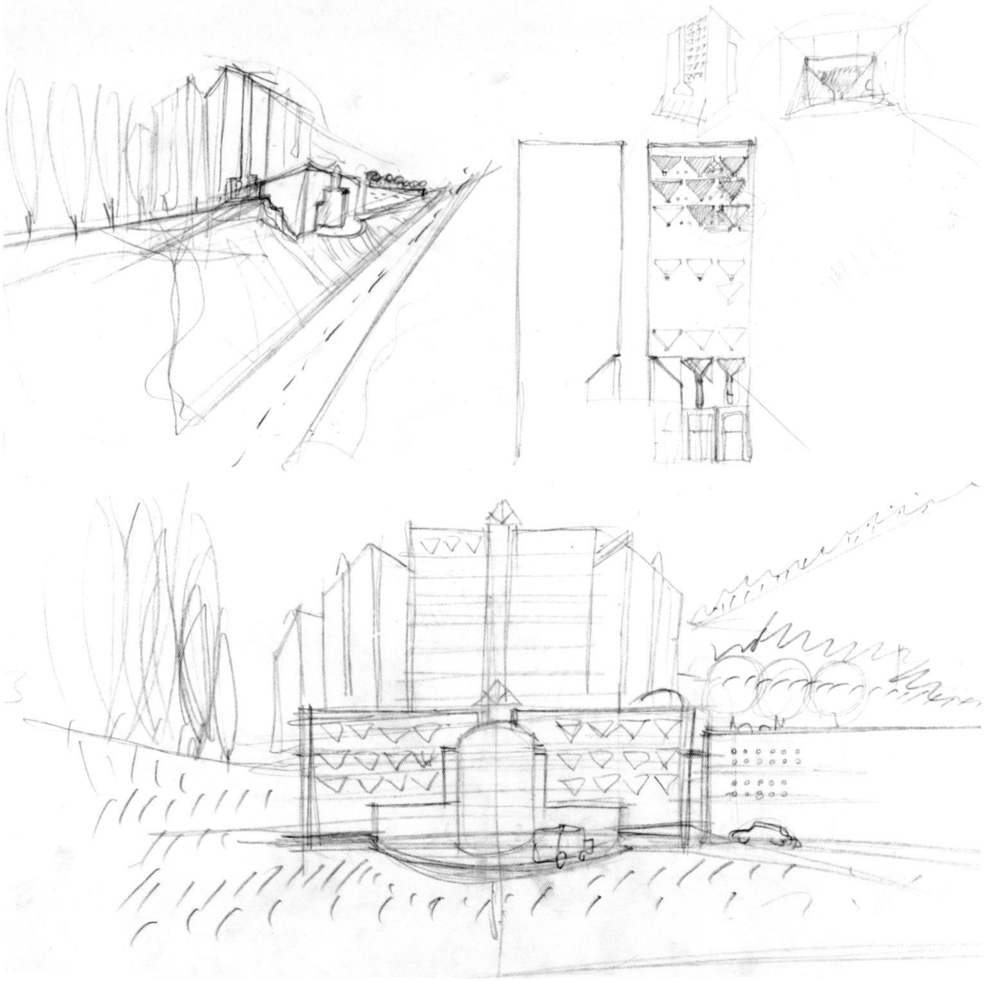

Preliminary study

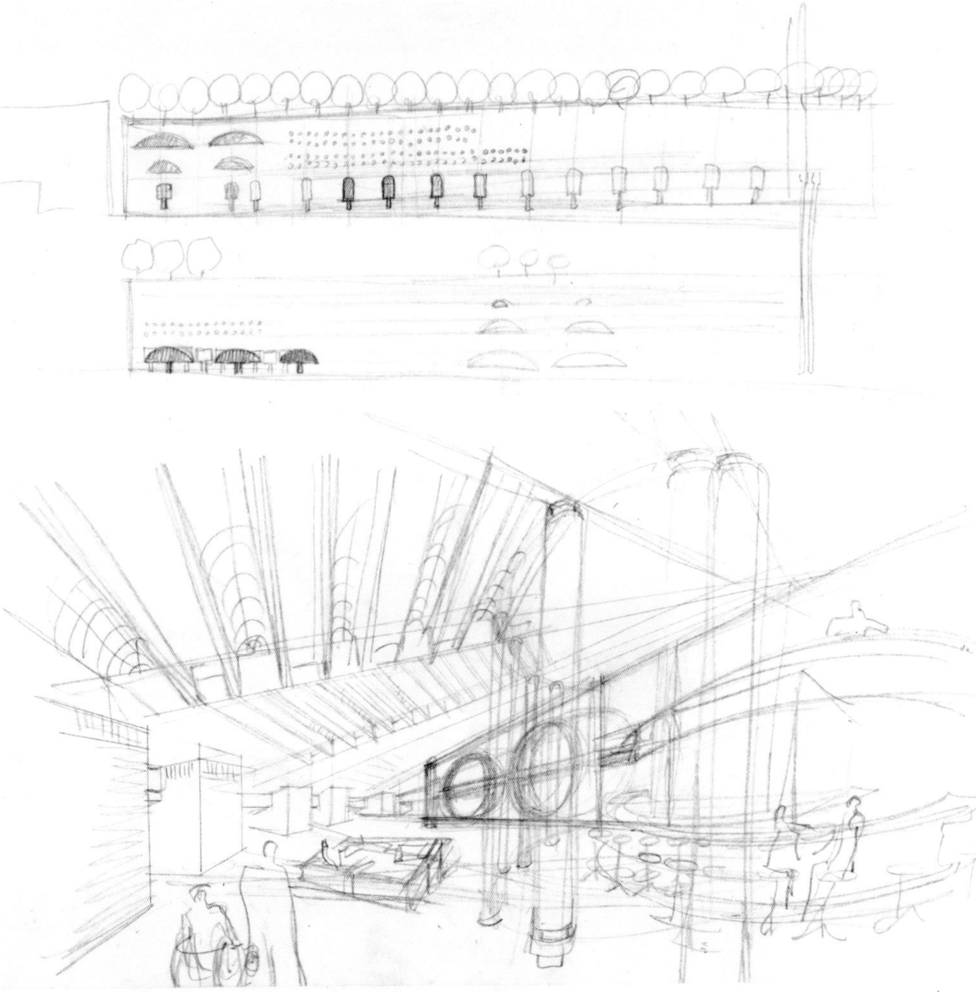

Preliminary study

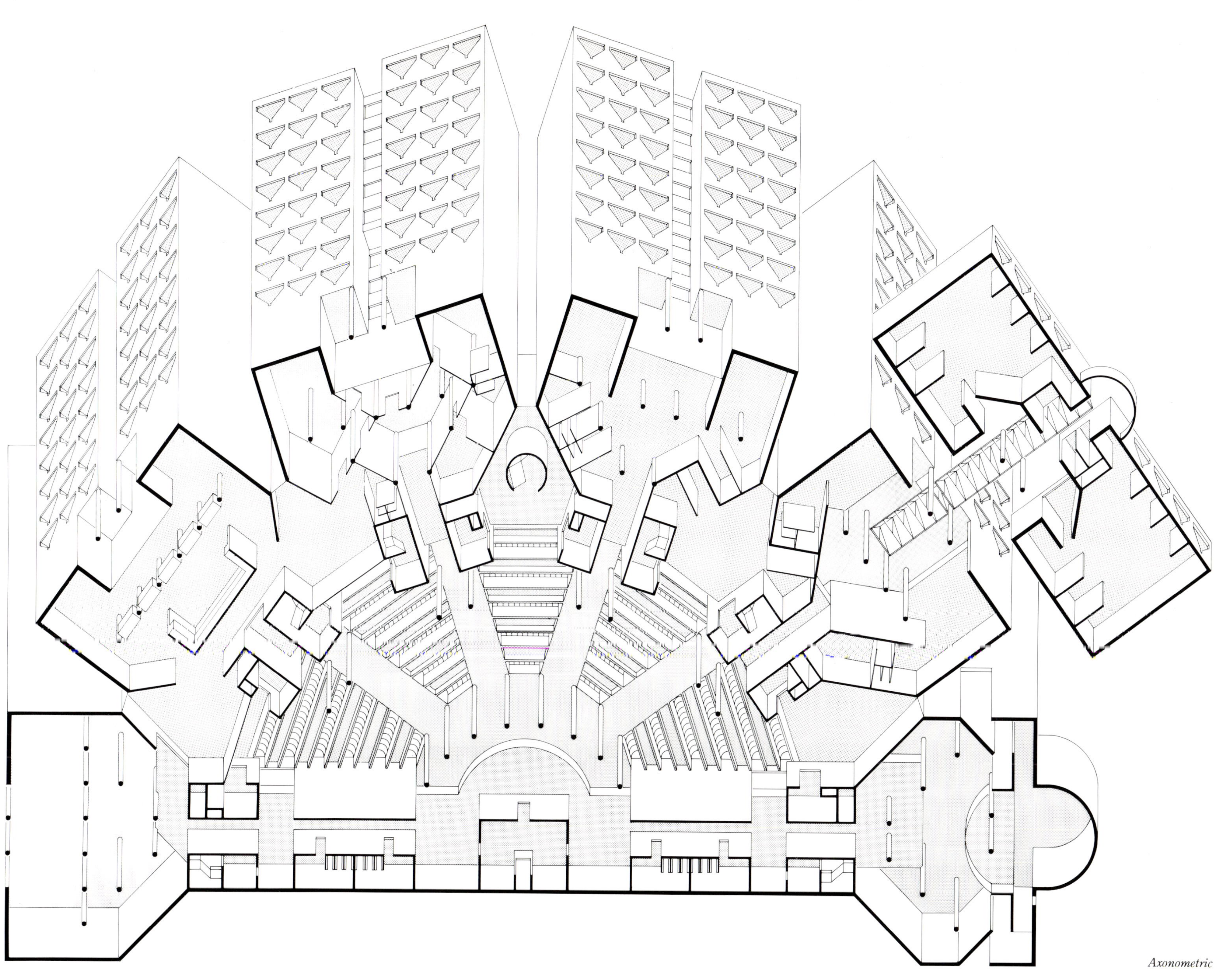

Axonometric

Crafts Center at Balerna, Switzerland, 1979 (project)

The site for which the center is projected has a triangular shape, with railroad tracks to the east and a stream and a street to the south. The project includes two buildings: the first, along the street, provides the entrance to the center through a wide central arch and houses apartments; the second, adjacent to the first, has artisans' workshops and storehouses.

The cylindrical and rectangular volumes of the center duplicate those of the museum projected for Guernica, with the difference that in Guernica the two volumes were, as in the Capuchin Library at Lugano, buried into the ground. Corresponding to the entrance, the cylinder housing the workshops is cut into two sections by a truck passage; this passage receives light from a central opening in the roof, the only space that links together the two independent semicircular volumes.

The wide arches allow the merging of the workshops' space with the central space; the thick perimetric wall, as in the house at Manno, has thin vertical incisions.

Preliminary study

Basement

Ground floor

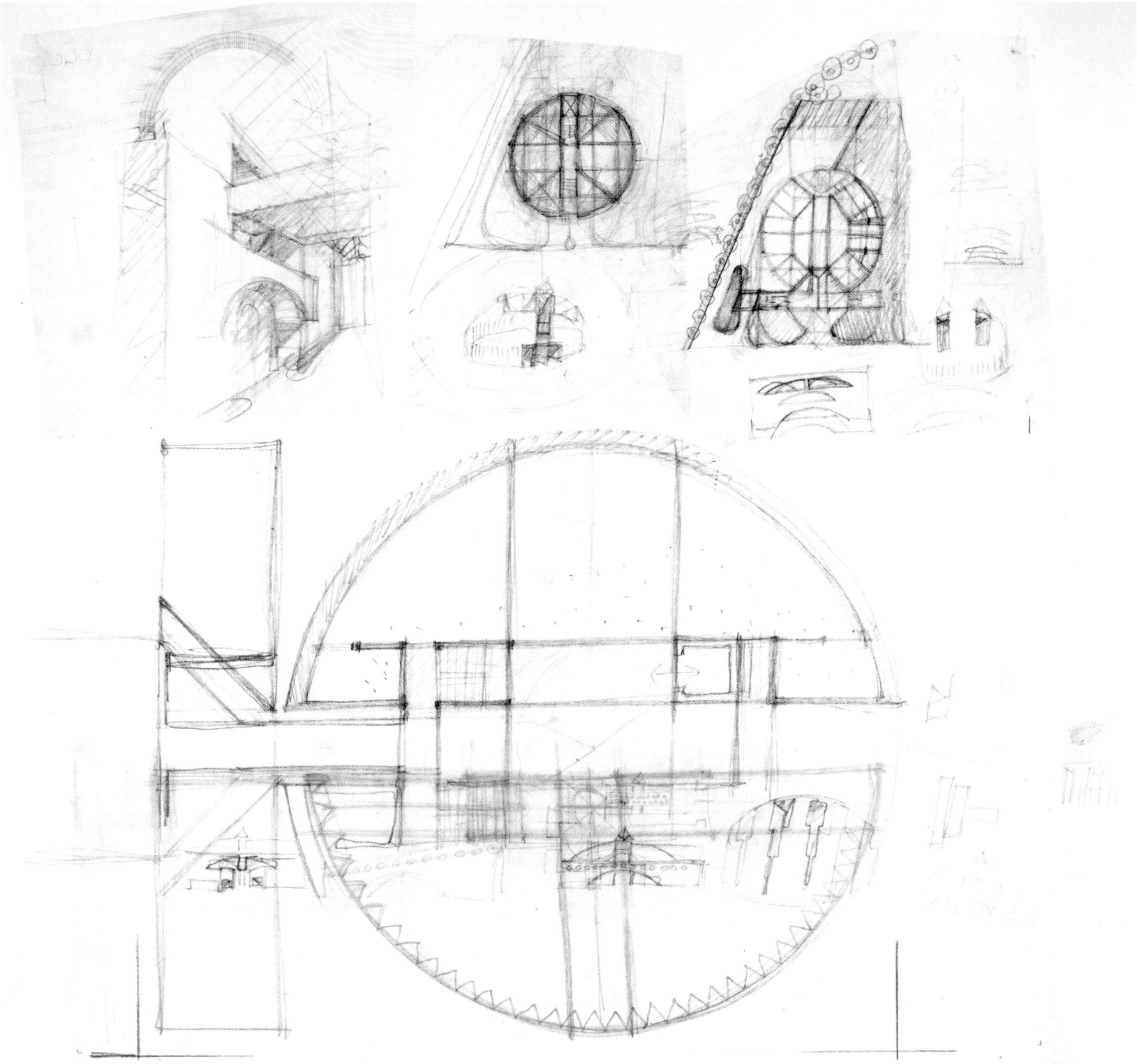

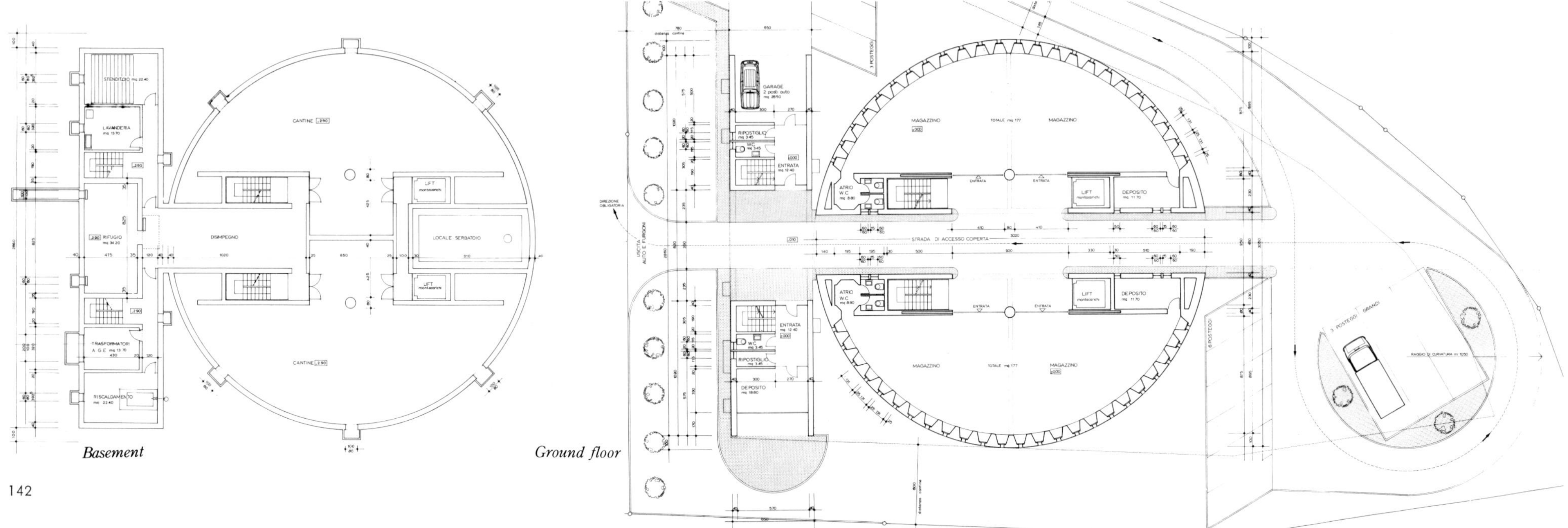

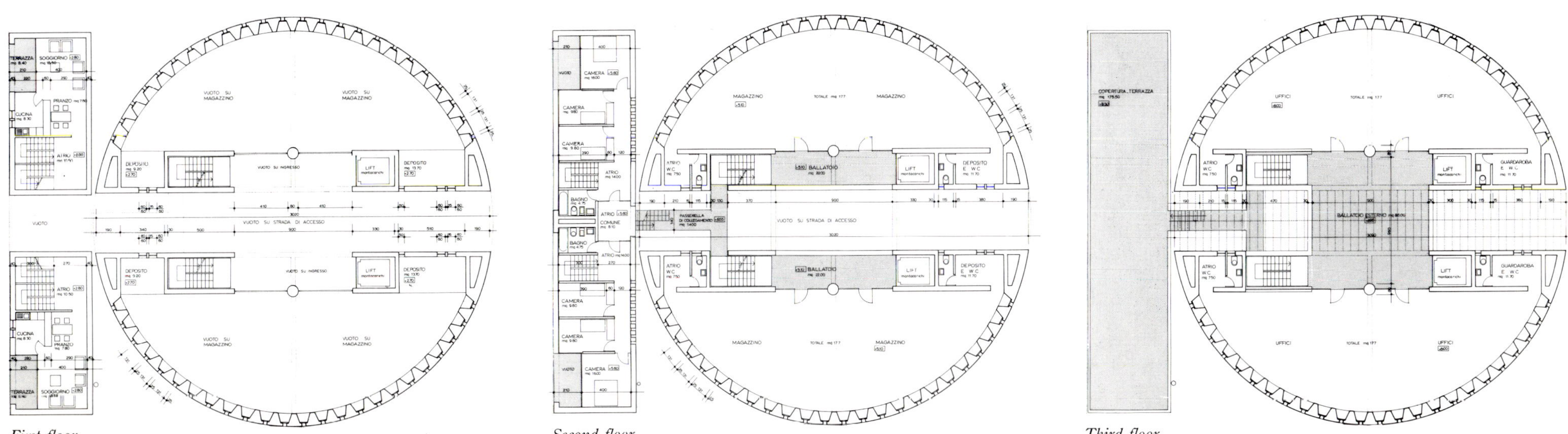

Preliminary study

First floor   *Second floor*   *Third floor*

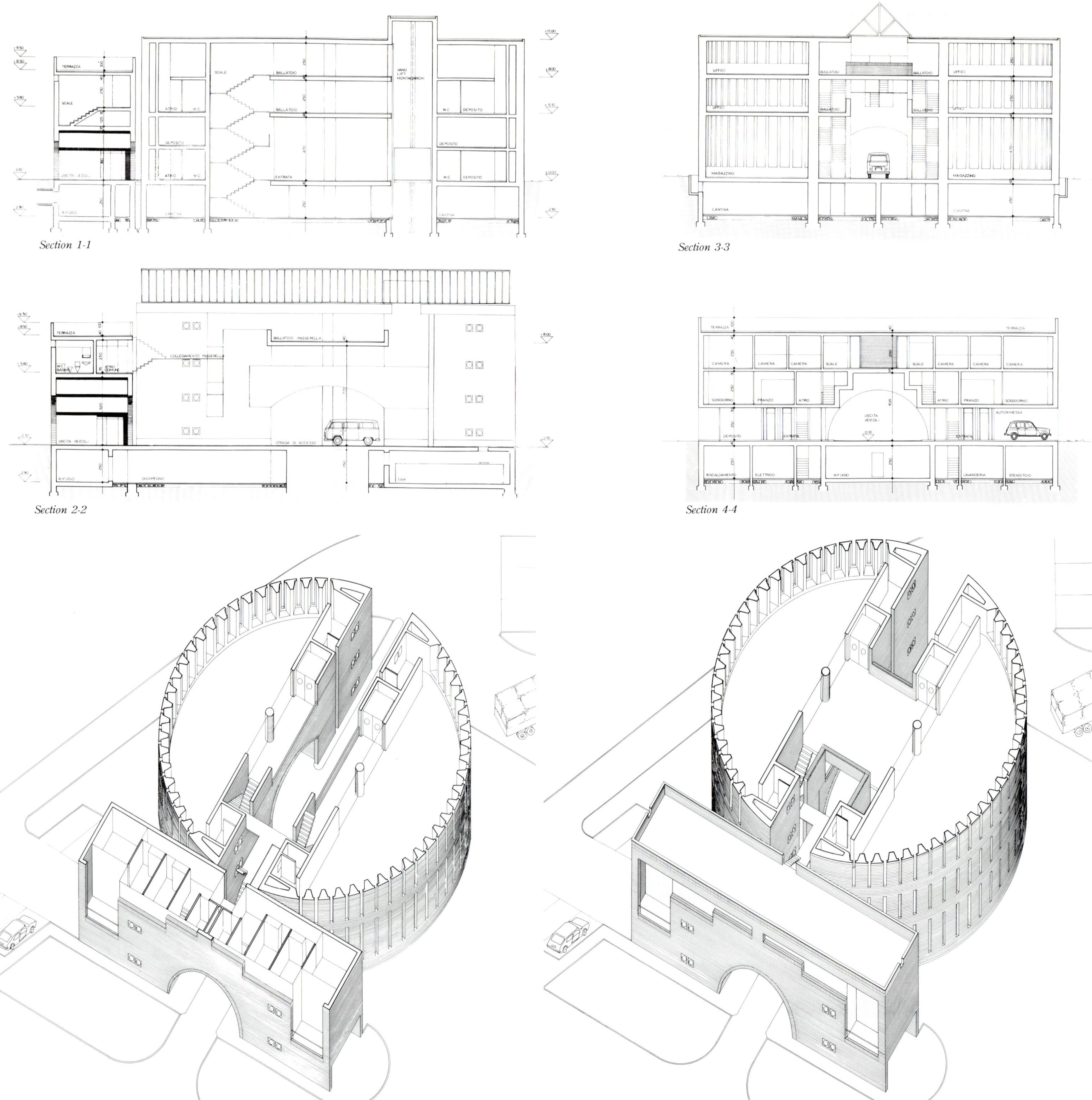

Section 1-1

Section 3-3

Section 2-2

Section 4-4

Axonometrics

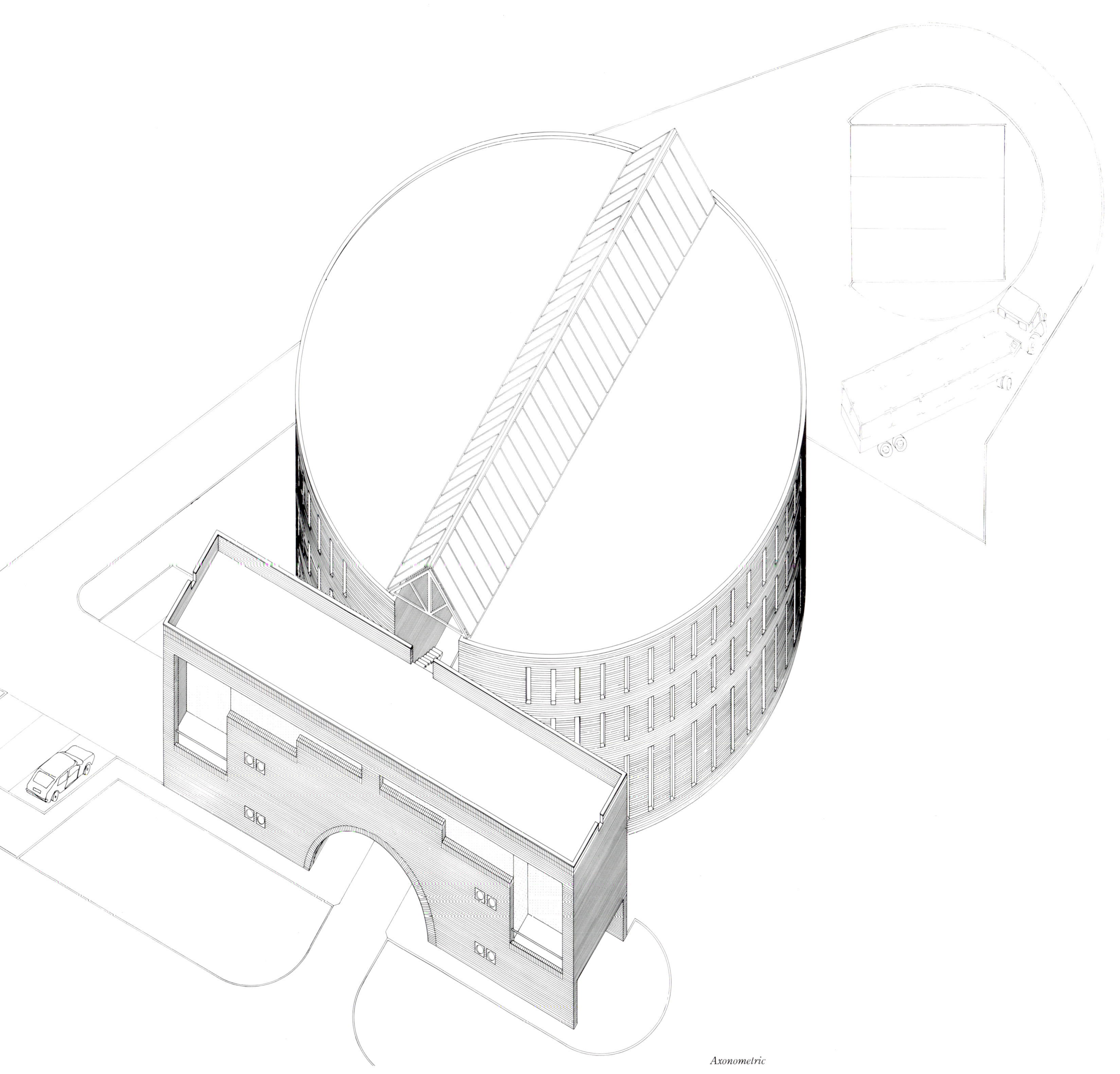

Axonometric

Berlin 1856

Berlin 1980

The area designated for the project is situated between the Nationalgalerie by Mies van der Rohe to the east; the Shell Haus by Fahrenkamp in the opposite direction; the Landwehrkanal to the south and the open space of the Tiergarten to the north. Other buildings in its proximity include the old Matthaikirche, the Philharmonia, and the Staatsbibliothek by Scharoun. The texture of the old historic city was completely destroyed by World War II and later interventions. The project proposes to recreate a compact, unified texture through a system of city blocks. The solid row of buildings will contrast on one side with the void of the canal, and on the other with the large open space of the Tiergarten.

The plan is divided into two parts: the first is the Science Center, along the canal and facing south; the second, toward the north, is a housing project. This second part includes a group of internal courtyards separated by transversal housing duplexes, and larger perimetric structures aligned with the Science Center. The triangular building toward the canal incorporates the existing building. Its front, which spreads toward the Shell Haus, consists of a continuous wall pierced by a large opening, the new entrance to the Center. On the opposite corner, toward the Nationalgalerie, the new structure does not extend to the existing building; the space left empty thus becomes a small square that faces the entrance to the museum.

The new L-shaped construction has room for different offices of various sizes located around a central arcade illuminated by a skylight on the roof, upon which there will be rows of trees. The building will be nineteen meters tall — the height of the existing building.

1900 : Diplomatic district

Present : Mixed use district

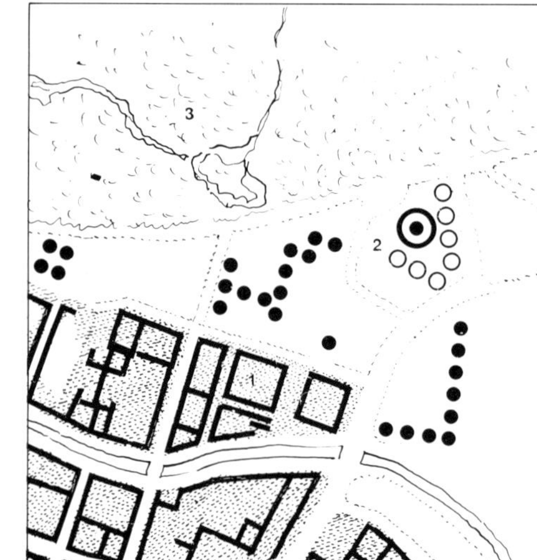

Site plan

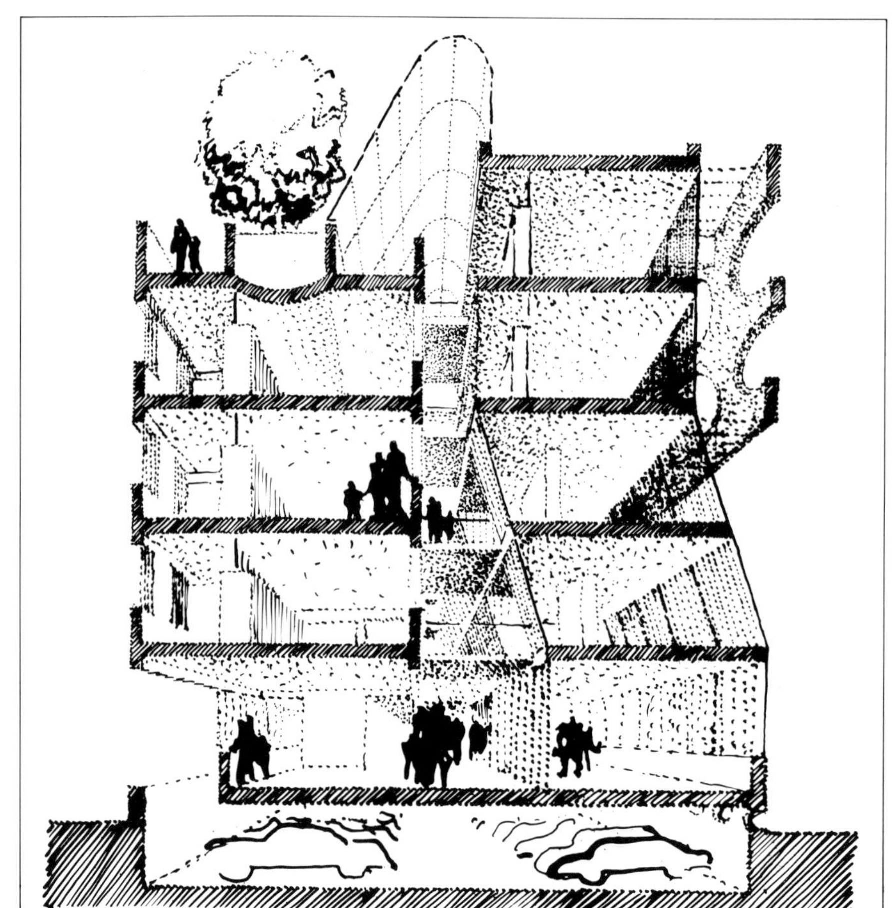

Perspective

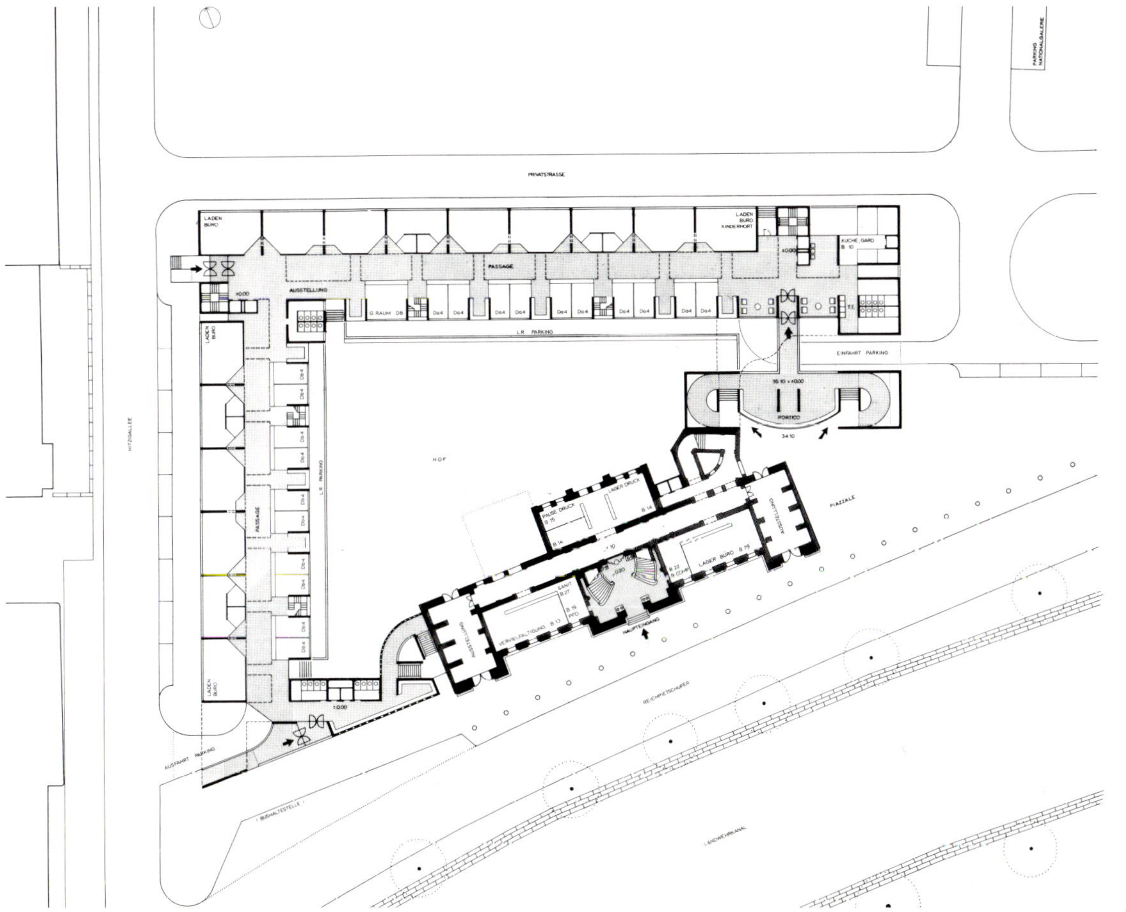

Perspective

Ground floor

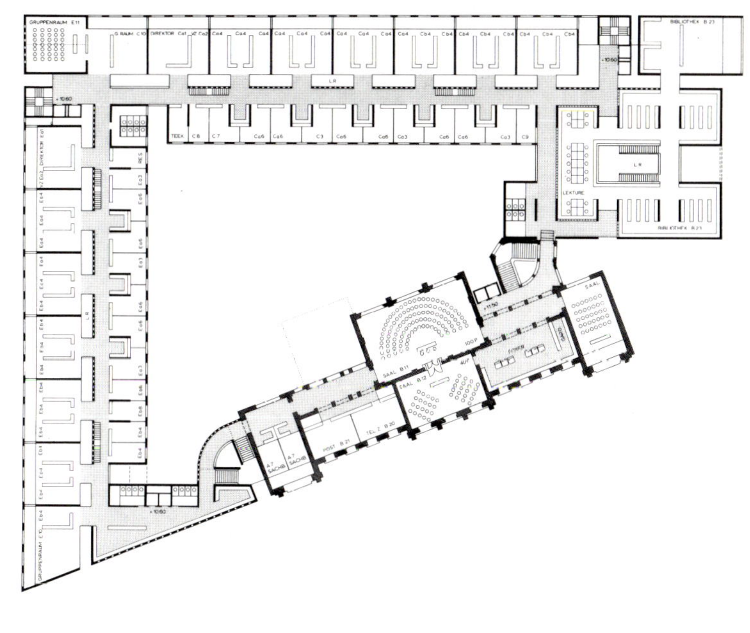

Third floor

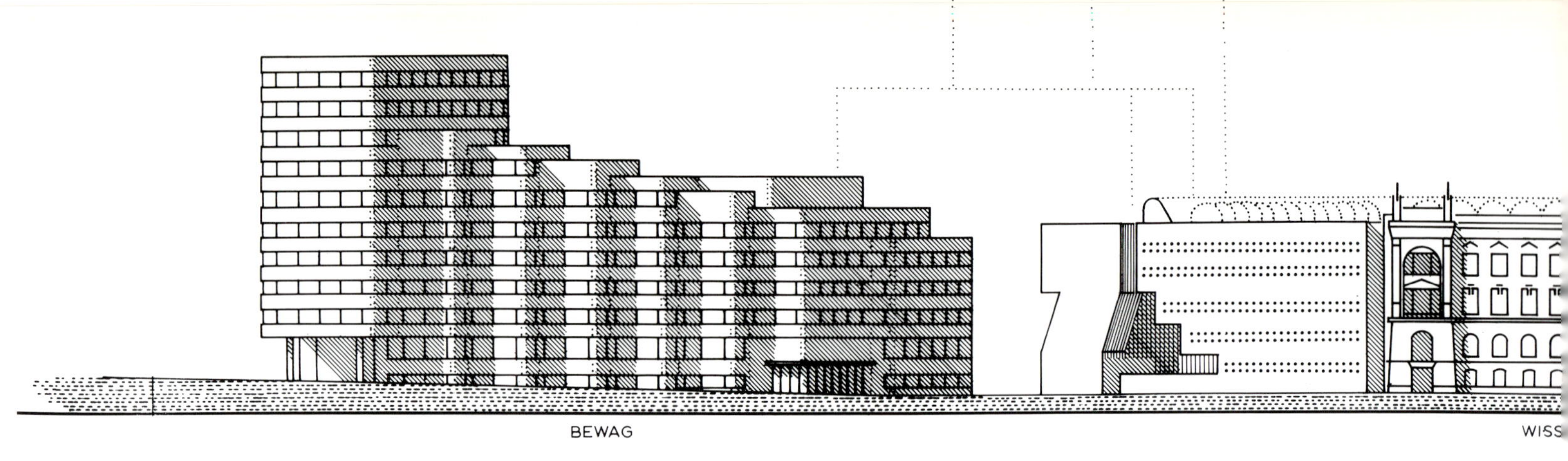

BEWAG
WISS

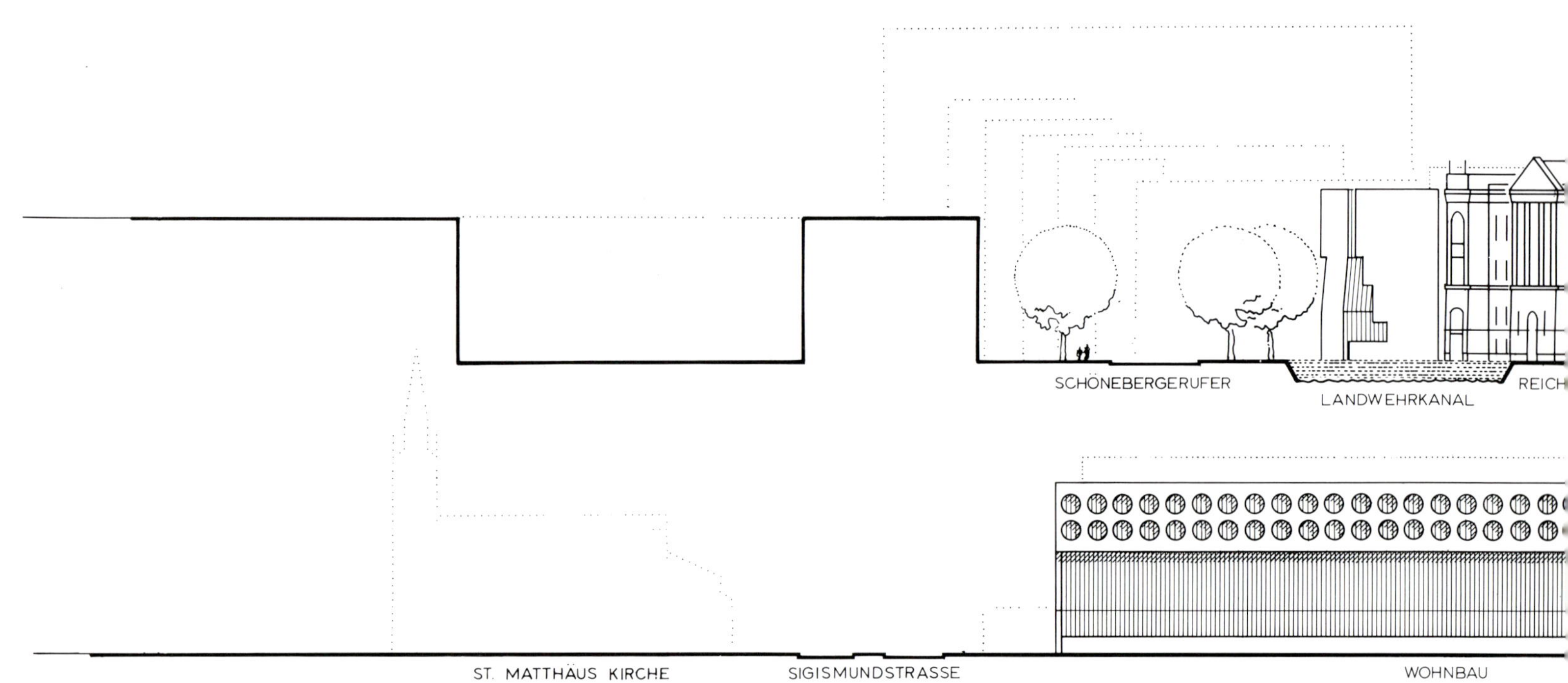

SCHONEBERGERUFER
LANDWEHRKANAL
REICH
ST. MATTHAUS KIRCHE
SIGISMUNDSTRASSE
WOHNBAU

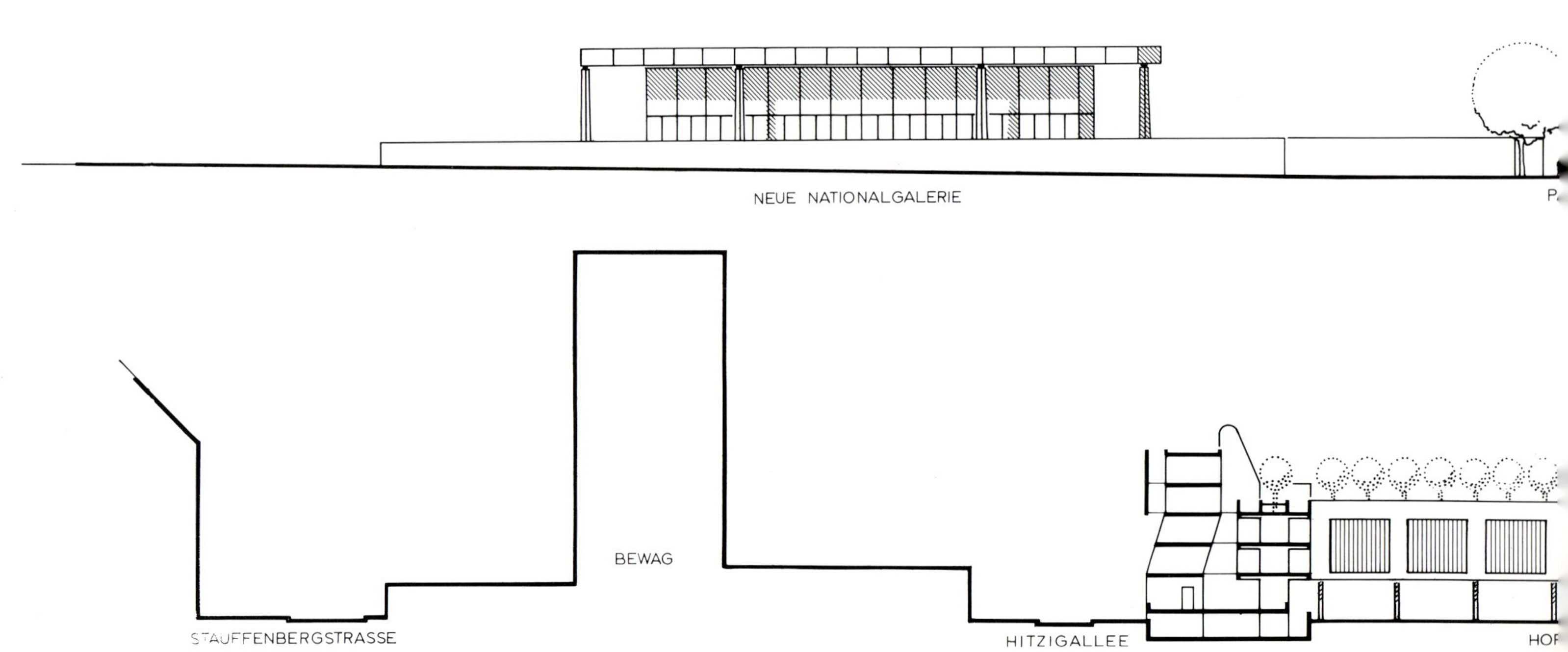

NEUE NATIONALGALERIE
P.
STAUFFENBERGSTRASSE
BEWAG
HITZIGALLEE
HOF

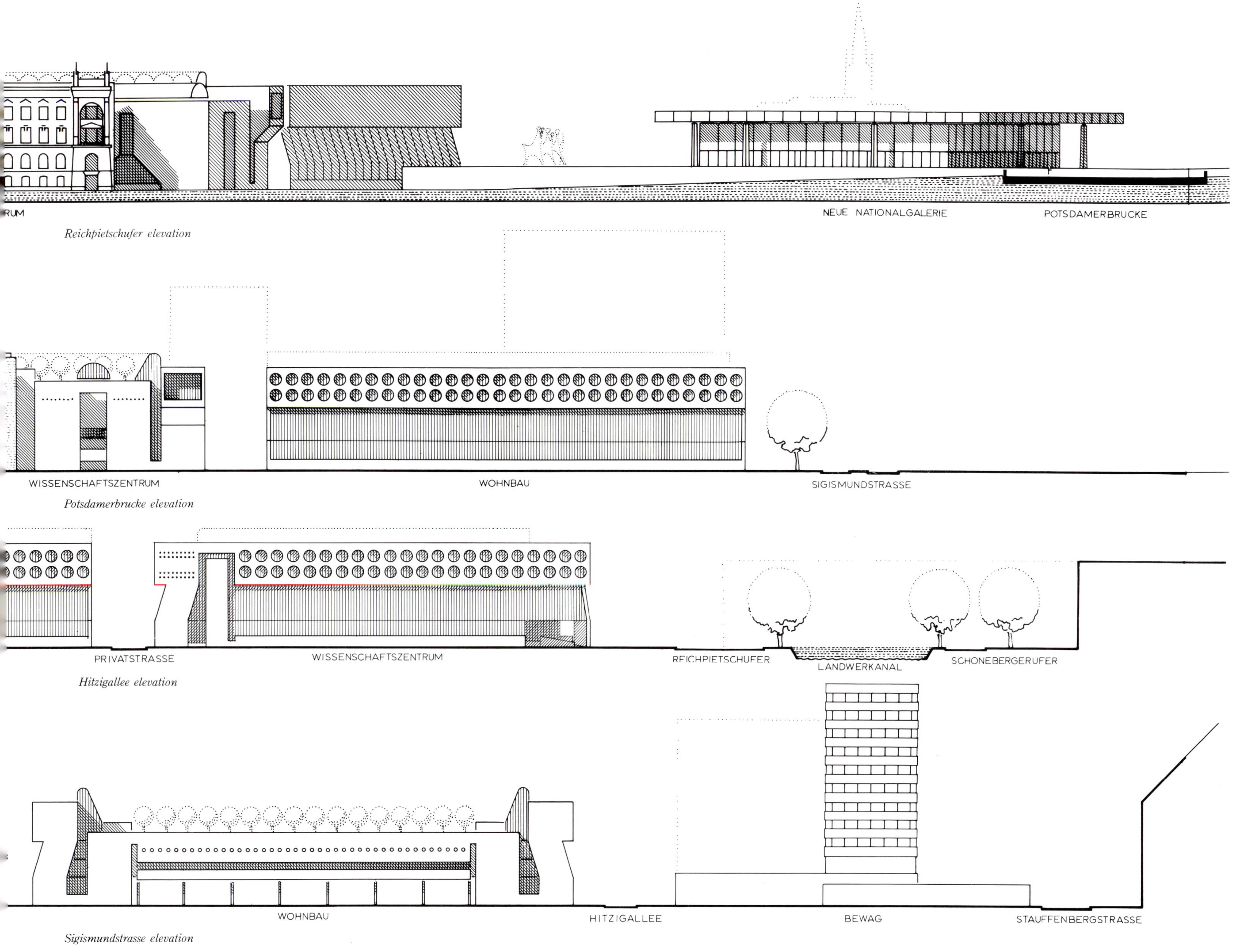

Reichpietschufer elevation

Potsdamerbrucke elevation

Hitzigallee elevation

Sigismundstrasse elevation

Section through Wohnbau

149

The competition for this project was held when the city was being considered as a permanent home for Picasso's painting *Guernica* and its seventy-two preparatory sketches. The site for the proposed museum is in the Plaza de la Union, next to the Cathedral and the Casa de la Giunta, which are the two most important institutions of the city.

The museum itself is dug into the ground at the center of the large courtyard in which the existing Neoclassical building (shaped like a C), presently housing a school, would eventually shelter the museum offices and related spaces. The covering of the museum reshapes the form of the square, whose open side is delimited by a long wall pierced by an arch. At the extremities of this new façade, opposite the two ends of the semi-circular building, are two volumes in which are located the stairs that link the underground museum and its offices.

From the street level two ramps lead either to the square or to the museum entrance. In the underground hall, along the curved, segmented wall, next to the ramps, the seventy-two sketches are exhibited, while on the main wall the painting, illuminated by the natural light descending from above, is constantly visible.

The other semicircular volume, also underground and accessible through an independent stairway, will be used as an auditorium.

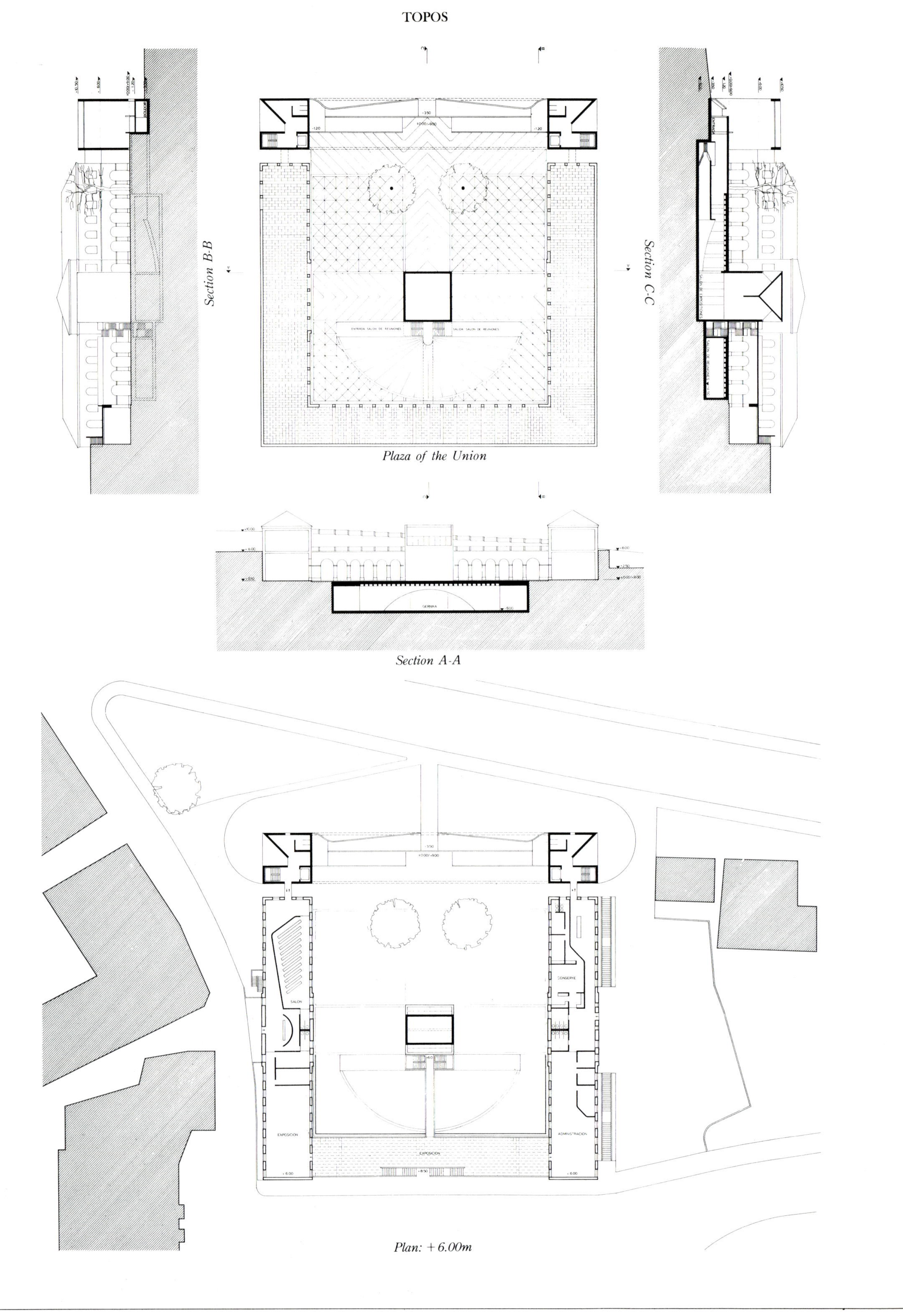

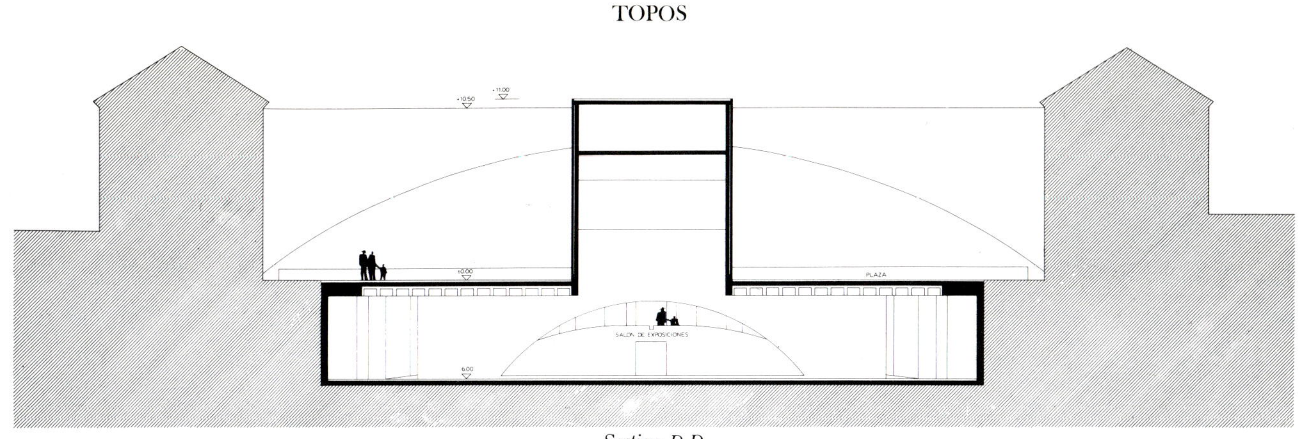

Section D-D

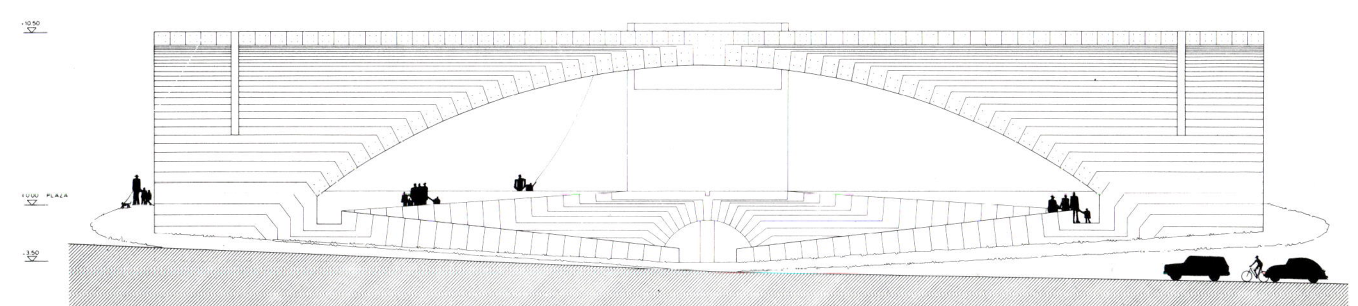

Elevation

Underground museum level

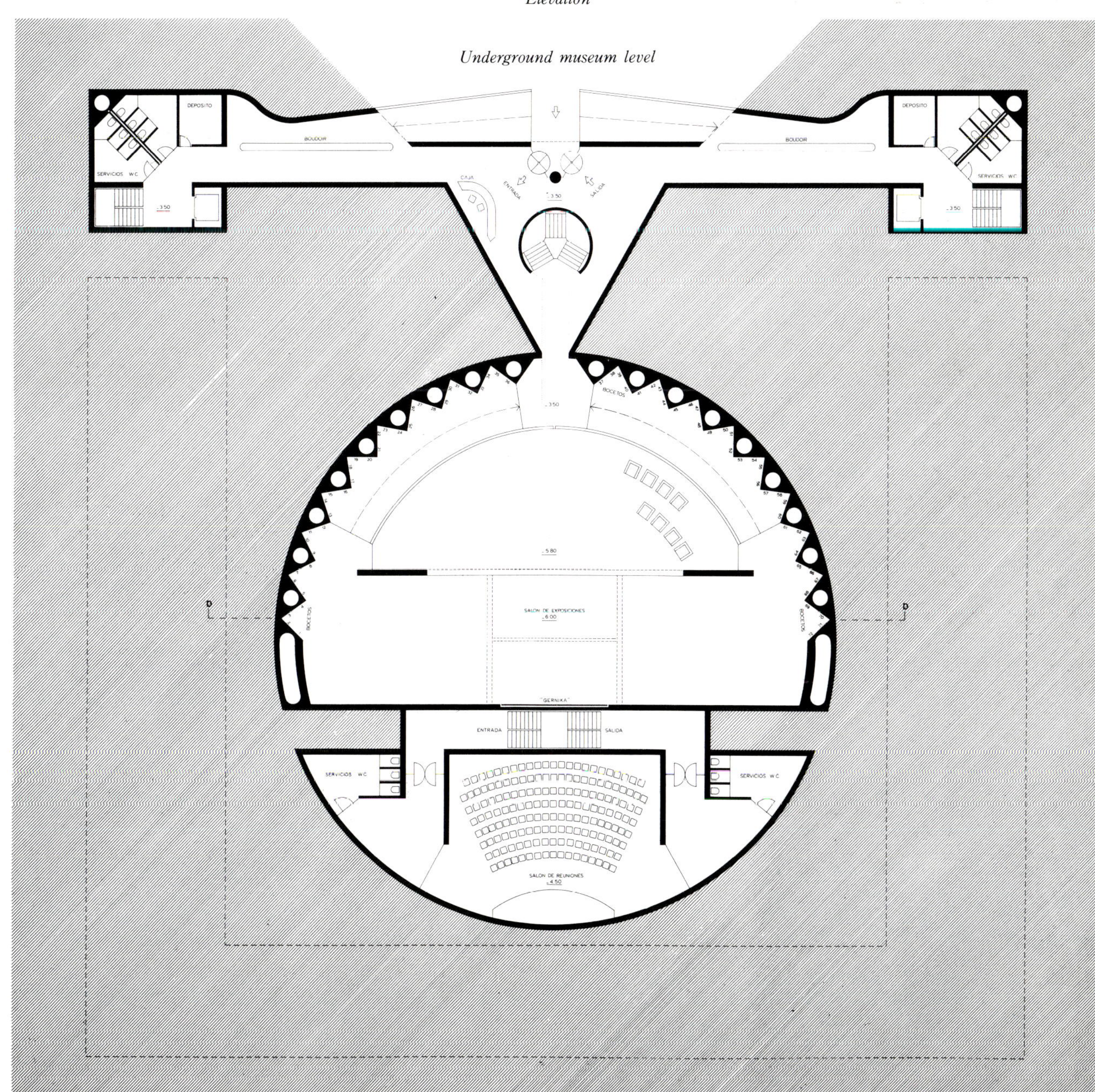

The house is located on a steep slope. The central volume, in which the stairs and secondary spaces are located, appears to lean against the mountain behind it and opens onto a valley through a large central aperture and two lateral cylindrical structures. As in the house at Viganello, cars can be parked on the road and a walk leads to the entrance, which is deeply cut into the central volume of the house. Bedrooms are on the ground floor; the living room and the covered terrace on the upper level extends over the top of the two semicylindrical volumes.

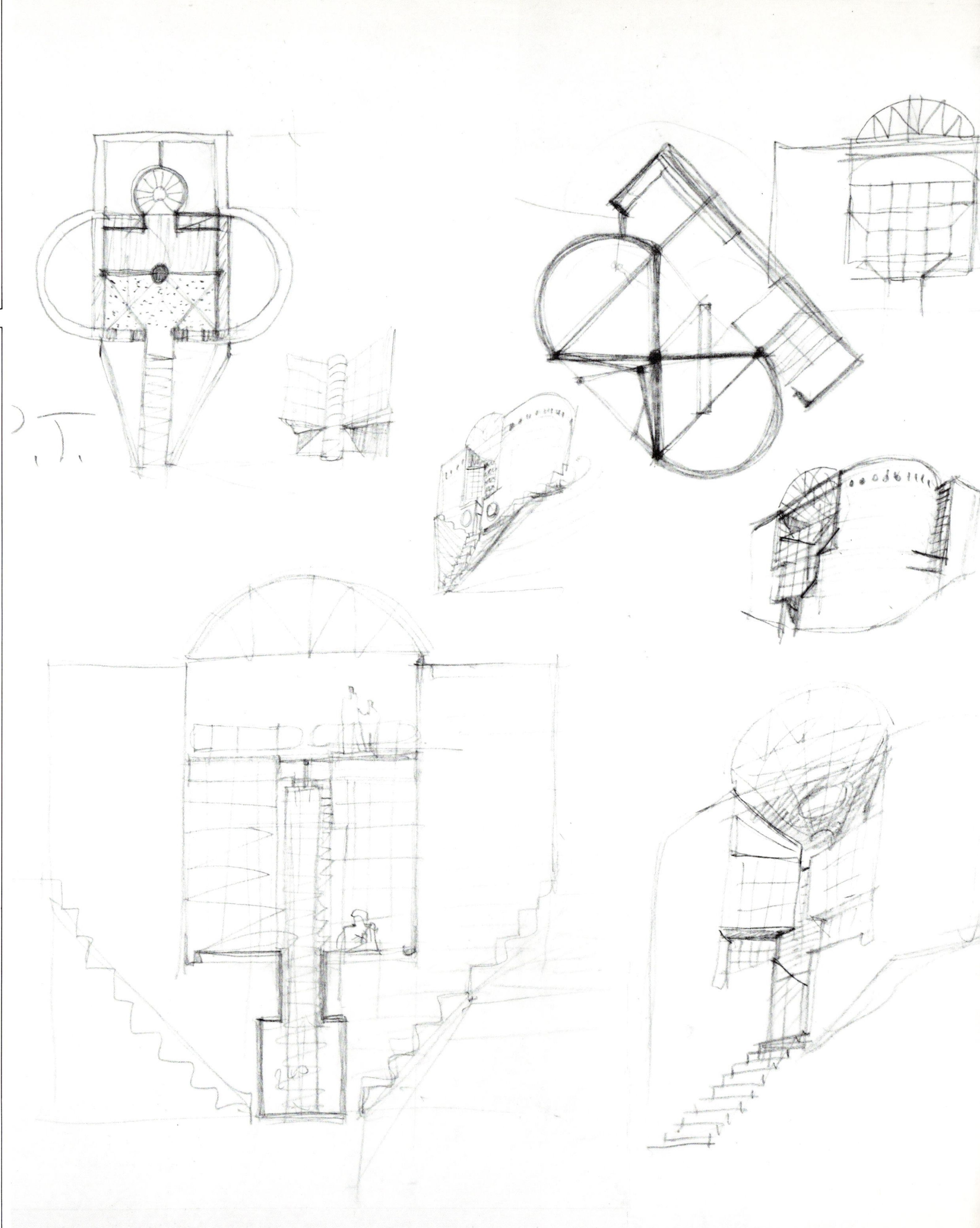

Preliminary study

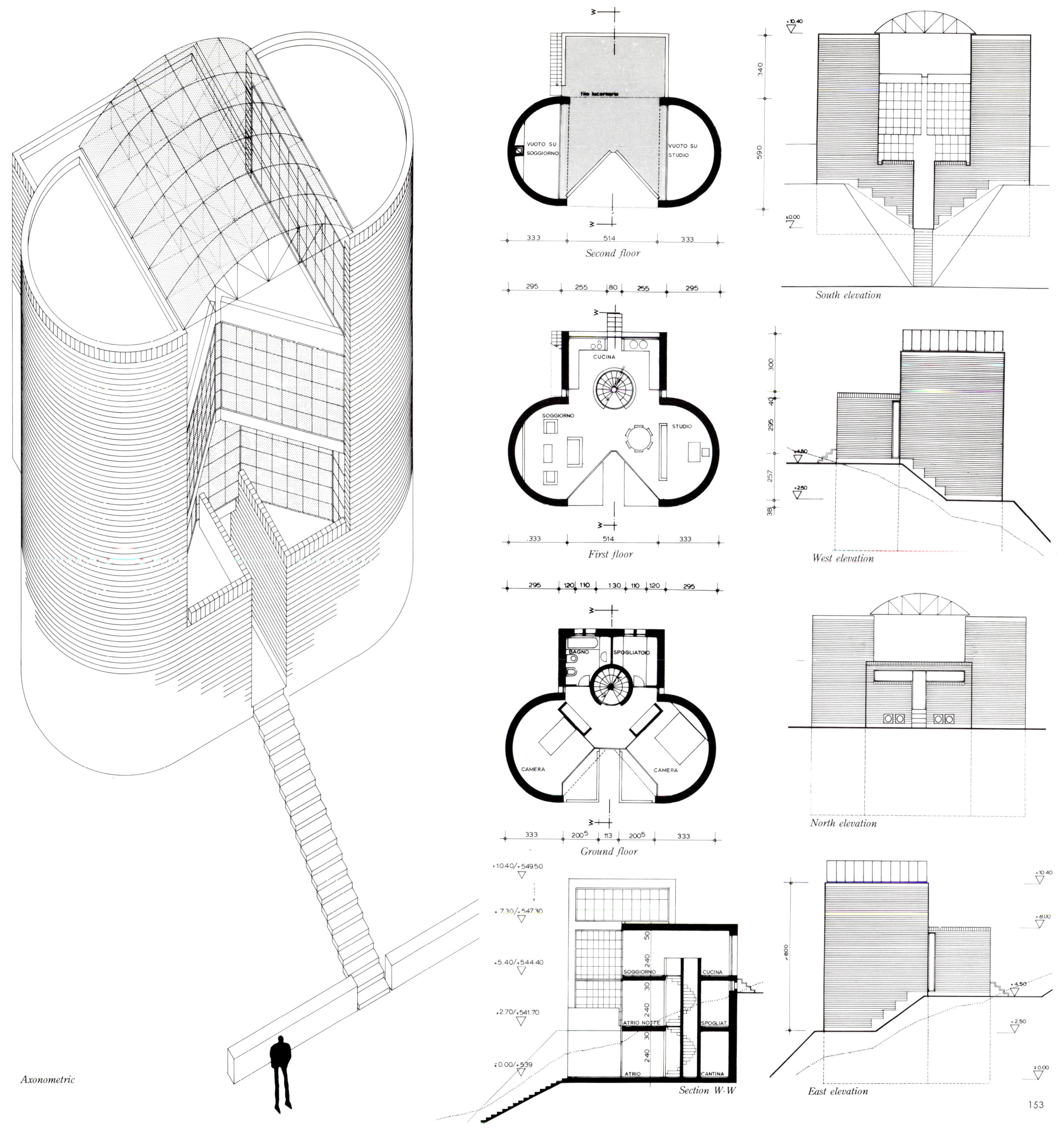

VUOTO SU SOGGIORNO
VUOTO SU STUDIO
333 514 333
Second floor
CUCINA
SOGGIORNO
STUDIO
295 255 80 255 295
333 514 333
First floor
BAGNO
SPOGLIATOIO
CAMERA
CAMERA
295 120 110 130 110 120 295
333 200⁵ 113 200⁵ 333
Ground floor
South elevation
West elevation
North elevation
+10.40/+549.50
+7.30/+547.30
+5.40/+544.40
+2.70/+541.70
+0.00/+539
SOGGIORNO
CUCINA
ATRIO NOTTE
SPOGLIAT.
ATRIO
CANTINA
Section W-W
East elevation
Axonometric

*Office Building at Lugano,
Switzerland, 1981–85
(under construction)*

The building, which at one of its corners overlooks a large square, reestablishes the unity of the nineteenth-century city block located next to the historic center of Lugano. As in the State Bank at Fribourg the theme of the "corner building" is solved through the separation of volumes into parts. In Fribourg three different volumes were combined and organized into a single whole; in this case, a single unified volume is carved up and, by taking parts from the whole, different volumes are created. Part of this single, unified volume, carved away from one of the corners of its matrix, becomes a tower that rises from the façade bordering the streets.

The system of external openings changes in every section of the building: the two negative volumes present a surface of continuous glass windows, while in the tower windows are located on corners. The paired windows overlooking the two streets recede strongly into the walls, the *chiaroscuro* effect created by full and empty spaces is increased by the particular arrangement of the rows of bricks. A tree grows atop the tower set on the corner of the structure.

On the ground floor of the building there is an area covered by a portico; the upper floors have two supporting walls (with circular windows) resting on the tower; to these two elements are attached sections of the two lateral façades. The stairs, the elevators, and secondary spaces are located in the section of the corner toward the courtyard. The two wings of the project house offices set on different levels, along a central corridor; natural light is planned to be the source of illumination for the upper floor.

The building is composed of reinforced concrete covered with a layer of bricks.

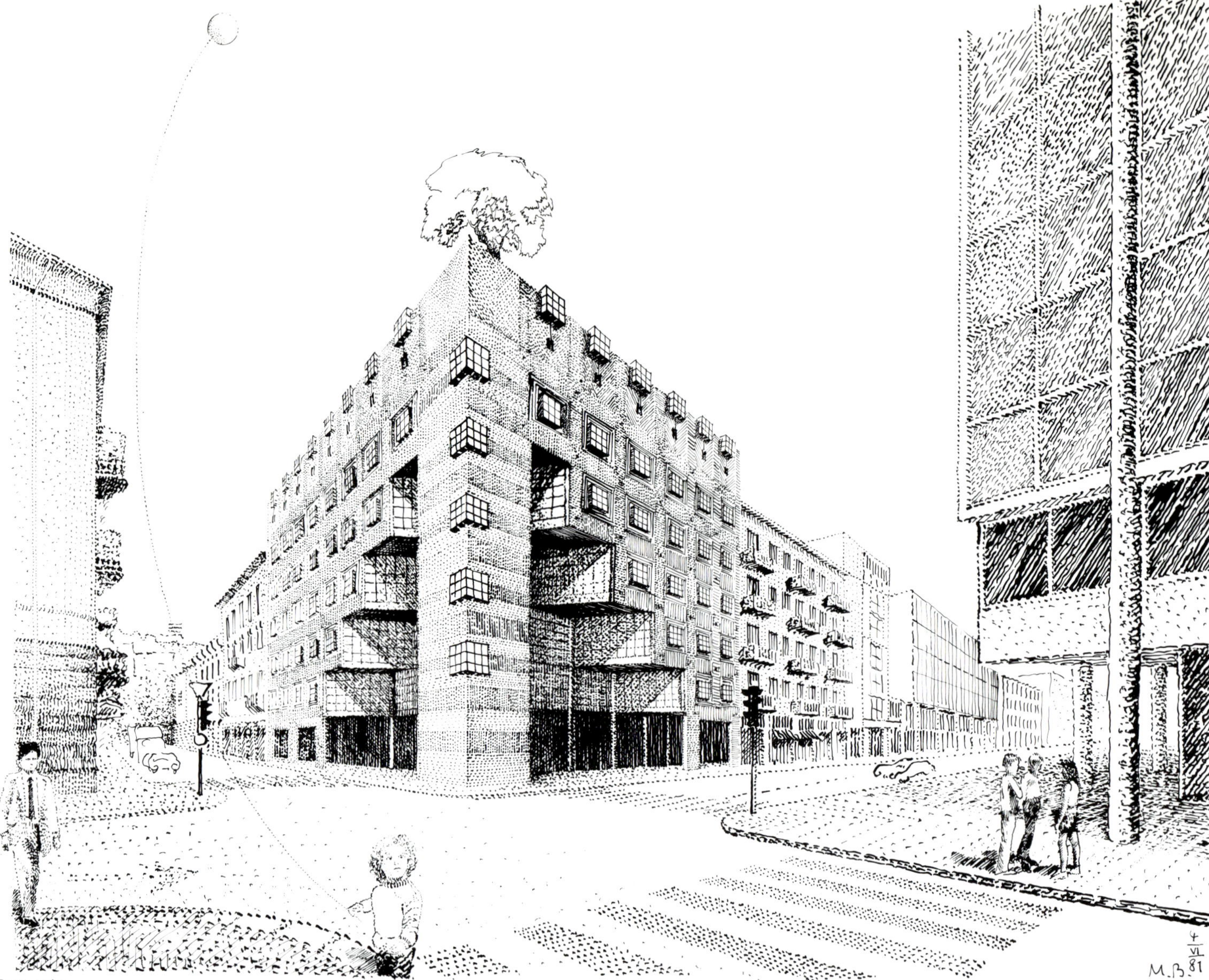

Perspective

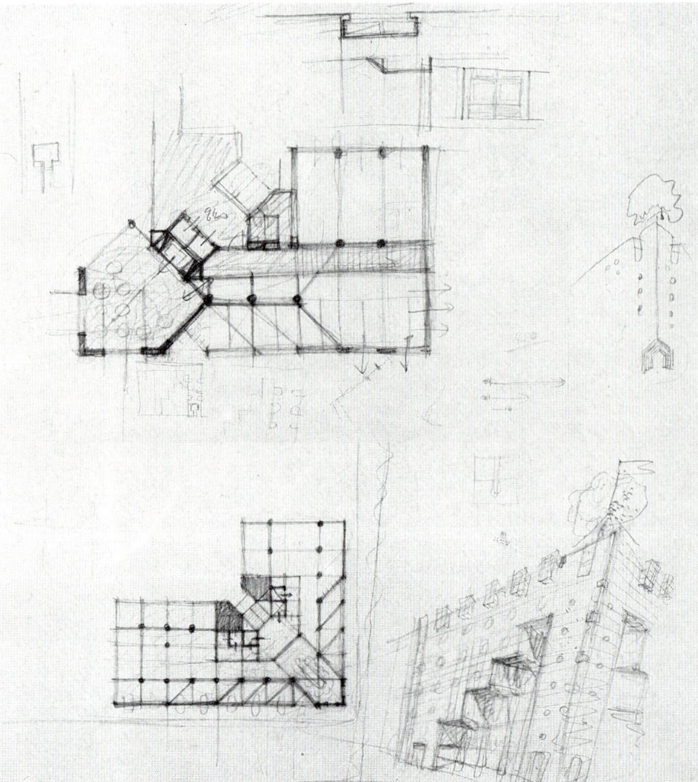

Preliminary study

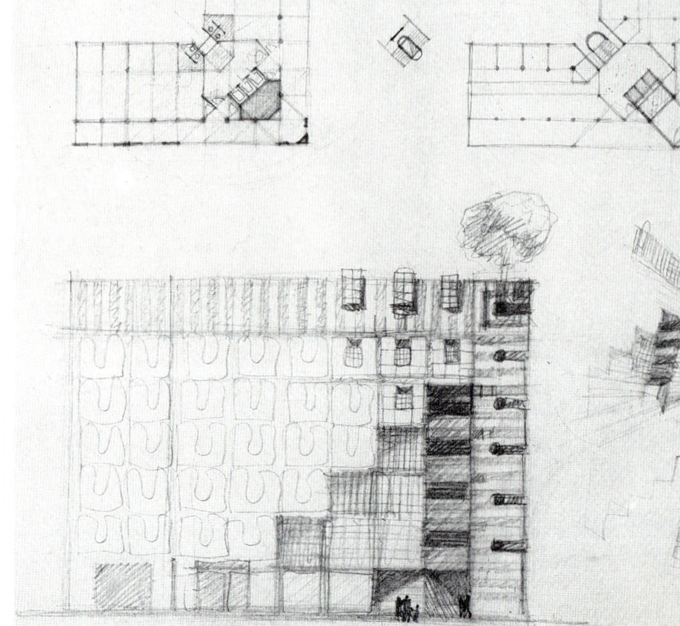

Preliminary study

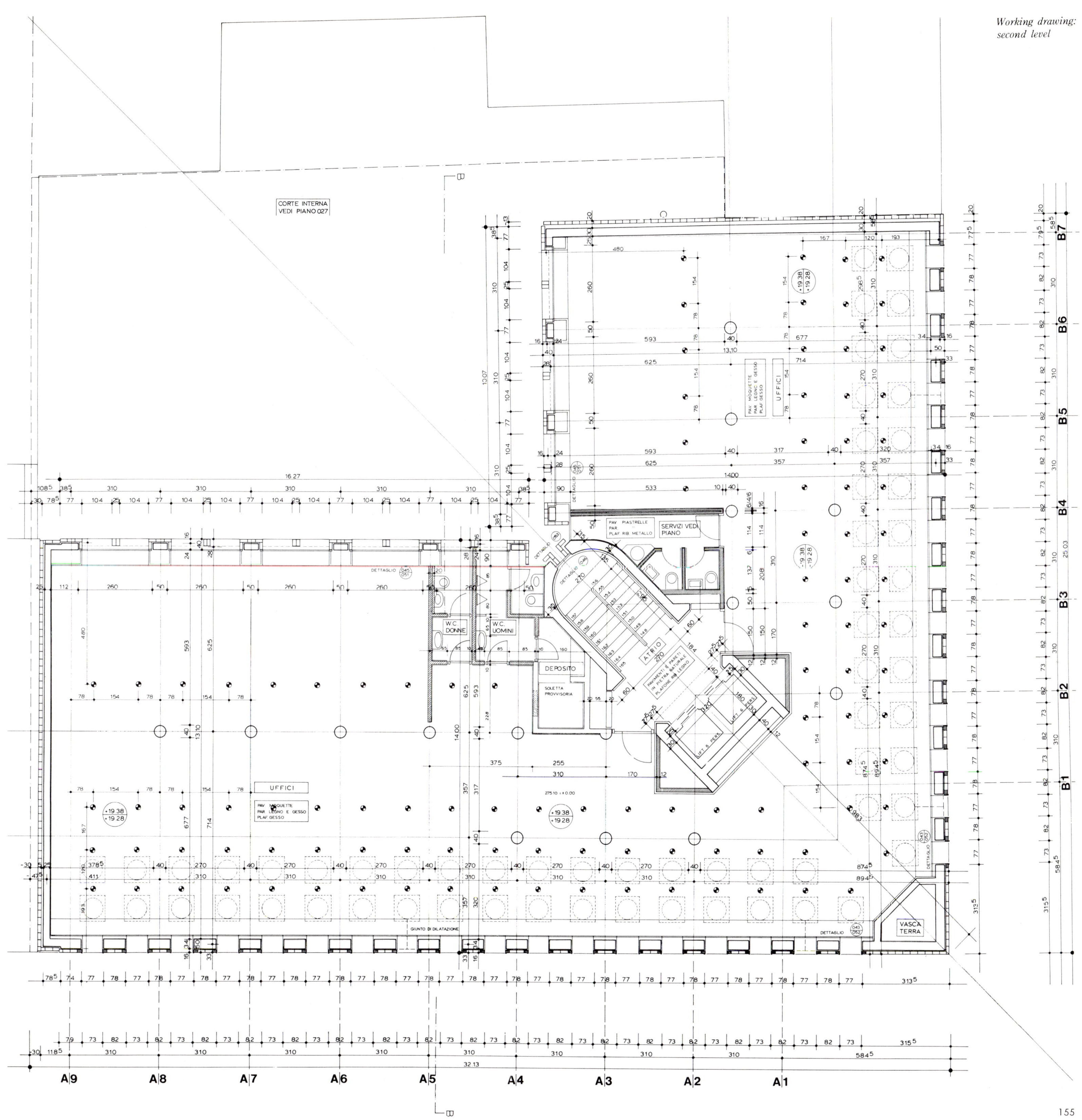

CORTE INTERNA
VEDI PIANO 027
UFFICI
PAV. MOQUETTE
PAR. LEGNO E GESSO
PLAF. GESSO
SERVIZI VEDI PIANO
PAV. PIASTRELLE
PLAF. RIB. METALLO
W.C. DONNE
W.C. UOMINI
DEPOSITO
ATRIO
SOLETTA PROVVISORIA
UFFICI
GIUNTO DI DILATAZIONE
VASCA TERRA
DETTAGLIO
A9 A8 A7 A6 A5 A4 A3 A2 A1
B1 B2 B3 B4 B5 B6 B7

△▽ *Model photos*

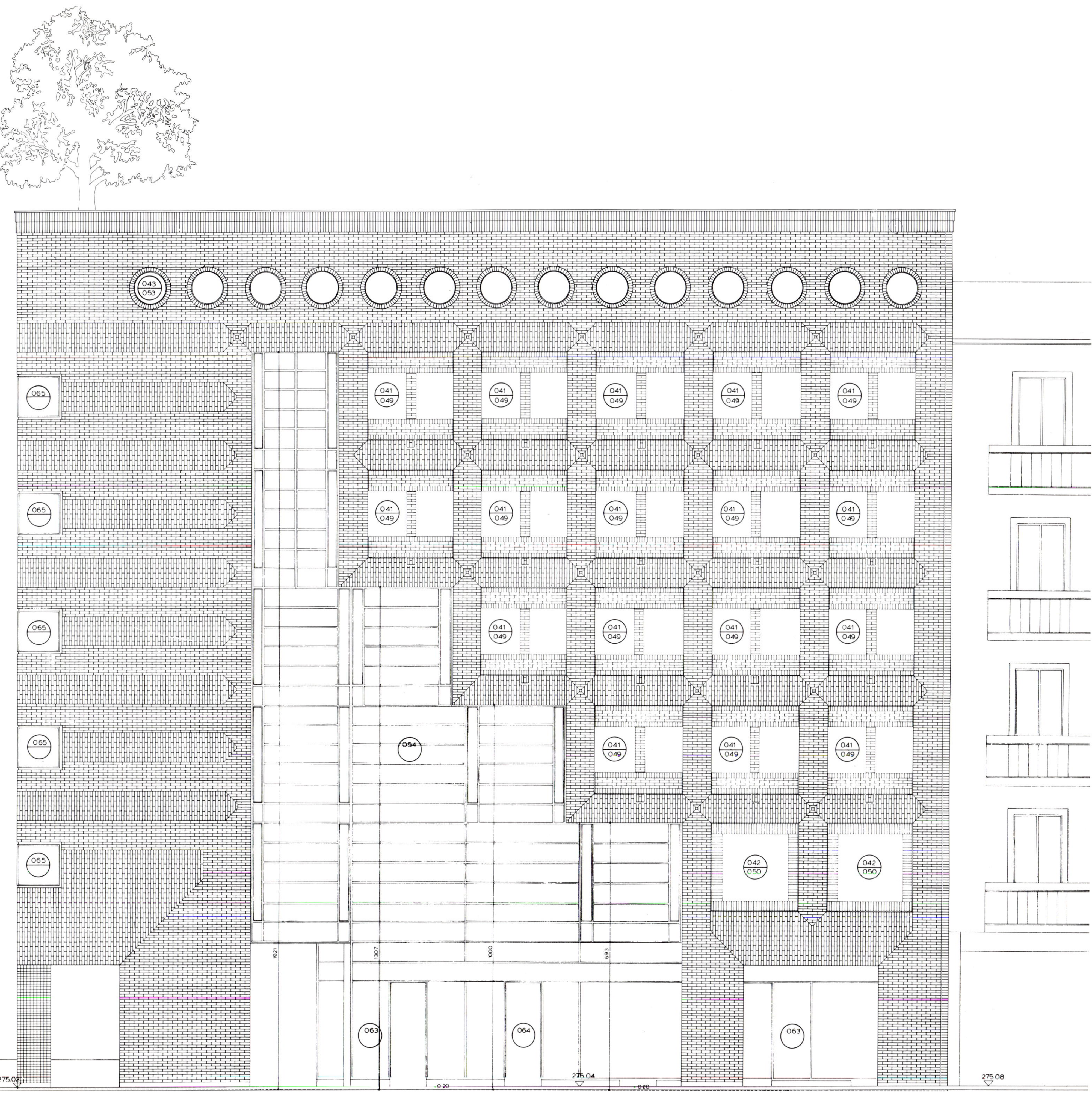

Street façade

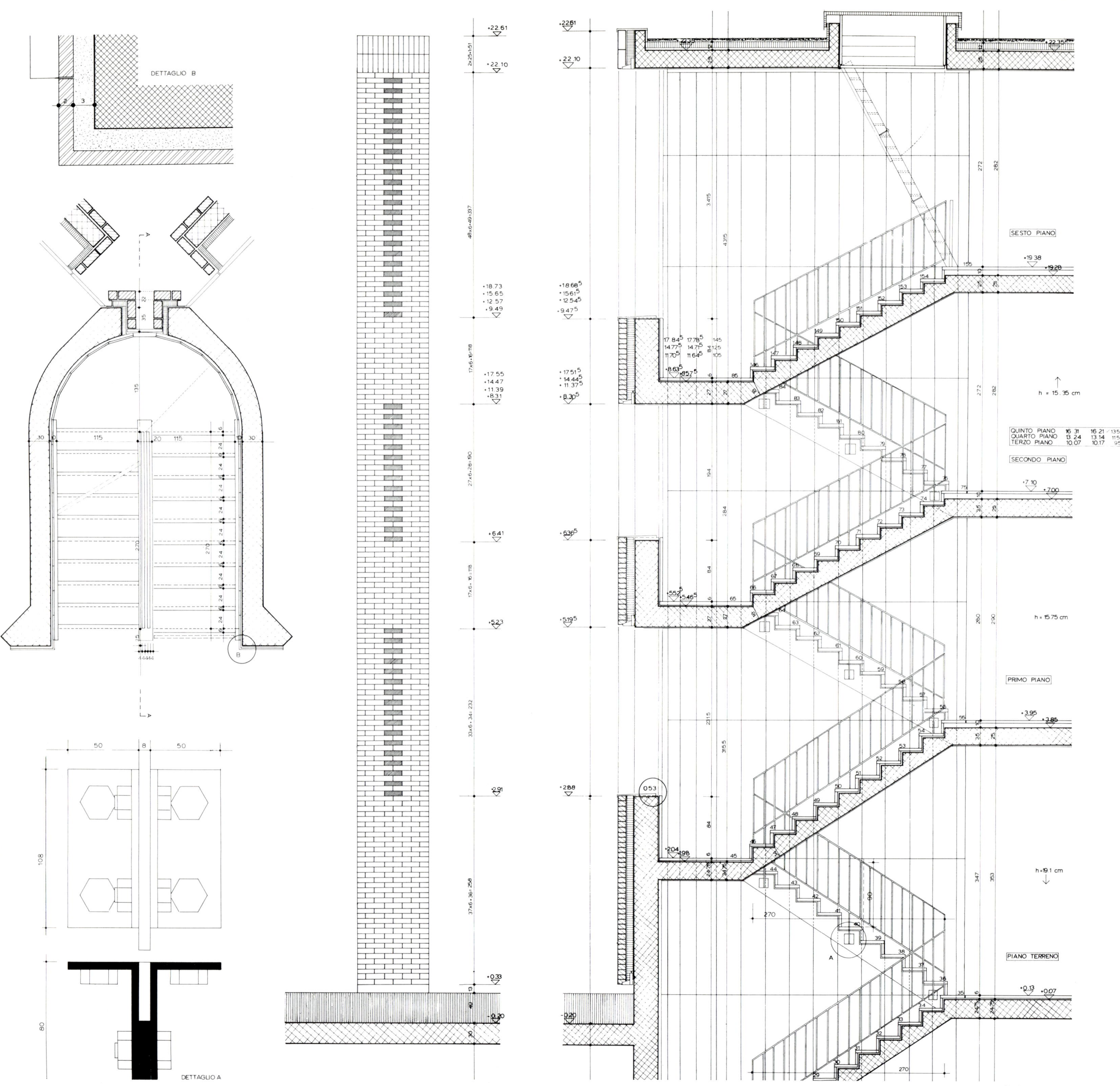

Staircase details

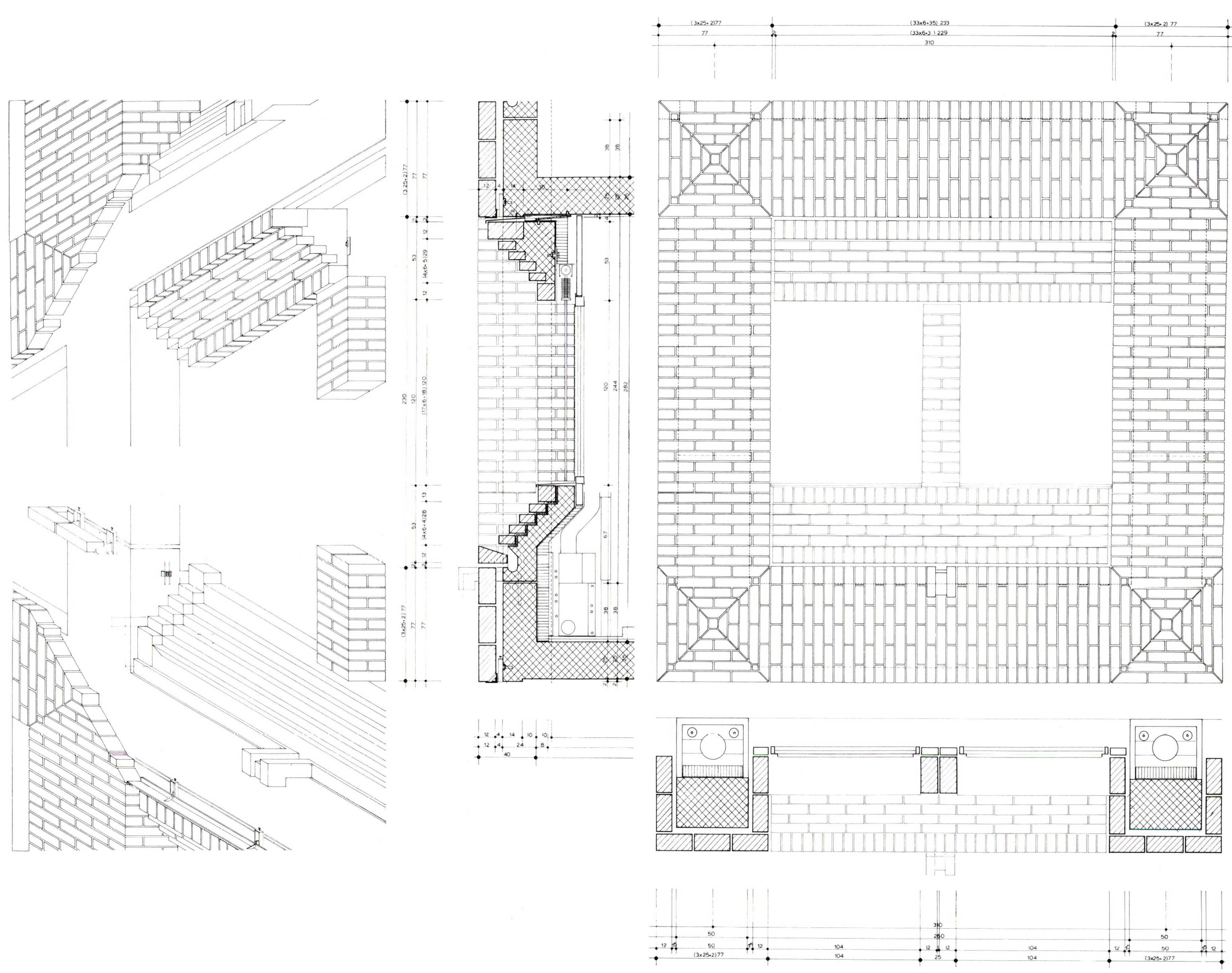

Window details

A single façade oriented toward the valley and a large central opening are the main characteristics of the building. Located on the slope of a hill, the house echoes in many ways some of the elements already present in the house at Viganello, on the hill opposite Massagno, near Lugano. Evident in both constructions is the intention to enliven the façade overlooking the valley; at Massagno this goal is achieved through the use of alternating bands of pink and gray bricks (this was already done in the house of Ligornetto). The two superimposed openings of the house at Viganello (the entrance and the loggia) become here geometric circular figures. In the house at Massagno the upper loggia, once the screens hidden in the thickness of the wall are drawn, can be transformed into a winter garden.

The entrance area, whose façade forms a 45-degree angle, seems cut into the volume standing between the external wall and the interior proper of the house. The two upper floors each have a large loggia (open also laterally) on which the rooms converge. All secondary spaces are placed along the wall facing the mountain; the cylindrical volume of the stair protrudes from the flat surface of the wall. There are two skylights on the roof: one above the stair; the other, enclosed like a luminous well between the two main walls, radiates light on all the three levels of the house.

The entrance and all secondary spaces are on the ground floor; the master bedroom and the children's room are on the upper level.

The masonry is executed in concrete brick, painted white on the interior; ceilings are of exposed reinforced concrete. Flooring is wood, doors and other openings are made of iron, painted black, with the exception of the loggia, where the screens are painted white.

View of south façade

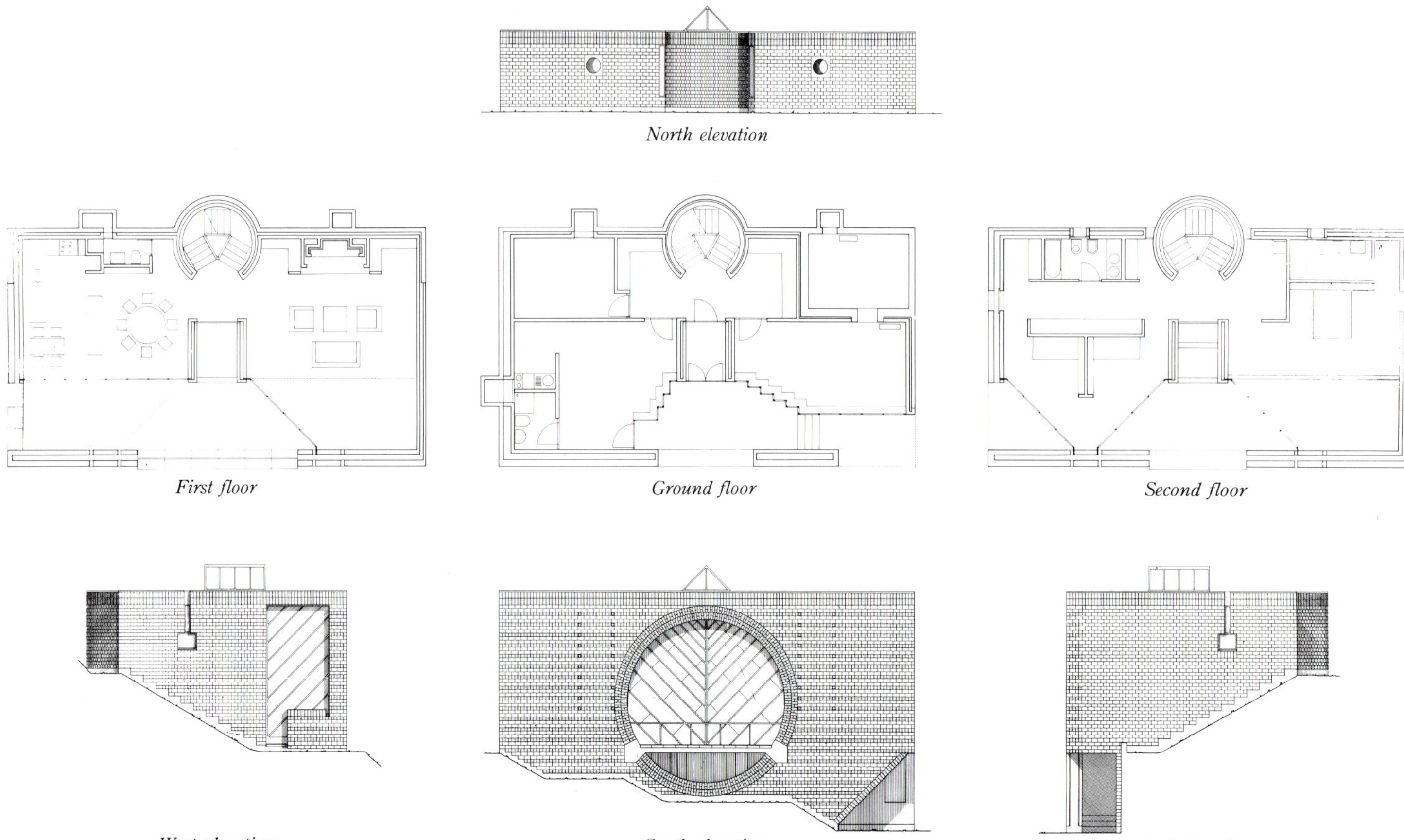

North elevation

First floor

Ground floor

Second floor

West elevation

South elevation

East elevation

Central opening

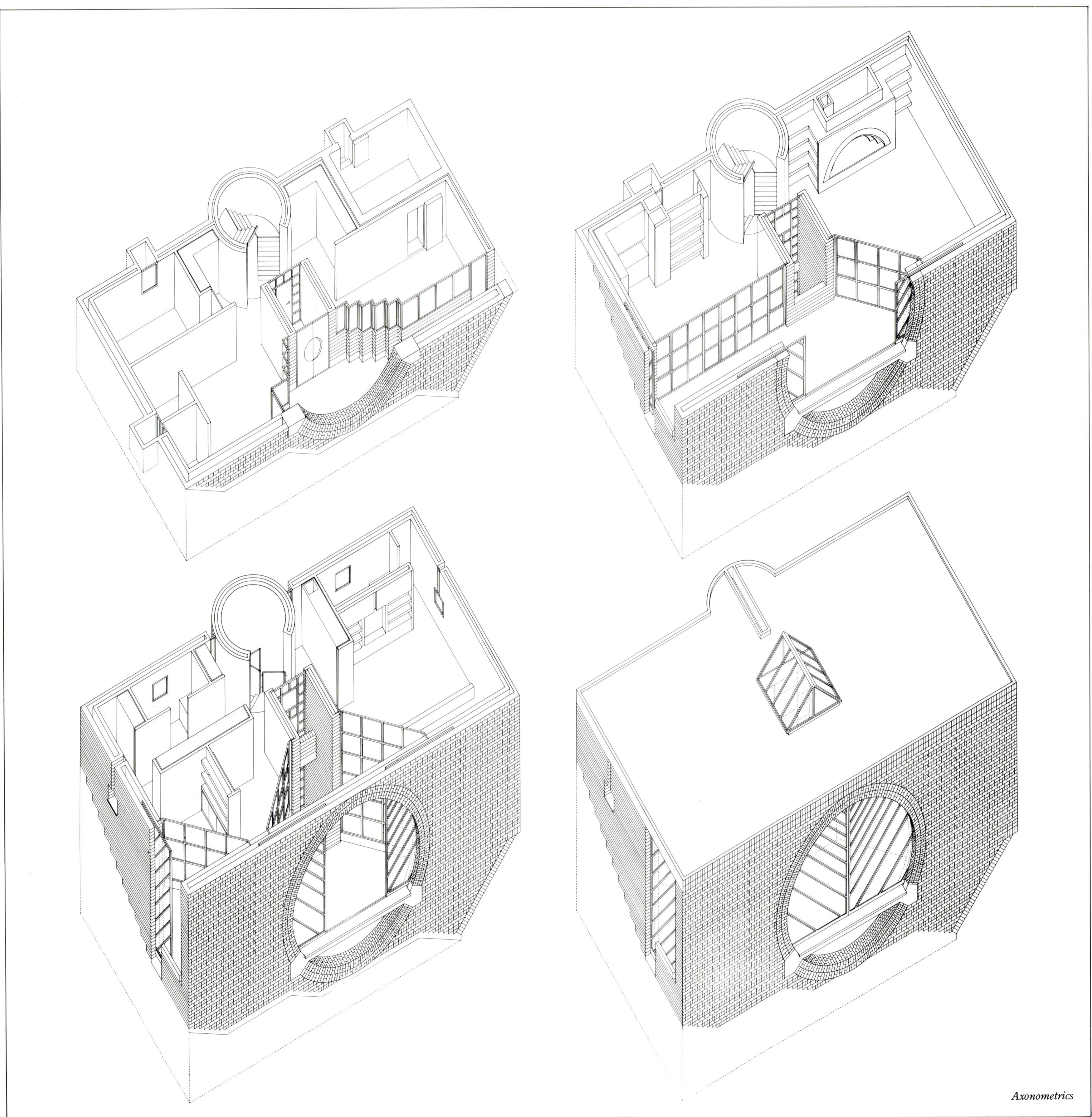

Axonometrics

Terrace on first floor

Living room fireplace

△ *View from living room*

△ *View from porch*

▽ *Staircase*

▽ *View from entrance hall*

◁ South elevation

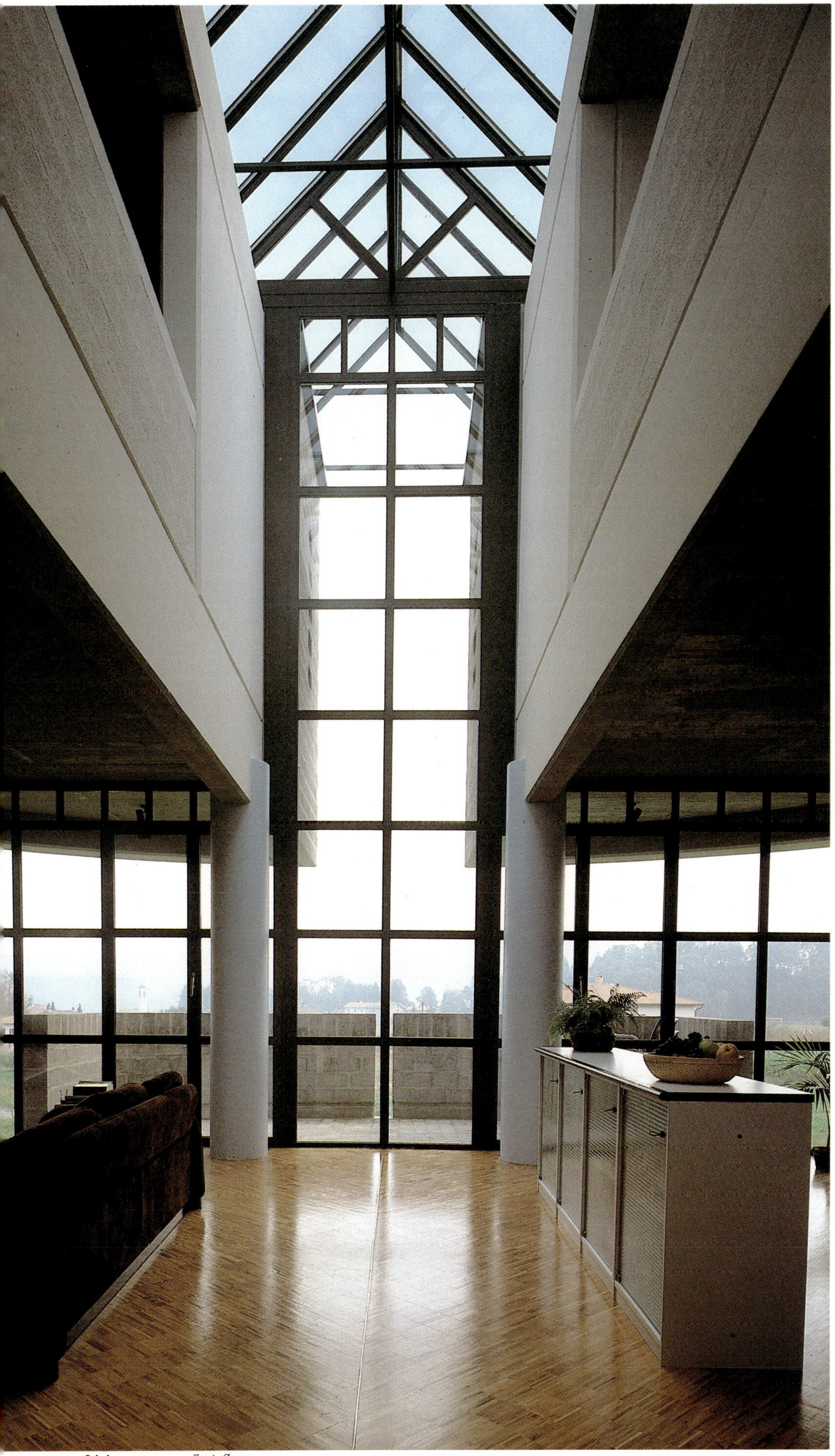

Living room on first floor

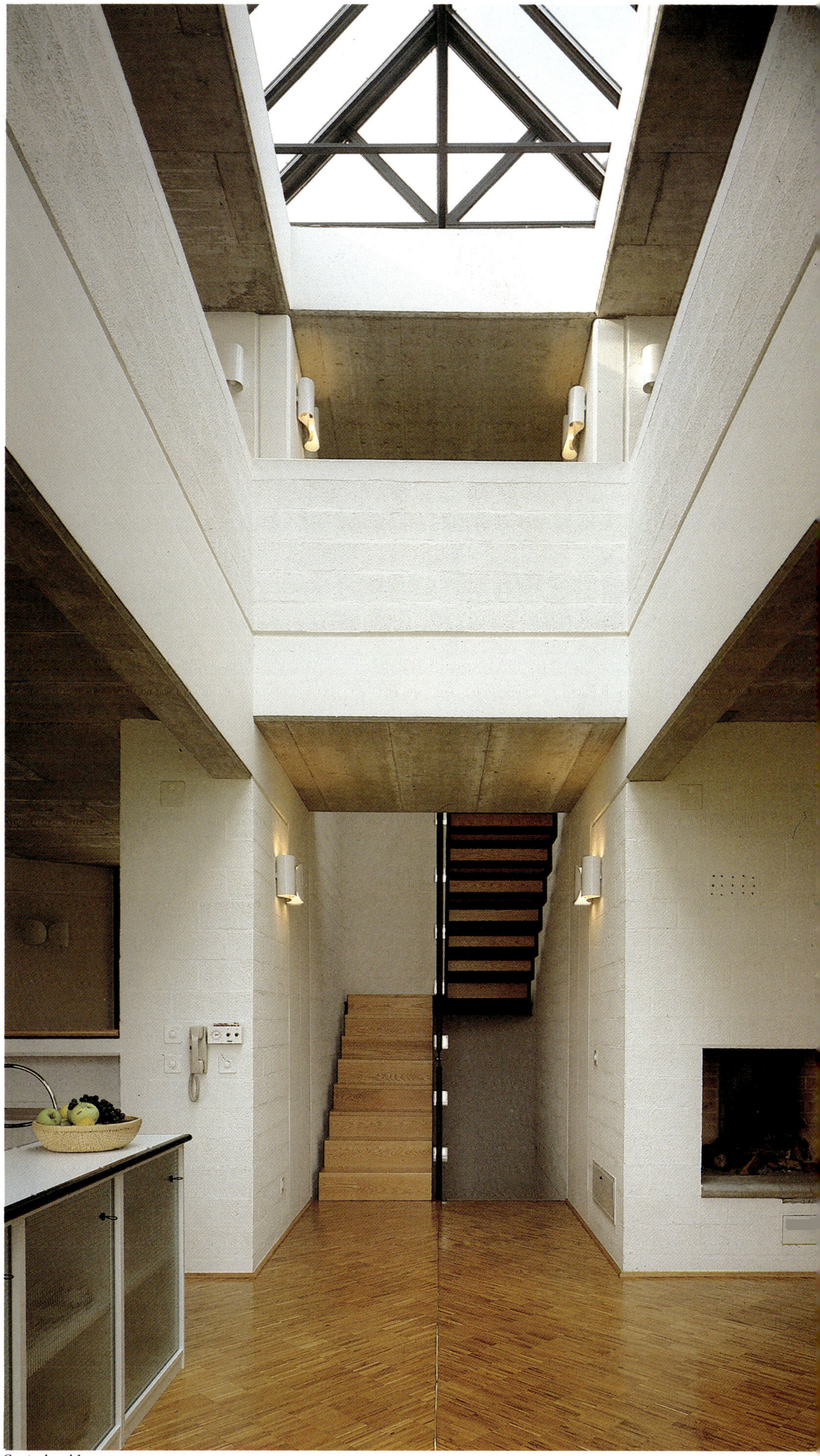

Central void

△ *View toward kitchen*　　　　　　　　　　　　　　　　　　　　　　▽ *Dining room*

Entrance hall

Staircase

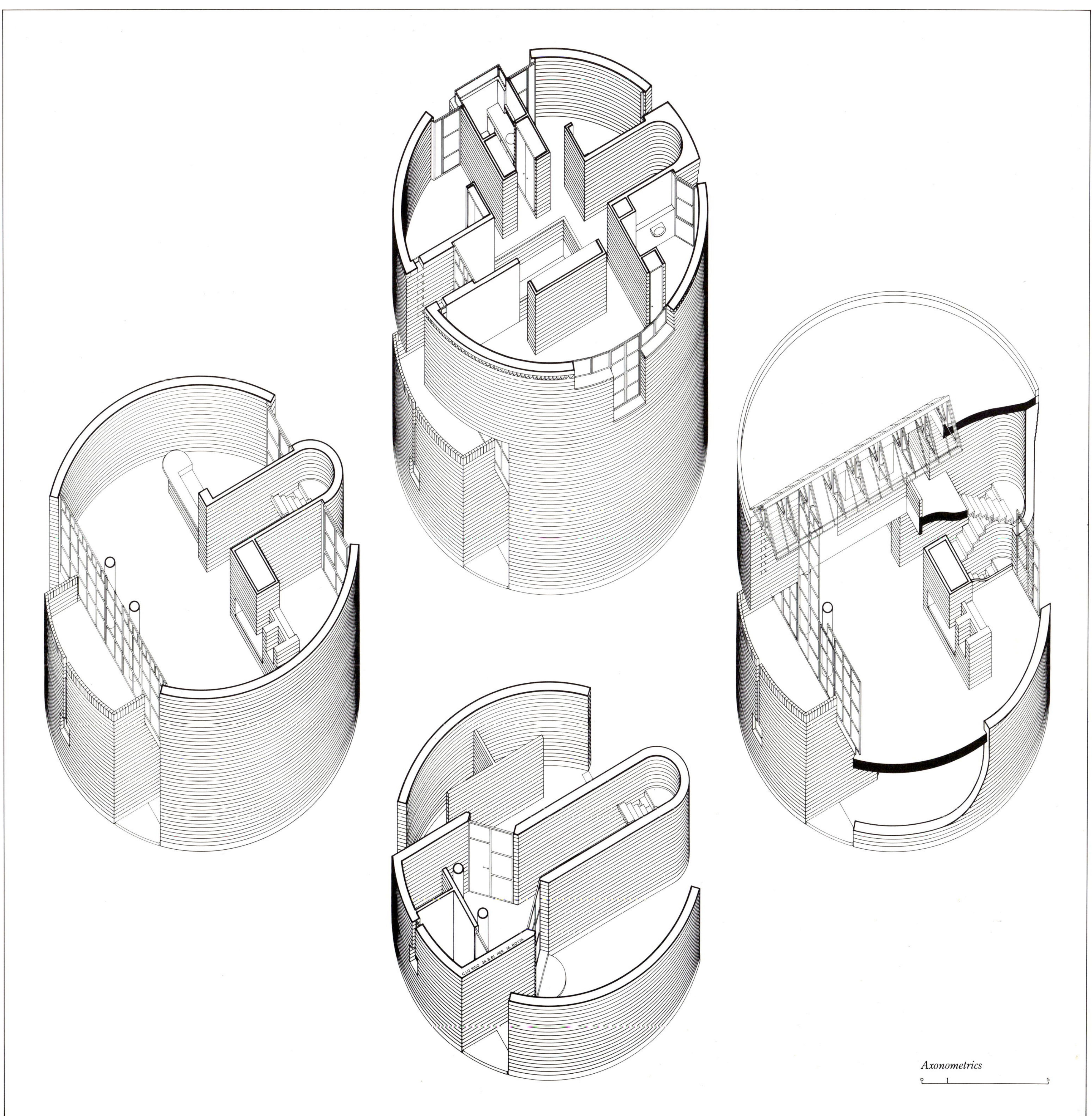

Axonometrics

The property on which the house is located slopes toward the west and the city of Lugano. The steep slope suggested space for parking cars along the nearby road; a walk leads from the road to the house. A small square in the front allows one last view of the landscape before the visitor enters and penetrates into the deep opening at the base of the building. Once the visitor has entered the house, stairs lead him to the first floor where he reaches a wide central opening overlooking the valley. All the rooms of the house and the balconies are directed toward this central space and its skylight above. Once closed, the two large screens, placed in the perimetric walls, transform this area into a winter garden.

The single façade of the house faces the valley. As if giving way under the thrust of the ground, the wall facing the mountain has a small protrusion, along which a beam of light descends from the skylight on the roof. The masonry of the wall facing the valley uses moldings and *chiaroscuro* to enrich the surface of the single real façade of the house. As in the farm at Ligrignano, part of the surface has blocks of concrete placed at 45-degree angles. The final crowning, as in the house at Stabio, is underlined by a row of bricks placed at 45-degree angles, and by two other rows, whose configuration of bricks resemble knife blades. On the two sides the protrusion of the chimney ducts reinforce the composition of the façade.

On the ground floor are the entrance and secondary spaces, on the first the living room and the kitchen; bedrooms are on the upper level. The stairway and service spaces are placed along the wall facing the mountain. The house is constructed with blocks of concrete, painted white on the interior; attics are made of exposed reinforced concrete. Floors are covered with black slate; doors and other openings are made of iron, painted black.

View of west façade

West façade detail

Central opening

Detail of column, central opening

△ View toward staircase from dining room

▽ Wardrobe: second floor

Staircase with bookshelf

Single-Family House at Origlio, Switzerland, 1982

The plan of the house is determined by the two east-west and north-south axes. In the center, which is double-height, is the living room, opening onto the valley to the west and the garden to the south. The large glass walls, pushed back toward the central core, are enclosed between the full volumes of the corners that emerge from the slope like gigantic columns surmounted by capitals.

The two cylinders, with their many vertical openings that accentuate the separation from the upper elements, contain two studies, while the bedrooms are in the superimposed cubes. The small square windows are oriented toward particular elements of the landscape: a distant church, a mountain. A skylight protects the open space overlooking the garden.

The stairs, the kitchen and services are placed along the wall facing north; the fireplace, set at the center of the building, seems to create an actual internal façade. On the ground floor there is a covered parking area and other spaces. The entrance is at the corner of the building that faces north.

The construction is made of bricks of concrete, painted white on the interior of the house; ceilings are of exposed reinforced concrete. Floors are tiled with the exception of the bedrooms, where they are of dark gray moquette. Doors and windows are made of iron, painted black; the skylight has a metal frame, painted white, and slabs of translucent Perspex.

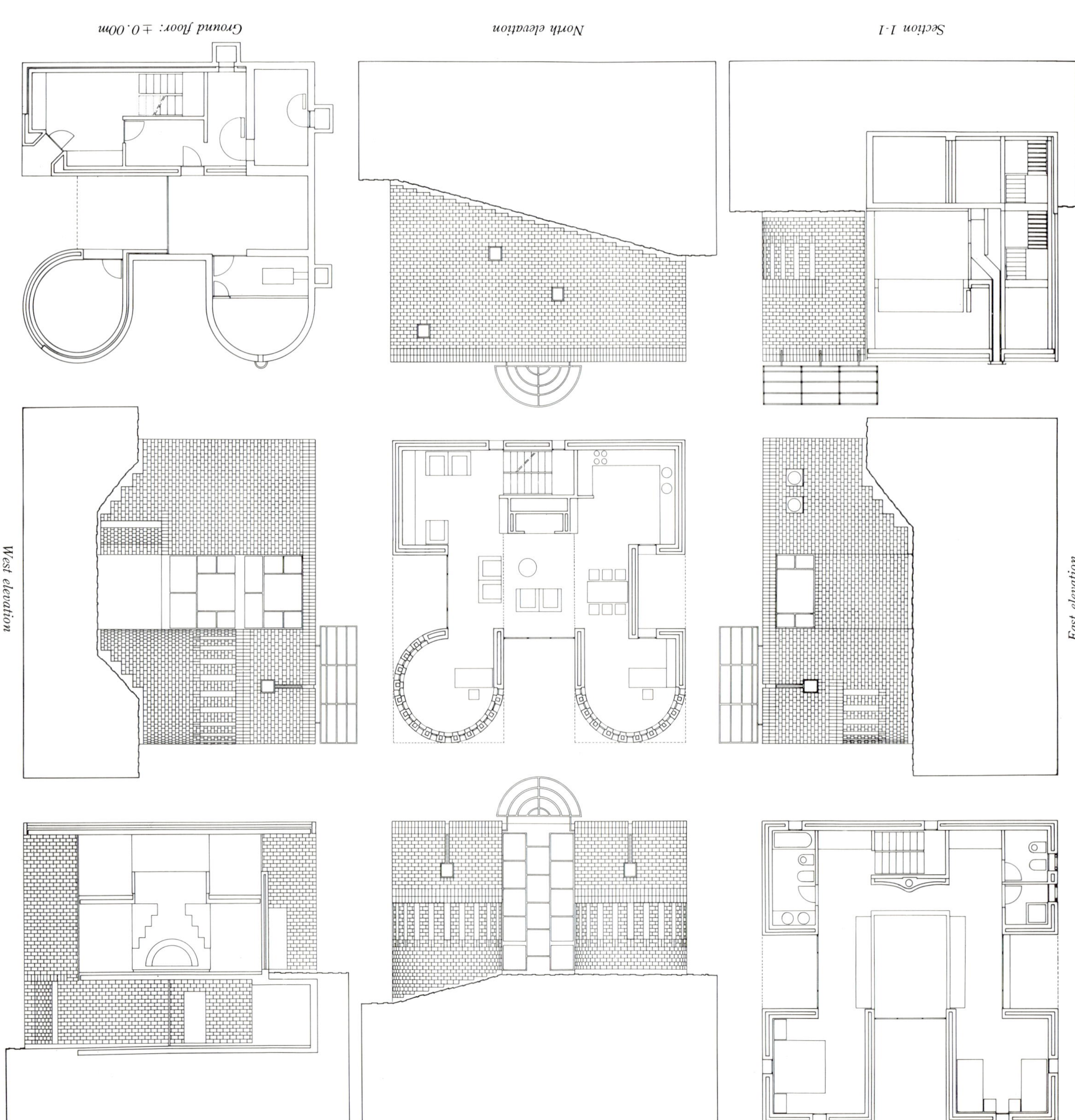

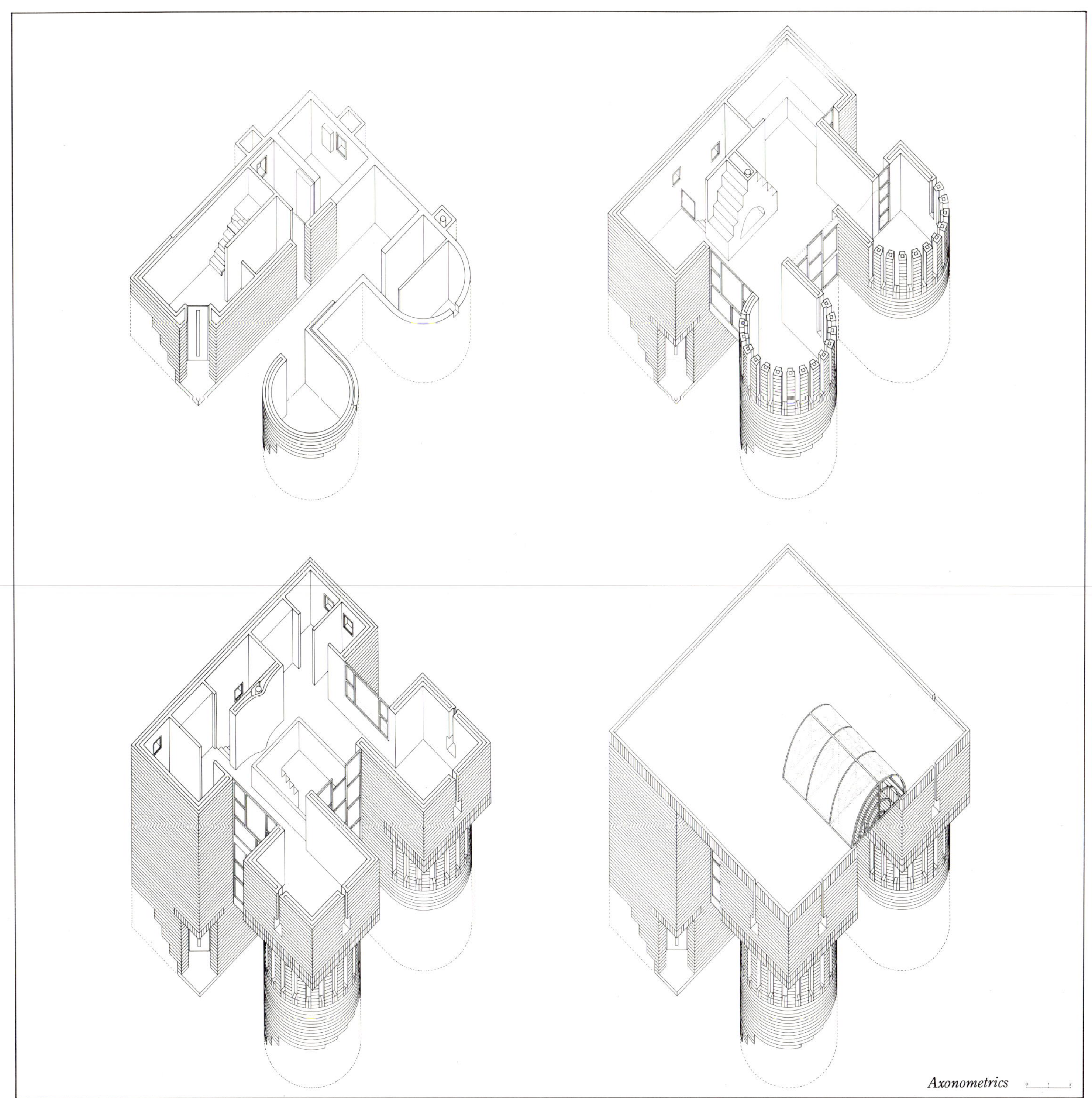

Axonometrics

General view from south

182

South façade detail

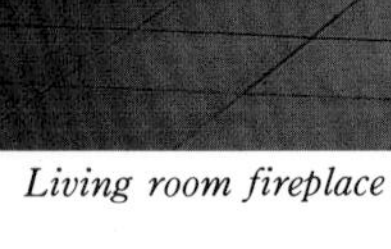

Living room fireplace

Dining room

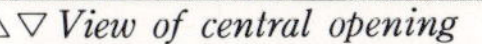

△▽ *View of central opening*

The existing building, a vacation house built in the 1950s, is located in a forest at the edge of a lake. The simple addition of a terrace and the creation of a new façade on the side overlooking the lake has completely changed the structure of the house and its relation with the surrounding landscape. The direction of the roof has been altered, from parallel to the mountain to perpendicular to it. The new roof rests on the perimetric walls of the terrace that opens onto the lake.

On the ground floor the old cellar has been transformed into a living room. The real interior of the house, above the living room, is reached through an outside stair. On the first floor is the fireplace, another living room, and the terrace; the kitchen and secondary spaces are located along the wall facing the mountain. On the upper level, beneath the roof, there is the bedroom and a second terrace that, like the one below, faces the lake.

The walls of the new construction are made of rough concrete blocks, the interiors are covered with a coat of white plaster. Flooring is gray polished granite; doors and other openings are made of iron, painted black.

General view from lake

Detail of façade

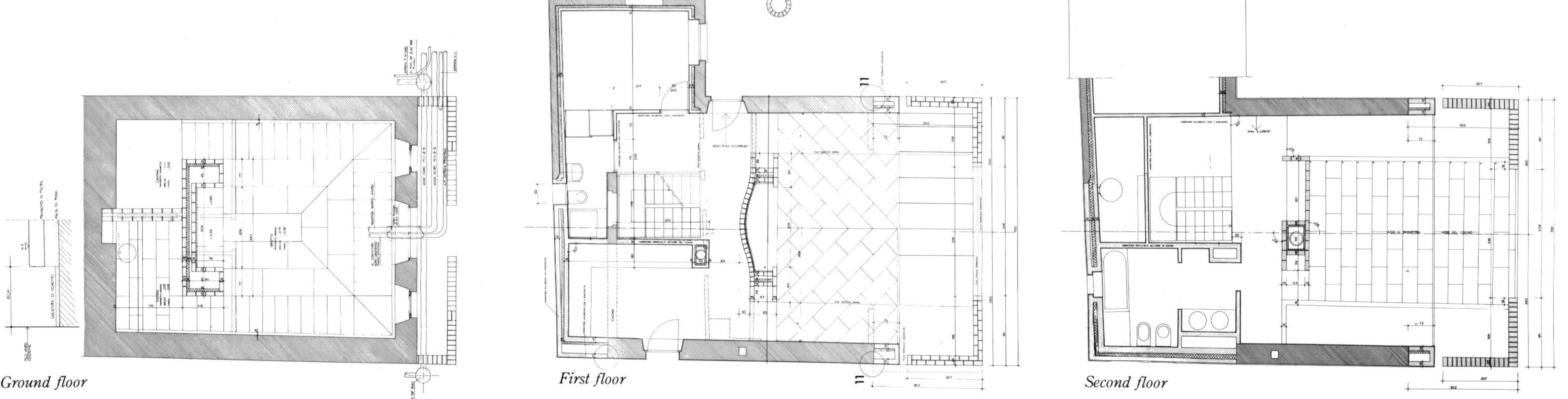

View of terrace

Ground floor　　　　*First floor*　　　　*Second floor*

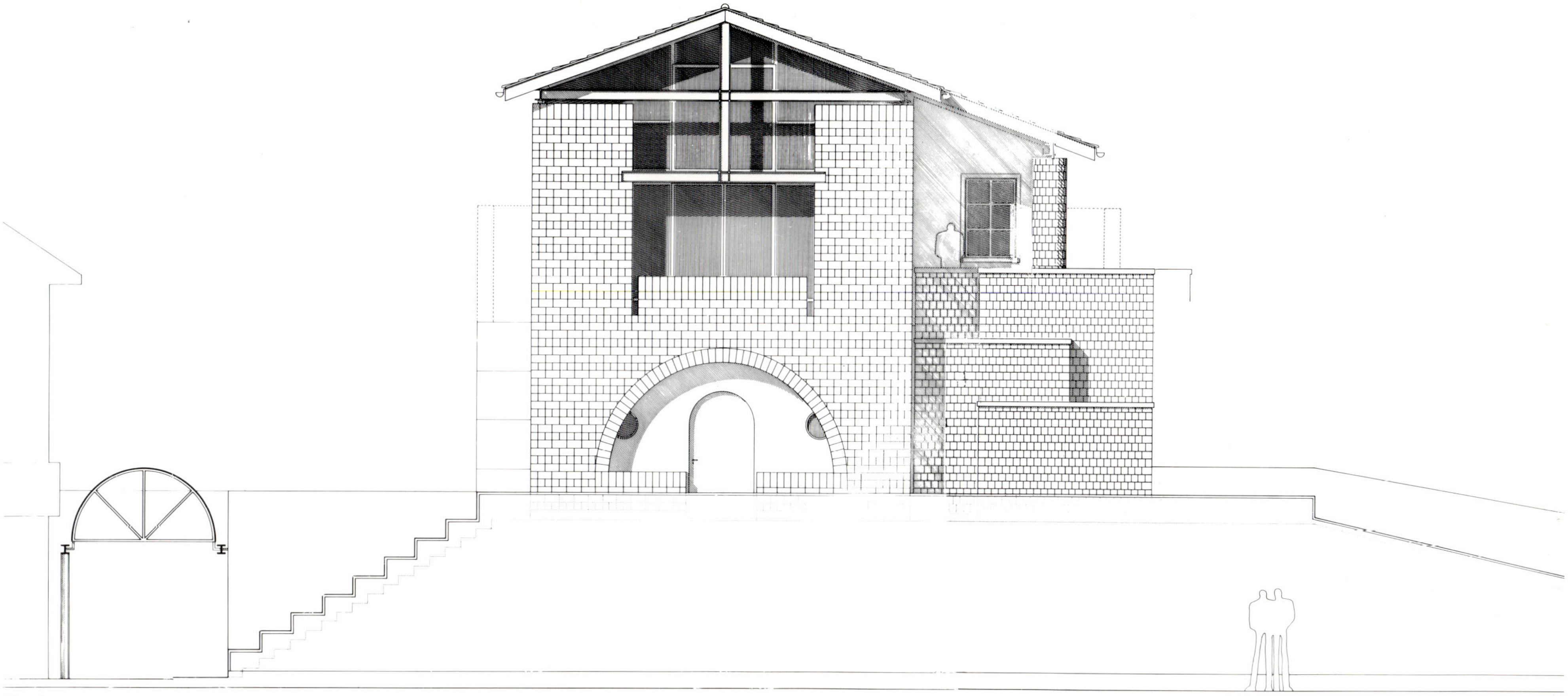

Elevation

Gallery

Stairs leading to gallery

The flat tract of land on which the house is built drops off abruptly. The house, located exactly on the border between flat and sloping ground, emerges only slightly from the flat land while it opens and offers itself to the landscape below, becoming a point of reference, a sign that articulates the surrounding space.

The southern façade, slightly concave, has alternating bands of bricks laid at 45-degree angles. This technique has already been employed in the house at Viganello. At Morbio Superiore this treatment is extended to all the façade and further accentuated by the silver color with which the concrete bricks are painted. A skylight located on the north-south axis gives light to the deep incision that cuts across the entire building and ends with the large opening of the wall toward the valley. On this level, besides a loggia, are the kitchen and living room; above, the bedrooms with their lateral loggias, and the curved volume housing secondary spaces are located. The entrance, preceded by a portico, is on the upper level of the house.

The building is composed of concrete bricks; floors are covered with slate, and ceilings are made of exposed reinforced concrete. Interior walls are painted white, doors and other openings are made of iron, painted black.

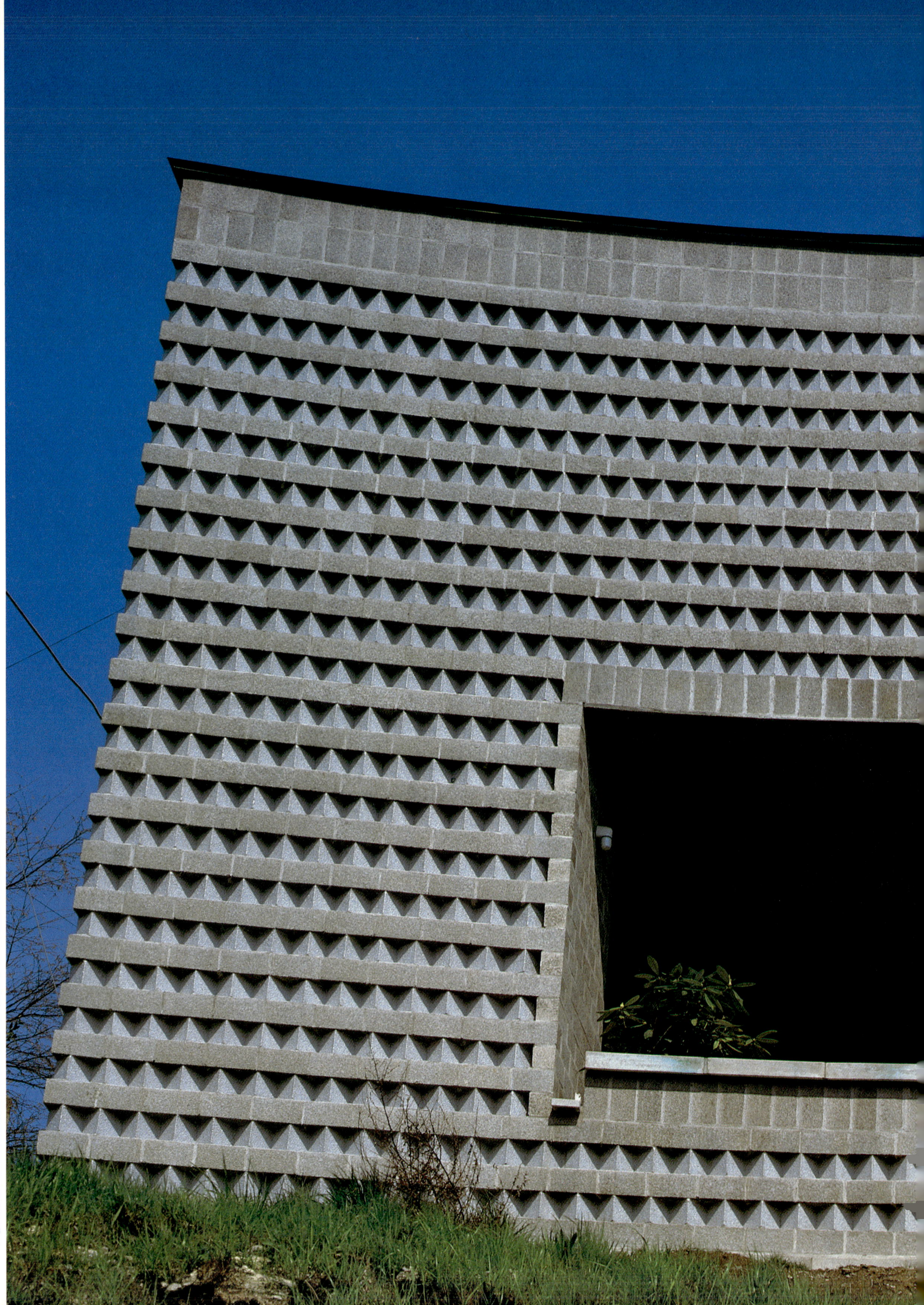

South façade

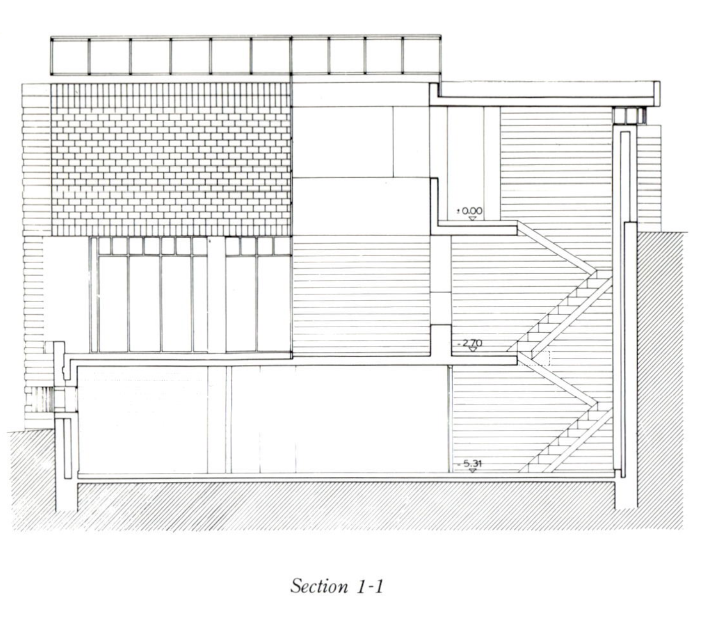

Section 1·1

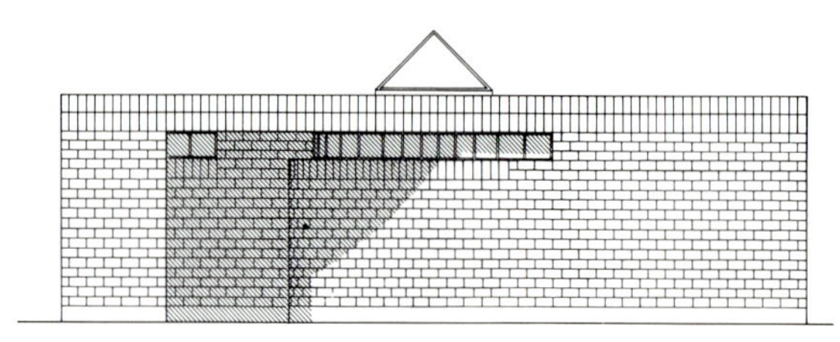

North elevation

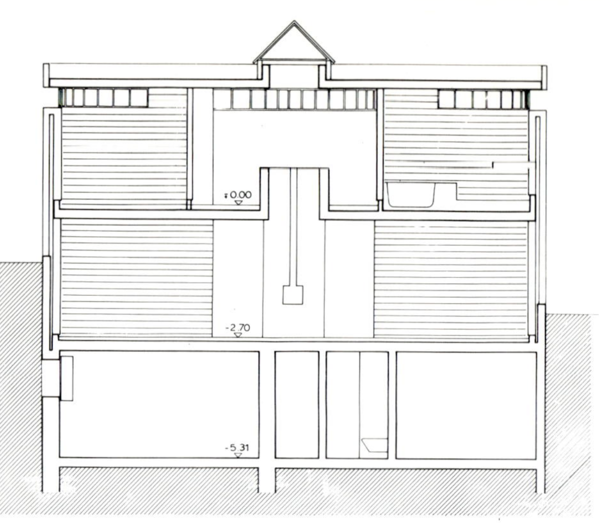

Section 2·2

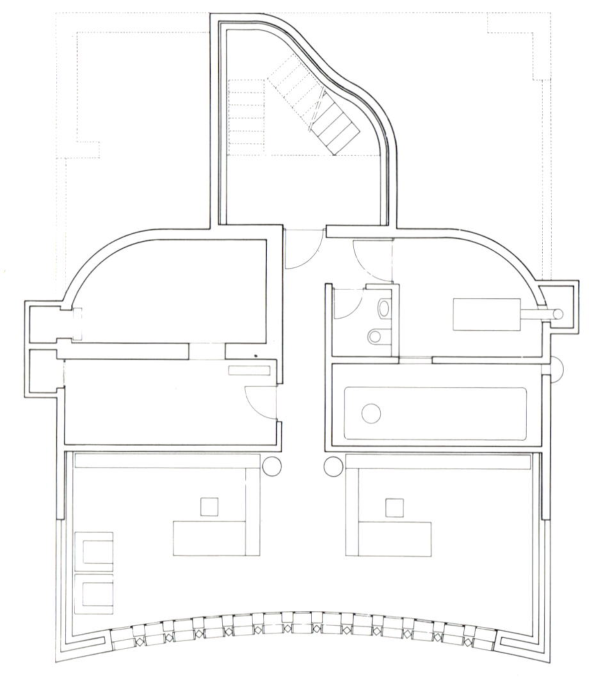

Basement: −5.31m

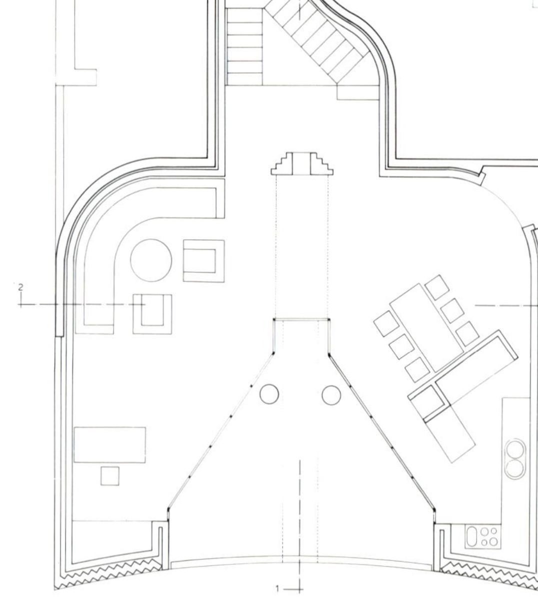

Ground floor: −2.70m

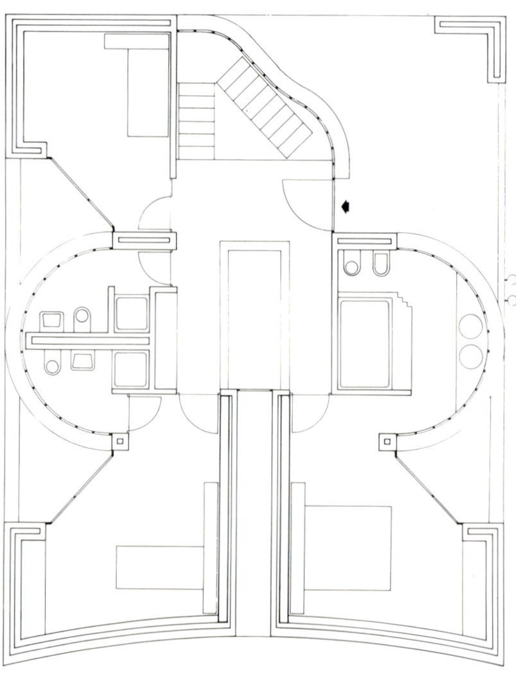

First floor: ± 0.00m

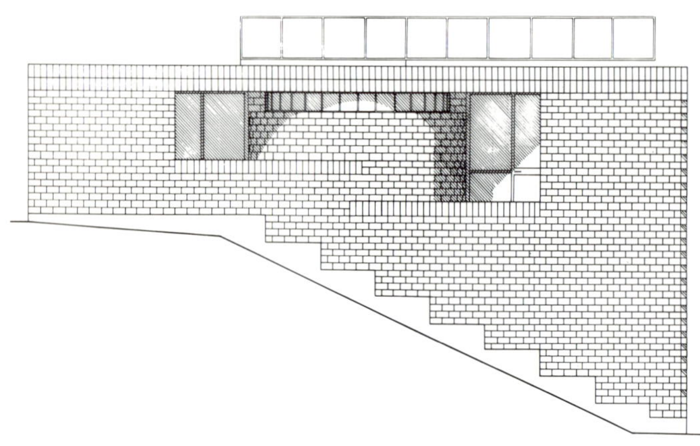

West elevation

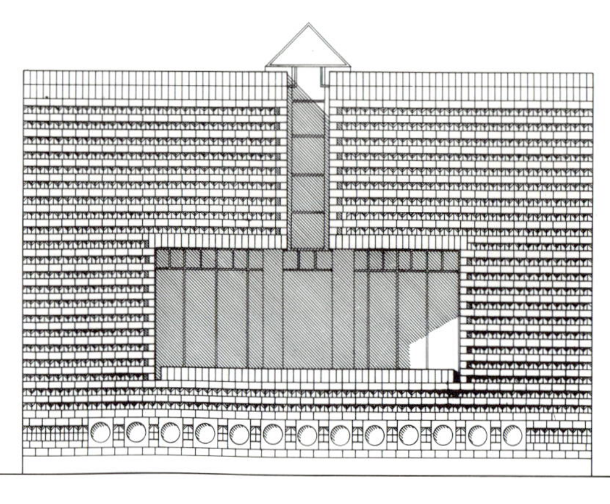

South elevation

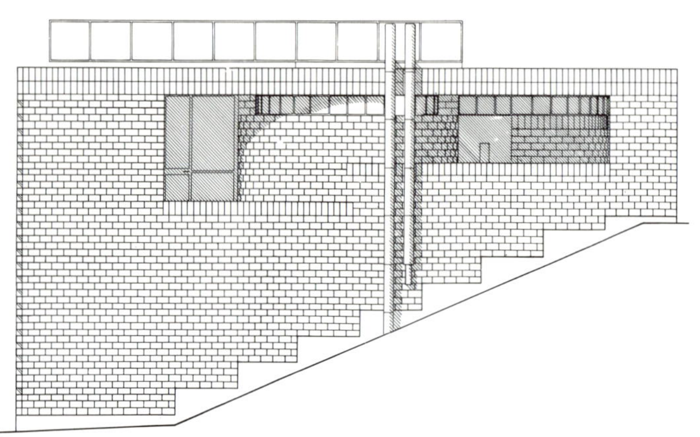

East elevation

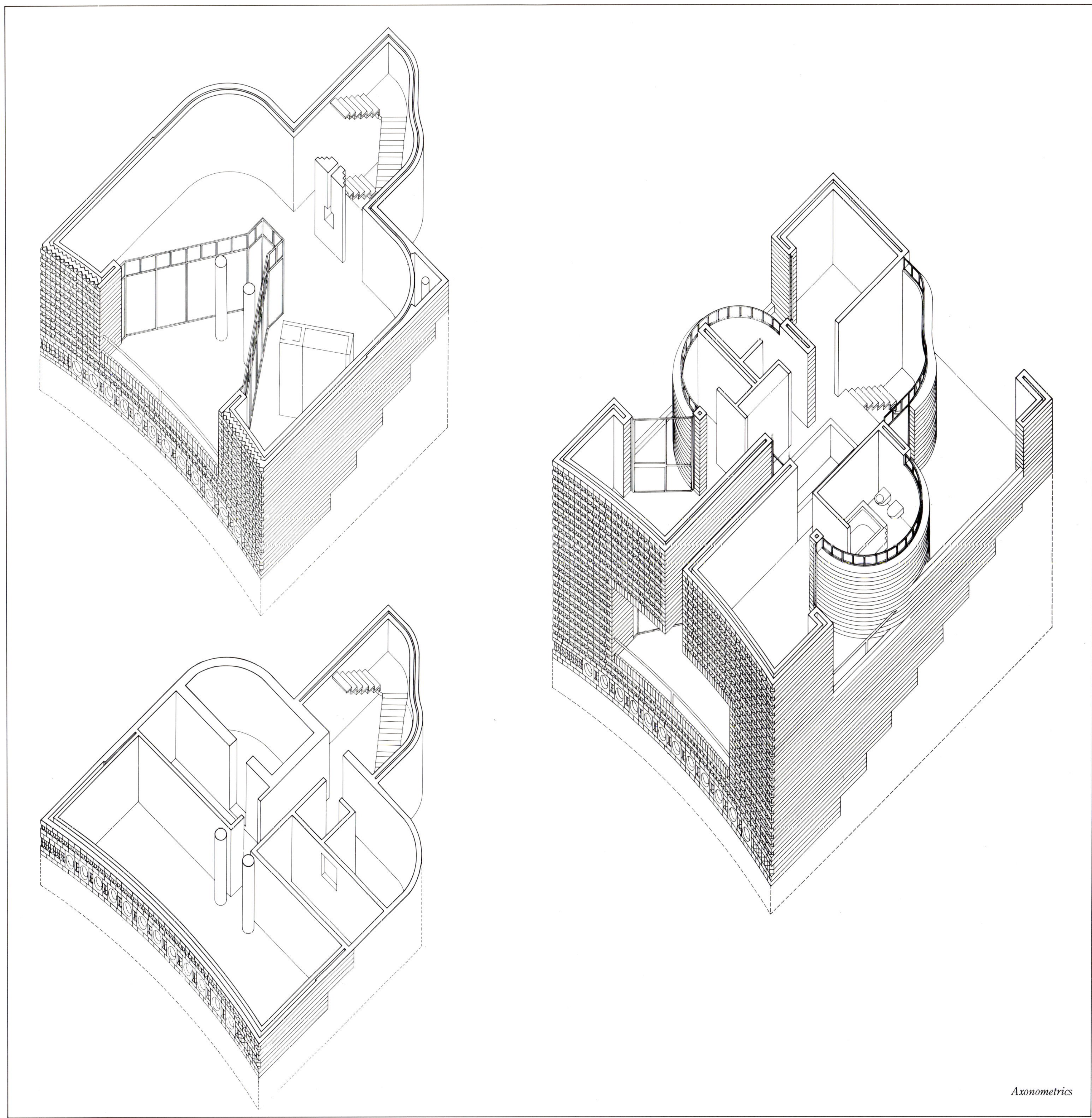

Axonometrics

Dining room beside terrace

View from first floor terrace

View of terrace

Model photo

The building presents itself as an auton-
omous object, located on the side of the
new square of the railway station, on a
street with heavy traffic. By its presence
the structure intends to establish the
physical limits of the square and, at the
same time, to function as a new entrance to
the railway station and an open window
overlooking the city. As already established
in the building at Brühl, the large central
opening transforms the building into a
gateway for the station directly behind it.
An elevated pedestrian walk links the
Information Center to other pedestrian areas
(also elevated) of nearby buildings.

The structure has two lateral volumes and
a central one covered with glass. On the
lower floors there will be space for an
auditorium, a hall for exhibitions, and
offices. The space of the upper floors will
be divided into offices; all secondary spaces
are located in the part of the building facing
the railway station. The parking lot, already
existing, is underground.

The structure will be composed of reinforced concrete, covered with a pinkish
stone, the color of the surrounding buildings.

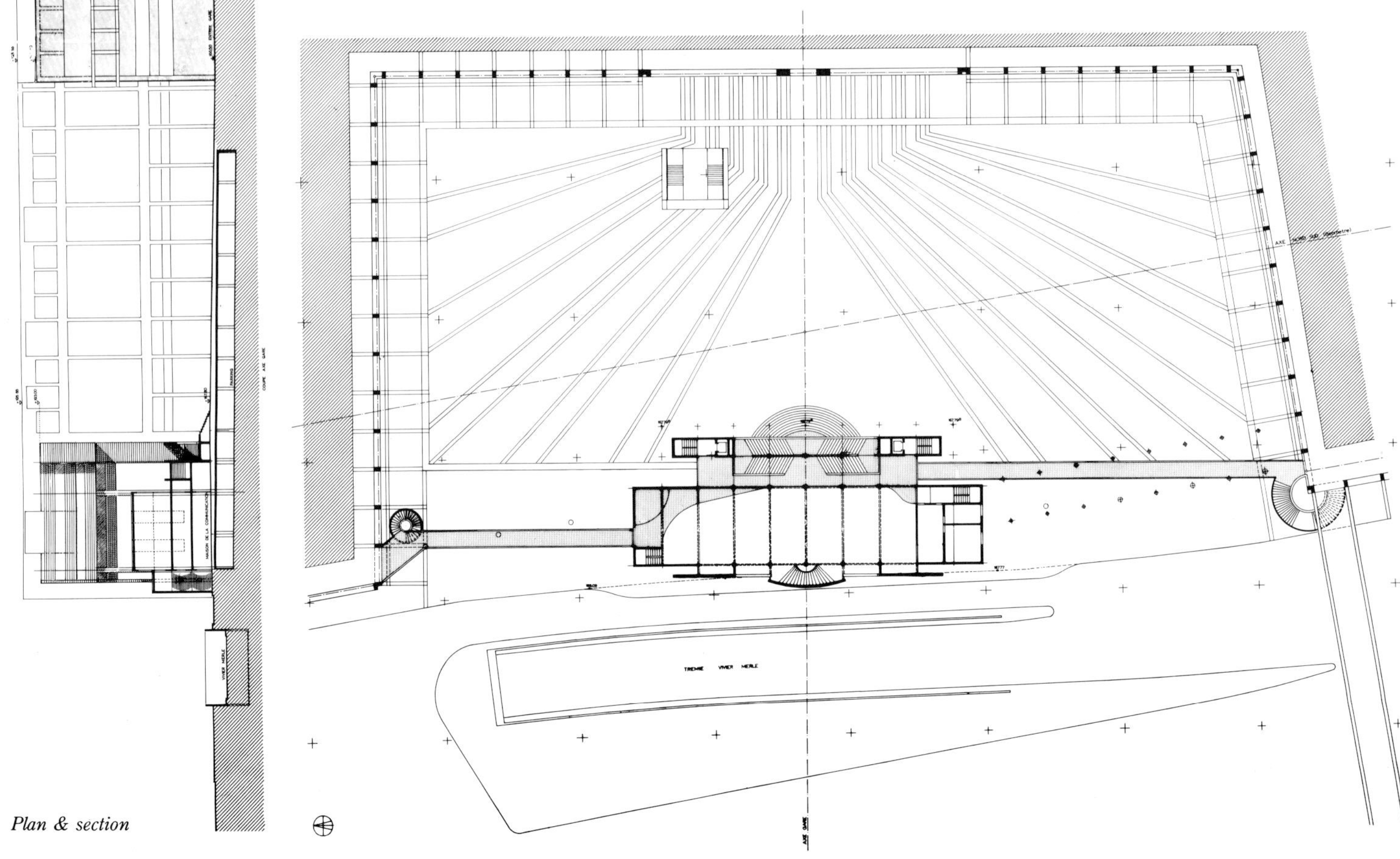

Plan & section

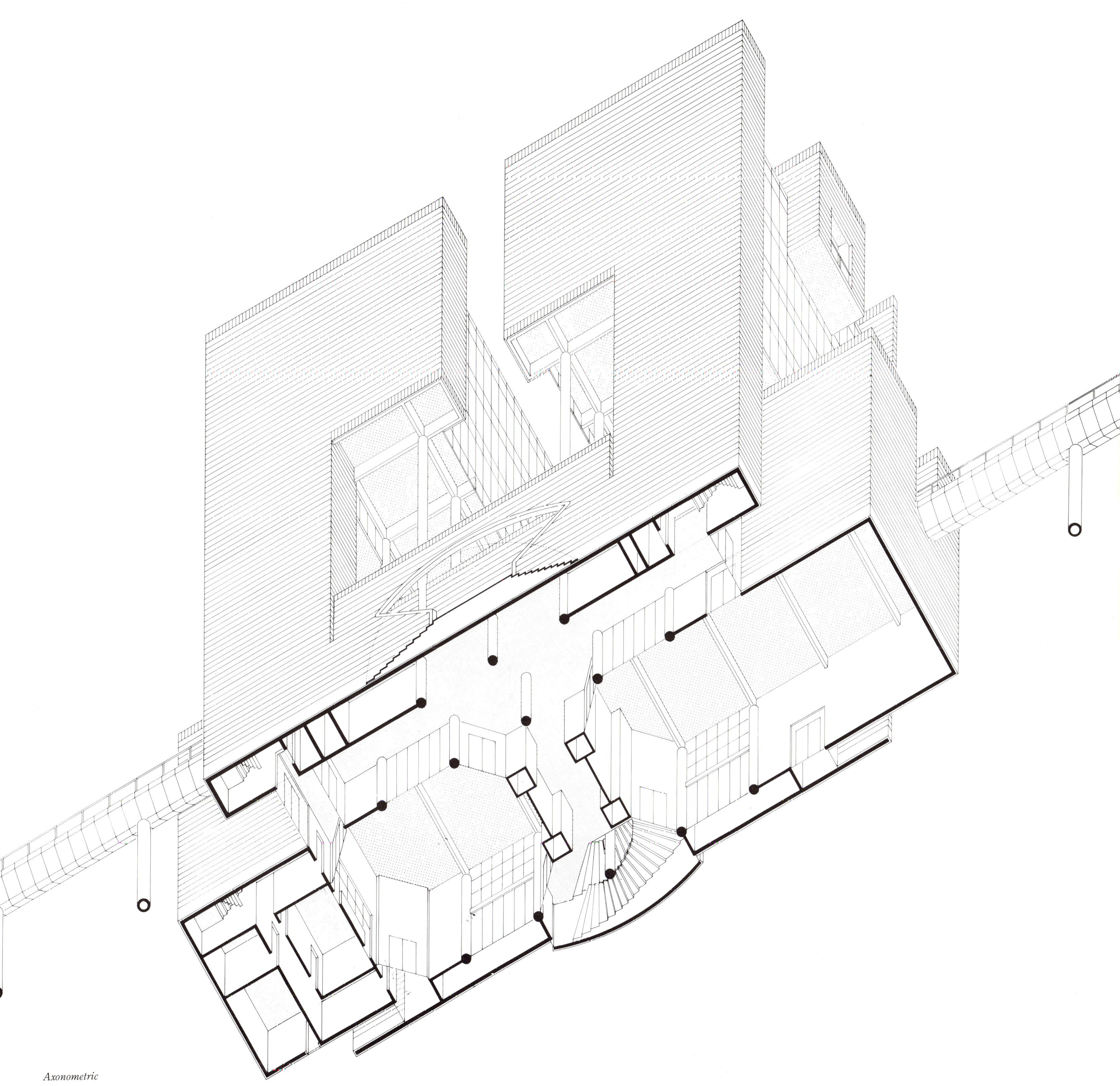

Axonometric

The two chairs, made of tubular steel frames, have a delicate perimetric structure and a flat seat of perforated sheet metal, while the backs are made of two rolls of polyurethane. The metal elements can be painted either gray or dull black. Botta's design for a chair was a way for him to begin working in new directions and, at the same time, to assess his previous accomplishments. As was the case with his buildings, Botta's chair is a prototype that can be developed further and reelaborated in future works. The table that goes with the chair is planned as the exact complement to the chairs, a large sculpture instead of a frail element. The table has a large tubular steel frame (14 cm. in diameter) upon which are laid three slabs of red Verona marble or Florentine breccia. Whereas the chair is designed to demonstrate its function in terms of the human body, the table relates sculpturally to the space of the surrounding environment.

《PRIMA》 601 Chair and 《SECONDA》 602 Armchair

《*SECONDA*》 *602 Armchair*

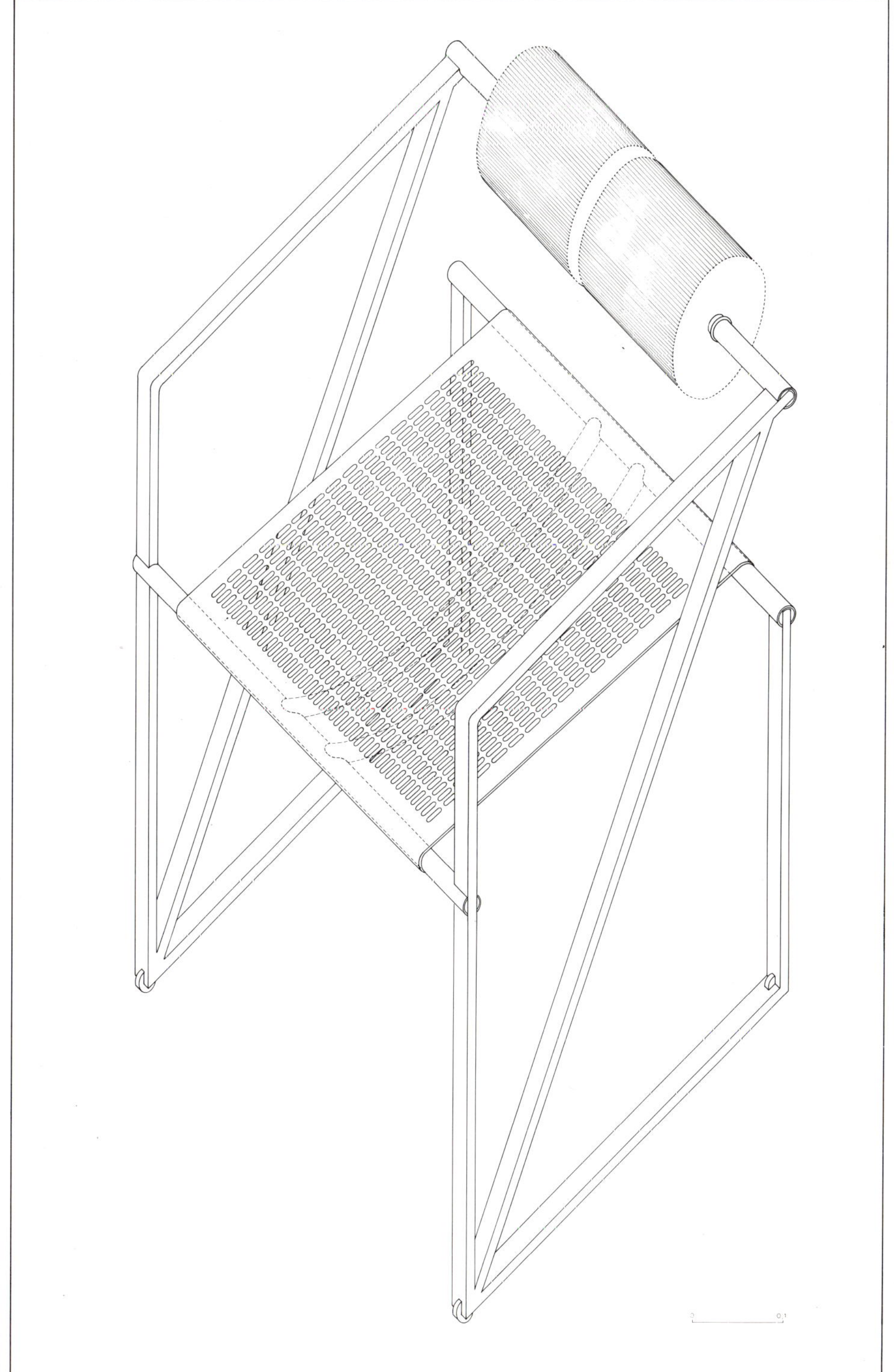

Axonometric

The competition required the construction of a new theater complex to be built near the old Napoleonic structure of the curial barracks, whose eastern wing was to be restored. The project will articulate the new complex into two different volumes: a semicylindrical one housing a theater with 900 seats, and a rectangular one for equipment and sets. The restored wing of the barracks, transformed into a foyer and atrium, is the third compositional element of the project.

The two new buildings are not axially aligned with the curial barracks but instead line the existing street; the link between the barracks and the theater is provided by a glass-covered passage that allows for a view of the surrounding city. Around the theater a distributive peripheral ring with stairs leading to the upper balconies mediates the passage between the two different axes. The curved wall of the new structure is set against the flat one of the barracks. At street level the surface of this wall is broken by a portico that acts as a mediating link between exterior and interior. The emergency stairway outside, placed between the volumes of the theater and of the storehouse, marks the small square formed by the barracks, the theater, the police headquarters, and a group of houses, still to be built, along the street.

The building is composed of reinforced concrete covered with slabs of stone.

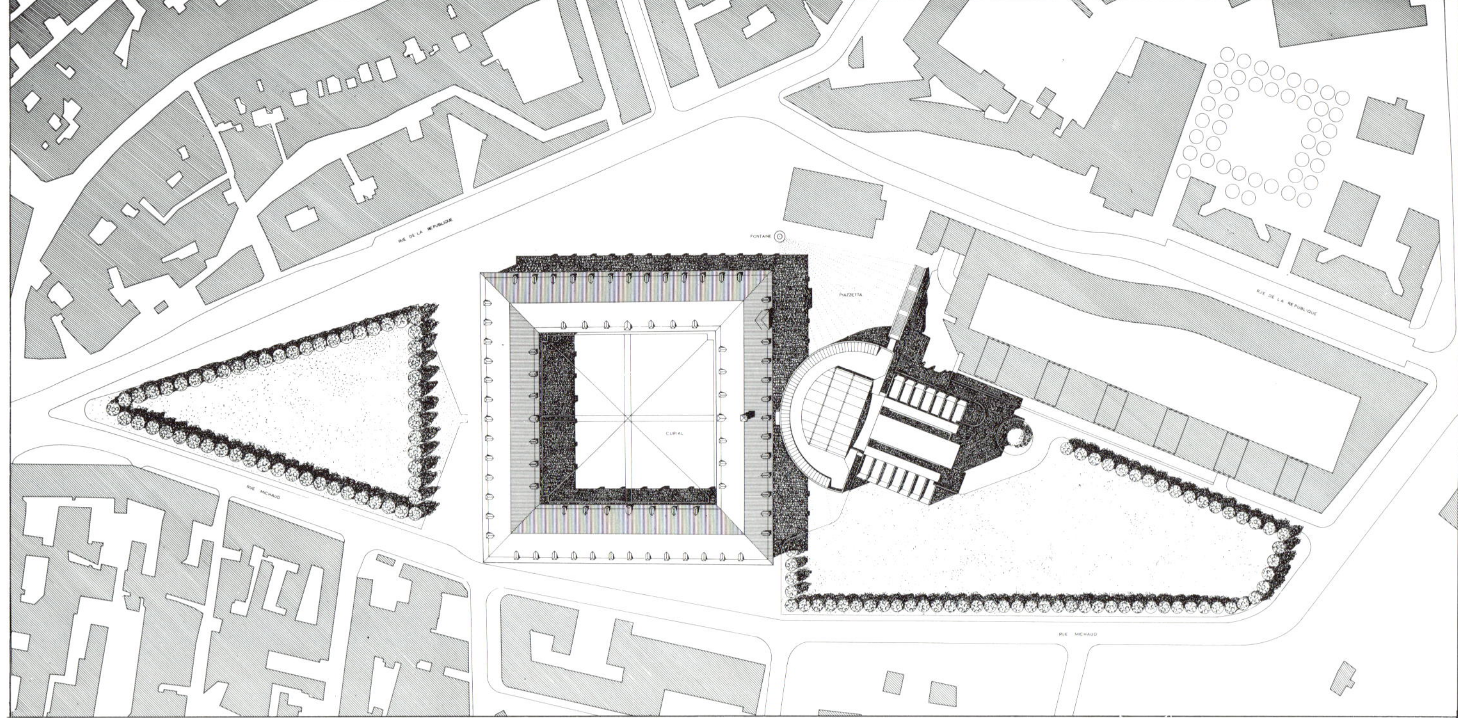

Site plans

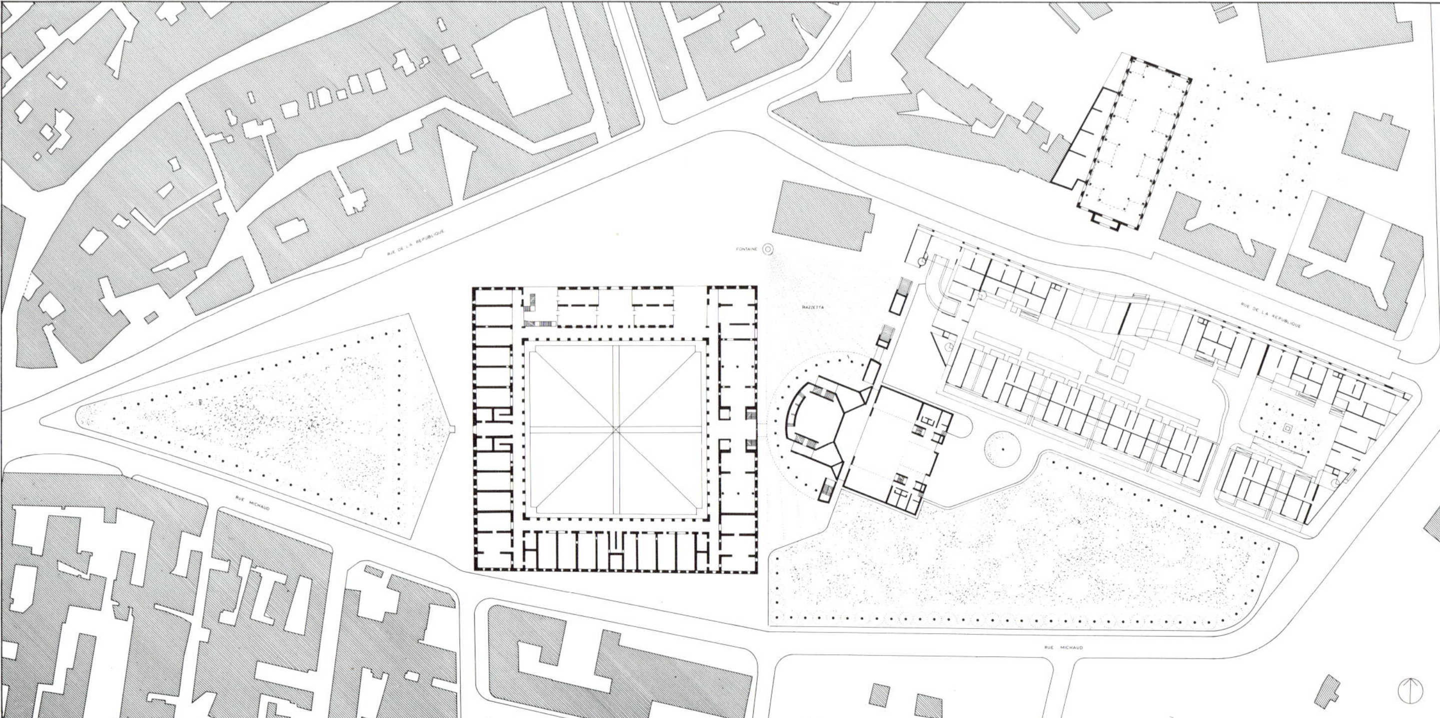

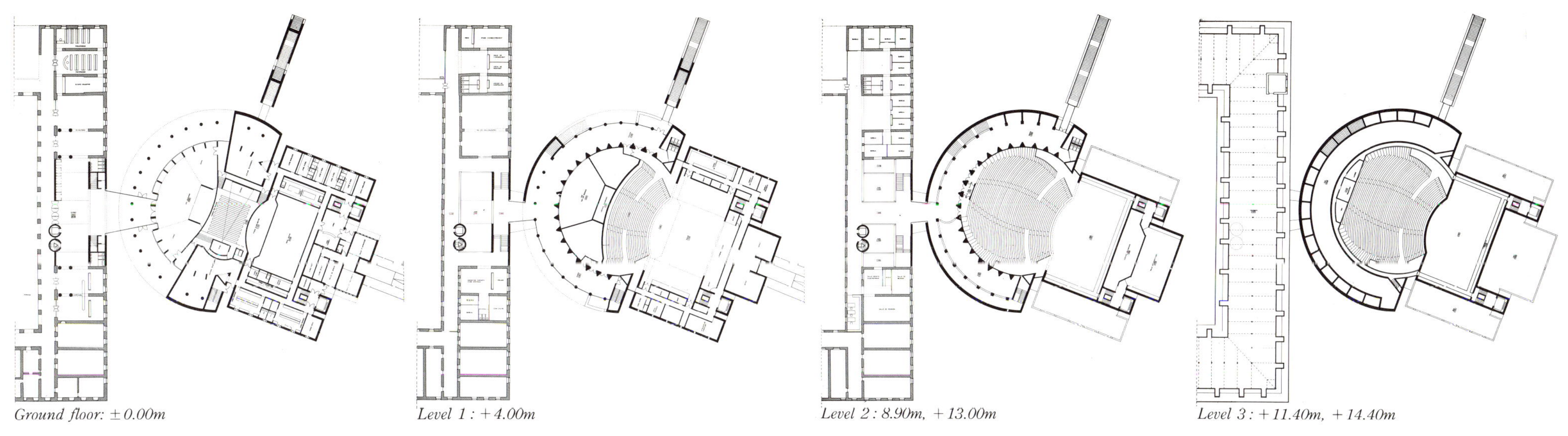

Ground floor: ± 0.00m

Level 1 : + 4.00m

Level 2 : 8.90m, + 13.00m

Level 3 : + 11.40m, + 14.40m

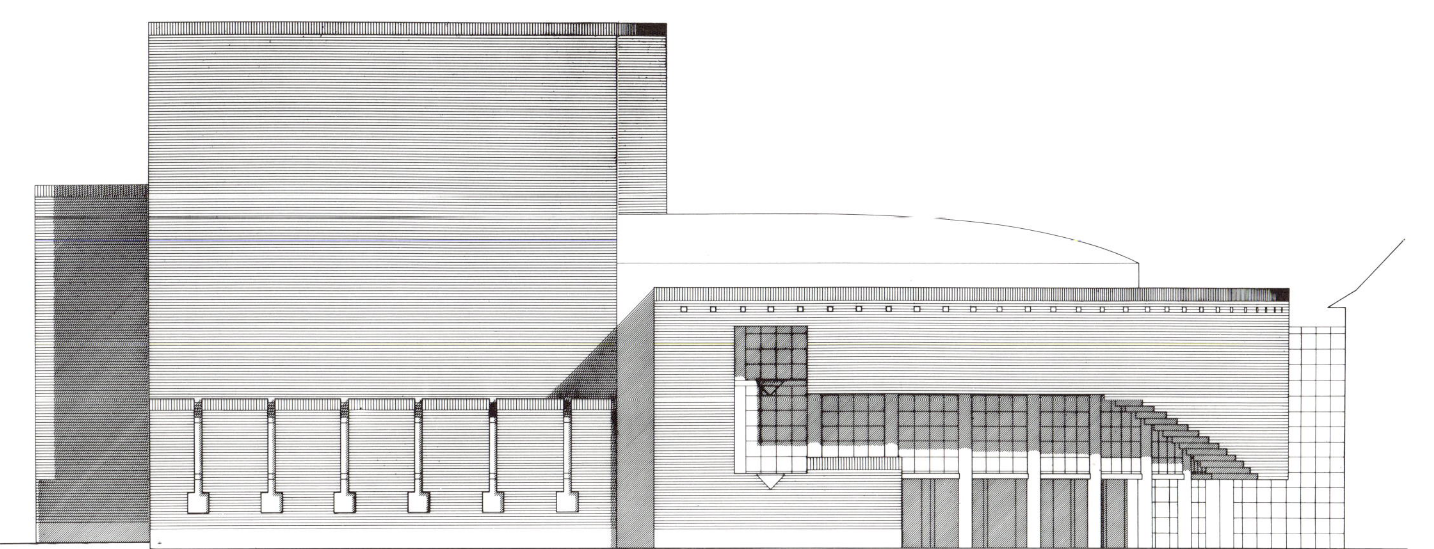

Elevation A-A

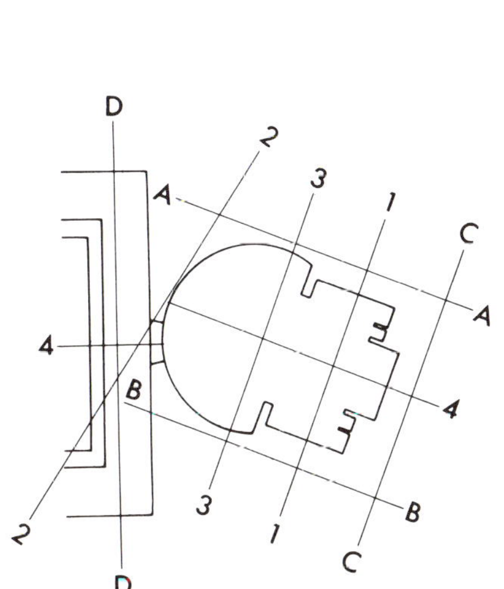

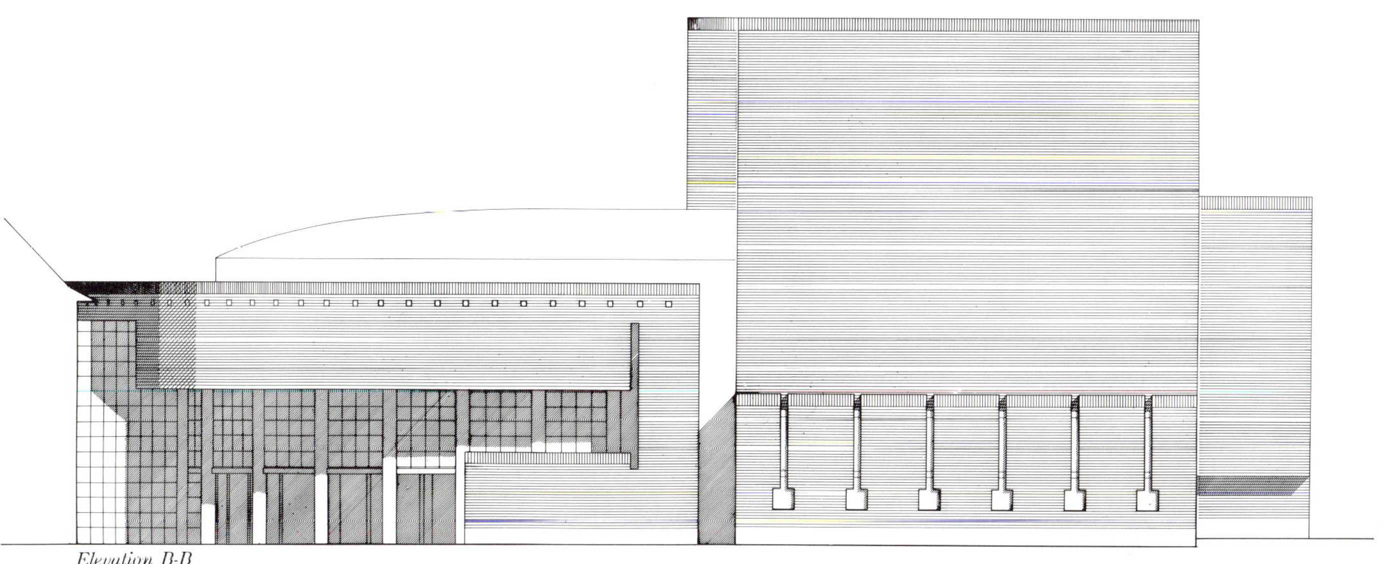

Elevation B-B

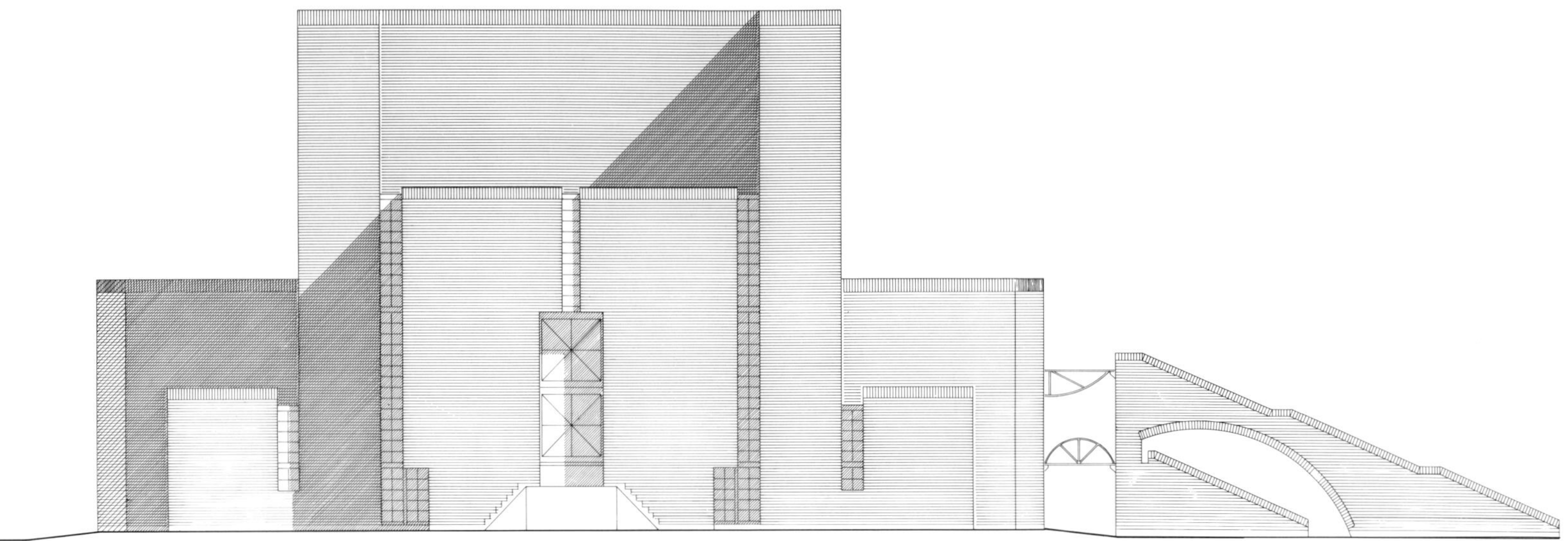

Model photo

Elevation C-C

Model photo

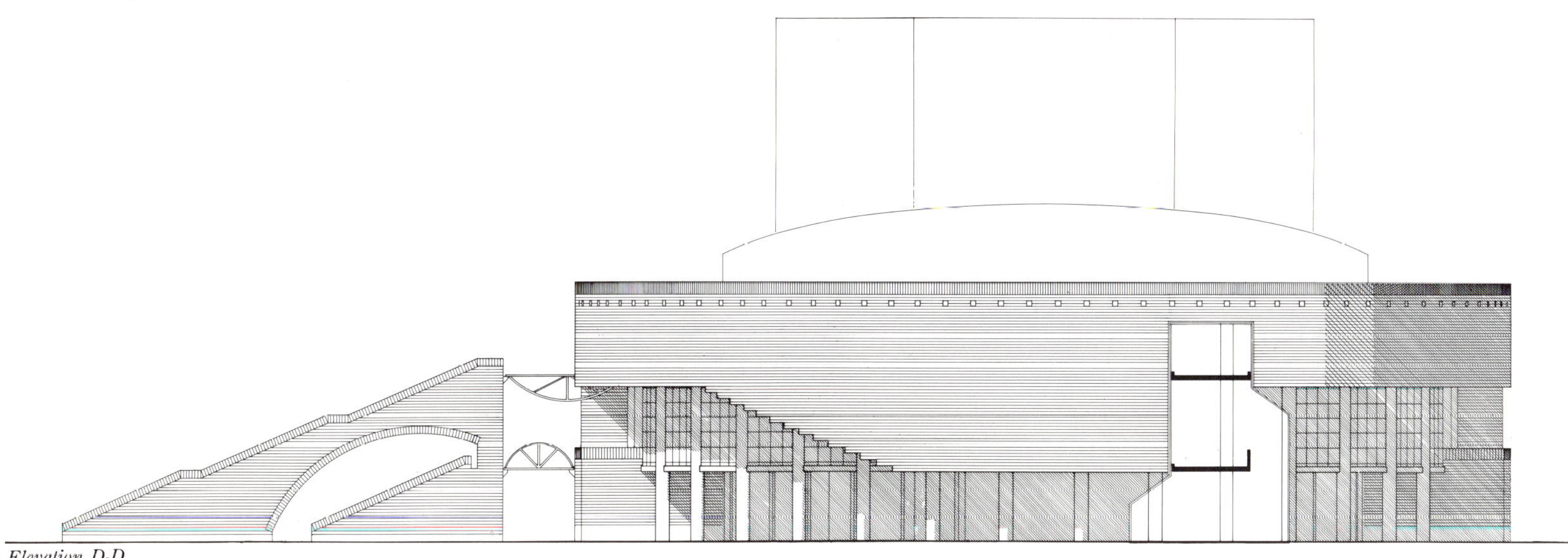

Elevation D-D

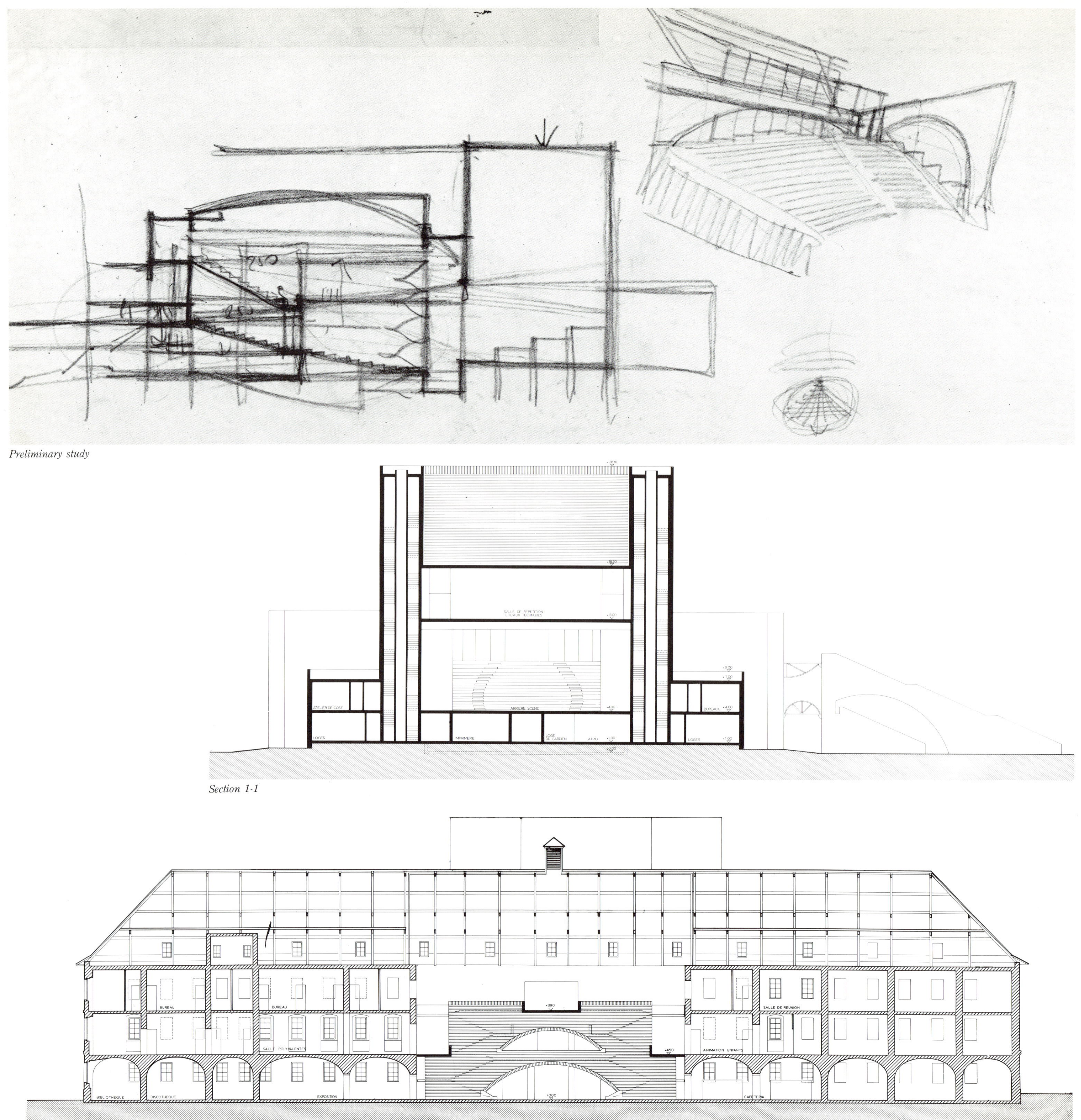

Preliminary study

Section 1-1

Section 2-2

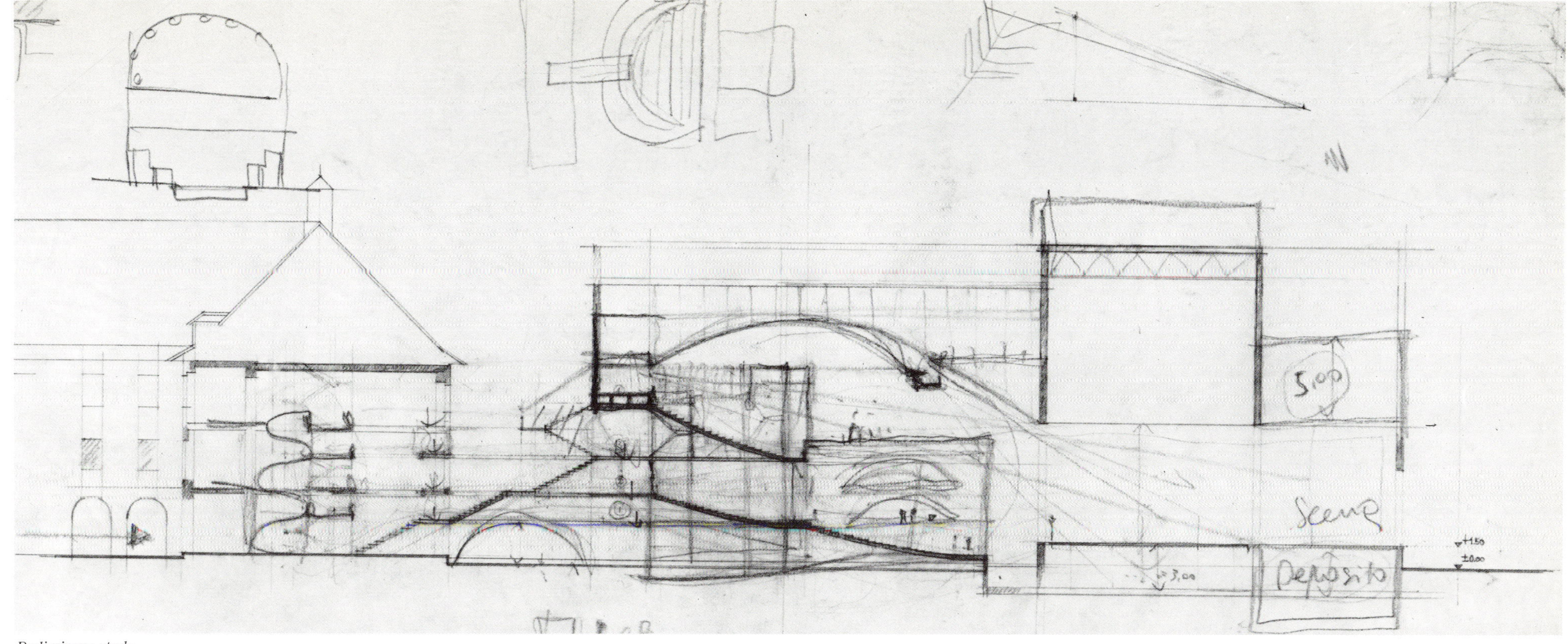

Preliminary study

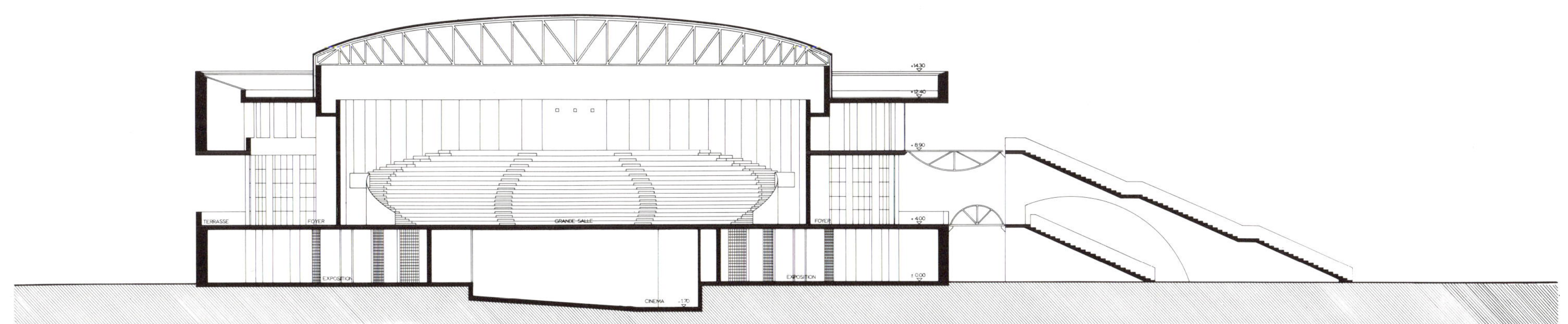

Section 3-3

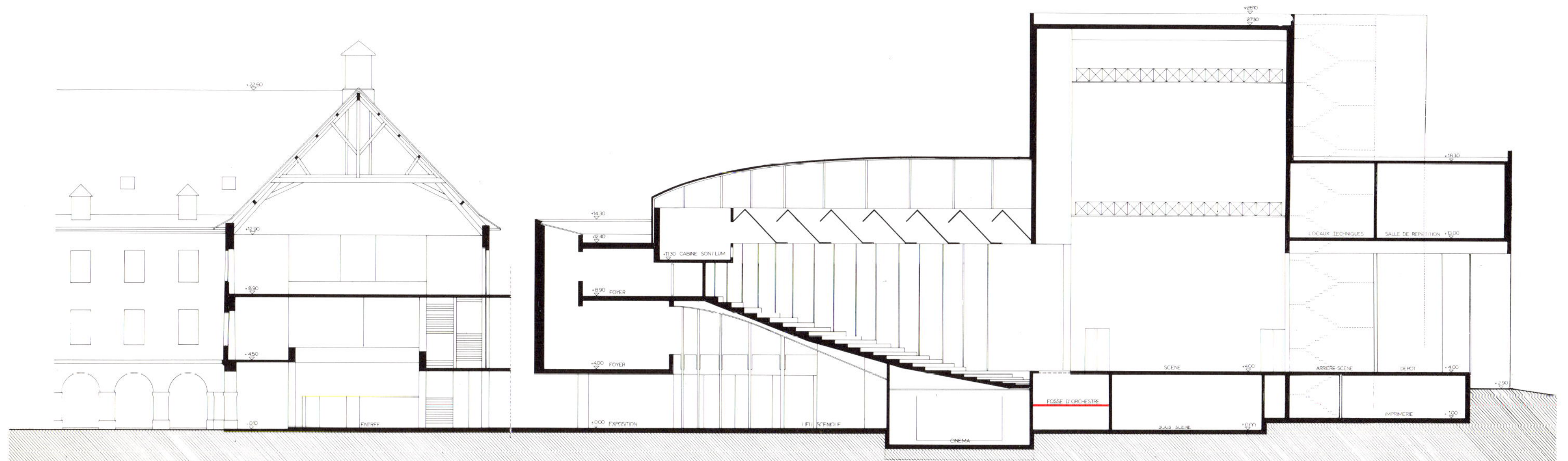

Section 4-4

Twenty years ago the creation of a new super-highway modified the existing texture of the site. The site is located on a section of a city block bisected by the new highway next to a couple of buildings already constructed. The project divides the building into two different structures, not because it was requested by the competition but in order to facilitate the insertion of the volumes into the city fabric. One element of the project is the building facing south that echoes in its plan the one of the building next to it, and reestablishes the continuity of the street front. The second part of the project follows the direction of the new highway, facing it with a continuous wall, while toward the interior the volume arcs toward the corners.

The particular solution adopted, two separate volumes, attempts to knit together the torn fabric of the city, while at the same time making a statement about the impossibility of a traditional building inside the area disrupted by the highway. Because of this, the entrance is not located on the side facing the street (which is treated as a mute background) but on the point of conjunction of the two volumes. From here one enters into the covered courtyard of the building facing south, eventually reaching, by ramp, the other building set along the street.

△▽ *Model photos*

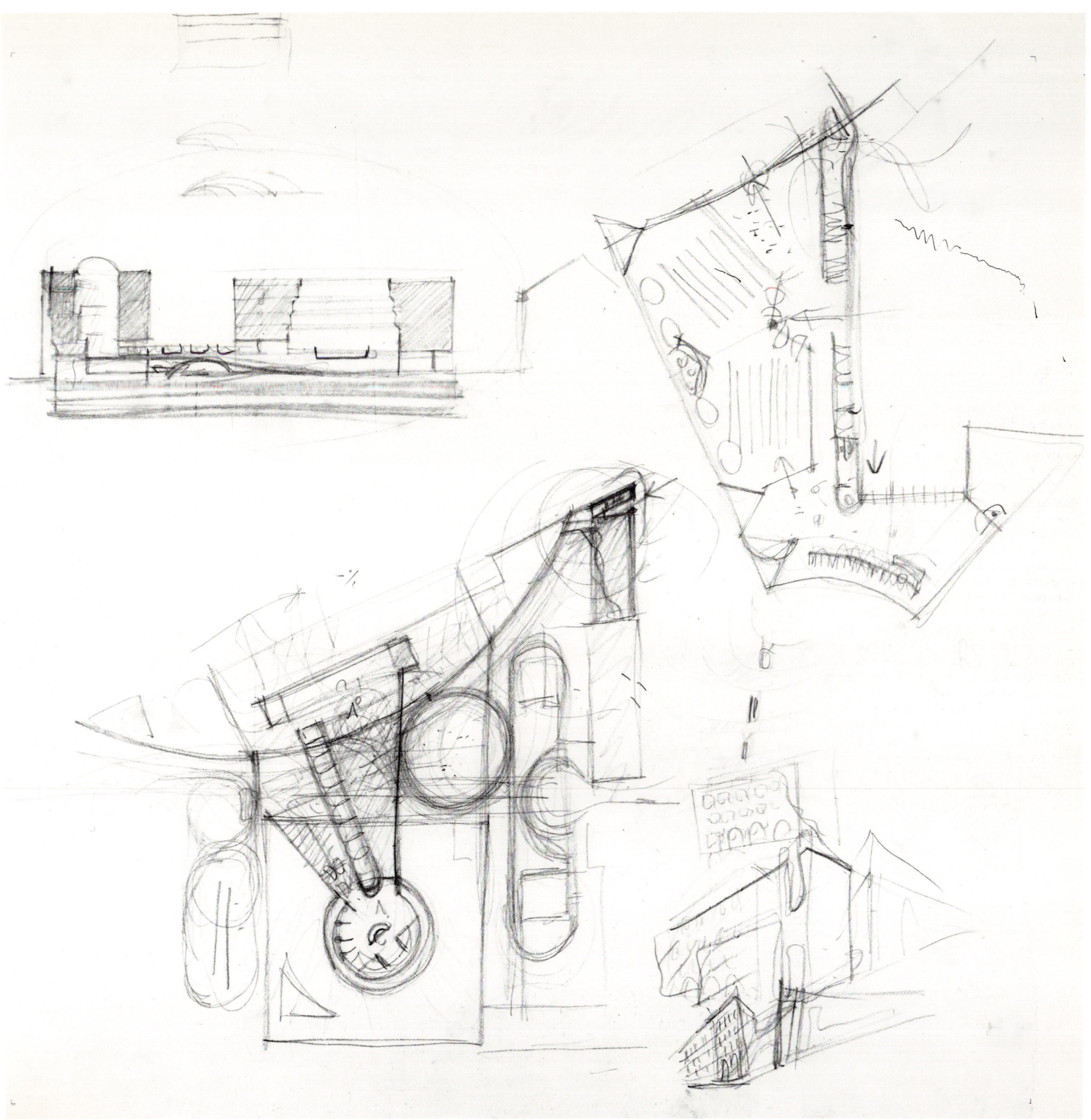

Preliminary study

München 1849

München 1983

Perspective from Oskar-von-Miller-Ring.

Urban Setting

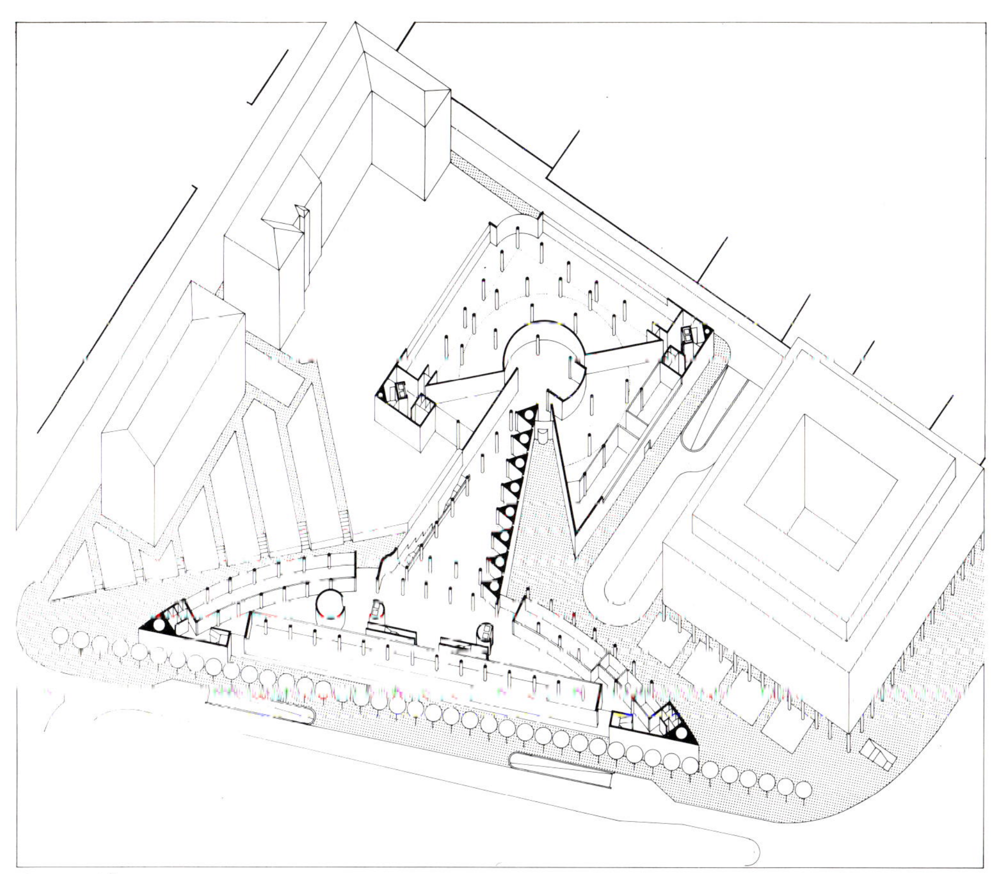

Axonometric

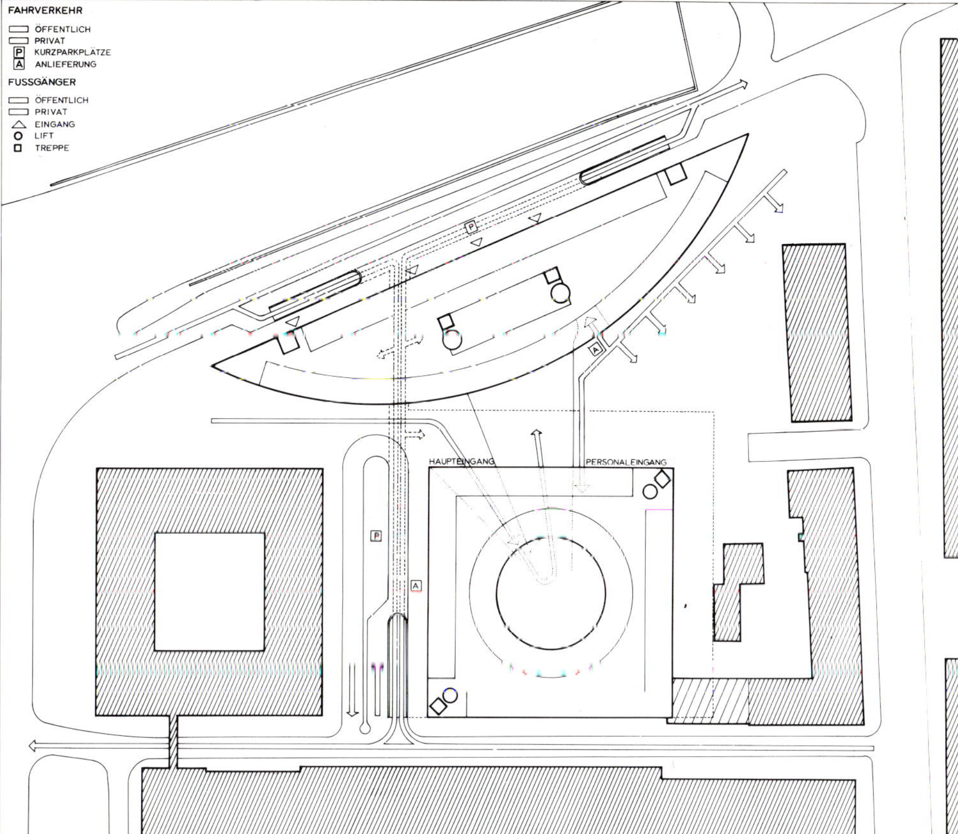

Traffic circulation

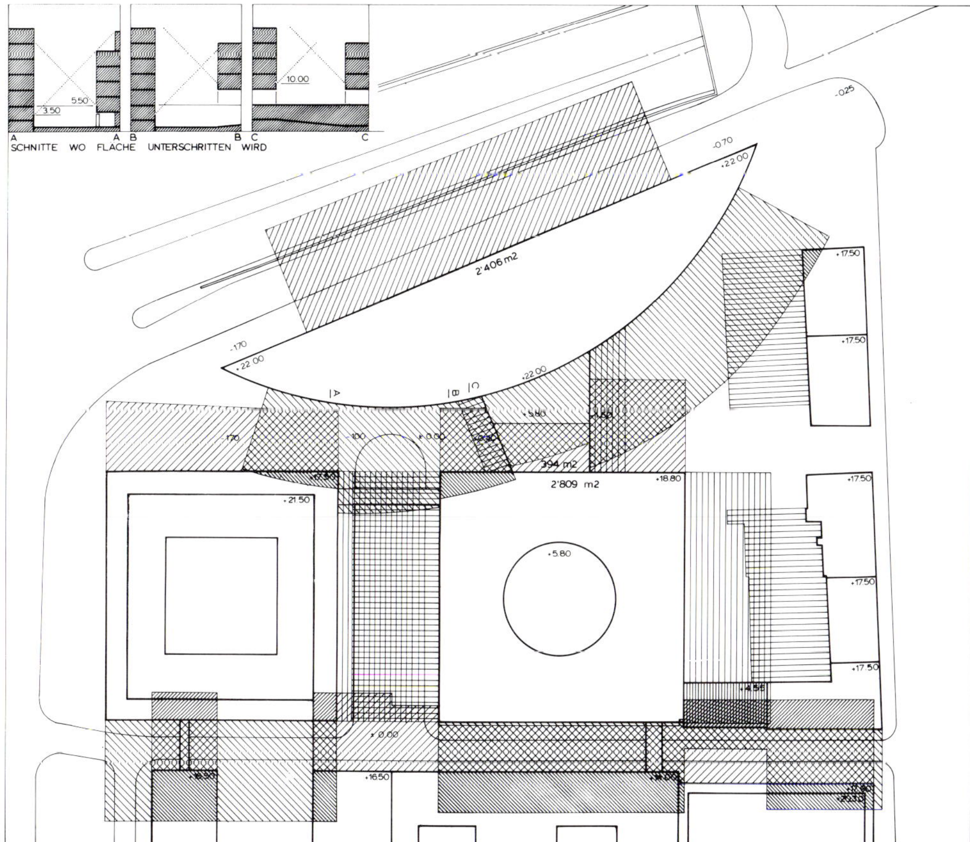

Floor levels : Floor areas 0.57 (< 0.6) : Eave heights

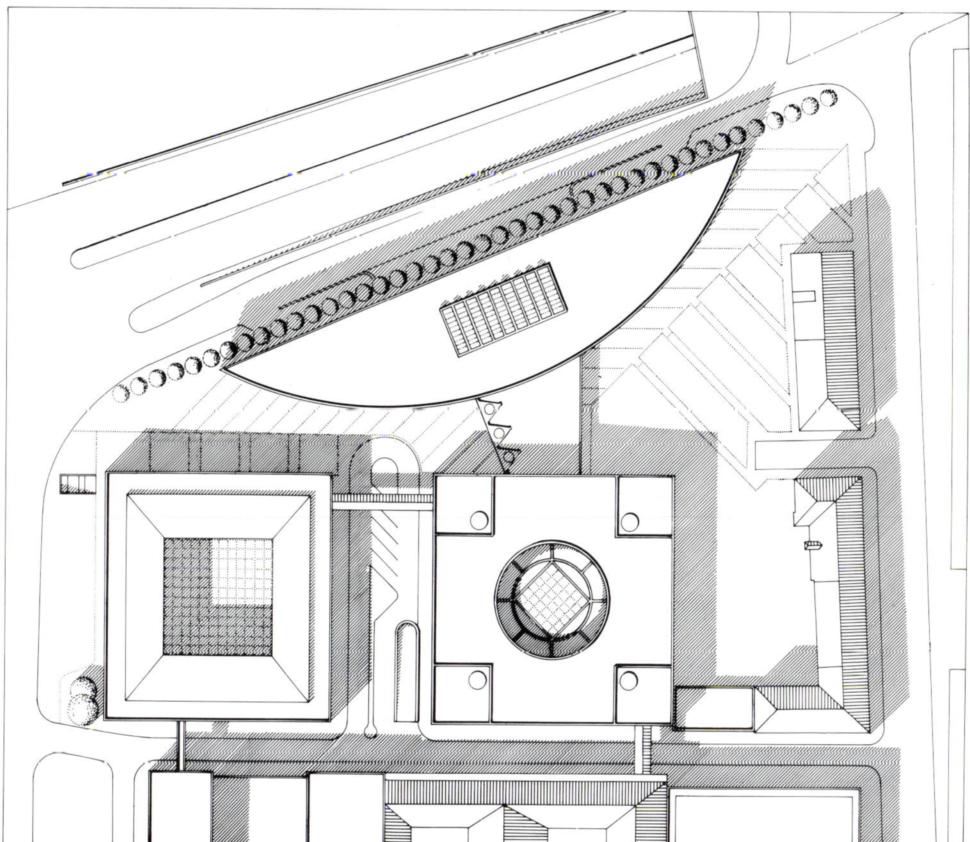

Site plan

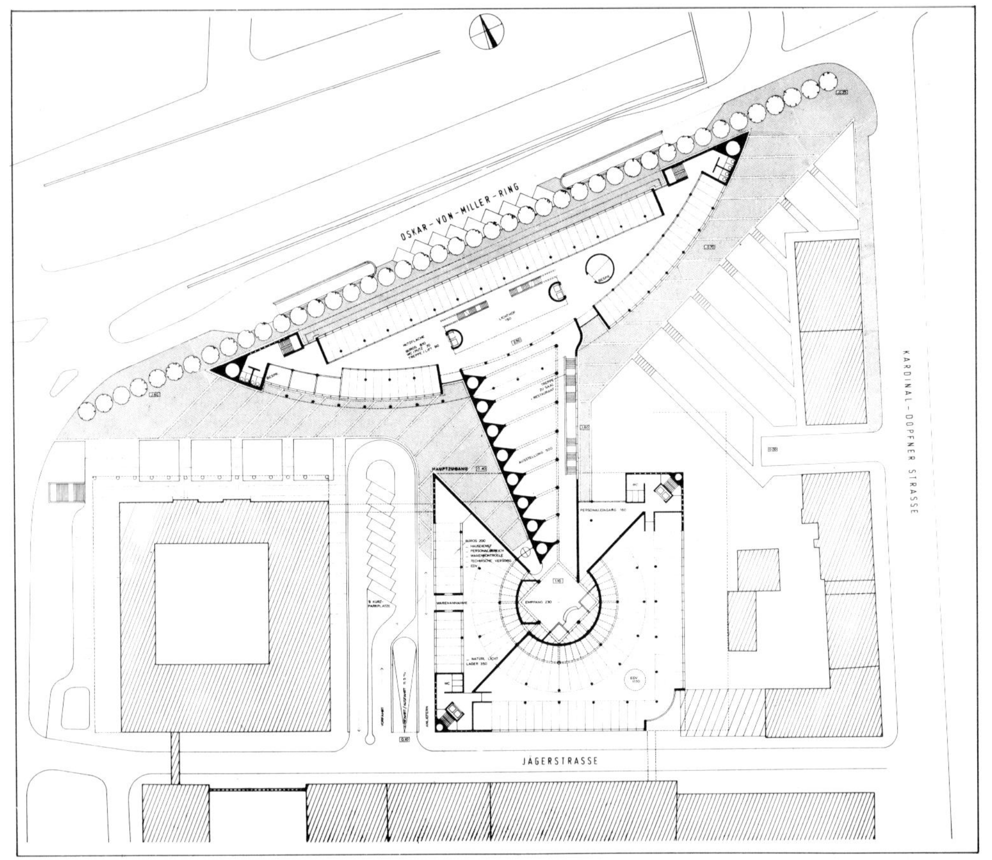

EG+: level +2.50m

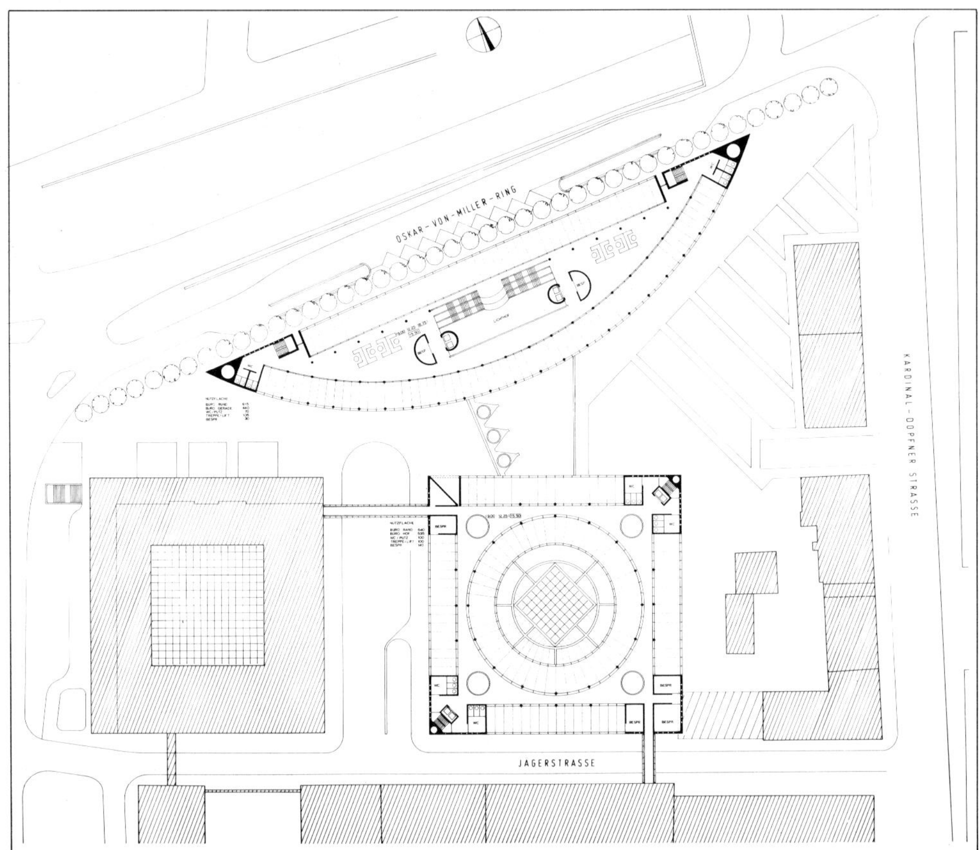

4.0G: level +15.50m

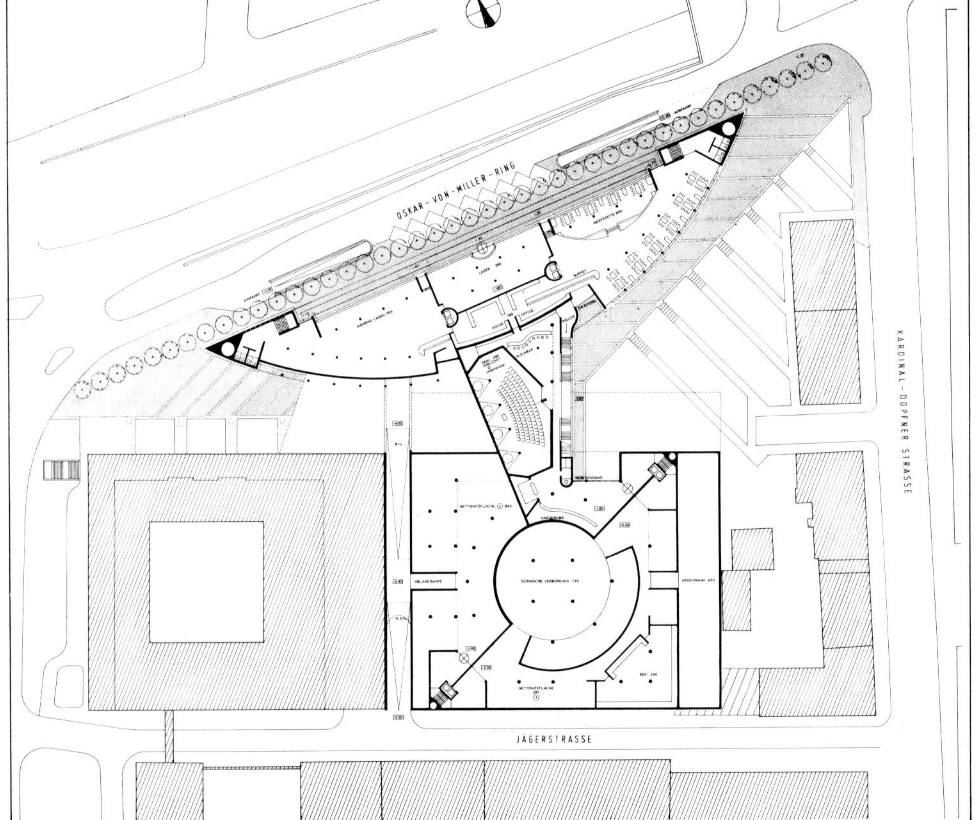

EG−: level −1.60m

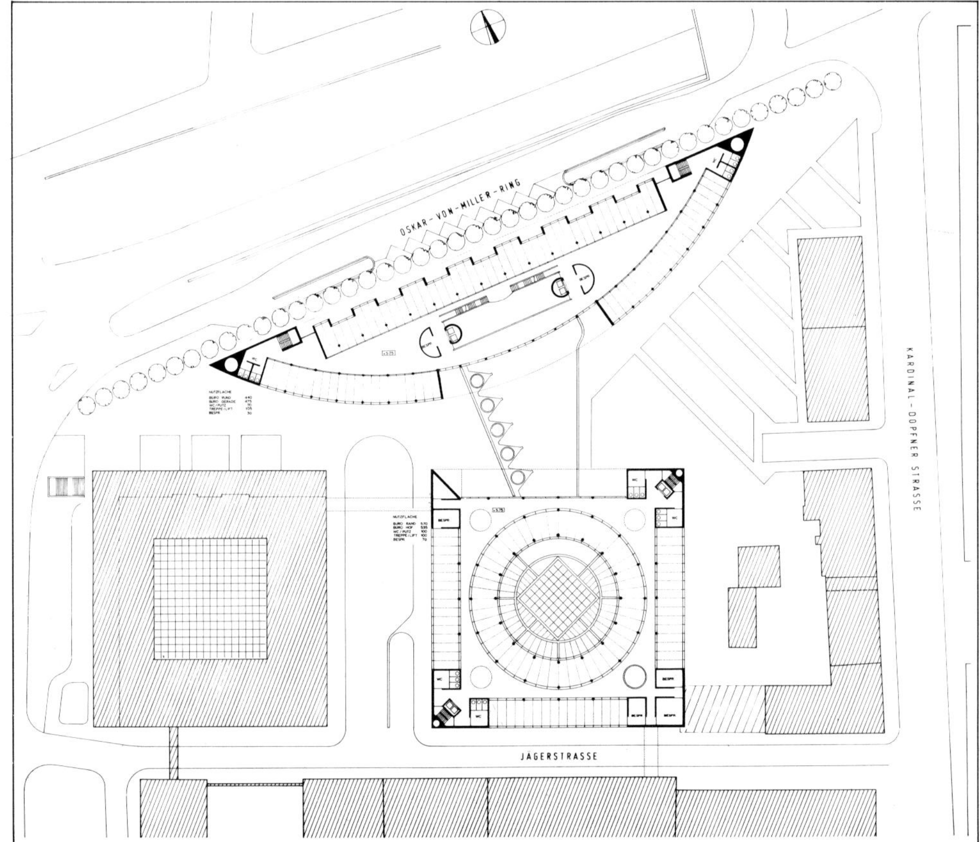

1.0G: level +5.80m

Elevation 1-1

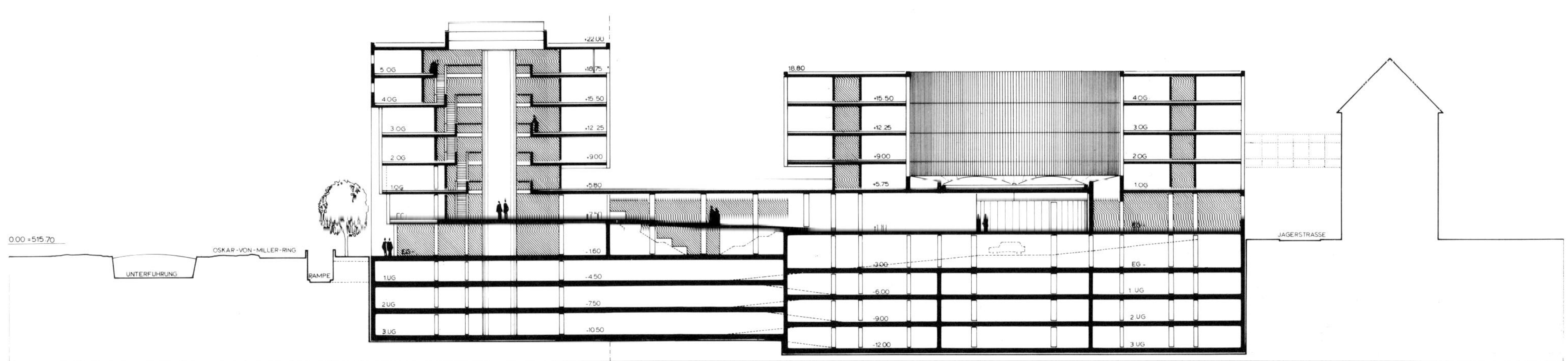

Section 2-2

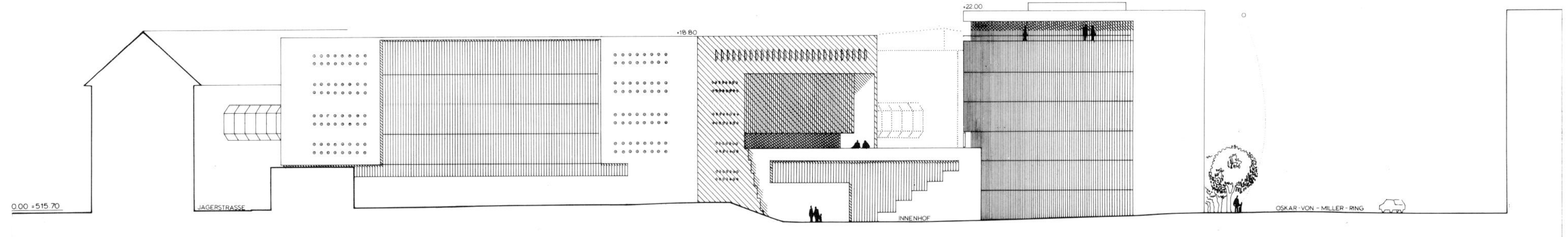

Elevation 3-3

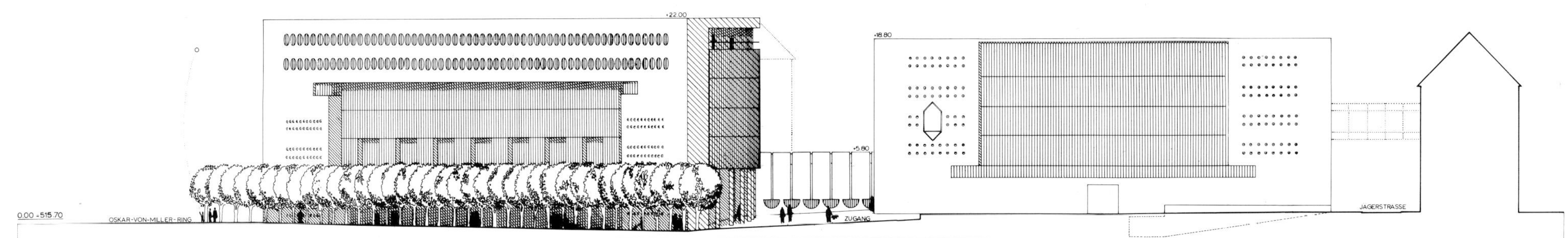

Elevation 4-4

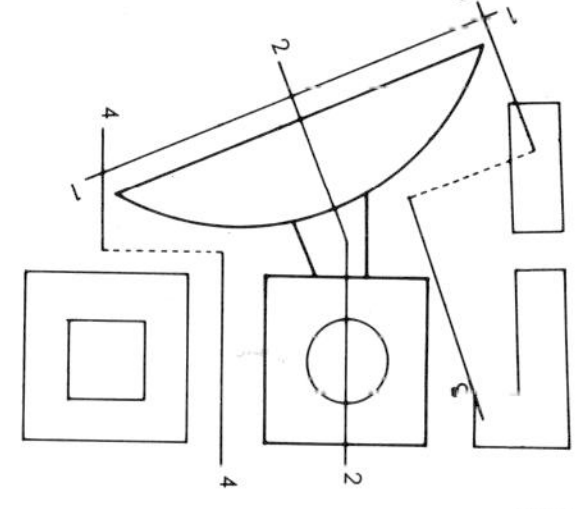

The project for Piazza Cavour allows for the creation of a link between two different sections of the city: the nineteenth-century upper level of the city around the Viale della Vittoria and the eighteenth-century section, built around the harbor, to the north. By exploiting the difference of levels, a sequence of public spaces is carved in the slope of the ground: an underground passage and a long bridge assure the continuity of the pedestrian walk set on the axis that links the Viale della Vittoria with the harbor.

The first element of the project is the new square for pedestrian use, between the post office and the city hall; the second is the triangular square of the bus station; the third is the large circular square (60 m. in diameter) that follows the conformation of the slope and around which there will be shops. At the center of this round space a stair brings one to the pedestrian bridge that, after crossing over the bus station, reaches the square of the city hall.

All existing trees at will be preserved.

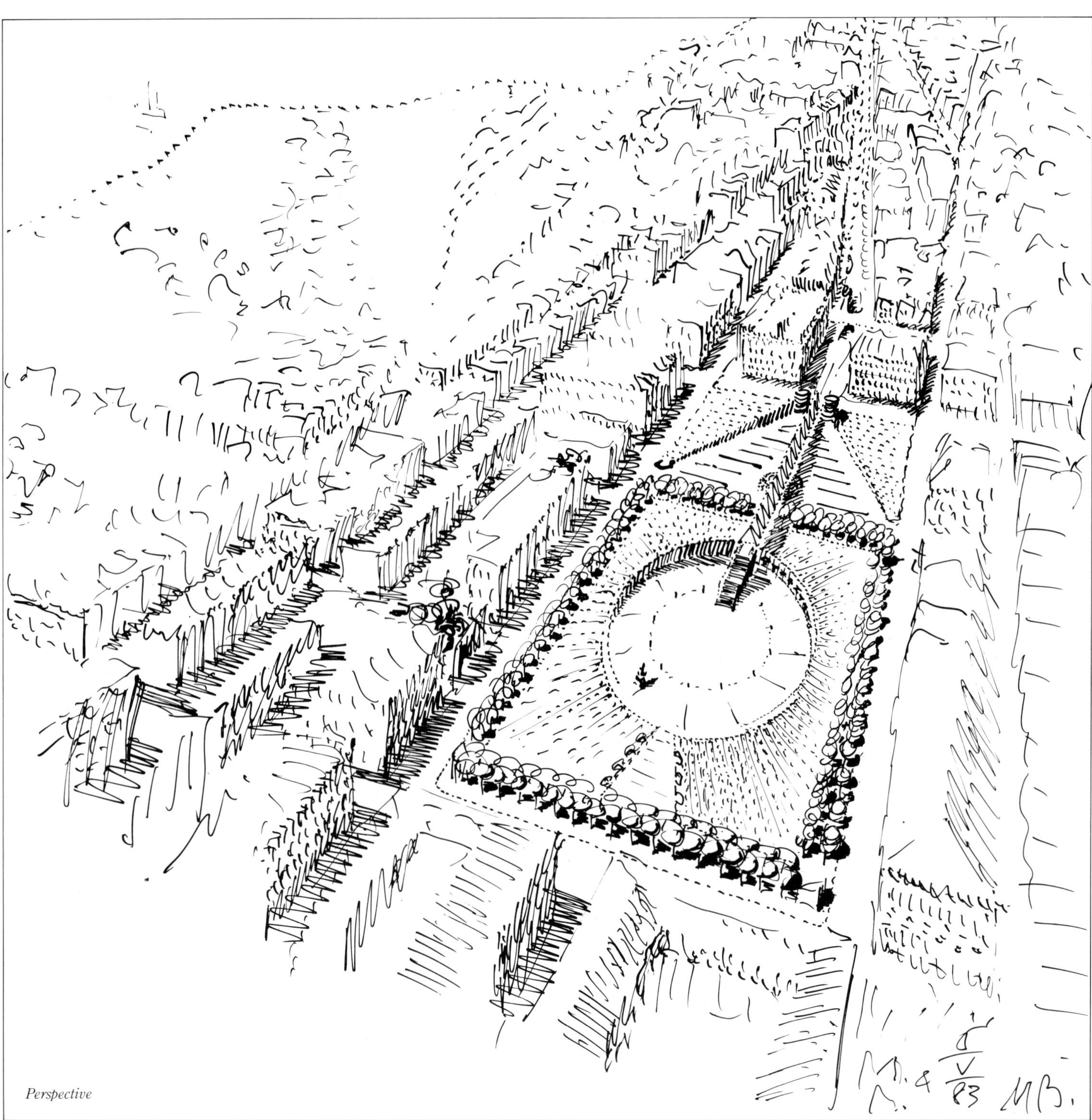

Perspective

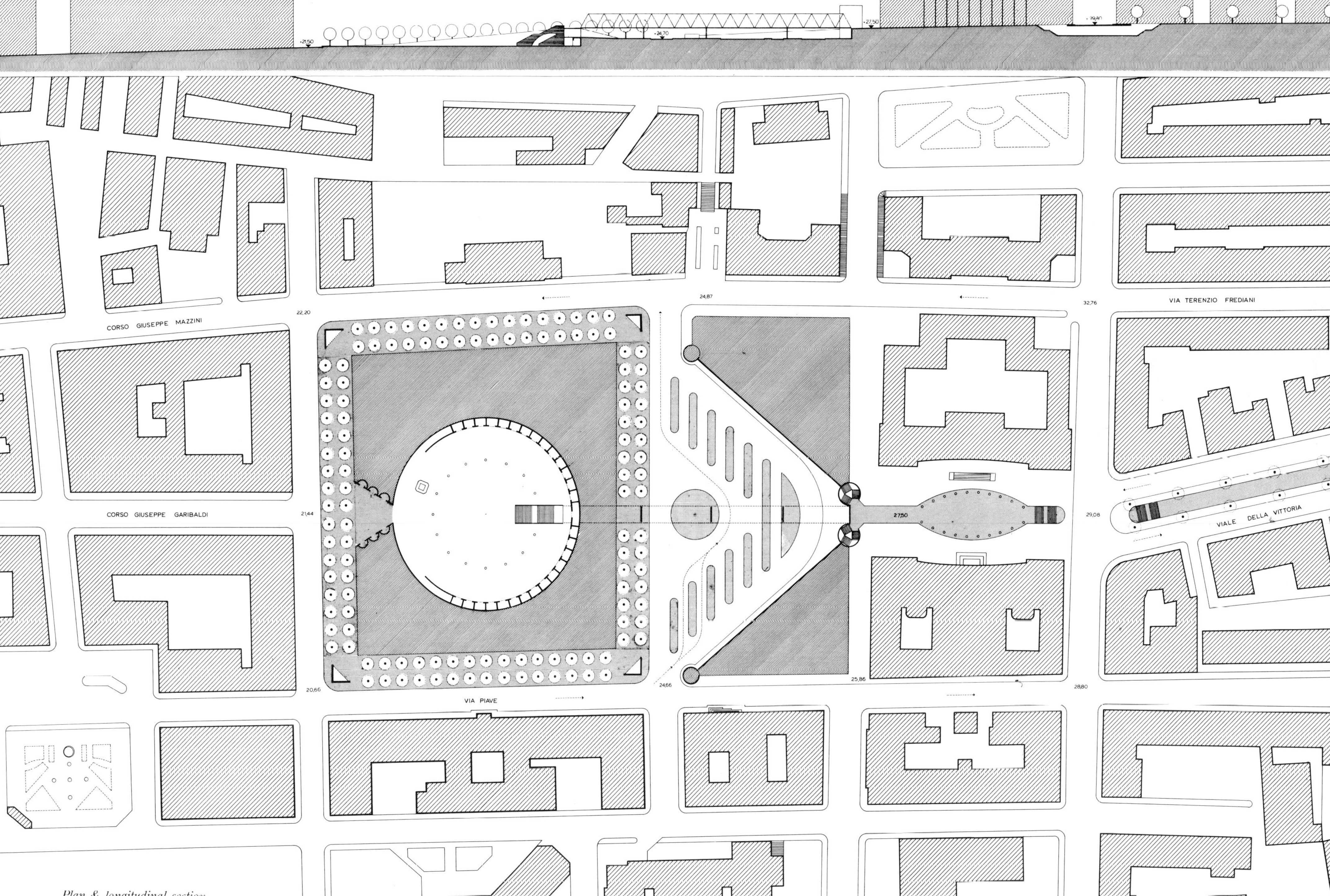

Plan & longitudinal section

213

Two of the three sections composing the new library recompose the unity of the street front and of the space behind it. The first element of the project houses the entrance, the stairs, and secondary spaces; its façade covered with stone in two colors perfectly merges into the row of street buildings. The second section of the library, behind the first, aligned with the buildings constructed two decades ago, houses the library's storerooms. The façades of this building are made of glass and concrete. The third element, a semicylindrical structure covered with stone, overlooks the internal courtyard.

In this section are located the reading rooms, which also face the courtyard. The large central space of this section is illuminated by a skylight; its walls are painted white. Stairs connect the reading rooms located on different levels, decreasing in size as they approach the upper floor.

Sixth level: Guardians' lodgings

Roof

Fourth level: Children's section

Fifth level: Periodicals

Second level: Adult section and gallery

Third level: Record library and audio section

Basement

First level: Adult section

North elevation

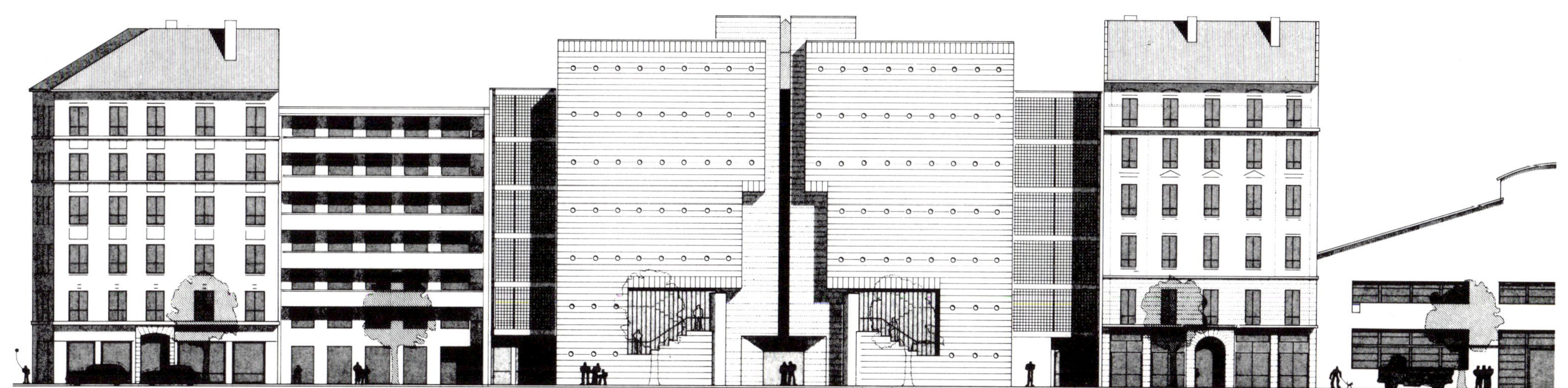

South elevation

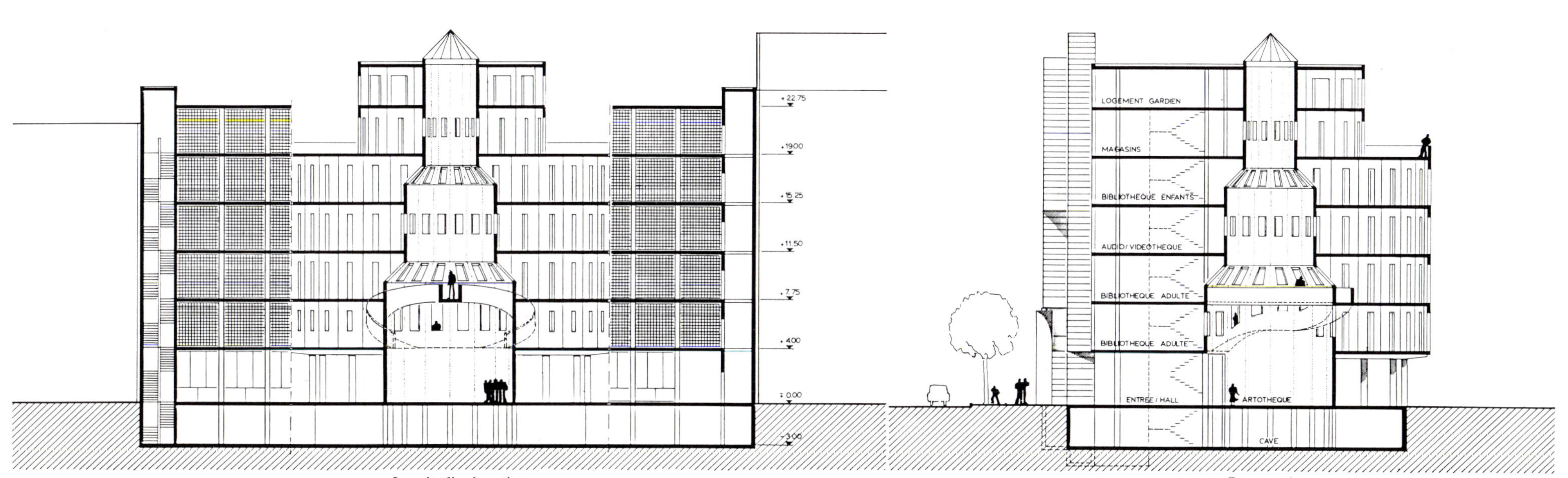

Longitudinal section   *Cross section*

In order to avoid a single long front along the street that would have been out of proportion with the existing texture of the city, the complex program requested by the bank was broken down into a series of four independent volumes, each one fronting the street. The façades are set back farther than the adjacent buildings; a new row of trees reestablishes the broken course of the avenue. The alternation of full volumes and smaller ones produces an aesthetically pleasing sequence along the street level.

Stairs and elevators are located in the smaller volumes set among the four different buildings; the sides toward the street are characterized by glass walls screened with a *brise-soleil* of concrete and stone. The four walls facing the street are lined with granite in shades of gray and rose.

A large triangular hall (repeated in every block) is at the core of the structures; around it there are stairs and, on all levels, offices. The offices, about 6 meters deep, are illuminated on one side by glass windows, on the other (toward the interior) by a skylight placed above on the roof of the triangular hall.

On the three floors below street level are parking lots, technical equipment, and bank vaults. On the ground floor are banking windows, a cinema, and a restaurant.

The structure will be composed of reinforced concrete covered with stone.

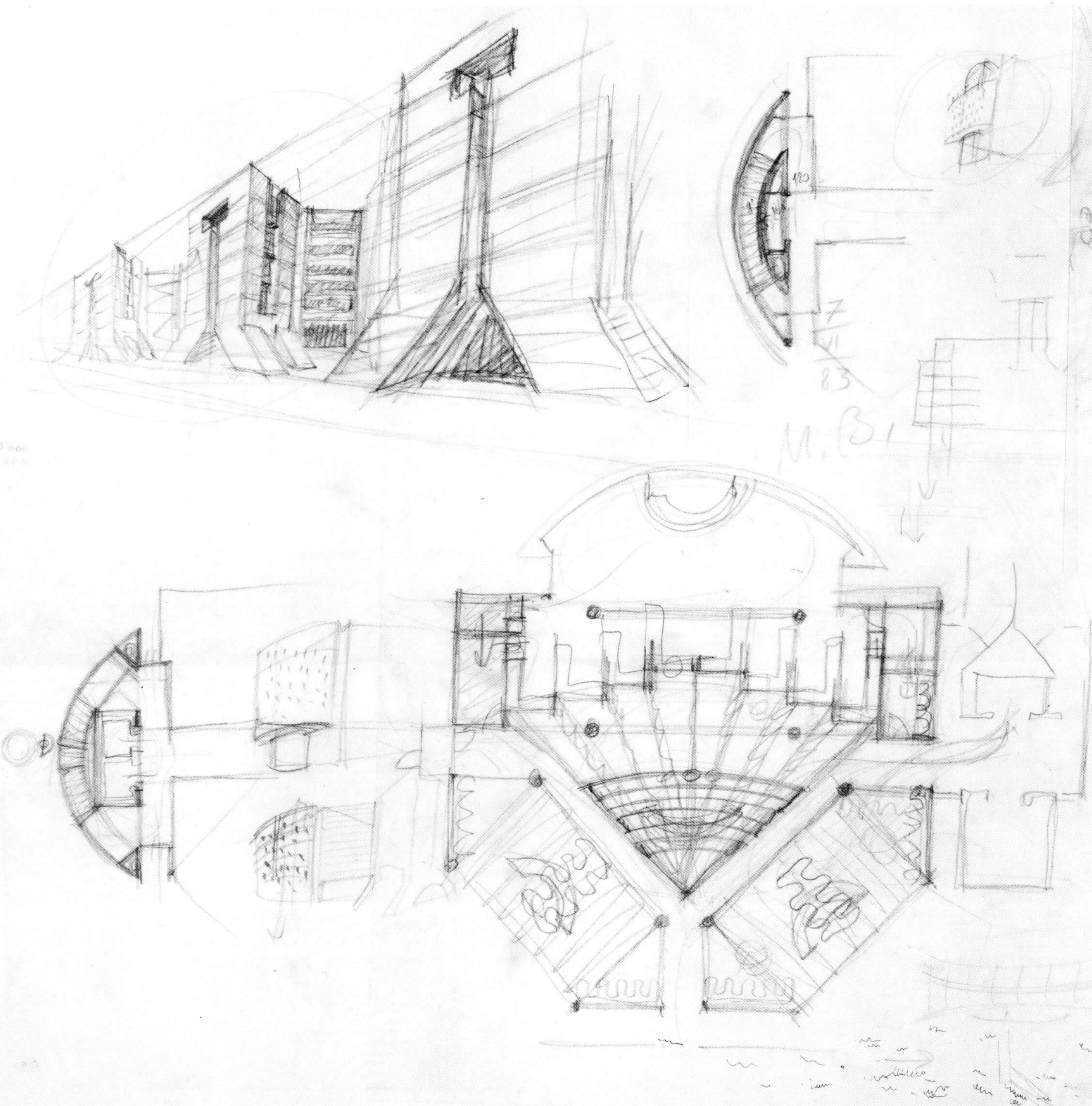

Preliminary study

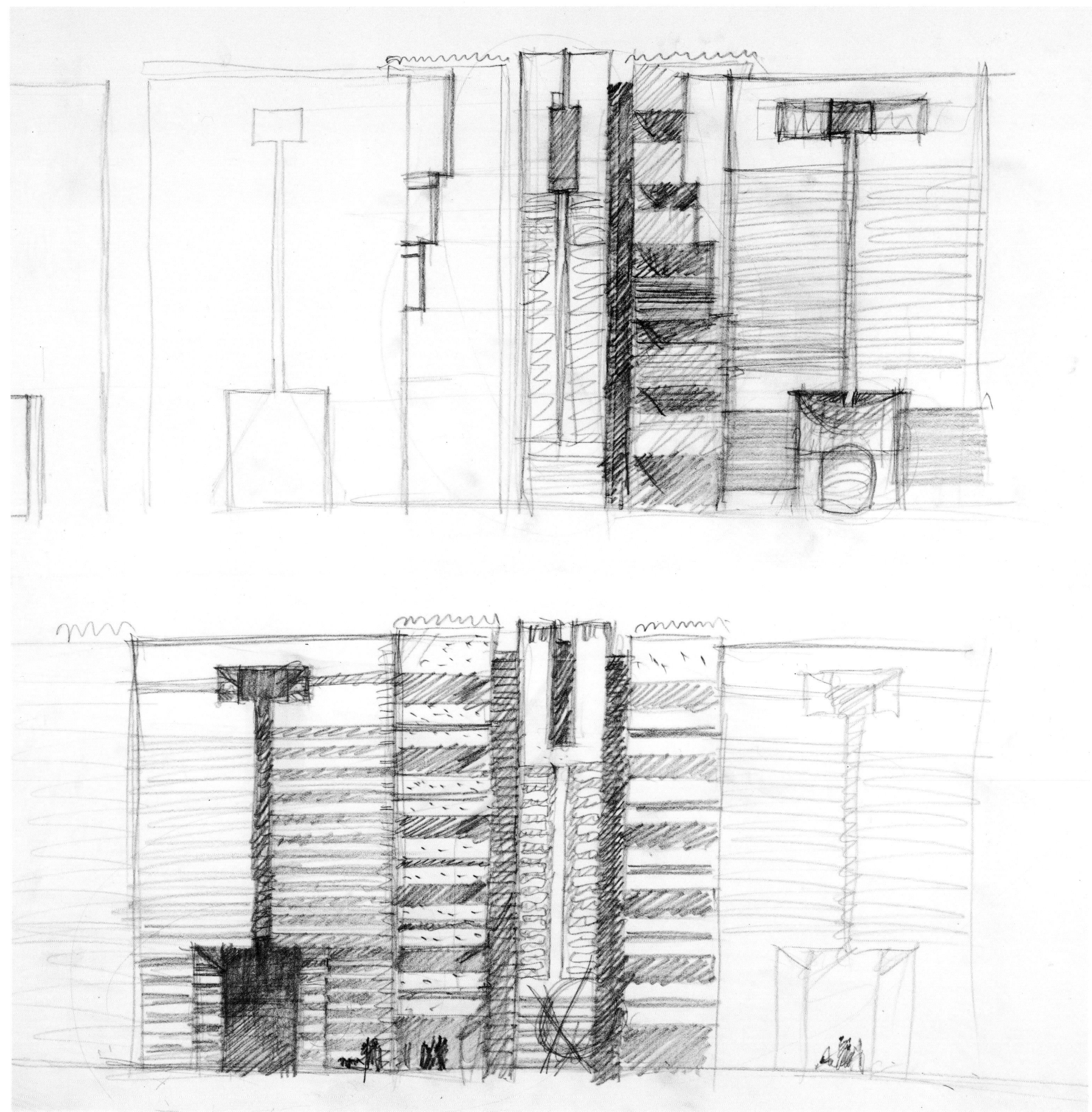

Preliminary study

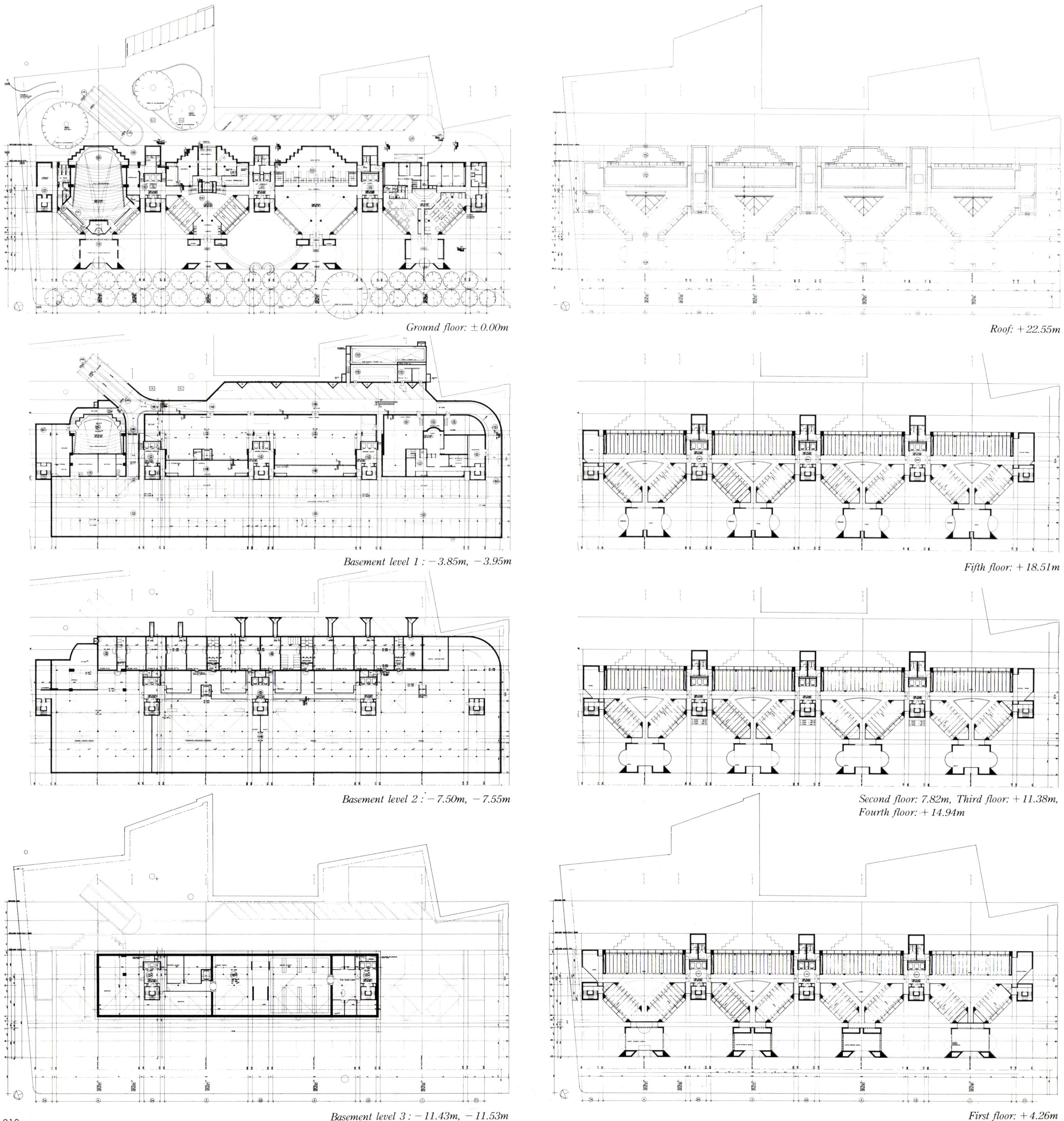

Ground floor: ± 0.00m

Roof: + 22.55m

Basement level 1 : − 3.85m, − 3.95m

Fifth floor: + 18.51m

Basement level 2 : − 7.50m, − 7.55m

*Second floor: 7.82m, Third floor: + 11.38m,
Fourth floor: + 14.94m*

Basement level 3 : − 11.43m, − 11.53m

First floor: + 4.26m

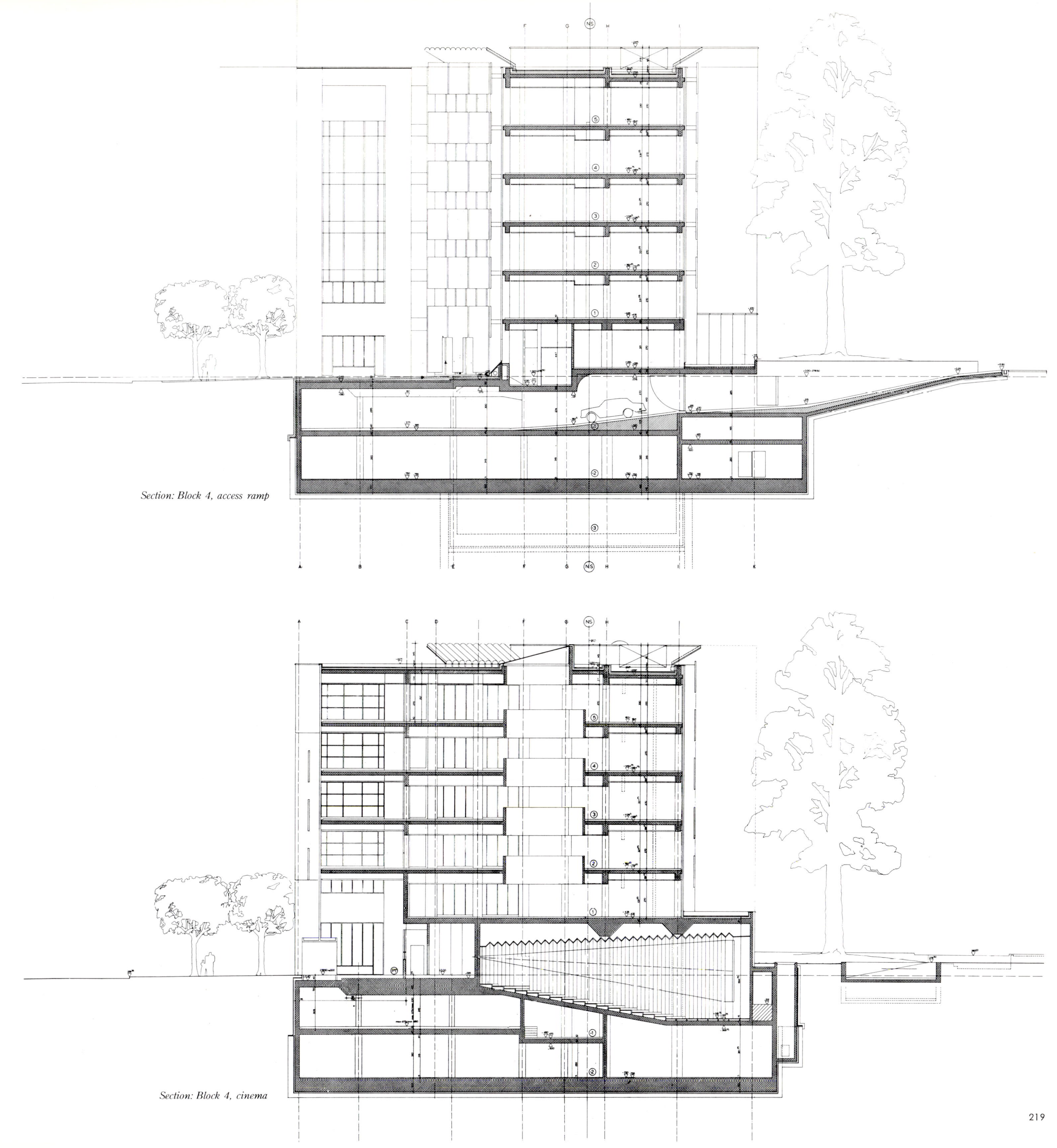

Section: Block 4, access ramp

Section: Block 4, cinema

West elevation

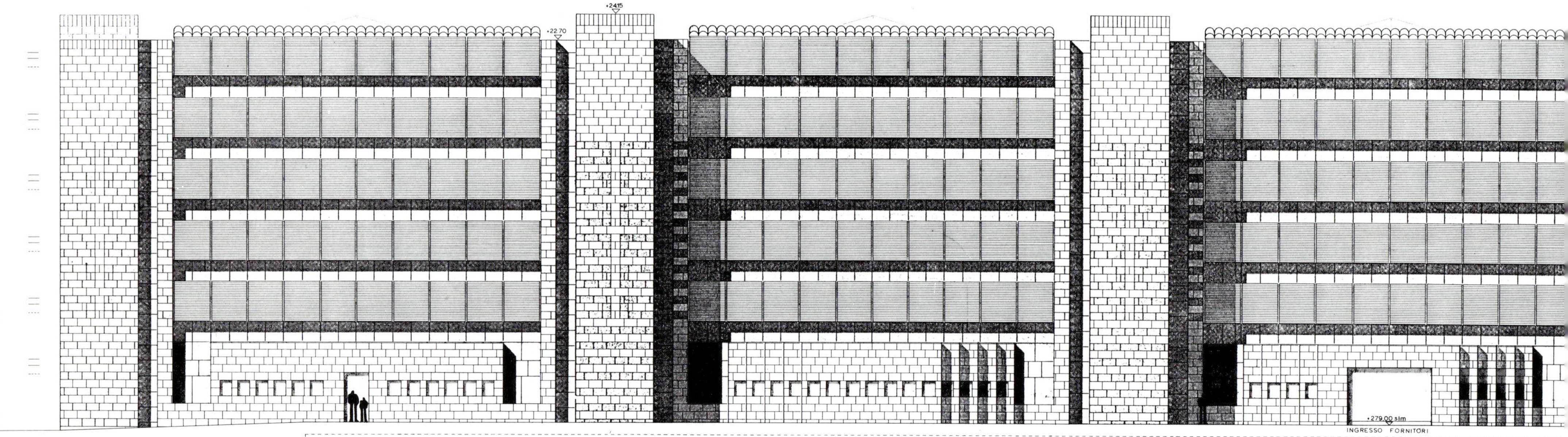

East elevation

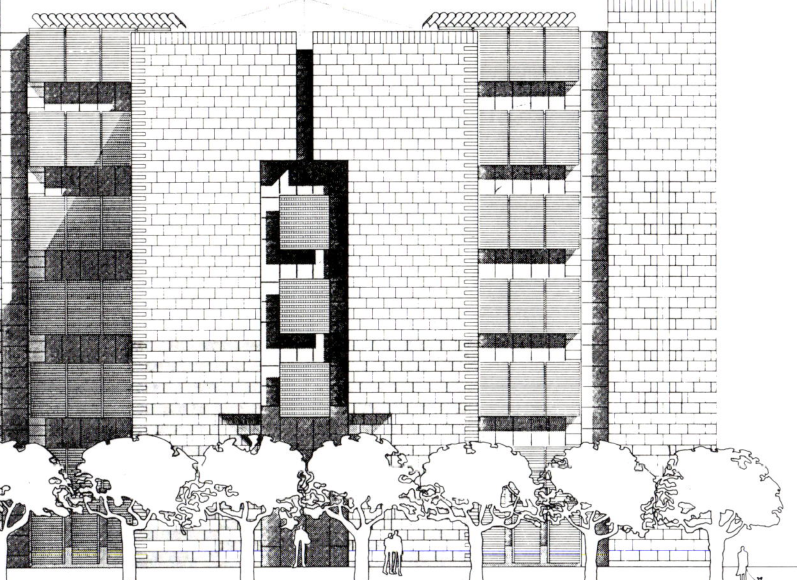

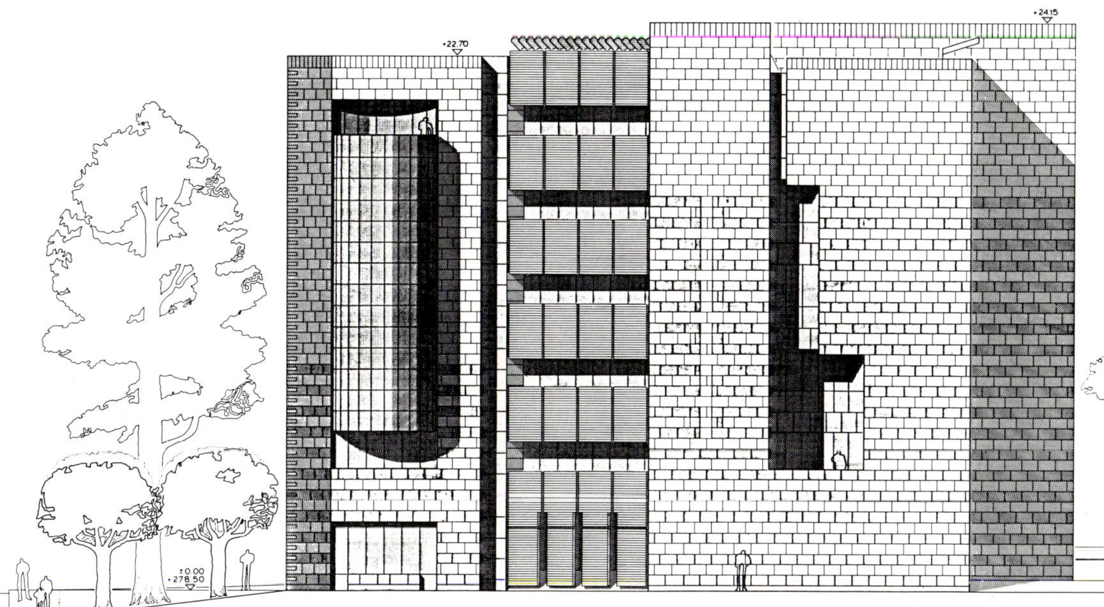

South elevation

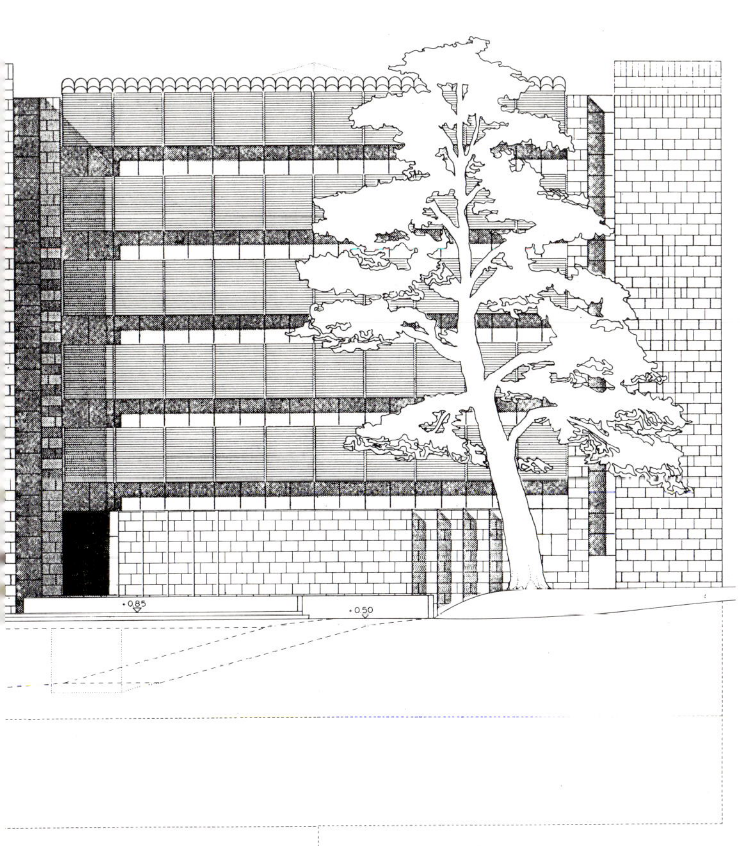

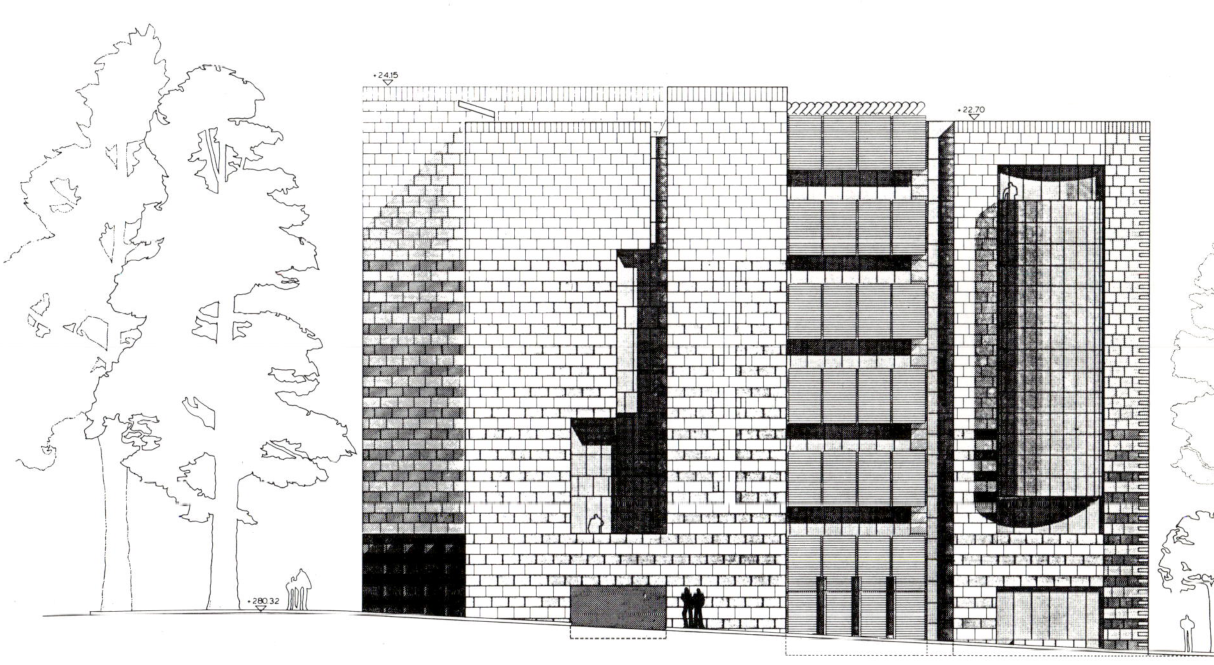

North elevation

Model photo
222

The house is built on a steep slope, with two roads running below and above it. The project allows for two sections: a lower one housing the entrance and the parking area, and one above it where the living quarters are located. The two sections are tied together by an open stairway and by an inclined elevator set into the ground. The stairway is placed above the elevator and its course traverses the entire garden.

The house has four elements: a curved structure, set against the mountain, where all secondary spaces are located; two cubes divided by a central space topped by a skylight; a semicylindrical element near the garden where the elevator and the stairway end; and, adjacent to this portion, a terrace overlooking the valley.

On the ground floor are different installations and spaces; on the first floor is a covered swimming pool from which a terrace can be reached. The kitchen, the study, and the living room are on the second floor; bedrooms are on the upper level. Two small cylindrical sections house the elevator and the stairs.

All the rooms of the house overlook the central loggia: the fireplace at the center is illuminated by a skylight.

The building will be composed of reinforced concrete for the sections below ground, and of concrete brick in the parts emerging from it.

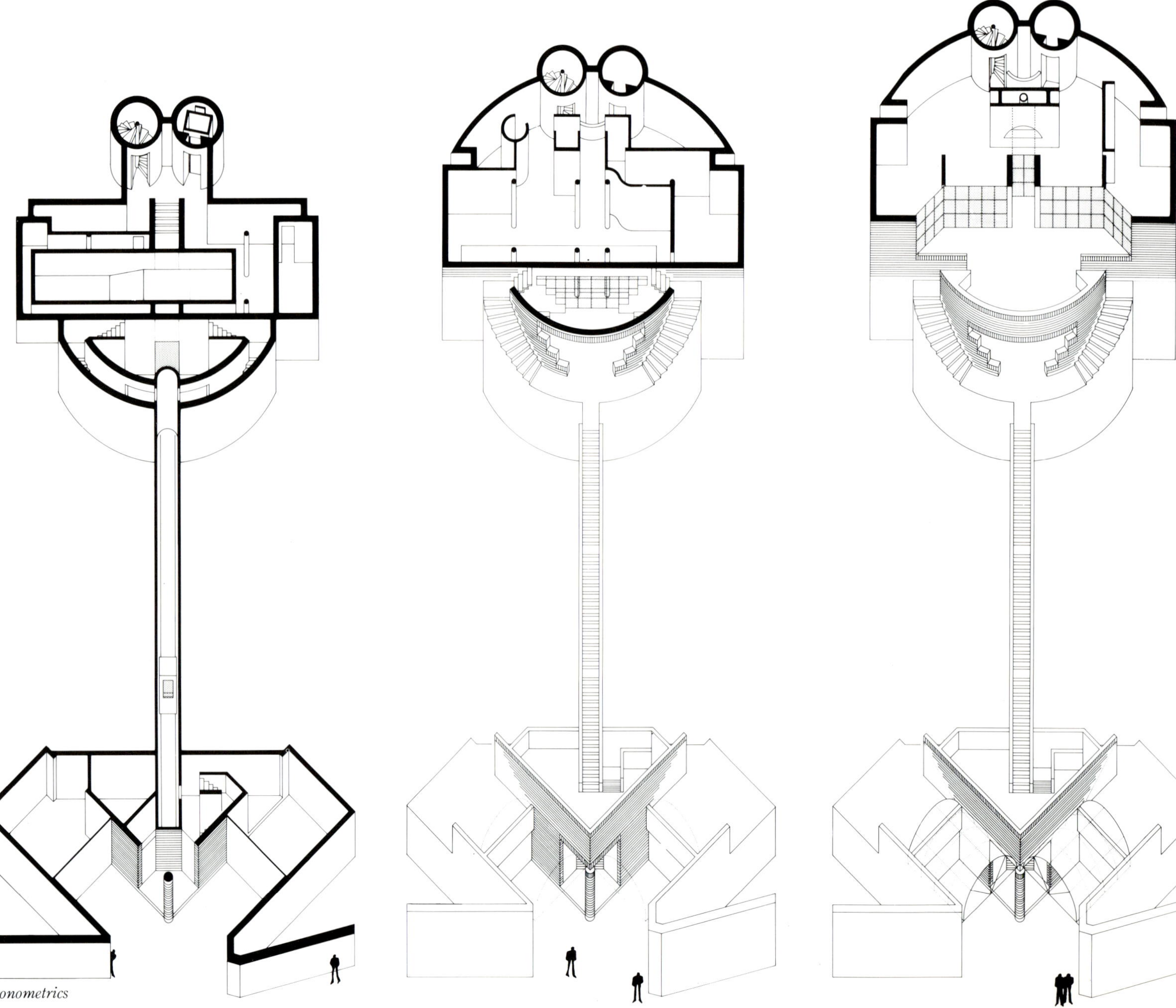

Axonometrics

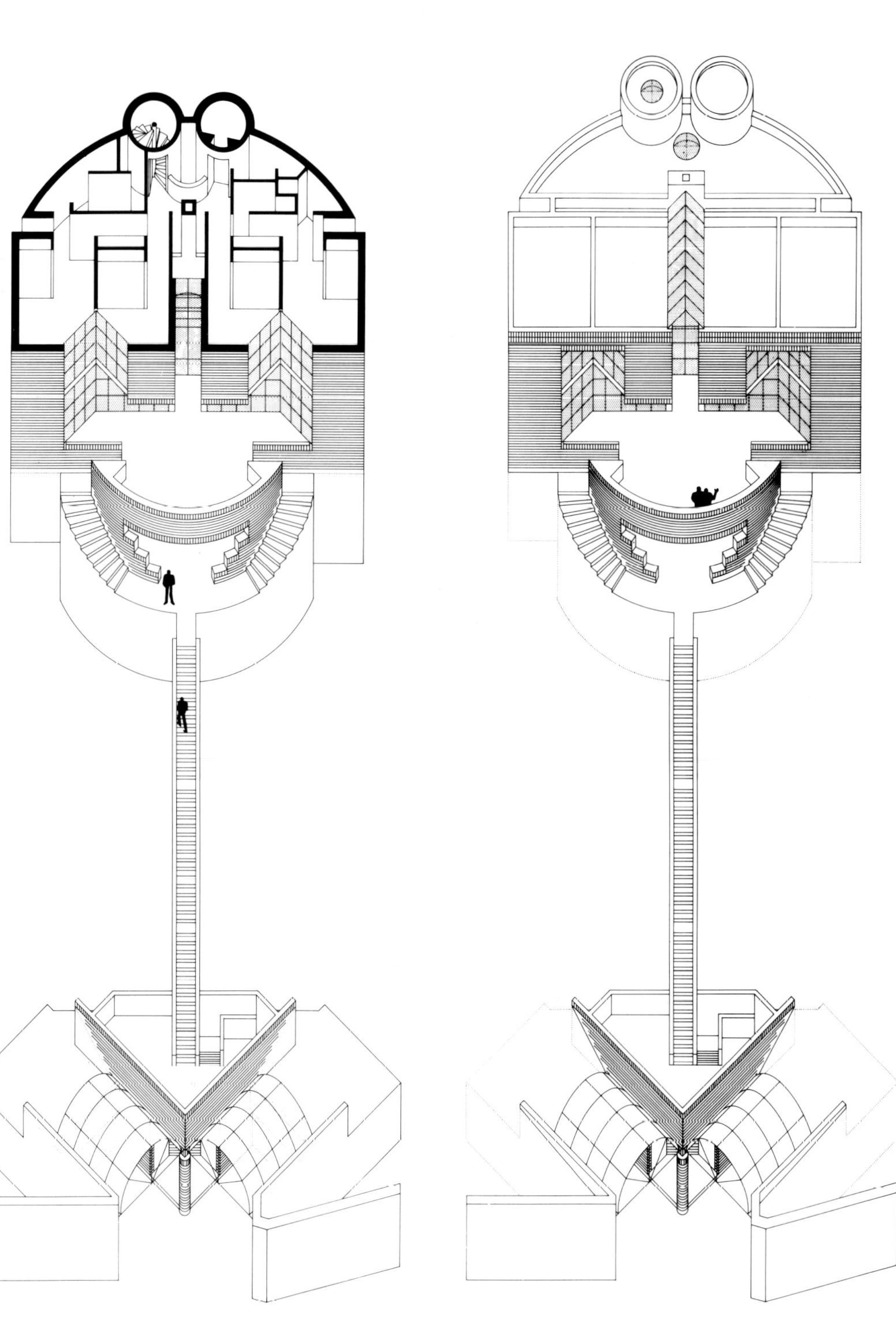

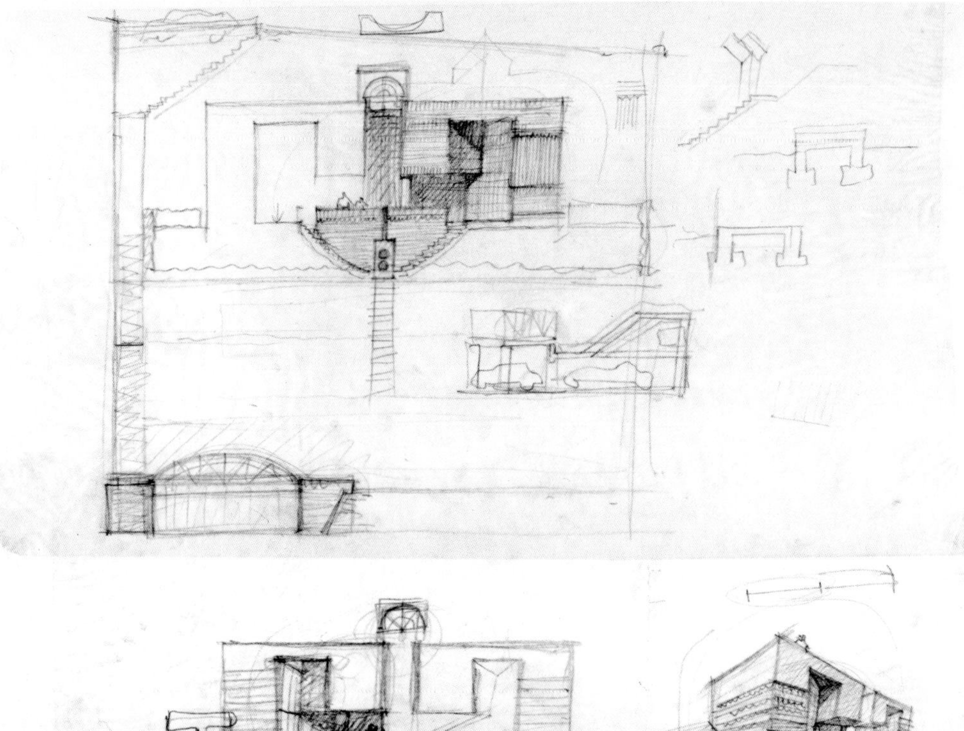

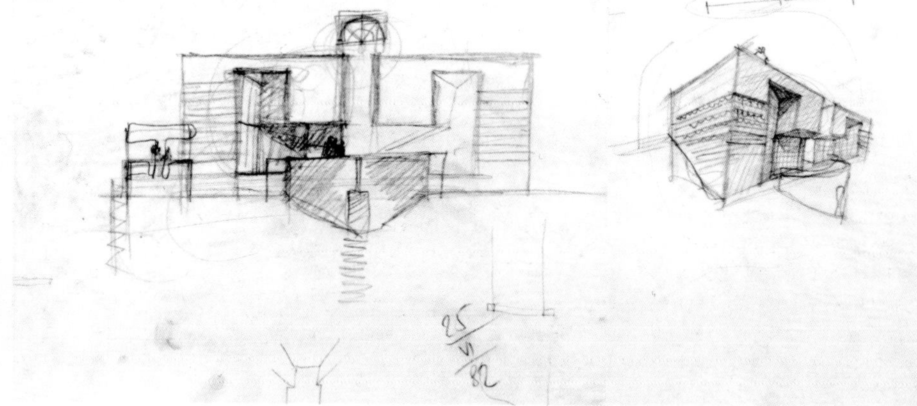

Preliminary study

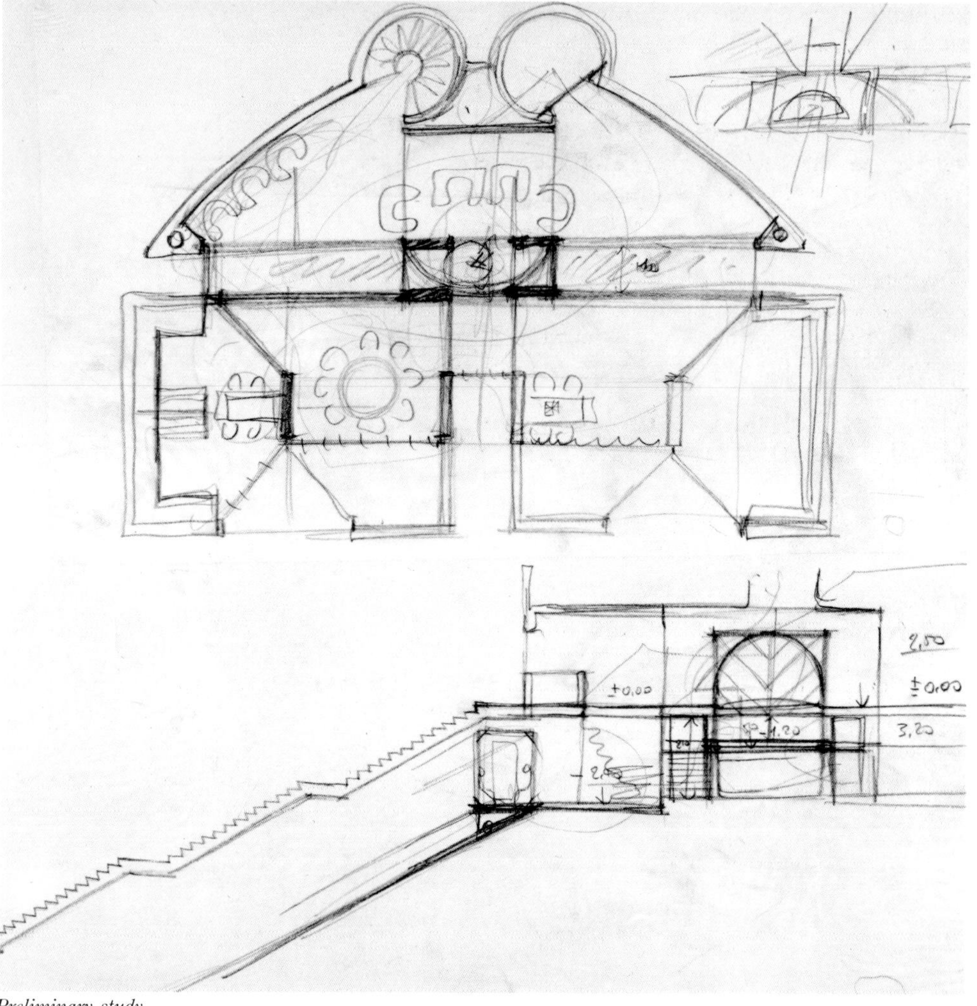

Preliminary study

The project was completed in 1980 and
slightly changed in 1984. The house, partially buried in the slope of the mountain,
shows on the side facing the valley a façade
enlivened by alternating bands of bricks
laid at 45-degree angles, and by a large opening that widens on top. The loggia behind
(as with the house at Massagno) has a lateral
opening that, in this case, faces south.

The house has three floors. The entrance
and a living room are on the ground floor;
the kitchen and another living room are
on the first; four bedrooms are on the upper
level. Stairs are placed in a cylindrical body
that follows the conformation of the terrain.
Another long stairway links the house with
the garage below, at street level.

The house will be composed of concrete
brick, the interior will be painted white.
Ceilings are of exposed reinforced concrete,
and floors are of black slate or granite.

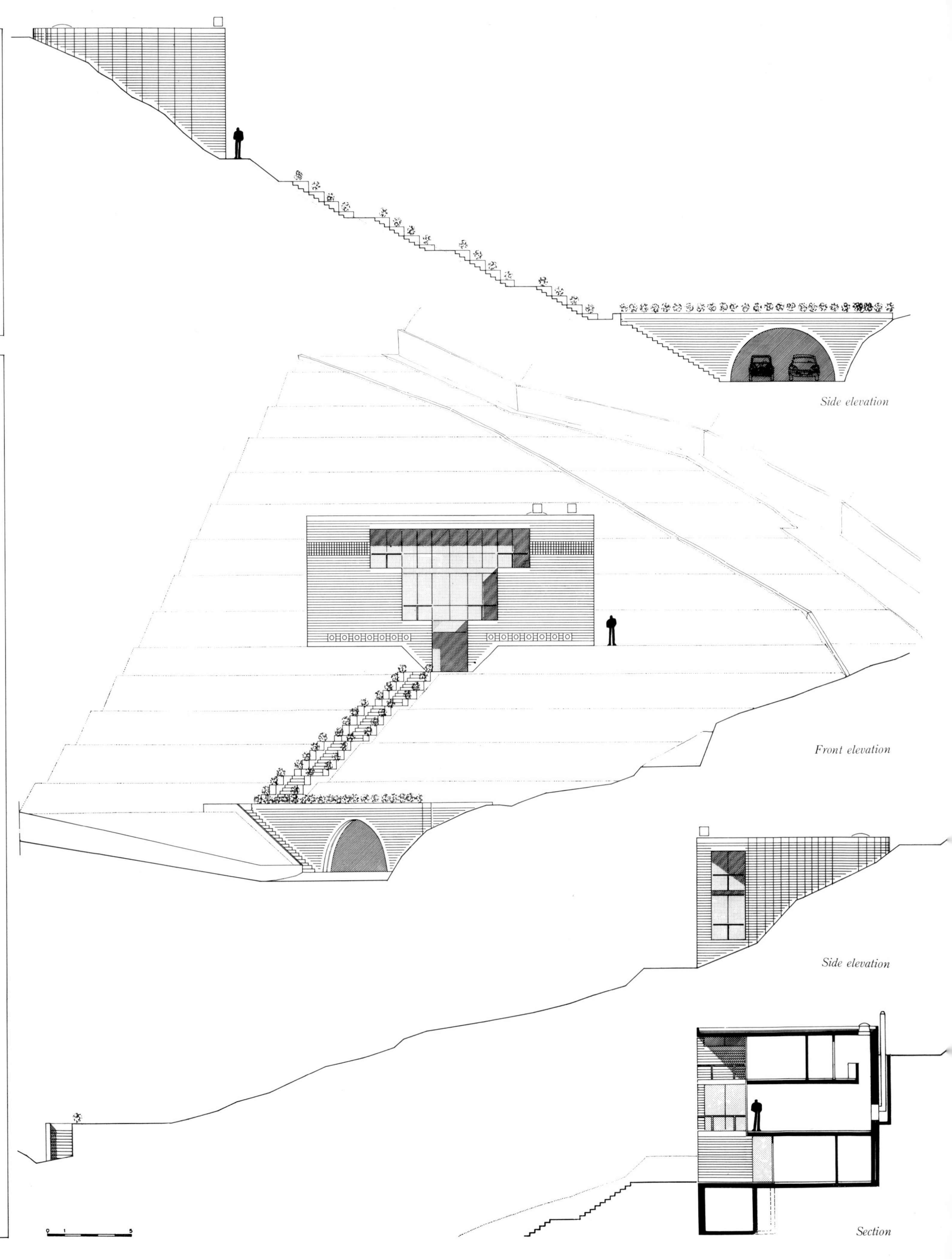

Side elevation

Front elevation

Side elevation

Section

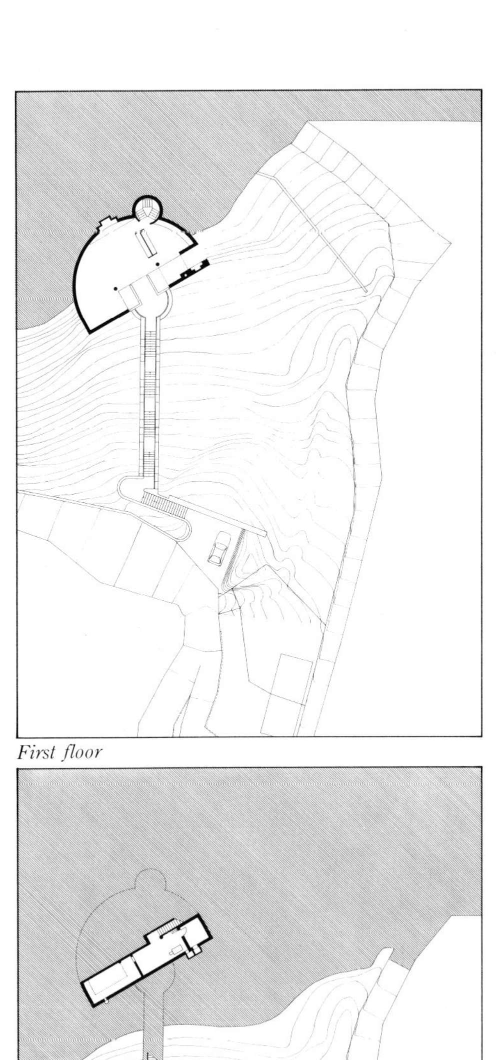

First floor

Second floor

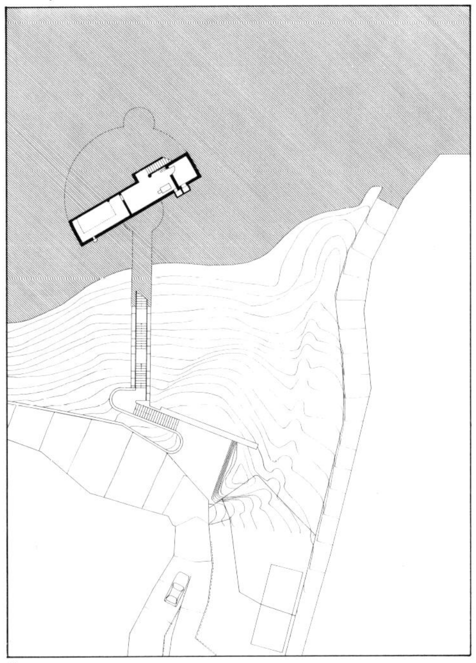

Basement

Ground floor

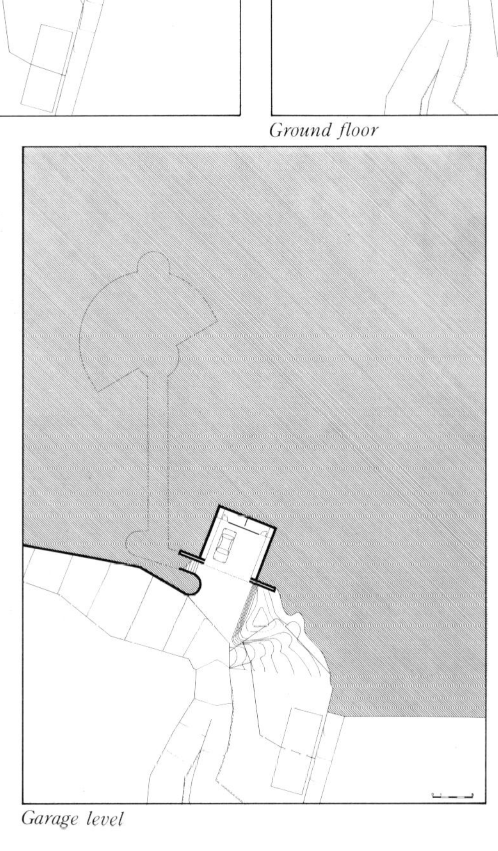

Garage level

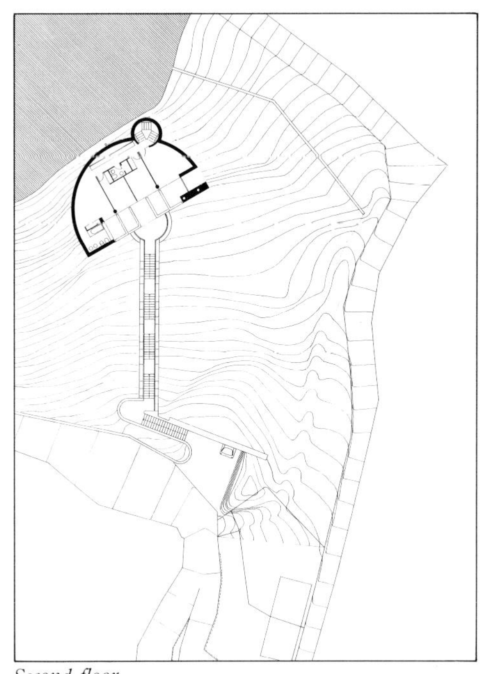

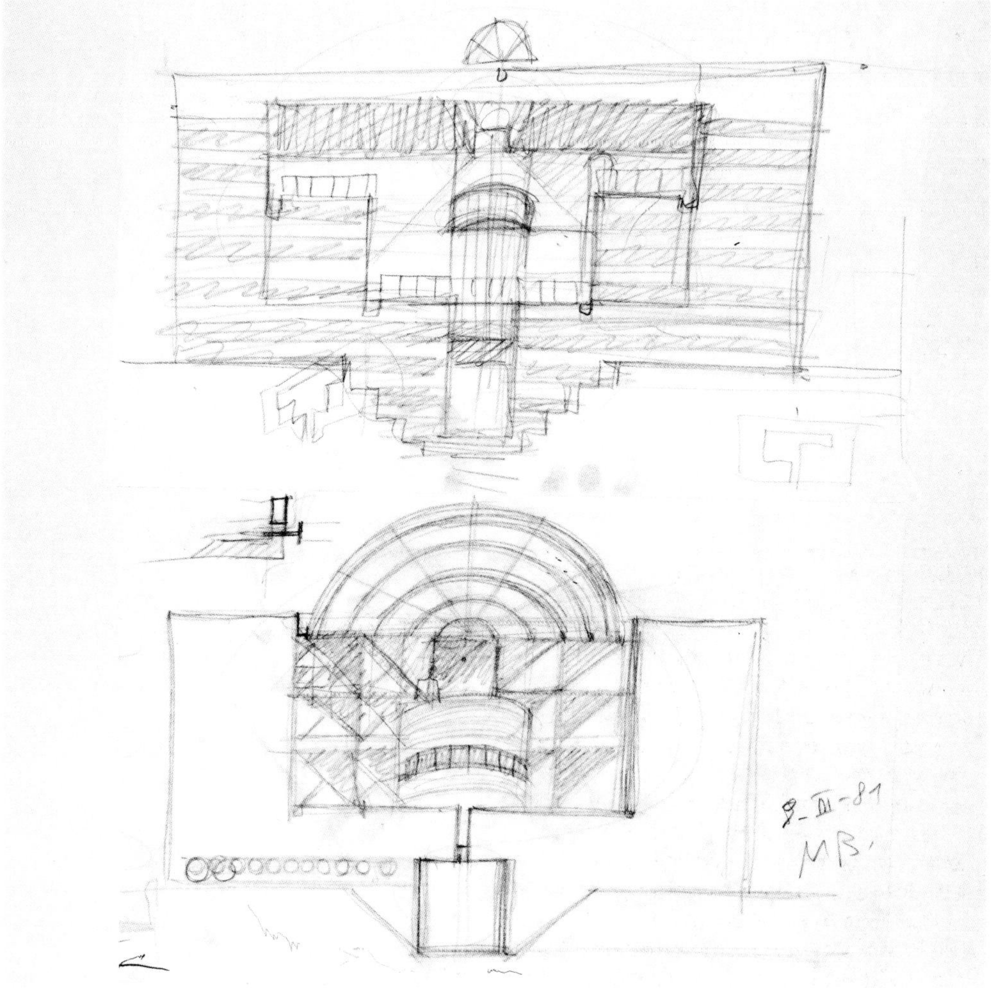

Preliminary study

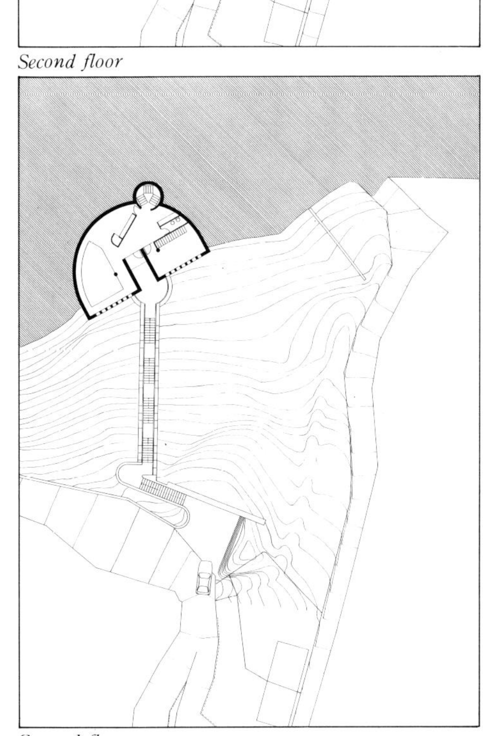

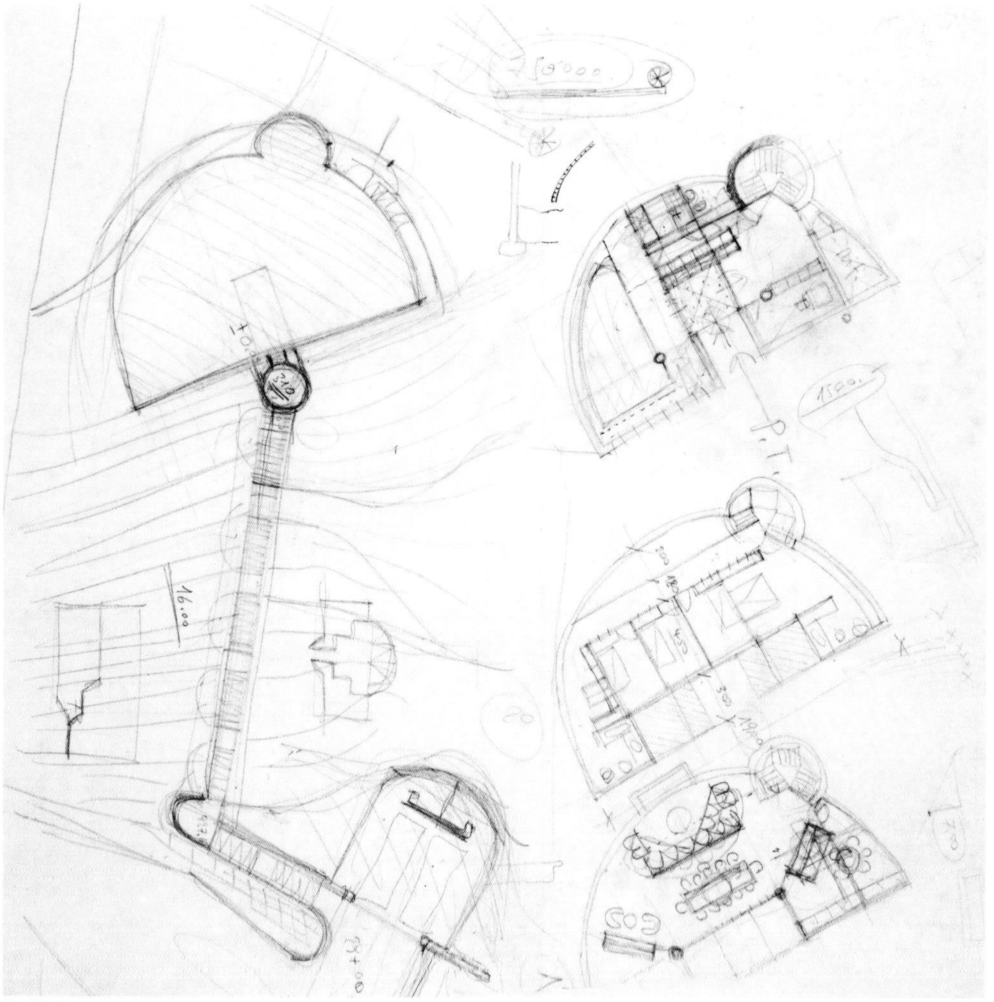

Preliminary study

Single-Family House at Breganzona, Switzerland, 1984 (project)

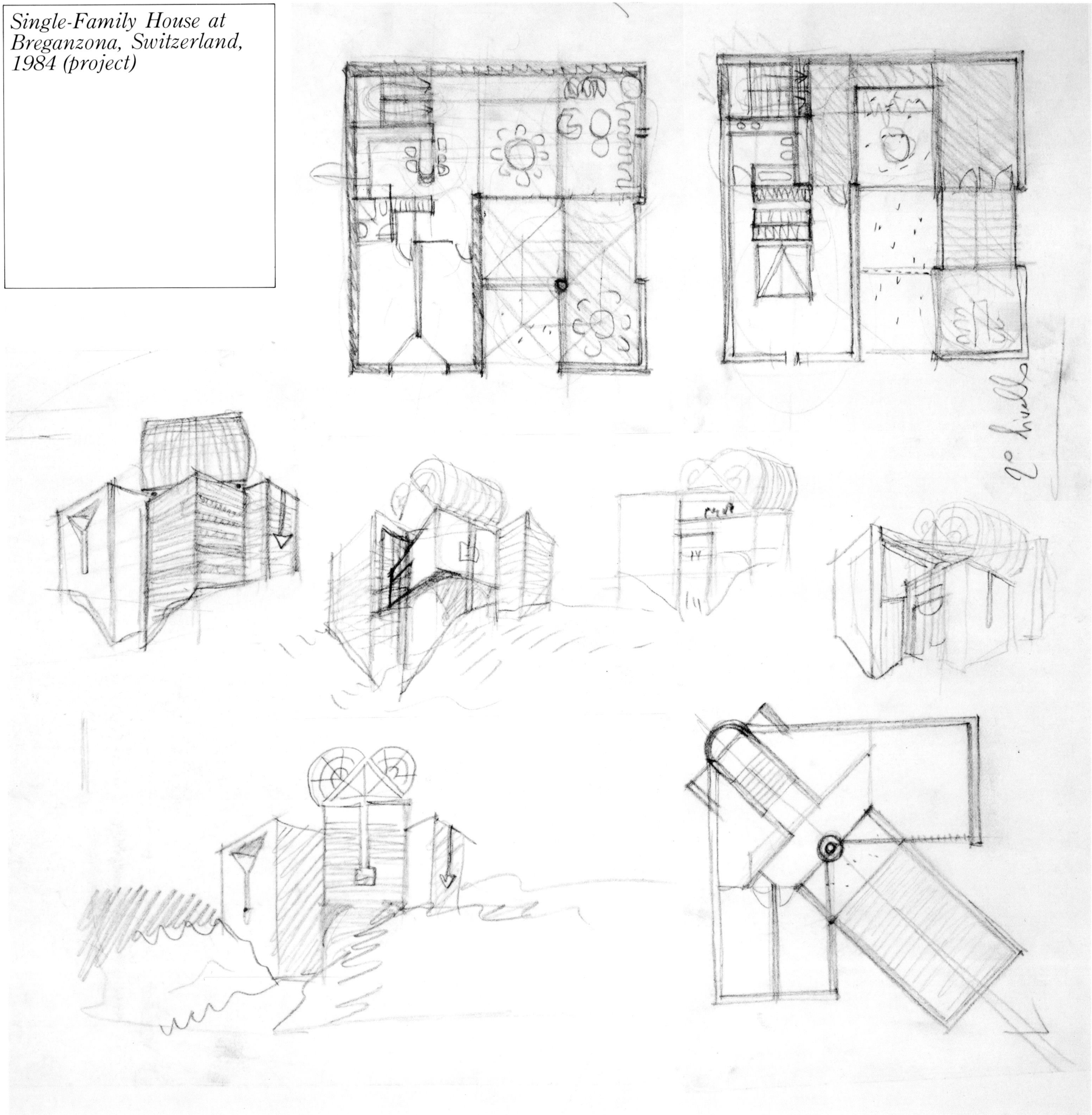

Preliminary study

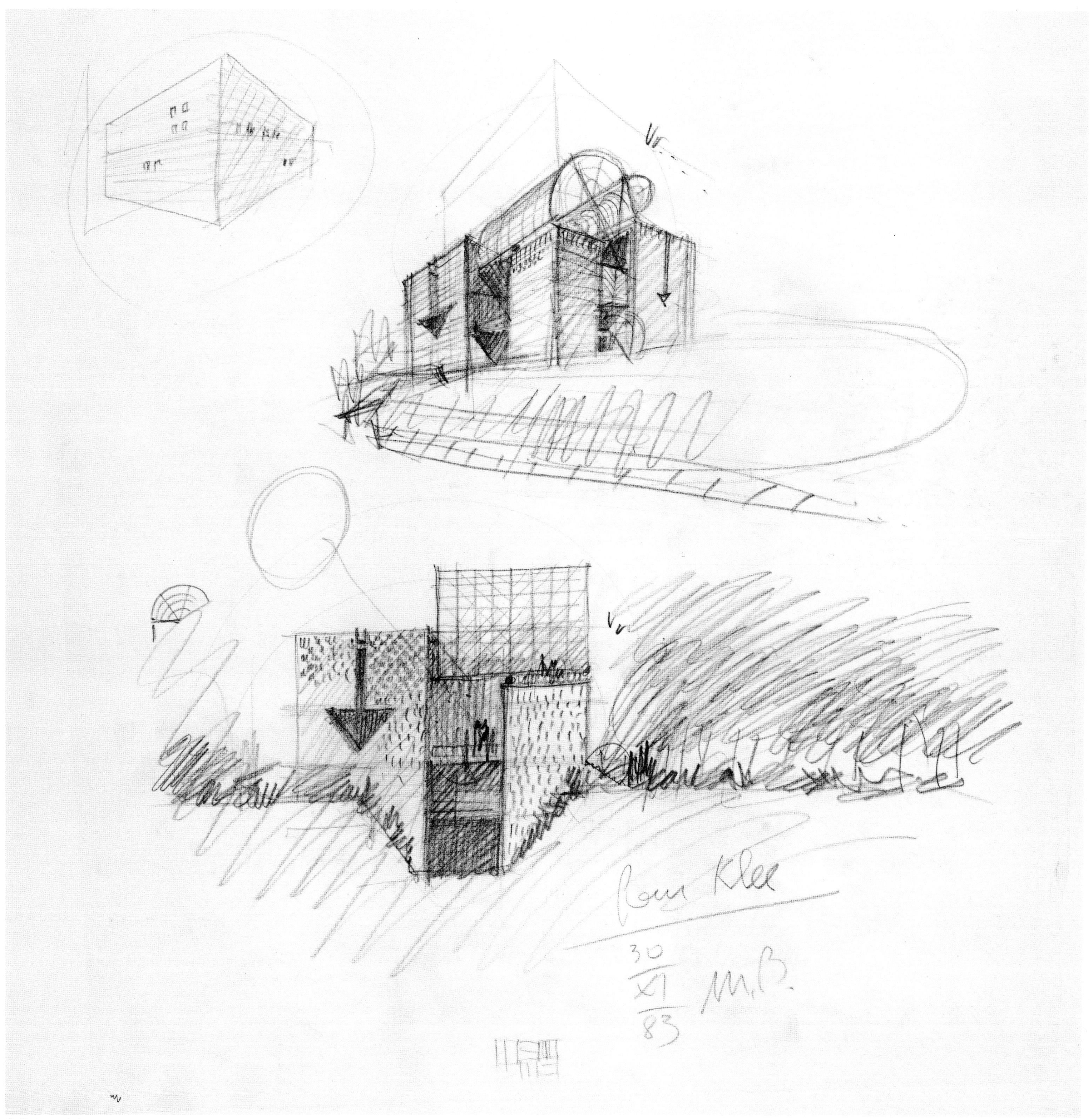

Preliminary study

1968
Alfieri, Bruno. "Una casa nel Ticino." *Lotus international,* no. 9, Venice, Italy.

1969
Mazzariol, Giuseppe. "Un fiore per Le Corbusier." *Werk,* no. 4, Zurich, Switzerland.

1974
Pedio, Renato. "Casa unifamiliare a Riva San Vitale." *L'Architettura,* no. 223, Rome, Italy.

1975
Borges, Mario. "Analyse d'une expérience." *Werk,* No. 1, Zurich, Switzerland.
Steinmann, Martin. *Tendenzen Neuere Architektur im Tessin.* (ETH catalogue), Zurich, Switzerland.

1976
Fujii, Hiromi, *Architecture and Urbanism,* no. 69, Tokyo, Japan.

1977
Berni, Lorenzo. "Scuola media unica a Morbio Inferiore." *Panorama,* no. 604, Milan, Italy.
Culot, Maurice. "Les maisons de Mario Botta." *Archives d'architecture moderne,* no. 12, Brussels, Belgium.
Dal Co, Francesco. "Critique d'une exposition." *L'Architecture d'Aujourd'hui,* no. 190, Paris, France.
Kultermann, Udo. "Schweizerische Architektur." *Die Architektur im 20. Jahrhundert,* Cologne, Germany.
Reichlin, Bruno and Steinmann, Martin. "Critique d'une critique." *L'Architecture d'Aujour'hui,* no. 190, Paris, France.
von Meiss, Pierre. "La maison et la ville." *Pro Fribourg,* no. 33, Freiburg, Switzerland.

1978
Croset, Pierre-Alain. "Dorigny: la question théorique de l'architecture." *Habitation,* no. 11, Lausanne, Switzerland.
Graf, Urs. "Aspects de l'architecture de Mario Botta." *Docu-Bulletin,* nos. 3-4, Blauen, Switzerland.
Mantero, Enrico. "Il luogo e l'edificio." *Domus,* no. 579, Milan, Italy.
von Moos, Stanislaus, "Notizen zu einigen neuen Schweizer Schulbauten." *Werk Archithese,* nos. 13-14, Zurich, Switzerland.

1979
Battisti, Emilio. "Esperienze d'architettura."
Mario Botta – Architetture e progetti negli anni 70, Electa Editrice, Milan, Italy.
———. "L'Intelligenza del mestiere." *Lotus international,* no. 22, Milan, Italy.
Berni, Lorenzo. "Progetti del concorso per l'ampliamento della Stazione di Zurigo." *Panorama,* no. 669, Milan, Italy.
Botta, Mario. "Architecture and 'environnement'." *Architecture and Urbanism,* no. 105, Tokyo, Japan.
Coenen, Jo. "Moderne Architektur En Oude Waarden." *Avenue,* October, Amsterdam, Netherlands.
Dal Co, Francesco. "Discepolo di Le Corbusier che piace ai giapponesi." *Rinascita,* no. 39, Rome, Italy.
den Hollander, Jord. "Mario Botta: Eén van de 'Tessiner' Architecten Dialoog Tussen Het Bestaande En Het Nieuwe." *De Architect,* no. 6, Hague, Netherlands.
Frampton, Kenneth. "La Tendenza a costruire." *Mario Botta – Architetture e progetti negli anni '70,* Electa Editrice, Milan Italy.
———. "Mario Botta and the School of the Ticino." *Oppositions,* no. 14, New York, U.S.A.
Nicolin, Pierluigi. "Mario Botta: architetture e progetti negli anni '70." *Triennale di Milano,* Galleria del Disegno, catalogue, Milan, Italy.
Trevisiol, Robert. "Mario Botta." *A Plus,* no. 61, Brussels, Belgium.
van Dijk, Hans. "Tessiner Architectuur." *Plan,* no. 5, Amsterdam, Netherlands.
———. "Mario Botta - Botta's Muren." *B-NWS,* 12-28, Technische Hogeschool Delft.

1980
Berni, Lorenzo. "Edificio per laboratori e residenze a Balerna." *Panorama,* no. 716, Milan, Italy.
Botta, Mario. "Il Disegno, il luogo e il progetto." *Am Rand des Reissbretts: 10 Schweizer Architekten, Skizzen, Zeichnungen, Grafik, Bilder.* catalogue, Chur, Switzerland.
———. "Une maison familiale encore!" *Werk, Bauen + Wohnen,* no. 5, Zurich, Switzerland.
Descloux, Charles. "Faire oeuvre d'architecte, c'est transformer le paysage." *La Liberté,* no. 202, Freiburg, Switzerland.
Dimitriu, Livio. "Swiss Transmission and Exaggerations: An Interview with Mario Botta." *Skyline,* vol. 2, no. 8, New York, U.S.A.
Dorn, Roland, "Moderne Architektur im Tessin." *Baumeister,* no. 1, Munich, Germany.
Frampton, Kenneth. "Architecture contemporaine." *Encyclopaedia universalis,* Paris, France.
———. "Place, Production and Architecture: Towards a Critical Theory of Building." *Modern Architecture: a Critical History,* London, Great Britain.
Glusberg, Jorge, "La Arquitectura de Mario Botta entre la historia y la memoria: el passado como amigo." *Centro de Arte y Communicacion (CAYC),* Buenos Aires, Argentina.
Hedgepeth, Michael. "Visit by Mario Botta." *Archetype IV,* San Francisco, U.S.A.
Jehle, Ulrike. "Avec les éléments de l'histoire – Zum Wettbewerb Wissenschafts zentrum Berlin (WZB)." *Werk, Bauen + Wohnen,* no. 6, Zurich, Switzerland.
———. "Mario Botta: Il Passato come un amico." *Werk, Bauen + Wohnen,* no. 3, Zurich, Switzerland.
Joedicke, Jürgen. "Rationalismus." *Architektur im Umbruch,* Stuttgart, Germany.
Lampugnani, Vittorio Magnago. *Architektur und Städtebau des 20. Jahrhunderts,* Stuttgart, Germany.
Ostinelli, Elio. "L'Architettura di Mario Botta." *"Popolo e libertà,* no. 133, Bellinzona, Switzerland.
Pizza, Antonio. "Mario Botta: archeologo o architetto?" *Dipartimenti architettura,* year 1, June, Venice, Italy.
Rayon, Jean-Paul. "Mario Botta 'S'il vous plait, dessine-moi une maison'." *Techniques et Architecture,* no. 332, Paris, France.
Reiser, Jean Marc. "Mario Botta." *Charlie-Hebdo,* no. 484, Paris, France.
Santini, Pier Carlo. "Mario Botta architetto ticinese." *Ottagono,* no. 58, Milan, Italy.
Steinmann, Martin. "Mario Botta: 'recherche patiente'." *Archithese,* no. 1, Zurich, Switzerland.
Trevisiol, Robert. "Un chàteau en Suisse." *A Plus,* no. 66, Brussels, Belgium.
van Dijk, Hans. "Botta's Muren." *Forum,* no. 1, Amsterdam, Netherlands.
Volonterio, Guglielmo. "Fare architettura equivale a trasformare l'ambiente." *Corriere del Ticino,* 7 January, Lugano, Switzerland.
Werner, Frank. (über neue Architektur im Tessin) "Lieder, die Man Nicht Erwartet." *Bauwelt,* no. 39, Berlin, Germany.
Zevi, Bruno. "La Poetica del muro." *L'Espresso,* no. 38, Rome, Italy. cf. also *Cronache di architettura,* no. 1341, Bari, Italy.

1981
Barten, Walter. "Neo-rationalistische architectuur van Botta en Grassi." *Het Financieele Vrijdablad,* 20 March, Amsterdam, Netherlands.
Beck, Haig. "A Home for Guernica's Return: Mario Botta's Competition Design." *International Architect,* no. 6, London, Great Britain.
Blaser, Werner. *Architecture 70/80 in Switzerland.* Basel-Boston-Stuttgart.
Botta, Mario. "Ein Raum für Gernika." *Werk, Bauen + Wohen,* no. 11, Zurich, Switzerland.
Cassarà, Silvio. "Biblioteca dei Cappuccini a Lugano." *Parametro,* no. 99, Bologna, Italy.
Disch, Peter. "Internationale Bauaustellung Berlin 1984 – Centro delle scienze di Berlino." and "Uno spazio per 'Guernika'." *Rivista Tecnica,* no. 10, Bellinzona, Switzerland.
Dominguez, Martin. "Une soirée à Morbio." *Quadernos,* no. 147, Barcelona, Spain.
Hinke, Roland. "Die moderne Klassik in der Architektur." *Das Haus,* Burda GmbH, Stuttgart, Germany.
Jehle, Ulrike and Reichlin, Bruno. "Mario Botta... Morbio Inferiore, Tessin. Bauernhof. Umbau 1977-79." *Architektur 1940-1980,* (Vogt-Jehle-Reichlin), Berlin, Germany.
Kleihues, Josef Paul. "Die Neubaugebiete-Dokumente. Projekte 2." *Internationale Bauaustellung Berlin 1981,* Berlin, Germany.
Kloos, Maarten. "Architectuur van Botta overtuigend." De Volkskrant, 31 March, Amsterdam, Netherlands.
Knobel, Lance. (Assistant Editor AR) "Botta." *AR The Architectural Review,* no. 1013, London, Great Britain.
Lüchinger, Arnulf. "Mario Botta, Mittelschule in Morbio Inferiore. CH, 1972-76." *Strukturalismus in Architektur und Städtebau,* Stuttgart, Germany.
Maxwell, Robert. "Hotel/Clinic, Agra: Function & Symbol." *International Architect,* no. 5, vol. 1, issue 5, London, Great Britain.
Meyhöfer, Dirk. "Das Streifenhaus von Ligornetto." *Architektur und Wohnen,* fasc. 2, Hamburg, Germany.
Moschini, Francesco. "Mestiere come professione." *Domus,* no. 620, Milan, Italy.
Nicolin, Pierluigi. "Un segno di profondità. Mario Botta: biblioteca a Lugano (Ticino)." *Lotus international,* no. 28, Milan, Italy.
Odermatt, Bruno. "Projektaufträge 'Pensione

di Cura' in Agra/TI." *Schweizer Ingenieur und Architekt*, no. 14, Zurich, Switzerland.

Pevsner, Nikolaus; Fleming, John and Honour, Hugh. *Dizionario di architettura*. (Italian edition edited by Renato Pedio Edizioni Einaudt) Turin, Italy.

Pilarski, Laura. *Nikkei Architecture*, 2-2, published by Nikkei McGraw-Hill, Inc. Tokyo, Japan.

Reinhart, Fabio. "Frei/Libre." *AS Architettura Svizzera*, no. 46, Anthony Krafft, Pully-Lausanne, Switzerland.

Reiser, Jean Marc. "La maison ronde de l'architecte Mario Botta" *Charlie Hebdo*, no. 579, Paris, France.

Sisto, Maddalena. "Una scultura per abitare. le sue luci. i suoi contrast." *Casa Vogue*, no. 117, Milan, Italy.

Specchio, Gruppo. "Intellectual Tradition 'Mario Botta'." *SD Space Design*, no. 3, Tokyo, Japan.

Trevisiol, Robert. "M.B." *A Plus*, no. 68, January-February, Brussels, Belgium.

————. "Kunstgrepen volgens de wetten van de natuur." *Knack Magazine*, no. 18, Antwerp, Belgium.

Werner, Frank. *Die Vergeudete Moderne: Europäische Architekturkonzepte nach 1950, die Papier geblieben sind*. published by DVA, Stuttgart, Germany.

1982

AA. VV. "Architecture: après la quantité, quelle qualité?" *Pignon sur rue*, no. 39, Lyon, France.

Arnell, Peter, "Mario Botta: Trans-Alpine Rationalist." *Architectural Record*, June, New York, U.S.A.

Botta, Mario. "Casa a Stabio." *Rivista tecnica*, no. 2, Bellinzona, Switzerland.

————. "Gernika." *Vergangenheit Gegenwart Zukunft*, catalogue, Stuttgart, Germany.

————. "L'Albero come eccezione." *Lotus international*, no. 31, Milan, Italy.

Caglio, Luciana. "Mario Botta: 'L'Architettura può diventare un'alleata del territorio'." *Azione*, 28 January, Lugano, Switzerland.

Casciani, Stefano. "La Casa Rotonda." *Domus*, no. 626, March, Milan, Italy.

Champenois, Michèle. "Botta à l'Institut d'architecture. Les maisons d'Adam au paradis." *Le Monde*, no. 11789, 24 December, Paris, France.

Chaslin, François. "Théâtres dans la ville." *Architecture*, no. 36, Paris, France.

Cirio, Rita. "Architetto, che stai architettando?" (debate between Paolo Portoghesi and Mario Botta) *L'Espresso*, nos.

27-28, Rome, Italy.

Croset, Pierre-Alain. "Mario Botta – La Banca dello Stato di Friburgo." *Casabella*, no. 484, Milan, Italy.

————. "Una casa de feudatari." *Casabella*, no. 482, Milan, Italy.

de l'Aulnoit, Béatrix. "Des architects à visiter. Vivre au milieu du pré." *Cosmopolitan*, no. 106, Paris, France.

Dimitriu, *Livio*. "Transfigurer of Geometry." *Progressive Architecture*, June, Stamford, U.S.A.

Echeverria, Emile Duhart. "Tessin une tradition moderne." *Décoration internationale*, no. 52, published by Rusconi S.A., Paris, France.

Glusberg, Jorge. "Mario Botta: o passado como amigo." *Modulo*, no. 71, Rio de Janeiro, Brasil.

Gmür, Otti. "Architekten unsere Zeit. Mario Botta, Lugano." *Vaterland*, no. 287, 11 December, Lucerne, Switzerland.

Grossman, Loyd. "Milan's Post-Modern Masters." *Harpers and Queen*, May, London, Great Britain.

Guenzi, Carlo. "La Sedicesima Triennale voce architettura e edilizia." *Annuario Rizzoli 1981*, Milan, Italy.

Kévés, György. "Mario Botta." *Mü Vészet*, Budapest, Hungary.

Krier, Rob; Nicolin, Pierluigi; Reiser; Sanguineti, Edoardo; Sartoris, Alberto; Trevisiol, Robert. *Mario Botta – La Casa Rotunda*. published by L'Erba Voglio, Milan, Italy.

Lamarre, François. "Mario Botta: parpaings et chocolat." *Architecture*, December.

Lampugnani, Vittorio Magnano. "Frammento di storia critica del disegno architettonico del ventesimo secolo." *La Realta dell'immagine*, (Verlag Gerd Hatje), Stoccarda, Germany.

Modes, Antonie. "Ein Privathaus im Tessin." *Das Schoene Heim*, vol. IV, Karl Thiemig AG, Munich, Germany.

Nicolin, Pierluigi. "La Firma dell'architetto. Oppure: l'uomo propone, l'architetto dispone." *Interni*, no. 323, Milan, Italy.

————. "Notes on the House at Stabio (1981) and the House at Pregassona (1979)." *Global Architecture Houses*, no. 10, Tokyo, Japan.

Nogueira, Mauro Neves. "Idea e construcao da Arquitectura de Mario Botta." *IAB Journal de Nucleo*, no. 1, October/November, Rio de Janeiro, Brazil.

Pasca, Vanni. "Una villa dal cuore di vetro." *Vogue*, no. 136, Milan, Italy.

Portoghesi, Paolo. "Guernica tolto a Guernica?" *Europeo*, no. 13, 29 March,

Milan, Italy.

Rapasch, Gudrun. "Wohn-Turm über Luganer See." *Das Haus, Burda*, GmbH, Stuttgart, Germany.

Rubino, Luciano. "Natura e volumi bloccati." *Tuttoville*, no. 72, Milan, Italy.

Werner, Frank. "Gegenwarts-Architektur." *Vergangenheit Gegenwart Zukunft*, catalogue, Stuttgart, Germany.

Zevi, Bruno. "Sua maestà il paesaggio." *L'Epresso*, no. 9, 7 March, Rome, Italy.

1983

Abercrombie, Stanley. "The Neo-Rationalists Are Coming." (an interview with Mario Botta) *Interior Design*, June, Marion, U.S.A.

Bergdoll, Bary. "Like a Fist on the Table." *Progressive Architecture*, March, New York, U.S.A.

Bernardis, M.A. "Que nul n'entre ici s'il n'est geometre: Mario Botta ou L'architecture de l'an 2000." *Lyone Poche*, no. 594, 27 July – 2 August, Villeurbanne, France.

Berta, Catherine. "Mario Botta et 'ses maisons d'images'." *24 Heures*, 8 February, Lausanne, Switzerland.

Bessenich, Wolfgang. "Bottas Erfolg – warum?" *Basler Zeitung*, no. 7, 10 January, Basel, Switzerland.

Bettini, Paolo. "Piazza Cavour ad Ancona." *Arredo Urbano*, no. 8, Rome, Italy.

Blatter, Marie Luise. "Eine starke Geometrie als Werkzeug." *Basler Magazin*, 12 February, Basel, Switzerland.

Blumer, Jacques, "Antwort auf einen Diskurs." *Werk, Bauen + Wohnen*, no. 3, March, Zurich, Switzerland.

Boissière, Olivier. "Mario Botta ou le parfum des îles Borromées." *Le Moniteur*, no. 1, Paris, France.

Botta, Mario. "Architettura e 'environment'." *Dopo L'Architettura Post-Moderna*, edited by L. Ferrario, published by Kappa, Rome, Italy.

Branche, Pierre. "Botta: des maisons rassurantes." *Le Figaro*, 28 January, Paris, France.

Büchi, Georg. "Die Bank, die Stadt und 'Pro Freiburg'." *Werk, Bauen + Wohnen*, January / February, Zurich, Switzerland.

Bühring, Alvaro. "Appunti sullo stato dell' architettura nel Ticino." *Rivista tecnica*, March-April, Bellinzona, Switzerland.

Carloni, Tita. "Architetto del muro e non del trilite." *Lotus international*, no. 37, Milan, Italy.

————. "Tra conservazione e innovazione." (specifically on the architecture in the district of Ticino from 1930 to 1980),

Ingegneri e architetti Svizzeri (Bulletin technique de la Suisse romande), October 1983, Losanna, Switzerland.

————. "50 Anni di architettura in Ticino: 1930-1980." published by Grassi, Bellinzona, Switzerland.

Castellano, Aldo, "Quando il passato diventa presente." *La Mia Casa*, July-August, Milan, Italy.

Châtenay, Maxime. "Mario Botta l'homme des cavernes." *Illustre*, 17 August, Lausanne, Switzerland.

Colbertaldo, Alessandro. "Architetture ticinesi." (Evocation and mannerism of the new professionalism of the Ticinese School.) *Interni*, no. 332, July-August, Milan, Italy.

Dagnino, Tomas. "El hombre necessita ligarse al valor esencial del vivir." *Clarin arquitectura, Ingenieria, Planeamiento y Diseno*, Friday, 11 November, Buenos Aires, Argentina.

————. "Mario Botta: la arquitectura encarda como una transformacion del naturaleza." *reportajes a la arquitectura*, 1983, ed. CAYC, Buenos Aires, Argentina.

de Monbrison, Pamela. "Regards sur l'architecture et le design." *Vogue*, December/January, Paris, France.

de Seta, Cesare. "Architettura libri." *Il Mattino*, Friday, 27 May, Naples, Italy.

Dimitriu, Livio. "Architecture and Morality: an interview with Mario Botta." *Perspecta 20, The Yale Architectural Journal*, MIT Press, Cambridge and London, Great Britain.

————. "Casa Rotunda." *House and Garden*, September, New York, U.S.A.

Frampton, Kenneth. "Le Régionalisme dans l'architecture contemporaine." *Architecture/Quebec*, August, Montreal, Canada.

Fumagalli, Paolo. "Zur Staatsbank in Freiburg." *Werk, Bauen + Wohnen*, January/February, Zurich, Switzerland.

Gmür, Otti, "Neubau der Freiburger Staatsbank in Freiburg." *Archithese*, 1 January, Zurich, Switzerland.

Goldberger, Paul. "Chairs, when successful, can become virtual trademarks for architects." *The New York Times*, March, New York, U.S.A.

Gravagnuolo, Bendetto. "Il mestiere (l'architettura di Mario Botta: ricerca logica e paziente e poi...)." *Il Mattino*, 27 May, Naples, Italy.

Jencks, Charles. "Mario Botta and the New Tuscanism." *Architectural Design*, no. 53, September/October, London, Great Britain.

Kaupp, Katia D. "Entre le rétro et le chichi"

Architectes, 4 February, Paris, France.

Knobel, Lance. "Botta in the City." *The Architectural Review,* May, London, Great Britain.

______. "Mario Botta Theme and Variations." *Architectural Review,* April, London, Great Britain.

Lietti, Anna. "Construis-moi une maison." *L'Hebdo,* no. 25, 23 June, Lausanne, Switzerland.

Lino, Aldo and Vanini, Aldo. "I mattoni dell'architetto." *L'Unione Sarda,* no. 157, Friday, 10 June, Sardinia, Italy.

Lipstadt, Hélène. "Swiss Shows at IFA." Skyline, February, New York, U.S.A.

Maia, Eolo. "Mario Botta: on a arquitectura do fazer presente." *Pampulha,* no. 8, Belo Horizonte, Brazil.

Maxwell, Robert. "Ten New Buildings." ICA (Institute of Contemporary Arts), February, London, Great Britain.

Meier, Marco. "Architekt Botta." *Weltwoche Magazin,* 16 February, Zurich, Switzerland.

Morita, Kazutoshi and Pelissier, Alain. "Mario Botta Talks on Recent Works." *Architecture and Urbanism,* April, Tokyo, Japan.

Norberg-Schulz, Christian. "Wiederaufnahme des Bildlichen." *Werk, Bauen* + *Wohnen,* January/February, Zurich, Switzerland.

Noseda, Margherita. "A colloquio con l'architetto Mario Botta." *Popolo e liberta,* 2 June, Lugano-Bellinzona, Switzerland.

Pelissier, Alain. "L'Unité poursuivie." AMC *(Architecture-Mouvement-Continuité),* May, Paris, France.

Peters, Paulhans. "Freiburger Staatsbank in Freiburg." *Baumeister,* June, Munich, Germany.

Rambert, Francis. "Le Chevalier de la maison ronde." *Architectes,* January/February, Paris, France.

Reiser, Jean Marc. "Botta." *Rivista tecnica,* March-April, Bellinzona, Switzerland.

Robert, Elena. "Architettura come provocazione." *Corriere del Ticino,* 29 January, Lugano, Switzerland.

Sachs, Raoul. "Architecture: les maisons 'laboratories' de Mario Botta." *Le Matin de Paris 1982,* 6 January, Paris, France.

Sartoris, Alberto. "Expressionismus und Rationalismus als Synthese." *Werk, Bauen + Wohnen,* January/February, Zurich, Switzerland.

Schifres, Alain. "Botta: je veux rentrer à la maison." *Le Nouvel observateur,* 21-27 January, Paris, France.

Schneider, Bruno F. "Wenn Wohnhäuser wie Raumstationen wirken." *Koelnische Rundschau – Bonner Rundschau,* no. 213, Wednesday, 14 September, Koeln, Germany.

Simeoforidis, G. "Regionalism and Contemporary Architecture." *Design and Art in Greece,* no. 14, Athens, Greece.

Soldini, Jean. "Una tipologia per laboratori e residenze artigiane: Balerna, 1977-1979, architettura di Mario Botta." *Cenobio,* January – March, Vezia, Switzerland.

Tolmein, Gabriele. "Der Wohnturm im Tessin." *Hauser,* January, Hamburg, Germany.

Valls, Santiago Calatrava. "Einfache Struktur – Komplexe Form." *Werk, Bauen + Wohnen,* January/February, Zurich, Switzerland.

Vanlaethem, France. "Il passato come amico. Entrevue avec Mario Botta." *Achitecture/Quebec,* February, Montreal, Canada.

Van Stein, Emmanuel. "Organische Einheiten." *Koelner Stadt – Anzeiger,* no. 209, Friday, 9 September, Koeln, Germany.

Viladas, Pilar. "Botta on Botta's Chair." *Progressive Architecture,* May, Connecticut, U.S.A.

von Meiss, Pierre. "Eine Schweizer Bank, anders als die anderen." *Werk, Bauen + Wohnen,* January/February, Zurich, Switzerland.

Wuthe, Elke. "Geometrie schützt vor Willkür und Zufall." *Die Welt,* no. 283, Monday 5 December, Hamburg, Germany.

Zardini, Mirko. "Il teatro e la città (an interview with Mario Botta), *Casabella,* no. 496, November, Electa Periodici, Milan, Italy.

Zietschmann, Ernst. "Brutalismus Kubismus Klassizismus." *Merian,* July, Hamburg, Germany.

1984

"Architecture, Culture, Mode et Morale." (an interview with Livio Dimitriu), *Euroscopie,* no. 1, 1st quarter, 1984, Paris, France.

Baleri, Enrico and Terzi, Anna. "I protagonisti Mario Botta." *Interni,* no. 339, April, Electa Periodici, Milan, Italy.

Benson, Gordon. "An Exhibition of Drawings for the Casa Rotunda and Other Projects at the Architectural Association Gallery, 11 January – 10 February 1984." catalogue, London, Great Britain.

Bessenich, Wolfgang. "Das einfache bei Bottas Bauten." *Basler Zeitung,* no. 119, Tuesday, 22 May, Basel, Switzerland.

Descloux, Charles. "Mario Botta, architecte." *La Liberté,* no. 204, 2 June, Freiburg, Switzerland.

Dobai, Katharina. "Geometrie als Schlüssel zu Architektur und Design." *Das Neue Wohnen,* no. 2, April/May, Zug, Switzerland.

Fumagalli, Paolo. "Der Stuhl dem Menschen, der Tisch dem Raum." *Werk, Bauen + Wohnen,* no. 3, March, Zurich, Switzerland.

"Geometrie – Sprache der Menschen." *MD Möbel Interior Design,* February, Leinfelden-Echterdingen, Germany.

Horat, Heinz. "Häuser als Skulpturen der Landschaft." *Neue Zurcher Zeitung,* no. 116, Saturday/Sunday, 19/20 May, Zurich, Switzerland.

Horat, Marco. "Per una sedia in più." (an interview with the architect Mario Botta), *Azione,* Thursday, 23 February, Lugano, Switzerland.

"Intervista di Vittorio Anselmi a Mario Botta." *Il Mestiere di architetto,* Editrice Cluva, April, Venice, Italy.

Jencks, Charles. "Mario Botta : the Spartan Classicist." *Connoisseur,* April, New York, U.S.A.

Loderer, Benedikt. "Der Architekt wurde zum Star." *Tages Anzeiger,* Friday, 25 May, Zurich, Switzerland.

Mackay, David. "La Casa unifamiliar." edited by Gustavo Gili, S.A. Rosellon 87-89, Barcelona, Spain.

Petrina, Alberto. "Mario Botta, o la poesia de la precision." *Summa,* no. 195/196, January/February, Buenos Aires, Argentina.

Pozzi, Giovanni. "Quelle 'caverne impellicciate' di Mario Botta." *Popolo e liberta,* no. 121, 26 May, Lugano-Bellinzona, Switzerland.

Rothen, Beat. "Rafforzare e non distruggere." *Der Schweizerische Hauseigentumer,* no. 9, 1 May, St. Gallen, Switzerland.

Schmitt, Karl Wilhelm. "Freiheit statt Zwang." *Deutsche Bauzeitung.* April, Stuttgart, Germany.

Tolmein, Gabriele. "Die grossen Architekten (13) Mario Botta." *Hauser,* no. 2, Hamburg, Germany.

"Una visita al nuovo Lingotto." (an interview with Mario Botta), edited by Mirko Zardini, no. 502, May, Electa Periodici, Milan, Italy.

Photographs in this volume are by Yukio Futagawa with the exception of the following:

Aldo Ballo: pp.198, 199
Giovanni Luisoni: p.37
Paolo Pedroli: pp.36, 40
Roberto Sellitto: p.172
Alo Zanetta: pp.202, 203
Provided by the Architect: pp.136, 140, 186, 196, 206